Aesthetics in the 21ˢᵗ Century

Speculations V

speculationsjournal@gmail.com
www.speculations-journal.org

EDITORS
Ridvan Askin
Paul J. Ennis
Andreas Hägler
Philipp Schweighauser

ISBN-10: 0692203168
ISBN-13: 978-0692203163

ISSN 2327-803X

Cover image by Blanca Rego
Untitled, Ilpo Väisänen
[Raster-Noton, 20' to 2000 series]

20' to 2000 consists of 20 minutes of experimental music meant to be
played during the last 20 minutes of the 20th century.

Images generated from sound files. No edition, just automatic data bending.
1. Save sound file as raw
2. Open raw in graphics editing program

Designed by Thomas Gokey

V 1.0

 punctum books * brooklyn, ny

PART 2: THE THEORY OF ART

Acknowledgements

T HIS SPECIAL ISSUE OF *SPECULATIONS* grew out of the conference *Aesthetics in the 21st Century* held in Basel in September 2012, generously funded by the Swiss National Science Foundation, the Freiwillige Akademische Gesellschaft Basel, the University of Basel's Ressort Nachwuchsförderung and its James Fenimore Cooper grant. The conference would not have been possible without the invaluable help of Daniel Allemann, Sixta Quassdorf, Jasmin Rindlisbacher and Andrea Wüst. The editors of this issue would like to thank the contributors to this volume, both those who originally presented at the conference and those who were not present in Basel but agreed to participate in this project for their commitment and enthusiasm. We would also like to thank the *Speculations* crew for offering their journal as a venue to publicise the results of this project. We hope that the reader will find them as exciting as we do.

The University of Minnesota Press generously granted permission to include Steven Shaviro's "Non-Phenomenological Thought," an excerpt from his forthcoming *The Universe of Things: On Speculative Realism*.

Introduction
Aesthetics after the Speculative Turn

Ridvan Askin, Andreas Hägler, and Philipp Schweighauser

University of Basel

Origins

ANY EXPLORATION OF ART AND sensuous cognition from a speculative realist perspective must contend with the legacy of not only Kant's first critique but also his third.[1] For a speculative realist *aesthetics*, Kant's legacy is a crucial foil for two related reasons: first (and this is the better-explored argument), because his radically anti-metaphysical demand "that the objects must conform to our cognition" is the most prominent and influential manifestation of what Quentin Meillassoux calls "correlationism" in *After Finitude*; second, and more specifically, because Kant's aesthetic theory is a theory not of objects but of the human response to natural and artistic beauty.[2] That Kant's aesthetics is as unreservedly subject-centred as his first critique

---

[1] The editors of this special issue would like to thank Daniel Allemann for diligently proofreading the whole issue and his helpful feedback on this introduction. Ralf Simon, Paul J. Ennis, Jon Cogburn, and Sjoerd van Tuinen deserve special thanks for their incisive comments on the text that follows.

[2] Immanuel Kant, "Preface to the Second Edition" in *Critique of Pure Reason*, trans. Paul Guyer and Allen W. Wood (Cambridge: Cambridge University Press, 2003), 110. Quentin Meillassoux, *After Finitude: An Essay on the Necessity of Contingency*, trans. Ray Brassier (London: Continuum, 2009), 5.

becomes immediately clear if we consider that the central term in the *Critique of the Power of Judgement* is "taste." In focusing on this most crucial notion of eighteenth-century reflections on art, Kant joins fellow aestheticians of the age in bidding farewell to onto-theological theories of beauty revolving around notions such as *harmonia, consonantia,* and *integritas* to develop experientially grounded accounts of the production and reception of art that employ a wholly different, subject-centred and sensually inflected vocabulary: aesthetic idea, aesthetic feeling, sensuous cognition, the imagination, genius, the sublime, and taste.[3] If Kant's Copernican revolution and its assertion that "we can cognize of things *a priori* only what we ourselves have put into them" relegated realist epistemology to the margins of philosophical inquiry for over two centuries, his theory of aesthetic judgment likewise shifts our attention away from real-world objects and towards the subject's experience.[4] In a related vein, Kant's notion of beauty is explicitly anti-metaphysical in that it locates beauty neither in artworks' correspondence with a divinely ordered cosmos nor in objects themselves. Instead, beauty is in the mind of the beholder; it is something we experience: we "speak of the beautiful as if beauty were a property of the object and the judgment logical (constituting a cognition of the object through concepts of it), although it is only aesthetic and contains merely a relation of the representation of the object to the subject."[5] More precisely, the pleasurable experience of beauty is an effect of the harmonious interplay of the cognitive faculties of understanding and imagination.[6] Finally, if Hartmut Böhme is correct in considering eighteenth-century theories of the sublime as an integral part of the Enlighten-

---

3 For a good account of this shift, see Monroe C. Beardsley's classic *Aesthetics from Classical Greece to the Present* (New York: Macmillan, 1966), 140-208.

4 Kant, "Preface," 111.

5 Immanuel Kant, *Critique of the Power of Judgment*, trans. Paul Guyer and Eric Matthews (Cambridge: Cambridge University Press, 2000), §6, 97.

6 See Paul Guyer, "Beauty and Utility in Eighteenth-Century Aesthetics," *Eighteenth-Century Studies* (2002), 35:3, 449-50.

ment's project of achieving mastery over unruly nature, of submitting *le grand dehors* under human beings' cognitive control, then Kant's reflections on the dynamical sublime, a feeling that grows out of the subject's pleasurable recognition that its reason ultimately prevails over awe-inspiring nature, are an integral part of that project.[7] Monroe C. Beardsley puts it aptly: "It is our own greatness, as rational beings, that we celebrate and enjoy in sublimity."[8]

For all these reasons, then, Kant has emerged as speculative realism's most prominent foil. Yet any attempt to think metaphysics and aesthetics together must contend with a second, equally formidable opponent, a somewhat earlier philosopher greatly admired by Kant: Alexander Gottlieb Baumgarten. Kant based his own lectures on metaphysics on what was then the German-speaking world's major treatise on that subject—Baumgarten's *Metaphysica* (1739)—and he inherited Baumgarten's understanding of aesthetic judgment as aesthetic (sensuous) cognition.

It was Baumgarten who coined the term "aesthetics" in his M.A. thesis *Meditationes philosophicae de nonnullis ad poema pertinentibus* (1735).[9] The brief definition he gives there, in §116 of his short treatise, will come as a surprise to many readers of these pages. In Karl Aschenbrenner and William B. Holther's translation,

> Therefore, *things known* are to be known by the superior faculty as the object of logic; *things perceived* [are to be known by the inferior faculty, as the object] of the science of perception, or *aesthetic*.[10]

[7] Hartmut Böhme, "Das Steinerne: Anmerkungen zur Theorie des Erhabenen aus dem Blick des 'Menschenfremdesten'" in *Das Erhabene: Zwischen Grenzerfahrung und Grössenwahn*, ed. Christine Priess (Weinheim: VCH, Acta humaniora, 1989), 160-92.

[8] Beardsley, *Aesthetics*, 219.

[9] This text has been published in English translation as *Reflections on Poetry/ Meditationes philosophicae de nonnullis ad poema pertinentibus*, trans. Karl Aschenbrenner and William B. Holther (Berkeley: University of California Press, 1954).

[10] Baumgarten, *Reflections*, §116, 78, original emphases. In the Latin/Greek

Baumgarten's distinction between the superior faculty (reason) and the inferior faculty (the senses) corresponds to Gottfried Wilhelm Leibniz's successive set of differentiations between obscure and clear, confused and distinct, inadequate and adequate, and symbolic and intuitive cognition. In Leibniz's scheme, in which the second term of each pair is always the preferred one, reason allows for clear and distinct cognition while the senses allow only for clear and confused cognition.[11] In Baumgarten's account, sensory perception allows us to know things with clarity but intuitively and thus without the conceptual distinctness of reason—without, in Baumgarten's words, "clarity intensified by distinction."[12] What makes Baumgarten's contribution exceptional in 1735 is that he not only joins Leibniz in refusing to follow Descartes' outright dismissal of clear but confused perception but strives to give sensuous cognition its rightful place within the philosophical system of rationalism. This comes out clearly in his better-known definition of "aesthetics" in his two-volume *Aesthetica* (1750/58), a work that can rightly be called the foundational text of modern aesthetics. In Jeffrey Barnouw's translation,

> Aesthetics, as the theory of the liberal arts, lower-level epistemology [*gnoseologia inferior*], the art of thinking finely [literally, beautifully, *ars pulchre cogitandi*], and the art of the analogy of reason [i.e., the associa-

original, "Sunt ergo νοητά cognoscenda facultate superiore objectum logices; αισθητά, 'επιστήης. αισθητιχης sive AESHETICAE." Baumgarten, *Reflections*, §116, 39.

[11] Gottfried Wilhelm Leibniz, "Betrachtungen über die Erkenntnis, die Wahrheit und die Ideen" in *Hauptschriften zur Grundlegung der Philosophie*, Teil 1, trans. Artur Buchenau, Philosophische Werke: in vier Bänden, ed. Ernst Cassirer, vol. 1 (Hamburg: Meiner, 1996), 9-15. Leibniz's set of distinctions further refine the Cartesian differentiation between the clear and distinct perceptions afforded by reason and the clear but confused perceptions afforded by the senses. See Descartes' famous wax example in his *Meditations on First Philosophy*, trans. Ian Johnston, ed. Andrew Bailey (Peterborough: Broadview Press, 2013), 46-52. See also Ralf Simon, *Die Idee der Prosa: Zur Ästhetikgeschichte von Baumgarten bis Hegel mit einem Schwerpunkt bei Jean Paul* (Munich: Fink, 2013), 30-31.

[12] Alexander Gottlieb Baumgarten, *Ästhetik* [*Aesthetica*], trans. Dagmar Mirbach, 2 vols. (Hamburg: Meiner, 2007), §617, II: 604, our translation.

9

tive or natural-sign-based capacity of empirical inference common to man and higher animals], is the science of sensuous cognition.[13]

Sensuous cognition, then, belongs to lower-level epistemology in that it depends on the inferior faculty of the senses. But it is structured analogous to reason, is subject to the same truth conditions as reason (the principle of sufficient reason and law of noncontradiction),[14] and accounts for such a great variety of human experience that the philosophical tradition from Descartes to Christian Wolff has disparaged it at its own loss. In Baumgarten's words, "A philosopher is a human being among human beings; as such, he is ill-advised to believe that such a great part of human cognition is unseemly to him."[15]

Baumgarten's valorisation of the senses and of sensuous cognition was daring for its time, especially for a rationalist philosopher. Yet it is precisely that boldness which puts him at odds with the speculative realist project. Baumgarten's aesthetics appears as subject-centred as Kant's: both conceptualise aesthetics as a question of human consciousness, be it under the heading of "taste" or "sensuous cognition." As such, both appear to be correlationist thinkers through and through.

The remainder of this first section of our introduction argues that this is a hasty judgment. Let us begin with Kant, for whose aesthetics the argument has already been made, and then turn to Baumgarten. Recently, one of the contributors to our special issue has made the suggestion that it is precisely Kant's much maligned notion of disinterestedness that sketches a way out of the correlationist circle as it describes

---

[13] Jeffrey Barnouw, "Feeling in Enlightenment Aesthetics," *Studies in Eighteenth-Century Culture* (1988), 18, 324; the square brackets are Barnouw's. In the Latin original, "AESTHETICA (theoria liberalium artium, gnoseologia inferior, ars pulchre cogitandi, ars analogi rationis) est scientia cognitionis sensitivae." Baumgarten, *Aesthetica*, §1, I:10.

[14] See Constanze Peres, "Cognitio sensitiva: Zum Verhältnis von Empfindung und Reflexion in A. G. Baumgartens Begründung der Ästhetiktheorie" in *Empfindung und Reflexion: Ein Problem des 18. Jahrhunderts*, ed. Hans Körner et al. (Hildesheim: Georg Olms Verlag, 1986), 31-39.

[15] Baumgarten, *Aesthetica*, §6, I:14, our translation.

a way for human beings to relate to the real world that does not subject it to conceptual thought. In *Without Criteria: Kant, Whitehead, Deleuze, and Aesthetics* (2009), Steven Shaviro writes,

> When I contemplate something that I consider beautiful, I am moved precisely by that something's separation from me, its exemption from the categories I would apply to it. This is why beauty is a lure, drawing me out of myself and teasing me out of thought ... The aesthetic subject does not impose its forms upon an otherwise chaotic outside world. Rather, this subject is itself *informed by* the world outside, a world that (in the words of Wallace Stevens) "fills the being before the mind can think."[16]

Kant distinguishes between three types of pleasurable experience: that of the agreeable, that of the good, and that of the beautiful. Only the last of these is disinterested; only "the beautiful" is "an object of satisfaction without any interest."[17] Disinterestedness here means that the experience of the beautiful involves neither desire for sensual gratification (as would Emmentaler cheese, which we may find agreeable) nor the satisfaction granted by the conceptual mastery of an object in view of its pragmatic purpose (as would a multifunctional bike tool, which we may find good because it is useful).[18] Shaviro notes that, unlike the judgment of the good, the judgment of the beautiful involves no subsumption of the object under a determinate concept (the concept of an end in our example of the bike tool). And it is for this reason that aesthetic experience and judgment gesture beyond the correlationist mantra that, in Meillassoux's words, "we only ever have access to the correlation between thinking and being, and never to either term considered apart from the

---

[16] Steven Shaviro, *Without Criteria: Kant, Whitehead, Deleuze, and Aesthetics* (Cambridge: MIT Press, 2009), 4-5, 12, original emphasis.

[17] Kant, *Critique of the Power of Judgment*, §6, 96.

[18] Of course, Kant distinguishes between two judgments of the good; our example does not cover the moral good, which is an end in itself. Our understanding of Kant's notion of disinterestedness is indebted to Paul Guyer, "Disinterestedness and Desire in Kant's Aestheticism," *The Journal of Aesthetics and Art Criticism* (1978), 36:4, 449-60.

other."[19] This is why, in Shaviro's reading, the Kant of the third critique, the Kant who proposes that "the judgment of taste is not a cognitive judgment (neither a theoretical nor a practical one), and hence it is neither grounded on concepts nor aimed at them," emerges as a potential ally of speculative realism.[20] In our volume, it is Francis Halsall who most explicitly engages with the Kantian notion of the judgment of taste and its relevance to today's debates within speculative realist circles.

More generally speaking, quite apart from either Kant's reflections on disinterested pleasure or Graham Harman's provocative declaration that "aesthetics becomes first philosophy," it may be in aesthetic thinking that we should look for a way out of the correlationist path laid out by Kant's first critique.[21] It is this supposition that prompted us to solicit papers for a special issue on speculative realist approaches to aesthetics in the first place. And it is that very same supposition that invites us to return to the origin of aesthetics in Baumgarten once more. True, the Baumgartian understanding of aesthetics as "the science of sensuous cognition" seems to lead us straight down the correlationist road. But it does so only if we disregard the provenance of Baumgarten's thinking about sense perception. Baumgarten was a philosopher trained in the rationalist tradition of Descartes, Leibniz, and Wolff. As such, he belongs to the very history of ideas in which Meillassoux situates his claims concerning the necessity of contingency: "I'm a rationalist, and reason clearly demonstrates that you can't demonstrate the necessity of laws: so we should just believe reason and accept this point: laws are not necessary—they are facts, and facts are contingent—they can change without reason."[22] And yet, as we will see, Baumgarten

---

[19] Meillassoux, *After Finitude*, 5.

[20] Kant, *Critique of the Power of Judgment*, §5, 95.

[21] Graham Harman, "On Vicarious Causation," *Collapse* (2007), 2, 221.

[22] Quentin Meillassoux, "Time Without Becoming," Speculative Heresy, http://speculativeheresy.files.wordpress.com/2008/07/3729-time_without_becoming.pdf (accessed June 26, 2013).

represents a rationalist tradition quite different from that evoked by Meillassoux (or Ray Brassier, for that matter).

In giving the senses their due, Baumgarten does not subscribe to the eighteenth-century empiricist (and thus by definition correlationist) creed of contemporaneous British aestheticians such as Francis Hutcheson and David Hume. Instead, he strives to establish a science of sensuous cognition from *within* the bounds of rationalist thought. That Baumgarten's aesthetics is ultimately metaphysical to the core becomes clearest in section XXXIV of the *Aesthetica* ("The Absolute Aesthetic Striving for Truth"). There, he writes,

> Indeed, I believe that philosophers can now see with the utmost clarity that whatever formal perfection inheres in cognition and logical truth can be attained only with a great loss of much material perfection. For what is this abstraction but loss? By the same token, you cannot bring a marble sphere out of an irregular piece of marble without losing at least as much material as the higher value of roundness demands.[23]

Four paragraphs later, Baumgarten adds a remarkable observation:

> Above all, the aesthetic horizon delights in those particular objects that exhibit the greatest material perfection of aestheticological truth, in the individuals and the most specific of objects. These are its woods, its chaos, its matter [*sua silva, Chao et materia*] out of which it chisels the aesthetic truth into a form that is not entirely perfect yet beautiful, always in the attempt to lose as little materially perfect truth as possible and rub off as little of it for the sake of tastefulness.[24]

Baumgarten has a remarkably strong notion of truth, which we have learned to distrust in the wake of Nietzsche and his post-structuralist heirs (on potential Nietzschean ramifications for speculative realism, see Theodor Leiber and Kirsten Voigt's contribution to this volume). As we will see in the second

---

[23] Baumgarten, *Aesthetica*, §560, I:538, our translation.

[24] Ibid., §564, I:542, our translation.

section of this introduction, it took Alain Badiou to return aesthetics to the question of truth. For Baumgarten, sensuous cognition allows us to glimpse something of that which reason's striving for abstraction and formal perfection denies us: the richness, multiplicity, plenitude, and particularity of things, the "woods," "chaos" and "matter" of the real world.[25] More precisely, not only sensuous but all cognition is ultimately based on what Baumgarten calls *"fundus animae"* (the dark ground of the soul), which is a repository for infinitesimally small pre-conscious, unconscious, and half-conscious sensuous perceptions (Leibniz's *petites perceptions*) that ensures the soul's continuing activity even when we sleep and mirrors the plenitude of the universe.[26] For Baumgarten, neither reason nor the senses can ever fully access the infinite universe, but the aestheticological truth of artworks approaches that ideal in that it gives form to the material perfection of things in their multiplicity and particularity: "Aestheticological truth brings the light of beauty into the *fundus animae* by working a beautiful form out of the chaotic woods."[27] In his contribution to our

---

[25] See Peres, "Cognitio sensitiva," 36.

[26] Baumgarten puts it thus in the *Metaphysica*: "There are dark perceptions in the soul. Their totality is called GROUND OF THE SOUL [*FUNDUS ANIMAE*]." Alexander Gottlieb Baumgarten, *Metaphysica*, 7th, rpt. ed. (Hildesheim: Georg Olms Verlag, 1963), §511, 176, our translation. For good discussions of the *fundus animae* and its relation to Leibniz's *petites perceptions*, see Hans Adler, "Fundus Animae—Der Grund der Seele: Zur Gnoseologie des Dunklen in der Aufklärung," *Deutsche Vierteljahrsschrift für Literaturwissenschaft und Geistesgeschichte* (1988), 62:2, 197-220; Peres, "Cognitio sensitiva," 39-40; Tanehisa Otabe, "Der Begriff der 'petites perceptions' von Leibniz als Grundlage für die Entstehung der Ästhetik," *JTLA* (2010), 35, 46-49; and Simon, *Die Idee der Prosa*, 26-46. Note also that while the *fundus animae* seems akin to what Freud would later call "the unconscious," Simon rightly insists that the two are categorically distinct (27-28).

[27] Ralf Simon, *Die Idee der Prosa*, 50, our translation. Note that the resulting artwork is not just form; it is *beautiful* form because it manages to retain something of the plenitude of things instead of reducing them to the sterile formulae of scholasticism (which Baumgarten disparages in §53 of the *Aesthetica*). See Baumgarten, *Aesthetica*, §§557-58, I:534-36; §§562-65, I:540-44. In Wolfgang Welsch's words in "Ästhetische Grundzüge im gegenwärtigen Denken" in *Grenzgänge der Ästhetik* (Stuttgart: Reclam, 1996), 81: "Aesthetics—which Baumgarten introduced as a Trojan horse into the fortress of the

volume, Sjoerd van Tuinen taps into this rationalist tradition to argue that artworks themselves can be speculative. Yet not even the aestheticological truth of art can capture the truth of the world in its totality; Baumgarten "liberates himself from the idea of total access, from the ideal of complete cognition and thus also from the traditional obsession with absolute assurance and certainty."[28] In this model, only God is able to cognise things simultaneously in their formal and material perfection; only he possesses metaphysical truth. Ultimately, then, Baumgarten turns out to be a rationalist quite different from Meillassoux: Baumgarten, too, aims at the real, but he does not presume that the absolute can be recuperated. Instead, he stresses human finitude, i.e., our ultimate inability to access the real. For that reason, even though Baumgarten is clearly no empiricist in its eighteenth-century sense, his thinking has the closest affinities not with Meillassoux's work but with those speculative realists we describe as—rather unusual—empiricists in the third section of this introduction (Harman, Shaviro, Iain Hamilton Grant, Tim Morton). Baumgarten's framing of aesthetics as a theory of experience, sensation, and sensuous cognition lays the ground for their expansion of aesthetic thinking into the non-human world.

Not unlike Kantian disinterested pleasure, sensuous cognition allows us to experience the real in its confused beauty rather than subjecting it to conceptual thought. Perhaps, it is in sensuous cognition and aesthetic experience that "intuitions without concepts" are *not* "blind" after all.[29] If, from the perspective of what N. Katherine Hayles in this issue calls the argumentative, philosophical variety of speculative aesthetics (an aesthetic theory born out of the spirit of speculative realism), one of the thorniest questions concerning

---

sciences—brings about a change in the concepts of science and cognition: henceforth, genuine cognition is aestheticological cognition, and genuine science cannot ignore its aesthetic determinants" (our translation).

[28] Steffen W. Gross, "Felix Aestheticus und Animal Symbolicum: Alexander G. Baumgarten—die 'vierte Quelle' der Philosophie Ernst Cassirers?" *Deutsche Zeitschrift für Philosophie* (2001), 49:2, 285, our translation.

[29] Kant, *Critique of Pure Reason*, 193-94.

aesthetics is that of human access to the real, then both Kant's and Baumgarten's inquiries into forms of access that are not primarily conceptual in nature at the very least allow us to imagine non-correlationist ways of relating to the universe of things. For a speculative realism that does not follow Meillassoux in trying to reclaim the absolute on purely rational grounds this is a crucial, though underexplored legacy.

But let us not jump too quickly from eighteenth-century aesthetics to the new metaphysicians. As the following section shows, the speculative realists are not alone among contemporary thinkers in returning to the original meaning of aesthetics as a theory of modalities of perception.[30]

Contemporary French and German Aesthetics

Aesthetic matters have generally witnessed a strong return in philosophy and other disciplines of the humanities in the last fifteen years.[31] In this section, we briefly survey some of the influential positions in contemporary aesthetics in order to establish what it means to pursue aesthetics in the twenty-first century and how these contemporary discourses in turn contribute to understanding the content, aims, and possible limits of speculative aesthetics.

Let us begin with two thinkers whose work has been greatly responsible for the present resurgence of aesthetics in philosophy, art history and criticism, media and literary studies: Alain Badiou and Jacques Rancière.

In the *Handbook of Inaesthetics*, Alain Badiou claims that what we lack today is a proper understanding of the relation between art, philosophy, and truth. In his view, three schemata have so far determined our understanding of this relation.

---

[30] For a similar assessment, see Ernst von Glasersfeld, "Farewell to Objectivity," *Systems Research* (1996), 13:3, 279-86.

[31] See John J. Joughin and Simon Malpas, eds., *The New Aestheticism* (Manchester: Manchester University Press, 1996); Isobel Armstrong, *The Radical Aesthetic* (Oxford: Blackwell, 2000); Jonathan Loesberg, *A Return to Aesthetics* (Stanford: Stanford University Press, 2005); Thomas Docherty, *Aesthetic Democracy* (Stanford: Stanford University Press, 2006).

He terms these schemata the "didactic," the "classical," and the "romantic." The didactic and the classical schemata have their origin in Greek philosophy, in Plato and Aristotle, while the third schema, as its name implies, was established in the Romantic age.[32] According to the didactic schema, art produces a "semblance" of truth while truth is in fact "external to art" and only conceivable in philosophy. In the romantic schema, "art *alone* is capable of truth," a truth that philosophy can only approximate. And in the classical schema, there is no truth to art at all—art is only cathartic, and "not at all cognitive or revelatory."[33]

Badiou holds that the major schools of thought of the twentieth century were but continuations of these schemata: Marxism was a continuation of the didactic schema—we see this in the work of Brecht, for whom art makes manifest an external, philosophical truth, that of "dialectical materialism"; German hermeneutics was a continuation of the romantic schema—we see this in the work of Heidegger, where only the poet truly "maintains the effaced guarding of the Open," meaning only art discloses the truth that philosophy can at best proclaim or register; and psychoanalysis was a continuation of the classical schema—we see this in the work of Freud and Lacan, for whom art is mainly therapeutic and has no claim to truth outside of the "imaginary."[34]

Crucially, Badiou holds that the twentieth-century continuations of the inherited schemata led to a "*saturation* of these doctrines." The major schools of thought in the twentieth century, while unable to establish a new schema for the relationship between art, philosophy, and truth, have all reached certain—political, quasi-theological, institutional—dead ends, ultimately relinquishing any claim to truth on the part of art. Badiou suggests that this is due to the fact that none of these schools of thought established a notion of artistic truth that

---

[32] Alain Badiou, *Handbook of Inaesthetics*, trans. Alberto Toscano (Stanford: Stanford University Press, 2005), 1-5.

[33] Badiou, *Handbook of Inaesthetics*, 2-4, original emphasis.

[34] Ibid., 5-7.

is *proper* to art itself. In his words, they missed out on articulating a notion of artistic truth that is both "immanent" and "singular"—a truth that is manifest *in* art and, in the particular form in which it is manifest, *only* in art.[35]

In the didactic schema, the truth of art is singular yet not immanent: singular because art is a semblance and because semblance is unique to art; yet not immanent because truth ultimately belongs to philosophy. In the romantic schema, the truth of art is immanent yet not singular: immanent because art (and only art) makes truth manifest; yet not singular because this is a truth that philosophy also aspires to. In the classical schema, the truth of art is neither singular nor immanent: art is merely therapeutic, without any claims to truth whatsoever. Yet only through a singular and immanent notion of artistic truth can we find a way out of the dead ends of the predominant aesthetic discourses of the twentieth century.[36]

Badiou holds that we can only arrive at such a notion if we give up the idea that *the work of art* is "the pertinent unity of what is called 'art.'"[37] Any notion of artistic truth that proceeds from the work of art as the bearer of that truth must necessarily fall back into the aporiae of the established schemata. Rather, Badiou suggests, we have to comprehend the pertinent unity of art as an

> Artistic configuration initiated by an evental rupture ... This configuration, which is a generic multiple, possesses neither a proper name nor a proper contour, not even a possible totalization in terms of a single predicate. It cannot be exhausted, only imperfectly described. It is an artistic truth, and everybody knows that there is no truth of truth.[38]

Badiou's evental notion of artistic truth cannot be exhaustively discussed here.[39] Yet what we can grasp from this brief

---

[35] Badiou, *Handbook of Inaesthetics*, 7-9, original emphases.

[36] See Ibid., 9.

[37] Ibid., 10.

[38] Ibid., 12.

[39] For a more extensive discussion of Badiou's inaesthetics and his evental

account is that Badiou perceives the major aesthetic discourses of the twentieth century to have reached certain historical limits, which in his view is based on their failure to properly comprehend the truth of art, that is, to establish a notion of artistic truth that is both singular and immanent, according to which art is "irreducible to philosophy,"[40] and in which philosophical aesthetics becomes an "inaesthetics," a thinking about art that "makes no claim to turn art into an object for philosophy."[41] And in order to achieve such a notion of artistic truth, we must first consider what we talk about when we talk about art: the author, the work, the recipient, or, as Badiou suggests, an event?

In the *Handbook of Inaesthetics*, Badiou returns to an issue that centrally concerned Baumgarten at the inauguration of aesthetics as a discipline—the relation between art, truth, and philosophy. How does Baumgarten's notion of this relation fare in the schemata of Badiou? Baumgarten seems to firmly remain within their limits, yet a clear assignment of his notion of artistic truth to one of the schemata seems quite difficult. As stated earlier, aestheticological truth has the advantage over the truth procedures of reason that it provides us with a material, concrete kind of truth that reason alone—because of its necessary abstraction—cannot deliver. This might suggest that we are dealing with an immanent yet not singular kind of truth here, i.e., with the romantic schema: art (the aestheticological truth procedure) aspires to the same kind of truth that philosophy (the truth procedure of reason) does, but whereas philosophy's truths are purely formal, art retains something of the plenitude of the universe in giving form to matter and thereby presenting a perhaps even more comprehensive form of truth. Yet one could also argue that this more material form of truth is in fact merely complementary: while art does bring forth a special kind of

---

notion of artistic truth, see Peter Hallward, *Badiou: A Subject to Truth* (Minneapolis: University of Minnesota Press, 2003), 193-208.

[40] Badiou, *Handbook of Inaesthetics*, 9.

[41] Ibid., epigraph.

truth, this kind of truth, because it is not strictly based in the procedures of reason, remains subordinated to philosophical truth—Baumgarten is a rationalist after all. This would then suggest the didactic schema: art is singular in that it produces a concrete, material kind of truth, yet truth in its highest form is not immanent to art, but only to philosophy.

The exact position of Baumgarten in the schemata of Badiou appears ultimately undecidable—it oscillates between the romantic and the didactic—but what is clear is that he certainly does not present a notion of artistic truth which is both singular and immanent, i.e., a kind of truth which in Badiou's view would do justice to a contemporary aesthetics that manages to overcome the dead ends of the major schools of thought of the twentieth century.

Since Badiou's schemata shed light on both the historical and the contemporary landscapes of aesthetics, relating speculative realism to them should prove illuminating with respect to its position vis-à-vis other contemporary currents. Given that speculative realism does not denote a unified doctrine, such juxtaposition should also shed some light on internal differences within the movement. This is a thread we will take up again in the third and last section of our essay. For now, let us continue with our brief and selective survey of contemporary positions by turning to another prominent French thinker: Jacques Rancière.

Whereas Badiou's work invites us to think about the relation between art, philosophy, and truth, with Jacques Rancière we are given the opportunity to address matters of politics and aesthetics. Arguably, the relation between politics and aesthetics is one of the central issues of Rancière's oeuvre. For the purpose of our brief survey, we will focus on Rancière's *The Politics of Aesthetics*—a book that nicely sums up his aesthetico-political project.

One obvious way to think about the relation between aesthetics and politics would be to think about the avant-garde, yet Rancière holds that "avant-garde thinking" has today turned into a form of "nostalgia"—a form of thought that only still claims the utopian in its absence.[42] This is best perceived in the work of Jean-François Lyotard, in which art becomes "witness to an encounter with the unrepresentable that cripples all thought" as a means to accuse or prevent the "arrogance of the grand aesthetic-political endeavour to have 'thought' become 'world'"—an endeavour that has become ideologically dubious, and must hence be rejected, which means for art to reject thought, or rather, to present that which cannot be attained by thought.[43] This however renders such an avant-garde thinking politically powerless.

Rancière's aim is not to proclaim, once more, "the avant-garde vocation of art or … the vitality of modernity that links the conquests of artistic innovation to the victories of emancipation."[44] Rather, he wants to develop a basic terminology by which we can properly understand the particular relation of aesthetics and politics. In order to achieve this, Rancière holds that we must first acquire a clearer conception of the term aesthetics.[45] Crucially, Rancière suggests that aesthetics must not be understood in its more narrow definition, as the philosophy of art, but more broadly and fundamentally, "in a Kantian sense … as the system of *a priori* forms determining what presents itself to experience."[46] Aesthetics in this sense is concerned with what Rancière famously calls "the distribution of the sensible": "the system of self-evident facts of sense perception that simultaneously discloses the existence of something in common and the delimitations that define the respective parts and positions within it."[47]

Rancière returns here to the very origins of aesthetics— and not only Kant's notion of aesthetics, but also to that of

---

[42] Jacques Rancière, *The Politics of Aesthetics*, trans. Gabriel Rockhill (London: Continuum 2004), 9.

[43] Ibid., 10.

[44] Ibid.

[45] Ibid.

[46] Ibid., 13.

[47] Ibid., 12.

Baumgarten as the science of perception. Yet Rancière gives this notion an emphatic political twist that both Kant and Baumgarten lack. With Rancière, a pleasurable experience can never be disinterested, but is always already interested, shaped by and in turn shaping the distribution of the sensible in pre-discursive—because it pertains to the very basic acts of perception—ways; likewise, whatever is formed out of the plenitude of the universe strives not after an absolute truth, but an ideological one: the aesthetic is not metaphysical, but political.

Rancière's *The Politics of Aesthetics* presents a fundamental rethinking of the relation between politics and aesthetics, which is, crucially, based on a general redetermination of what aesthetics is concerned with: not just with art practices, but more fundamentally with modes of sense perception. Only through such a return to the origins of aesthetics can we finally understand the political import of artistic practices. Rancière's point is that at its very core, the aesthetic act is political: sense perception is always an act that is itself structured and structures that which is perceived, granting the visibility of some objects and rendering others invisible (which affirms the power of some social groups at the cost of others), promoting some genres of art and disqualifying others. Aesthetics *means* the distribution of the sensible.

This very claim—that aesthetics cannot be separated from politics, but is, at its core, entwined with it—is a particularly interesting one to consider with regard to speculative realist thought. Like Rancière, some of the representatives of speculative realism also return to the origins of aesthetics as the science of perception and sensuous cognition in order to newly determine its basic character and thereby general import for philosophy and adjacent disciplines. Yet whereas this redetermination in Rancière suggests that the aesthetic is essentially political, in speculative realism it leads to a marginalisation, if not erasure, of the political. Of course, the basic *non-human* approach of speculative aesthetics might necessitate this: in its establishment of an aesthetics that goes beyond the human scope of things and addresses relations of objects regardless of our investment in them, the political—arguably an essentially human realm—gets dropped from its list of concerns.

Such an assessment of aesthetics after the speculative turn might make one assume that it is an *apolitical* project that attempts to re-establish a newly purified aesthetics, which from a partisan position would render it potentially problematic on ideological terms. Yet such an assumption would be quite short-sighted. For even though the non-human aims of speculative aesthetics disengage it at its core from any political relations, this must not mean that political issues might not re-enter the discussion. It might even be that precisely such a program might help us gain a new understanding of how political action takes place, which is what one of our contributors, Thomas Gokey, suggests. Gokey's essay is interesting for a further reason, because he conceives the speculative possibilities of political action in terms of an avant-garde practice—precisely the practice that is declared obsolete by both Rancière and Badiou.[48] Furthermore, the fact that Harman in his essay engages with the question of what the next avant-garde might look like solidifies our assumption that a speculative aesthetics might pose not just one but several challenges to other popular aesthetic discourses of our time.

We will now move from France to Germany for our last discussion of a contemporary position, and consider the recent developments in aesthetics there. Very helpful in this respect is the collection of essays titled *Falsche Gegensätze: Zeitgenössische Positionen zur philosophischen Ästhetik*. This book brings together essays by some of the major figures in contemporary German aesthetics—Andrea Kern, Jens Kulen-kampff, Christoph Menke, Martin Seel, Ruth Sonderegger, and

---

[48] See Rancière, *The Politics of Aesthetics*, 9-10. Badiou holds that the avant-garde, despite its attempt of being a proper twentieth-century aesthetic, did not manage to overcome the obsolete schemata, but rather formed a combination of two of them: the avant-garde was "didactico-romantic." Badiou, *Handbook of Inaesthetics*, 8.

Albrecht Wellmer—and in the editors' introduction contains a concise statement of their common pursuit.

The basic gesture of recent German aesthetics is similar to that of Badiou and Rancière: it presents a fundamental challenge to some of the persistent premises of modern aesthetic theory. In this, it is specifically concerned with the relation of aesthetics to theoretical and practical philosophy (according to the modern division of philosophy). As Andrea Kern and Ruth Sonderegger claim in their introduction to *Falsche Gegensätze*, we are confronted today with two problematic understandings of this relation.

The first understanding claims that aesthetics assesses a kind of experience which is autonomous and therefore stands in no relation whatsoever to a "theoretical and practical experience of the world," because to argue that there is such a relation would undermine the distinctiveness of aesthetic experience and thereby also of the discipline of aesthetics. The authors hold that such a view implies a "marginalisation" of aesthetic experience for our everyday life, and of aesthetics for philosophy. Aesthetic experience thus at best ends up being just a form of "relief from the ordinary, a diversion, a distraction."[49]

The second understanding assesses the relation between aesthetic, theoretical, and practical experience in a diametrically opposed way. Here, aesthetic experience is no longer conceived as autonomous, "irreducible to the ordinary experience of the world," but conversely represents "the highest form of precisely those experiences that theoretical and practical philosophy also want to comprehend." For in aesthetic experience, the world appears to us "in the whole fullness and variety of possible interests and purposes," rather than being approached under particular aspects, as in practical or theoretical philosophy. Such an understanding however implies that aesthetics, which assesses this experience, is no

---

[49] Andrea Kern and Ruth Sonderegger, "Einleitung" in *Falsche Gegensätze: Zeitgenössische Positionen zur philosophischen Ästhetik*, ed. Andrea Kern and Ruth Sonderegger (Frankfurt a. M.: Suhrkamp 2002), 7-8; this and all subsequent translations are ours.

longer just one of the major disciplines of philosophy, but rather attains the status of "the only *true* philosophy."[50]

The main problem that Kern and Sonderegger perceive here is that these positions are often assumed to be "mutually exclusive"—that it seems impossible to conceive of an aesthetic experience which is both autonomous *and* informative for our everyday lives and the other domains of philosophy. Yet this is the view that the contributors to *Falsche Gegensätze* want to establish. Even more emphatically, they argue that "precisely through the particular way by which it is related to ordinary, everyday experience," aesthetic experience "turns into an autonomous one."[51]

Kern and Sonderegger suggest three central concepts for determining this particular relation of aesthetic experience to other experiences: "reflection, aporiae, and play." The terms themselves already suggest why aesthetic experience is not congruent with ordinary experience—not because it has no relation to it at all, but because it "*relates* itself to it" in a special way—reflectively, aporetically, playfully. The authors hold that this is a crucial point, for it implies that there is a close link between aesthetic experience and the basic gesture of philosophy itself: in philosophy, as in aesthetic experience, "we relate ourselves … to our *relation* to the world."[52]

Such a reconception of aesthetic experience leads to a fundamental redefinition of the position aesthetics takes among the other domains of philosophy: aesthetics is no longer either marginal nor of the highest significance to practical and theoretical philosophy, but now instead stands in a "reciprocal relation" to them. Yet the status of aesthetics does remain special. Because of the philosophical character of aesthetic experience, aesthetics transcends the status of being merely one of the major disciplines in philosophy, but rather becomes the discipline for the contemplation *of* philosophy: in its reflection of aesthetic experience, aesthetics "cannot

---

[50] Kern and Sonderegger, "Einleitung," 8-9, original emphasis.

[51] Ibid., 9-10.

[52] Ibid., 10, our emphasis in second quote, original emphasis in third quote.

forbear to reflect the relation of its subject *to* philosophy and with that to reflect philosophy itself."[53]

We register here a further attempt to fundamentally renegotiate some of the central terms of traditional aesthetics, in this case the relation of aesthetics to practical and theoretical philosophy. Importantly, the contributors to *Falsche Gegensätze* put forward not only that we need a new understanding of this relation, but also that such a new understanding might imply that the discipline of aesthetics claims a special status inside philosophy. Such a diagnosis is reminiscent of Harman's already quoted assertion that aesthetics become "first philosophy." Yet Kern and Sonderegger's assessment is of a markedly different character: whereas in Harman's program, aesthetics becomes *metaphysics*, in Kern and Sonderegger it attains a *metaphilosophical* status.

Summing up our survey of recent French and German contributions to aesthetics and their relation to speculative realist concerns, we can say that one of the fundamental gestures of contemporary aesthetics, by which it attempts to reinvigorate debates about art, is to reconnect such debates to the original concerns of the discipline—to the questions of sensation, sense perception, and sensuous cognition that already occupied Baumgarten and, subsequently, Kant. Connecting again these two divisions of aesthetics—the philosophy of art and the science of sensuous cognition—seems to be one distinctive characteristic of the current writings on aesthetics that creates new valences and yields prolific new ways by which to renegotiate both the relation of aesthetics to the other domains of philosophy and the more specific matters of aesthetics itself. It comes as no surprise, then, that several of the contributions to this issue straddle this division as they ask some of the most fundamental questions about aesthetics and sensuous cognition even as they engage with specific works of art: Roberto Simanowski on digital art, Magdalena Wisniowska on Samuel Beckett's television

---

[53] Kern and Sonderegger, "Einleitung," 10-11, original emphasis.

plays, van Tuinen on mannerist painting, Robert Jackson on the modernist legacy in contemporary video and sculpture work, Harman, Bettina Funcke, and Gokey on avant-garde art. Together with Halsall's reflections on Kant's third critique, these essays make up the second part of our volume, "The Theory of Art," where we bring together those texts that engage most directly with artistic concerns.

Where precisely contemporary reformulations of aesthetics should lead us is a matter of dispute, and the various approaches apparent in aesthetics today vary greatly in terms of their specific aims. Yet they all seem to share something in their pursuits, namely that they all attempt to re-establish the aesthetic in its *distinctiveness*. This means to establish the aesthetic as something *specific*, as in Badiou's claim that art has its own proper truth that is irreducible to other discourses and can never be appropriated by them (which consequently turns any truthful philosophy of art into an inaesthetics); and also as something of *special importance*, as in Rancière's suggestion that politics is always (also) grounded in aesthetics, and in Kern and Sonderegger's claim that aesthetics is the exceptional discipline of philosophy in which philosophy and its other disciplines can be reflected.

Like the other contemporary aesthetic discourses, speculative aesthetics also lays claim to the distinctiveness of the aesthetic, putting forward equally programmatic statements about the particularity of its status precisely by bringing together matters of sensation with matters of art, which consequently enables an extensive re-evaluation of the proper matters of aesthetics, which, as in Claire Colebrook's contribution to our volume, might very well turn out to be the inherent aestheticism of matter itself. The first part of our issue, entitled "The Art of Theory," assembles these more programmatic interventions featuring, besides Colebrook's essay, the contributions of Shaviro, Leiber and Voigt, Matija Jelača, Hayles, Jon Cogburn and Mark Allan Ohm, and Miguel Penas López.

Speculations V
Aesthetics and Speculative Realism

Having traced the historical origins and, by means of paradig-matic examples, the contemporary landscape of the discipline of aesthetics and the attendant problems and questions it grapples with, we will now try to determine the place of the recent speculative turn in continental philosophy within this field.[54] In order to do so, both historically and systematically, let us first return to the beginnings of aesthetics and its early eighteenth-century prehistory in the discourse on taste.

In his entry in the *Stanford Encyclopedia of Philosophy*, James

---

[54] Of the original four speculative realists, Graham Harman has undoubtedly been the most explicit advocate of aesthetics. His claim that aesthetics has to be viewed as first philosophy and his theory of allure are well known by now. In addition to the already mentioned "Vicarious Causation" see also his "Aesthetics as First Philosophy: Levinas and the Non-Human," *Naked Punch* (2007), 9, 21-30 and particularly his *Guerrilla Metaphysics: Phenomenology and the Carpentry of Things* (Chicago: Open Court, 2005), 101-44. Quentin Meillassoux in turn has recently given us his reading of Mallarmé's *Coup de dés* in Quentin Meillassoux, *The Number and the Siren: A Decipherment of Mallarmé's Coup de Dés*, trans. Robin Mackay (Falmouth: Urbanomic, 2012). And while Iain Hamilton Grant has not explicitly written on aesthetics per se yet, given his Deleuzo-Schellingian dynamic process philosophy, it is safe to say that aesthetics plays a crucial role in his metaphysical project. One need only remember that Schelling pronounced "aesthetic intuition" as "merely transcendental intuition become objective" and art thus consequently "at once the only true and eternal organ and document of philosophy" (F. W. J. Schelling, *System of Transcendental Idealism*, trans. Peter Heath (Charlottesville: The University Press of Virginia, 1978), 231), and that for Deleuze aesthetics is the "apodictic discipline" (Gilles Deleuze, *Difference and Repetition*, trans. Paul Patton (London: Continuum, 2004), 68). From the original four, only Ray Brassier has voiced his disdain for aesthetics ("Against an Aesthetics of Noise," *Transitzone*, nY, http://ny-web.be/transitzone/against-aesthetics-noise.html (accessed September 18, 2013)). To these four thinkers, one should add Steven Shaviro and Reza Negarestani, the latter engaging aesthetic form directly by means of theory fiction. See Steven Shaviro, *Without Criteria* and Reza Negarestani, *Cyclonopedia: Complicity with Anonymous Materials* (Melbourne: Re.press, 2008). In addition, Timothy Morton just published his *Realist Magic: Objects, Ontology, Causality* (Ann Arbor: Open Humanities Press, 2013) that takes up Harman's philosophy in order to develop an aesthetic account of causality. Finally, one should mention Armen Avanessian's project of a speculative poetics and the book series related to this project: *Spekulative Poetik*, http://www.spekulative-poetik.de/ (accessed September 18, 2013).

Shelley emphasises the antagonistic stance theories of taste adopt vis-à-vis rationalist theories of beauty. He describes the situation thus:

> Rationalism about beauty is the view that judgments of beauty are judgments of reason, i.e., that we judge things to be beautiful by reasoning it out, where reasoning it out typically involves inferring from principles or applying concepts … It was against this … that mainly British philosophers working mainly within an empiricist framework began to develop theories of taste. The fundamental idea behind any such theory—which we may call *the immediacy thesis*—is that judgments of beauty are not (or at least not primarily) mediated by inferences from principles or applications of concepts, but rather have all the immediacy of straightforwardly sensory judgments; it is the idea, in other words, that we do not reason to the conclusion that things are beautiful, but rather "taste" that they are.[55]

In this vein, if one were to paint a broad-brush picture of speculative realism, one could maintain that what we are witnessing today, what is discernible now that the very first wave of the speculative turn has hit the shore and the ripples have subsided, is a new struggle between rationalism and empiricism *within* contemporary speculative philosophy in general and its take on aesthetics in particular. In fact, aesthetics is the domain that brings to light precisely this divide. Devoting a special issue to speculative realism and aesthetics thus not only provides an opportunity to survey what the speculative turn in all its variety might bring to the discourse on aesthetics, but comes with the added value of sharpening the focus on this variety itself. In analogy to Shelley's account, one could thus say that for the contemporary rationalists, mathematics (Meillassoux) and science (Brassier) dictate the discourse on and the place of aesthetics within the larger framework of epistemology with the concomitant intent to hunt down any manifestation of the, in their view, illusory "immediacy

---

[55] James Shelley, "The Concept of the Aesthetic," *The Stanford Encyclopedia of Philosophy* (Fall 2013 Edition), http://plato.stanford.edu/archives/fall2013/entries/aesthetic-concept/ (accessed September 23, 2013), original emphasis.

thesis." The empiricists (Harman and Grant, but also Shaviro and Morton) in turn insist upon "immediacy" and a theory of taste in disguise holding that we immediately taste something before we conceptually know it. Brassier voiced this divide within speculative realism precisely along these lines in a 2009 interview, where he said that he is

> Very wary of "aesthetics": the term is contaminated by notions of "experience" that I find deeply problematic. I have no philosophy of art worth speaking of. This is not to dismiss art's relevance for philosophy—far from it—but merely to express reservations about the kind of philosophical aestheticism which seems to want to hold up "aesthetic experience" as a new sort of cognitive paradigm wherein the Modern (post-Cartesian) "rift" between knowing and feeling would be overcome … Some recent philosophers have evinced an interest in subjectless experiences; I am rather more interested in experience-less subjects.[56]

This passage indeed seems to suggest that aesthetics is the domain where the differences among the speculative realists are most acutely on display. In addition, Brassier's juxtaposition highlights the inverse importance accorded to experience (empiricism) on the one hand and the subject (rationalism) on the other, thus confirming our labelling of the two opposing camps as empiricists and rationalists respectively. Resuming our genealogical recovery of the empiricist notion of taste from a contemporary point of view, let us emphasise that we spoke of a theory of taste in disguise since this traditional expression is barely ever mentioned in the respective speculative realist writings.[57] Furthermore, these theories of taste would

---

[56] Brassier, "Against an Aesthetics of Noise," n.pag.

[57] Morton, while not discussing it in detail, does refer to it in passing several times in his latest monograph. Morton, *Realist Magic*, 77, 89, 131, 168, 201. Shaviro in turn discusses taste more extensively, particularly throughout the first chapter of his *Without Criteria*. Shaviro, *Without Criteria*, 1-16. Both treat taste in the context of Kant's analytic of the beautiful precisely, as already indicated in our first section, because 1) Kantian judgments of taste are not regulated by concepts, and 2) because Kantian judgments of taste are disinterested. This moment in the discourse on taste is attractive to these thinkers because it seems to offer a potential entryway to things as they are, that is, reality itself.

have to be de-humanised as they apply to the fabric of reality
as such, not just the realm of the human faculty of judgment.
It becomes clearer what we are trying to say if we complement
taste with intuition, sensation, and perception (as it actually
happened in the history of aesthetics itself, as Baumgarten's
aesthetics qua sensuous cognition followed on the heels of
early British reflections on taste).[58] Thus, in Harman's (and
Morton's) object-oriented framework, aesthetics, as manifested
in the theory of allure, refers to one object tasting, intuiting,
sensing, perceiving another object; in Grant's Schellingian
transcendental naturalism, aesthetics concerns the tasting,
the intuition of nature's forces and potencies; and in Shaviro's Whiteheadian cosmology, which he further develops
in his contribution to this volume, it adequately describes
the domain of prehension, that is, the domain of relationality per se. For all these thinkers, any encounter whatsoever
is always the site of aesthetic experience (and the emphasis
rests on both of these terms equally). In these philosophies,
aesthetics is other to conceptual knowledge, and prior to it.
Given the expansion of aesthetics into the non-human realm,
this is also the moment when aesthetics is pushed from the
domain of human epistemology into that of general ontology. Ceasing to be a particular kind of human relation to the
world, it becomes a general descriptor of relationality of/in[59]
the world. As López argues in his contribution to this volume,
Gilbert Simondon's relational ontology has ventured into
this terrain half a century before the speculative realists. It
is in exploring that same space, albeit under the banner of a
substance ontology, that Harman has ventured to call aesthet-

---

[58] One would have to mention Joseph Addison and Richard Steele, *The Spectator,
with Notes, and a General Index*, 2 vols. (New York: Printed by Samuel Marks,
1826), Anthony Ashley Cooper (Third Earl of Shaftesbury), *Characteristics of
Men, Manners, Opinions, Times*, ed. Lawrence E. Klein (Cambridge: Cambridge
University Press, 1999), and Francis Hutcheson, *An Inquiry into the Origin of
Our Ideas of Beauty and Virtue*, ed. Wolfgang Leidhold (Indianapolis: Liberty
Fund, 2004), all of which were published between 1711 and 1725 and thus
well before Baumgarten coined the term "aesthetics" in 1735.

[59] The choice of the preposition depends on whether one favours a relational
ontology (of) or a substance ontology (in).

ics first philosophy: in this framework, human epistemology only builds on and comes after the general aesthetic structure of/in being. Indeed, "subjectless experience" underlies and comes to determine cognising subjects.

It is this centrality of aesthetic experience that the rationalists dispute. They view such a hypostatisation of aesthetic experience beyond the human realm as illegitimate and unfounded. Why use terms such as perception or intuition for describing non-human relations? According to the rationalists, this not only confuses a very human trait for a trait of reality in general; much worse, it actually impedes and hinders the rational inquiry into human and non-human relations, just as Jelača argues in staging a face-off between Sellars and Deleuze in his contribution. Thus, for the rationalists, epistemology qua rational inquiry governs and determines aesthetics. By their lights, any immediate "tasting" of anything is but a human fiction. Consequently, they do not have much to say in this regard, as Brassier himself makes unmistakably clear in the passage quoted above. All they have to offer for this discourse is to call it out for its "irrationalism."

Our neat dichotomy of rationalists vs. empiricists is too neat, though, and needs to be complicated. After all, the advent of Kant's transcendental philosophy separates this older debate from everything that came afterwards. Nothing remained the same after Kant's invention of the transcendental. His Copernican revolution marks the decisive turning point in the history of modern philosophy *as it intervenes precisely in this debate between rationalism and empiricism*. It is in this context that Meillassoux's diagnosis of correlationism, a diagnosis all speculative realists agree on, needs to be located. As Paul J. Ennis has convincingly shown,[60] the charge of correlationism is precisely directed against transcendental philosophy.[61] Thus, we have to add transcendental philosophy

---

[60] Paul J. Ennis, *Continental Realism* (Winchester: Zero, 2010).

[61] This is also the reason why Meillassoux has ventured to propose the term subjectalism as a complement to the earlier correlationism in one of his recent essays, Quentin Meillassoux, "Iteration, Reiteration, Repetition: A Speculative Analysis of the Meaningless Sign," http://oursecretblog.com/

to the mix. What we are witnessing in speculative realism is to a large extent a reworking of the transcendental. What all of the speculative realists retain from the Kantian invention of the transcendental is its *immanence*.[62] All speculative realists are firmly concerned with this world and their respective philosophies are thisworldly. What they all reject is Kant's Copernican revolution, which Meillassoux in *After Finitude* denounced as a "Ptolemaic counter-revolution."[63] What is rejected is thus the centrality of *human experience* and its *conditions of possibility*. However, while one part of speculative realism particularly rejects the *human* in human experience, the other side rejects precisely the *experience*. On the one side, what results is an *ontological* recasting of the transcendental as it applies to reality per se: a transcendental empiricism (Grant, Harman, Morton, Shaviro); on the other side, we have an *epistemological* account of the powers of human thought to pierce this very same reality: a transcendental rationalism (Brassier, Meillassoux). As such, both of these strains of thought are to a certain extent already present in Kant. This is why Kant, harking back to the very beginning of this article, is both speculative realism's worst enemy *and* best friend.

With respect to aesthetics, we could also recast this divide in terms of Badiou's tripartite division discussed above. In this vein, the transcendental empiricist camp of speculative

txt/QMpaperApr12.pdf (accessed October 24, 2013). A revised version is forthcoming in *Genealogies of Speculation: Materialism and Subjectivity since Structuralism*, ed. Armen Avanessian and Suhail Malik (London: Bloomsbury, 2015). The neologism serves to recuperate and subsume within his sweeping critique both idealist and vitalist philosophies whose point of origin Meillassoux ultimately traces to the pre-transcendental idealism of Berkeley.

[62] Already Gilles Deleuze acknowledged and emphasised this point in his own critique of Kant: "Kant is the one who discovers the prodigious domain of the transcendental. He is the analogue of a great explorer—not of another world, but of the upper or lower reaches of this one." Gilles Deleuze, *Difference and Repetition*, trans. Paul Patton (London: Continuum, 2004), 171.

[63] Meillassoux, *After Finitude*, 119. It is perhaps worth noting that this is not Meillassoux's coinage and has been in use at least since Bertrand Russell's original publication of *Human Knowledge* in 1948. See Bertrand Russell, *Human Knowledge: Its Scope and Limits* (London: Routledge, 2009), 1. Of course, discussions of Kant's "revolution" date to even earlier.

realism would be engaged in a radical reworking of the Badiouian romantic schema, while the transcendental rationalist camp could be said to either propose a renewal of the classical schema or a development of Badiou's own inaesthetics. The lack of publications that explicitly take up aesthetics makes it difficult to assess Brassier and Meillassoux on this point. Risking a judgment, it seems to us that Brassier could be said to endorse the classical schema, while Meillassoux seems to be more in line with Badiou. Admittedly, we are on very thin ice here. These diagnoses are based on Brassier's rejection of the category of experience on the one hand, and Meillassoux's following remarks from "Iteration, Reiteration, Repetition" on the other:

> My materialism is so far from being hostile to empiricism, that in fact it aims to found the absolute necessity of the latter. My only disagreement with the empiricist is that I affirm that he [sic] is *absolutely* correct: If you want to know or think what is, you must *necessarily* (from my point of view) do so by way of a certain regime of experience: scientific experimentation (the sciences of nature), historical and sociological experience, but also literary and artistic experience, etc. And here, my role is to prevent a certain philosophical regime from contesting the sovereignty of those "disciplines of experience" I have enumerated.[64]

Meillassoux, like Badiou, defends the disciplines' autonomy both from one another and from philosophy. As a result, it seems to us that Meillassoux should be sympathetic to Badiou's inaesthetics project. Also, note that while Meillassoux thus carves out a space of truth pertaining to art, this space remains purely empirical—it is given ("what is") and thus a manifestation of facticity. Meillassoux, however, is interested in founding the absolute necessity of the contingency of such facts—the "speculative essence" or "factiality" of facticity which itself is not a fact.[65] This is why Meillassoux is not an empiricist. It is also the reason why he is not that much

---

[64] Meillassoux, "Iteration, Reiteration, Repetition," 12, original emphases.

[65] Meillassoux, *After Finitude*, 79.

interested in art.[66] He is happy to leave discussions about art to the experts in the respective "disciplines of experience," that is, aesthetics and theory of art.

This is consistent with the fact that Meillassoux just published an extensive reading of Mallarmé's *Coup de dés*: the truth of the poem is intrinsic to literary (or artistic) practice, but this intrinsic truth it produces is indicative of another, philosophical, truth—and this is where Meillassoux's interest lies. According to Meillassoux, Badiou reads the uncertainty and hesitation in Mallarmé's poem as congruous with his own notion of the event. In this vein, the word "perhaps" as employed in the poem points to a future to come, "awaiting a truth that would come to complete it in the same time as abolish it, replacing its hypotheticity with an effective certitude."[67] Meillassoux thinks that this leads to "devaluing or relativizing the interest of [Mallarmé's] poetry" as it integrates and cuts down to size the function of the "perhaps," which, according to Meillassoux's own reading, lies in its hypostatisation: the absolutisation of chance.[68] Such diagnosis, of course, is not very far from Meillassoux's "necessity of contingency" thesis—hence his interest in *Coup de dés*.[69] In the context of

---

[66] The same holds true of Meillassoux's relation to the sciences—this goes a long way towards explaining the lack of actual scientific discourse in *After Finitude* despite its initial appeal to the sciences in its discussion of the arche-fossil.

[67] Quentin Meillassoux, "Badiou and Mallarmé: The Event and the Perhaps," trans. Alley Edlebi, *Parrhesia* (2013), 16, 38.

[68] Ibid., 38.

[69] How the aesthetic is to be situated in relation to contingency in Meillassoux's overall philosophical system is hinted at in the excerpts from *L'inexistence divine* included in Harman's study of Meillassoux. There, Meillassoux employs the notion of beauty as *the* indicator of the justness of a possible future world of justice and thus, in Kantian fashion, inextricably ties the aesthetic to the moral. Where in Kant the experience of beauty parades the world before our eyes "as if [it] had been created in conformance with … moral ends" and thus opens up the possibility of God, in Meillassoux, assuming that a perfect just world were incarnate at some future point in time, it would—in accordance with his principle of unreason and the necessity of contingency—reveal *"the emergence without reason of an accord between reason and the real."* The experience of beauty would thus be an indicator

our discussion, what is remarkable in Meillassoux's account is that he castigates Badiou for not being faithful enough to the truth of the poem, that is, for failing to live up to his own inaesthetics. Meillassoux then proceeds to out-Badiou Badiou himself.

A similar picture to that drawn from Badiou's tripartite classification of aesthetic discourse emerges from Kern and Sonderegger's introductory survey. When Kern and Sonderegger contest both the notion that aesthetics is the "only *true* philosophy" and the idea that it is but philosophy's servant,[70] they reject the romantic and classical schemata of art. In turn, their recasting of aesthetics as metaphilosophical could possibly even be seen as a reworking of the didactic schema as aesthetics thus provides philosophy with the mirror to observe itself as it is engaged in its epistemic project.[71] If we take these recent trends into account, it seems that Badiou's diagnosis of the death of the three aesthetic schemata is ill-fated as all three seem to be well and alive. A Badiouian might of course maintain that these strands are helplessly lost as they are caught in their dead ends and that only a proper inaesthetics provides the royal road of escape. Whatever the repercussions, it seems to be clear that speculative realism is divided between a retrieval (in the Harmanian sense elaborated in his contribution to this issue) of romantic aesthetics and its complete dismissal (Brassier); or, minimally, a profuse lack of interest towards it (Meillassoux).

---

of the contingency of justice incarnate, and only a world that offers this experience would be a just world. Quentin Meillassoux, "Excerpts from *L'inexistence divine*," trans. Graham Harman in *Quentin Meillassoux: Philosophy in the Making* by Graham Harman (Edinburgh: Edinburgh University Press, 2011), 218-19, original emphasis.

[70] Kern and Sonderegger, "Einleitung," 8-9.

[71] It is telling that Kern and Sonderegger do not have a word to say about ontology and only evoke ethics (practical philosophy as concerned with the good) and epistemology (theoretical philosophy as concerned with truth) as the other central disciplines of philosophy besides aesthetics. Equating theoretical philosophy with epistemology, their understanding of philosophy is very much in line with twentieth century's anti-metaphysical outlook. Philosophy is indeed reduced to an epistemic project.

The speculative realist retrieval of romantic aesthetics as expounded by its transcendental empiricist wing also goes a long way towards explaining the lack of an explicit discourse on politics. A short juxtaposition with Rancière's position should prove illuminating in this respect. From the point of view of the speculative realist retrieval of romanticism, Rancière's *socio-political* notion of the distribution of the sensible has to be recast in *metaphysical* terms. It is due to speculative realism's larger metaphysical outlook that aesthetics becomes divorced from the political; or, rather, the political becomes just one tiny field within being where the aesthetic plays out and politics can thus not assume a central role in its determination. Against advocates of a politics of being who argue for an inherently political structure of being and thus might object to such an argument, we agree with the speculative realists that politics needs some rudimentary form of *polis* to take place, and a mere congeries of things—what object-oriented thinkers call Latour Litanies—does not make a *polis*. Thus, distribution has to be recast as a *neutral* ontological, not *partial* socio-political activity (or occurrence; or process—pick your favourite term).

With this observation, we have reached the end of our short foray into the historical and systematic ramifications of the contemporary aesthetic landscape. As a means to conclude this survey, let us return once more to the heyday of aesthetics that started with Kant and continued through all of German Idealism. We have stated that speculative realism in large parts amounts to a retrieval of just this tradition, an argument that Cogburn and Ohm present in much more detail in their Whig history of speculative realism, which serves to introduce their own concerns with truth and fiction in their contribution to this special issue. In this vein, aesthetics in the twenty-first century, at least in its speculative guise, amounts to *either* a radical reworking of German Idealism (the speculative realist transcendental empiricists) *or* it amounts to nothing much at all (the speculative realist transcendental rationalists). Strikingly, the latter position comes close to Jens Kulenkampff's diagnosis in his contribution to *Falsche Gegensätze*. Having dismissed both Kant's and Hegel's metaphysical commitments as obsolete, Kulenkampff closes his essay with the following provocative remark:

> European aesthetics before Kant is in truth but a prehistory to philosophical aesthetics, and philosophical aesthetics from Hegel onwards is nothing but a variant of either Kantian or Hegelian aesthetics. If, however, Kant and Hegel are no longer available as reference figures for a philosophical aesthetics, then aesthetics might indeed survive as a sub-discipline within academic philosophy, and the label "Philosophical Aesthetics" continue to exist, but a philosophical aesthetics worthy of the name is long dead.[72]

Contra Kulenkampff (and contra the transcendental rationalist wing of speculative realism), however, speculative realism's transcendental empiricists testify to the ongoing relevance of the Kantian and post-Kantian tradition as can be witnessed in their central reworking of the transcendental and the importance of figures such as Schelling and Kant himself. Let us be clear on this point, then, and state it as succinctly as possible: speculative aesthetics in the twenty-first century *is* German Idealism redux.

---

[72] Jens Kulenkampff, "Metaphysik und Ästhetik: Kant zum Beispiel" in *Falsche Gegensätze*, 80, our translation.

Part 1: The Art of Theory

Non-Phenomenological Thought

Steven Shaviro

Wayne State University

Q UENTIN MEILLASSOUX, WHO invented the term *correlationism*, initially defines it as "the idea according to which we only ever have access to the correlation between thinking and being, and never to either term considered apart from the other."[1] This would seem at first to be an entirely symmetrical formulation. Subject and object, or more generally thought and being, are regarded by the correlationist as mutually co-constituting and co-dependent: "not only does it become necessary to insist that we never grasp an object in itself, in isolation from its relation to the subject, but it also becomes necessary to maintain that we can never grasp a subject that would not always-already be related to an object."[2] Described in this manner, the correlation would seem to move indifferently in either direction, from thinking to being or from being to thinking.

However, this turns out not to be the case. Meillassoux's formulation is not symmetrical or reversible, but rather unidirectional. When thought and being are correlated, thought is always the active and relational term, the one that actually *performs* the correlation. Being, on the other hand, just *is*; this makes it the dumb and passive term, the one that merely suffers being apprehended by, and thereby correlated to, some sort of consciousness or subjectivity outside of itself.

---

[1] Quentin Meillassoux, *After Finitude: An Essay on the Necessity of Contingency*, trans. Ray Brassier (New York: Continuum, 2008), 5.

[2] Meillassoux, *After Finitude*, 5.

In other words, subjectivity implies *intentionality*: which is to say, a primordial orientation *towards* an object beyond itself. Objectivity, in contrast, is supposed to be able to stand alone. In Meillassoux's account, thought always refers to being, while being in itself remains indifferent to thought. Thinking per se is correlational, insofar as it necessarily implies a "relation-to-the-world." Anti-correlationism therefore comes to be equated with positing "an absolute that is at once external to thought and in itself devoid of all subjectivity."[3] We can only escape correlationism by affirming "the pure and simple *death*, with neither consciousness nor life, without any subjectivity whatsoever, that is represented by the state of inorganic matter."[4]

In his critique of correlationism, therefore, Meillassoux seems very nearly obsessed with purging thought and subjectivity altogether from the universe of things. In order to step outside of the self-confirming "correlationist circle," Meillassoux says, we need to step outside of thought altogether.[5] We must reach a position "which takes seriously the possibility that there is nothing living or willing in the inorganic realm," and for which "absolute reality is an *entity without thought*."[6] Beyond the correlation, existence is "totally a-subjective."[7] If "ancestral" reality does not exist *for us*, this is because it does not exist *in thought* at all: it is "anterior to givenness" and refuses any sort of "manifestation" whatsoever.[8]

For Meillassoux, correlationism, no less than naive common sense, begins with a radical "decision": the assertion "of the essential inseparability of the act of thinking from its content." Once this decision has been made, it is already

---

[3] Quentin Meillassoux, "Iteration, Reiteration, Repetition: A Speculative Analysis of the Meaningless Sign," talk at Freie Universität Berlin, 20 April 2012, oursecretblog.com/txt/QMpaperApr12.pdf (accessed 11 April, 2013), 2.

[4] Meillassoux, "Iteration," 6, original emphasis.

[5] Meillassoux, *After Finitude*, 5.

[6] Ibid., 38, 36.

[7] Ibid., 38.

[8] Ibid., 14.

too late: "all we ever engage with is what is given-to-thought, never an entity subsisting by itself."[9] Meillassoux, as Graham Harman has noted, takes seriously the sophism according to which thinking of something means transforming that something into an object of thought. The paradoxical task of speculative philosophy, for Meillassoux, is therefore to think against the very "decision" that inaugurates thought. The aim is to attain a thought that turns back upon and erases itself. Meillassoux seeks to operate the dialectical reversal by means of which "thought has become able to think a world that can dispense with thought, a world that is essentially unaffected by whether or not anyone thinks it."[10]

Such a position can easily be aligned with scientific reductionism or eliminativism. Meillassoux argues that "empirical science is today capable of producing statements about events anterior to the advent of life as well as consciousness."[11] That is to say, science literally and objectively presents us with a reality that cannot be in any way correlated with thought: a world that is *anterior to givenness itself* and *prior to givenness in its entirety.*[12] Empirical science and mathematics intimate to us "a world crammed with things and events that are not the correlates of any manifestation, a world that is not the correlate of a relation to the world." The "primary qualities" disclosed by science are entirely nonrelational, and not *for us*.[13] Meillassoux therefore claims that "the mathematization of nature" performed by the physical sciences allows us, as other modes of understanding do not, "to know what may be while we are not ... What is mathematizable cannot be reduced to a correlate of thought."[14] Indeed, "all those aspects of the object that can be formulated in mathematical terms can be meaningfully conceived as properties of the object in itself"

[9] Meillassoux, *After Finitude*, 36.

[10] Ibid., 116.

[11] Ibid., 9.

[12] Ibid., 20-21.

[13] Ibid., 26, 1.

[14] Ibid., 115, 117.

rather than being "secondary qualities" that are added to the object by our own mental activity in perceiving it.[15]

I would like to compare this, for a moment, with Ray Brassier's position. Brassier, much like Meillassoux, rejects the privilege that traditional philosophy has accorded to subjectivity, experience, and thought. And Brassier, again like Meillassoux, turns to the physical sciences as a way to escape from correlationism. But where Meillassoux takes correlationist logic seriously, and thinks that he can only defeat it by emptying it out from within, Brassier is altogether dismissive of this logic. Brassier scornfully denounces what he describes as the "fatal non-sequitur at the root of every variant of correlationism": its slippage from the "trivially true" claim "that my thoughts cannot exist independently of my mind" to the entirely unsupported claim "that *what* my thoughts are about cannot exist independently of my mind."[16] To the contrary, Brassier argues, thought never coincides with its intentional content; it never corresponds with the thing that it is about. Correlationism is therefore ludicrous *a priori*. Indeed, Brassier insists that "thought is not guaranteed access to being; being is not inherently thinkable"; we live in "a world that is not designed to be intelligible and is not originarily infused with meaning."[17] Consequently, there is always a "gap," or a "discrepancy," between "what our concept of the object is and what the object is in itself."[18]

This very gap or discrepancy grounds Brassier's robust and thoroughgoing scientism. Neither science nor metaphysics can overcome the non-coincidence between things themselves, and the ways that these things are represented in our thought. But for Brassier, even philosophies that affirm this fundamental non-coincidence—like that, most notably, of Gilles

---

[15] Meillassoux, *After Finitude*, 3.

[16] Ray Brassier, "Concepts and Objects" in *The Speculative Turn: Continental Materialism and Realism*, ed. Levi Bryant, Nick Srnicek, and Graham Harman (Melbourne: Re.press, 2010), 63.

[17] Ibid., 47.

[18] Ibid., 55.

Deleuze—remain idealist and correlationist, to the extent that they posit this originary difference as a difference *for thought* itself.[19] Against this, Brassier's "transcendental realism" makes the case that this inevitable difference—the one between a concept and that to which it refers—can never be conceptualised itself, but itself always remains nonconceptual.[20] For science, Brassier says, "the reality of the object determines the meaning of its conception"; whereas metaphysics argues the reverse.[21] The difference of reality from how it is thought "is at once determining for thought and irreducible to thinking."[22] Science, therefore—unlike metaphysics—actually "allows the discrepancy between that reality and the way in which it is conceptually circumscribed to be measured."[23] The world is meaningless; but through science "it is possible to *understand* the meaninglessness of existence."[24] That is to say, science is able to understand this meaninglessness without turning it into yet another source of meaning. For Brassier, "this capacity to understand meaning as a regional or *bounded* phenomenon marks a fundamental progress in cognition."[25]

Through the progress of scientific knowledge, therefore, thought is increasingly compelled to recognise its own irrelevance and impotence. Once it is no longer correlated to being, "thought becomes the locus for the identity of absolute objectivity and impersonal death."[26] This means that scientific knowledge, achieved through thought, leads ultimately to the extinction of thought—or, more precisely,

---

[19] Ray Brassier, *Nihil Unbound: Enlightenment and Extinction* (New York: Palgrave Macmillian, 2007), 203.

[20] Ibid., 118.

[21] Brassier, "Concepts and Objects," 55.

[22] Ibid., 203.

[23] Ibid., 55.

[24] Ray Brassier, "I am a nihilist because I still believe in truth," *Kronos* (2011), http://www.kronos.org.pl/index.php?23151,896 (accessed September 17, 2013), original emphasis.

[25] Ibid.

[26] Brassier, *Nihil Unbound*, 204.

to thought's recognition of its own extinction. Not only is the philosopher mortal; "the subject of philosophy must also recognize that he or she is *already* dead."[27] When "the absence of correlation" itself becomes "an object of thought," it thereby "transforms thought itself into an object," so that "extinction indexes the thought of the absence of thought."[28] For Brassier, the consequence of rejecting correlationism is to confront a universe that is not only irreducible to thought, but fatally inimical to thought.

The contrast between Brassier and Meillassoux is telling. Brassier sees critical and rational thought—embodied in mathematics and science—as inevitably precipitating its own demise. Meillassoux, in contrast, recruits positivistic science and mathematical formalisation in order to turn them opportunistically against thought. That is to say, mathematical formalisation is not really the last word for him. Indeed, science and mathematics are arguably not important to Meillassoux at all. The physical sciences give Meillassoux the argument that ancestral objects exist, prior to any sort of manifestation for a subject. And Cantor's theory of transfinites provides the basis for his demonstration (following Badiou) that the set of possible future events does not constitute a totality and therefore cannot be understood probabilistically. But once these arguments have been established, science and mathematics no longer play a crucial role. Meillassoux himself concedes (or more accurately, boasts) that his own speculative materialism "says nothing as to the factual being of our world."[29] When Meillassoux praises Badiou for "us[ing] mathematics itself to effect a liberation from the limits of calculatory reason," he is saying something that applies even more fully to his own philosophy.[30]

Indeed, Meillassoux's major claim—that the "laws of nature" are entirely contingent, and that at any time they "could

---

[27] Brassier, *Nihil Unbound*, 239, my emphasis.

[28] Ibid., 229-30.

[29] Meillassoux, "Iteration," 13.

[30] Meillassoux, *After Finitude*, 103.

actually change for no reason"—would seem to undermine scientific rationality altogether.[31] Science cannot work without assuming the validity of relations of cause and effect—which is to say, without some degree of confidence or faith (however attenuated) in the "principle of sufficient reason" that Meillassoux rejects.[32] We can therefore conclude that Meillassoux does not embrace mathematisation because it helps to give us scientifically valid and objective (non-correlational) results. Rather, the point of mathematisation for Meillassoux is to get rid of subjective experience altogether, by giving us an account of nature "stripped of its sensible qualities."[33] The point is to abstract the world away from everything that our minds might add to it. This is why Meillassoux is so concerned with reinstating Descartes' doctrine of primary and secondary qualities, in order to separate the former from the latter. Meillassoux admits "those aspects of the object that can give rise to a mathematical thought (to a formula or to digitization)," while rejecting those that give rise, instead, "to a perception or sensation."[34]

Today, scientistic eliminativism no longer uses the terminology of "primary" and "secondary" qualities. But it still seeks to dismiss subjective impressions as illusory, and to explain them as mere effects of underlying physical processes. Daniel Dennett tells us, for instance, that "qualia," or the intrinsic phenomenal characteristics of subjective experience, do not really exist.[35] The only real difference between Dennett and Brassier is that Dennett refuses to follow through and acknowledge the radically nihilistic vision of extinction that Brassier rightly deduces as the inevitable consequence of scientistic reductionism and the bifurcation of nature.

But Meillassoux—unlike Brassier, and unlike most analytic

[31] Meillassoux, *After Finitude*, 84.

[32] Ibid., 60 et passim.

[33] Ibid., 124.

[34] Ibid., 3.

[35] Daniel Dennett, "Quining Qualia," http://ase.tufts.edu/cogstud/dennett/papers/quinqual.htm (accessed September 17, 2013).

philosophers of science—is not interested in demystifying and naturalising our theories of mind, nor in reducing subjectivity to its ostensible microphysical causes. He rejects what he calls "naturalism," or the grounding of philosophy upon a "state of science that has no more reason to be thought definitive today than it did yesterday."[36] Far more radically, Meillassoux seeks to achieve a total purgation of thought from being. In other words, Meillassoux does not value the physical sciences and mathematics for their own sakes, but only because—and to the extent that—they allow us to reject the categories of subjectivity and experience. Science and mathematics, in other words, are tools that Meillassoux uses in order to get rid of phenomenology. Where Nietzsche fears that we are not getting rid of God because we still believe in grammar, Meillassoux fears that we are not getting rid of correlationism because we still believe in phenomenal experience.

But do we really need to eliminate experience, and sentience, in order to get away from correlationism? The problem, I think, is with the asymmetry that I have been discussing. Consider another one of Meillassoux's formulations. The problem with correlationism, he says, is that "we never, according to this type of philosophy, have access to any intended thing (understood in the most general sense) that is not always-already correlated to an act of thinking (understood, again, in the most general sense)."[37] What I would like to do is to try a small experiment. I will invert Meillassoux's statement, in order to create a complementary proposition, as follows: the problem with correlationism is that we never, according to this type of philosophy, have any act of thinking (understood in the most general sense) that is not always-already correlated with access to an intended thing (understood, again, in the most general sense). But we cannot imagine Meillassoux saying any such thing. This is because he has already defined "access" and "correlation" as operations of thought, and of thought alone.

---

[36] Meillassoux, "Iteration," 11.

[37] Ibid., 2.

This is why the particular pretensions of human thought have (justifiably) been the target of speculative realist critique. And yet, in the very act of rejecting one side of the Cartesian duality, we have tended to reaffirm the other side. Nobody believes in *res cogitans* any longer, but we largely continue to accept Descartes' characterisation of *res extensa*. Despite the admonitions of Henri Bergson, Alfred North Whitehead, Deleuze, and (today) Jane Bennett, our default ontology still insists that, in the absence of transcendent mind, the world is composed of nothing but passive, inert, and indifferent matter. Whitehead calls this the "misconception" of "vacuous actuality, devoid of subjective experience."[38] Such a doctrine of "vacuous actuality" lies behind much analytic philosophy, as well as behind Meillassoux's and Brassier's assumption that the "great outdoors" must be entirely devoid of life and thought. And, despite Harman's rejection of "undermining" reductionism and of "smallism," he still echoes this logic when he declares that objects only "have psyches accidentally, not in their own right."[39]

Meillassoux's purgation of subjectivity and experience allows him to posit an altogether different notion of thought. For Meillassoux, true philosophical thought has no empirical basis whatsoever, and no relation to the body. It has no ties to sensibility or to affect. Rather, this thought is purely rational and theoretical; it provides us with a "veritable *intellectual intuition* of the absolute."[40] In order to be extricated from correlationism, thought must achieve an entirely exceptional status. It must be absolutely disconnected from the physical world. In accordance with this, Meillassoux claims that thought cannot be grounded in physical matter, nor even in life. Not only must we reject the panpsychist claim that thought is an

---

[38] Alfred North Whitehead, *Process and Reality* (New York: The Free Press, 1978), 29.

[39] Graham Harman, "Intentional Objects for Nonhumans," talk at Pour une approche non-anthropologique de la subjectivité conference, 18 November 2008, http://www.europhilosophie.eu/recherche/IMG/pdf/intentional-objects.pdf (accessed September 17, 2013).

[40] Meillassoux, *After Finitude*, 82, original emphasis.

inherent quality of matter, we also cannot explain the origin of thought, or its seeming greater complexity as we move from single-celled organisms to human beings, in continuist or evolutionary terms. Rather, Meillassoux separates thought from life as radically as he separates life from nonliving matter. He claims that human beings acquired thought *ex nihilo*, for no reason, without any prior basis, and out of sheer contingency.[41] Meillassoux celebrates the sheer gratuitousness of a mode of thought that is non-experiential, and beyond any correlation with being. This thought becomes the basis for a new sort of hyper-Platonism: "humans acquire value because they know the eternal ... Value belongs to the act of knowing itself; humans have value not because of *what* they know but *because* they know."[42]

More recently, Meillassoux has refined his analysis; he now modifies his formulations from *After Finitude* by more clearly distinguishing what he calls *subjectalism*, which in-cludes vitalism, from correlationism *strictu sensu*.[43] Where correlationism disallows the absolute, subjectalism is the philosophy that Meillassoux characterised in *After Finitude* as "absolutizing the correlation."[44] Life, thought, or some other subjective term becomes the new absolute. Meillas-soux claims that, in subjectalism, "thought thinks thought as the absolute."[45] According to Meillassoux, the claim of subjectalism is that "we always experience subjectivity as a necessary, and hence eternal, principle from which no one can escape."[46] But is not Meillassoux still wrongly assuming that any such subjective term is necessarily both intentional/(cor)relational, and unified rather than plural or multiple?

---

[41] Quentin Meillassoux, "Excerpts from *L'inexistence divine*," trans. Graham Harman in *Quentin Meillassoux: Philosophy in the Making* by Graham Harman (Edinburgh: Edinburgh University Press, 2011), 175-238.

[42] Ibid., 211.

[43] Meillassoux, "Iteration," 3.

[44] Meillassoux, *After Finitude*, 60.

[45] Meillassoux, "Iteration," 3-4.

[46] Ibid., 8.

Meillassoux is wrong to maintain that, in so-called subjectal-ism, "everything is uniformly subject, will, creative becoming, image-movement, etc."[47]

It is because he assumes the identity of thought with inten-tionality that Meillassoux does not even dismiss, but altogether ignores, the prospect of *uncorrelated thought*. For Meillassoux, thought in its essence is relational or correlational, while mere being need not be. To do away with correlationism then means to eliminate all thinking *about* the object, in order to allow the object just to *be*, in and of itself. Heidegger's sense of being as unveiling is maintained, even as his ruminations on the co-appurtenance of thought and being are rejected. A non-correlated entity is not manifested to any consciousness whatsoever. It "withdraws" from contact, and escapes any possibility of being captured by thought. For Harman and Meillassoux alike, the "great outdoors," the world beyond correlation, can therefore only consist in a-subjective objects. Meillassoux simply takes for granted the phenomenological doctrine of intentionality: thinking is always *about* something.

We might say, therefore, that Meillassoux's entire program is to enforce, as radically and stringently as possible, the very "bifurcation of nature" that Whitehead denounced as the most serious error of modern Western thought.[48] For Whitehead, the bifurcation of nature arises precisely out of the very distinction that Meillassoux seeks to rehabilitate in the opening pages of *After Finitude*: the Cartesian and Lockean distinction between "primary" and "secondary" qualities.[49] The bifurcation of nature consists in radically separating sensory experience from the physical causes that generate that experience. Thus, Whitehead says, we divide "the perceived redness and warmth of the fire" on the one hand, from "the agitated molecules of carbon and oxygen" and "the radiant

---

[47] Meillassoux, "Iteration," 15.

[48] Alfred North Whitehead, *The Concept of Nature* (Amherst: Prometheus Books, 2004), 26-48.

[49] Ibid., 27; Meillassoux, *After Finitude*, 1-3.

energy from them" on the other.[50] The first is said to be a subjective illusion, while only the second is objectively real.

But at this point in Meillassoux's analysis, there is a slight, yet crucial, slippage. Meillassoux claims that a non-correlationist philosophy—or what he also calls "speculative material-ism"—rejects "the closure of thought upon itself" and instead "acced[es] to an absolute that is at once external to thought and in itself devoid of all subjectivity."[51] The slippage comes in the way that Meillassoux implicitly moves from an object, or a world, that is independent of anything that *our* subjec-tivity imposes upon it, to one that is also devoid of thought in itself, devoid of any subjectivity of its own. The objects that are not correlated with *our* thought must also, in and of themselves, "have no subjective-psychological, egoic, sensible or vital traits whatsoever."[52] Meillassoux "absolutizes the pure non-subjective—the pure and simple *death*, with neither consciousness nor life, without any subjectivity whatsoever, that is represented by the state of inorganic matter."[53] This slippage in Meillassoux's account would seem to result from the assumption that thought and subjectivity are exclusively human attributes.

I want to suggest that this one-sidedness is not really justi-fied. The derogation of thought in Meillassoux and Brassier is itself a reaction against older ideas. Correlationism itself has generally assumed, not just the co-dependency of thought and world, or of subject and object, but also the priority of the former element of each pair over the latter. It has always taken for granted the supremacy of the mental, or the prior-ity of the act of perception over the things perceived. We can trace this tendency back, beyond Kant's transcendental logic, to our very habit of (in the words of Whitehead) "decisively separating 'mind' from 'nature,' a modern separation which

---

50 Whitehead, *The Concept of Nature*, 32.

51 Meillassoux, "Iteration," 2.

52 Ibid., 2.

53 Ibid., 6.

found its first exemplification in Cartesian dualism."[54] Ever since Descartes, we "moderns" (to use this term in the manner suggested by Bruno Latour) have divided the world between mentalities, which actively think and perceive (*res cogitans*), and bits of matter in homogeneous space, which make up the passive objects of all their acts of perception (*res extensa*).[55] The speculative realist rejection of the privileges of thought is therefore a necessary, and unsurprising, reaction against the traditional modernist and humanist exaltation of thought. There are few philosophers today who would actually accept Cartesian substance dualism; yet the legacy of this dualism still persists in our everyday "common sense" approach to the world.

In order to get away from this deadlock, we need to recognise that thought is not, after all, an especially human privilege. This is one of the driving insights behind panpsychism. Also, recent biological research indicates that something much like thinking—an experiential sensitivity, at the very least—goes on in such entities as trees, slime mould, and bacteria, even though none of these organisms have brains. I have also mentioned George Molnar's claim that even inanimate things display a sort of "intentionality." If things have powers (or dispositional properties) at all, as Molnar argues that they do, then by this very fact they exhibit a certain *aboutness*.[56] Salt has the power to be dissolved in water; and this is a real property of the salt, even if it never encounters water, and therefore never actually gets dissolved. A kind of intentional orientation, or prospect of "aboutness," exists even in the absence of any actual correlation between subject and object. For all these reasons, we can draw the conclusion that thought is not as grandiose, or as unique, as Cartesianism and correlationism have led us to

---

[54] Alfred North Whitehead, *Adventures of Ideas* (New York: The Free Press, 1967), 210.

[55] Bruno Latour, *We Have Never Been Modern*, trans. Catherine Porter (Cambridge: Harvard University Press, 1993).

[56] George Molnar, *Powers: A Study in Metaphysics* (New York: Oxford University Press, 2007), 72.

suppose. We should reject both the inflated, idealist notion of thought, and the "misconception" of "vacuous actuality" which is all that remains behind, once thought has been evacuated.[57] We need to affirm values, meanings, and thought, but see these in a deflationary way.

What is the alternative to the "misconception" denounced by Whitehead? I do not wish to embrace outright idealism any more than I wish to return to correlationism. Nor can I imagine simply inverting Meillassoux's formula of *being without thought* into some notion of *thought without being*— since I have little idea of what this latter phrase could possibly mean. But I still maintain that if, in spite of the paradoxes of reference, we can posit "an object in itself, in isolation from its relation to the subject," standing apart from whatever we might think about it, then we should also be able to posit a non-correlational subject, one that "would not always-already be related to an object," but would instead exist independently of any object whatsoever.[58] In order to do this, we need to grasp *thinking* in a different way; we need, as Deleuze might put it, a new "image of thought."[59]

This new image of thought would maintain that *aisthesis*, or precognitive feeling, precedes *noesis*, or cognitive apprehension. In Whitehead's language, "sense-reception" is more basic than "sense-perception."[60] In sense-reception, Whitehead says, "the sensa are the definiteness of emotion: they are emotional forms transmitted from occasion to occasion."[61] This means that "sensa"—Whitehead's term for what today are more commonly called "qualia"—are felt noncognitively, as singular aesthetic impressions. They are not referred beyond themselves, and do not have the status of representations. Particular things are not understood and identified as such.

---

[57] Whitehead, *Process and Reality*, 29.

[58] Meillassoux, *After Finitude*, 5.

[59] Gilles Deleuze, *Difference and Repetition*, trans. Paul Patton (New York: Columbia University Press, 1994), 129-67.

[60] Whitehead, *Process*, 113.

[61] Ibid., 114.

Rather, under these conditions, "the feeling is blind and the relevance is vague."[62] It is only in some rare and subsequent instances of what Whitehead calls "adequate complexity" that these bursts of feeling are transmuted into cognitions, so that sense-reception is supplemented by sense-perception as it is commonly understood.[63]

In his first of his two *Cinema* volumes, Deleuze proposes a contrast, arising in the very heart of modernity, between two crucial images of thought. He writes of the "historical crisis of psychology" that arose at the turn from the nineteenth to the twentieth century, at the very moment of the invention of cinema.[64] The crisis concerned the relation between mind and body, or between thought and matter; it had to do with the "duality of image and movement, of consciousness and thing."[65] Everyone recognised that this dualism had come to a "dead end."[66] Everyone realised that, as William James put it at the time, "there is only one primal stuff or material in the world, a stuff of which everything is composed."[67] This meant, James went on, that "consciousness ... does not denote a special stuff or way of being." Indeed, James concludes that "thoughts in the concrete are made of the same stuff as things are."[68] But how can we render this identity? Deleuze does not cite James directly in his account of philosophical psychology. But he notes that efforts were made by "two very different authors," Husserl and Bergson, "to overcome" the "duality" of thought and matter.[69] "Each had his own war cry:

---

[62] Whitehead, *Process*, 163.

[63] Ibid., 113-14.

[64] Gilles Deleuze, *Cinema 1: The Movement-Image* (Minneapolis: University of Minnesota Press), 56.

[65] Ibid., 56.

[66] Ibid., 56.

[67] William James, *Essays in Radical Empiricism* (Lincoln: University of Nebraska Press), 4.

[68] Ibid., 25, 37.

[69] Deleuze, *Cinema 1*, 56.

all consciousness is consciousness *of* something (Husserl), or more strongly, all consciousness *is* something (Bergson)."[70]

The first of these solutions leads to a phenomenological aesthetics: one that is concerned with sensible experience "as an embodied and meaningful existential activity."[71] Phenomenological criticism not only works to overcome the duality of Kant's two senses of aesthetics; it also effectively counters the excessively formalist and cognitivist tendencies both of much twentieth century modernism and avant-gardism, and of late-twentieth century structuralist approaches to aesthetics. It returns aesthetics from conceptual and epistemological concerns back to the lived reality of the flesh. However, the price that phenomenological aesthetics pays for these achievements is to remain embedded within correlationism.

But Deleuze, following Bergson's alternative, offers an anti-phenomenological account of consciousness. As Deleuze puts it elsewhere, "it is not enough to say that consciousness is consciousness of something";[72] rather, we must reach the point where "consciousness ceases to be a light cast upon objects in order to become a pure phosphorescence of things in themselves."[73] Deleuze's suggestion that "all consciousness *is* something"[74] offers a powerful response, not just to turn-of-the-twentieth-century anxieties about the relation of mind and matter, but also to turn-of-the-twenty-first-century anxieties about the nature of the real. Just as the invention of the phonograph and the cinema coincided with worries about the material and the immaterial, so our contemporary elaborations of digital technologies coincide with worries about whether the real even exists, and whether we have access to it.

---

[70] Deleuze, *Cinema 1*, 56.

[71] Vivian Carol Sobchack, *The Address of the Eye: A Phenomenology of Film Experience* (Princeton: Princeton University Press, 1992), xvii.

[72] Deleuze, *Difference*, 220.

[73] Gilles Deleuze, *The Logic of Sense*, trans. M. Lester and C. Stivale (New York: Columbia University Press, 1969), 311.

[74] Deleuze, *Cinema 1*, 56.

To follow these clues from Whitehead and Deleuze (and through them, James and Bergson) would mean to posit a sort of thought that is nonrelational—or even "autistic." This means developing a notion of thought that is pre-cognitive (involving "feeling" rather than articulated judgments) and non-intentional (not directed towards an object with which it would be correlated). Such a non-phenomenological (but also non-intellectual) image of thought can be composed on the basis of Whitehead's notion of *prehension* as an alternative to Husserlian intentionality. Such a thought is nonreflexive, probably nonconscious, and even "autistic"; it is not correlative to being, but immanently intrinsic within it. At this primordial (or better, humble) level, thought *just is*, without having a correlate.

In this way, noncorrelational thought is an immanent attribute or power of being. It involves what Whitehead calls "feelings," rather than articulated judgments or Heideggerian implicit preunderstandings.[75] It is non-intentional in that it is not directed towards, or correlated with, particular objects—though it may well be entwined or implicated with such objects. It experiences singularities that are, as Kant says of aesthetic sensations, "intrinsically indeterminable and inadequate for cognition."[76] And it apprehends a "beauty" that, in the words of Thomas Metzinger, "is so subtle, so volatile as it were, that it evades cognitive access in principle."[77] In all these ways, noncorrelational thought is *aesthetic*. And under such circumstances—to agree at least in this point with Graham Harman—"aesthetics becomes first philosophy."[78]

---

[75] Whitehead, *Process*, 40-42

[76] Immanuel Kant, *Critique of Judgment*, trans. Werner S. Pluhar (Indianapolis: Hackett Publishing, 1987), 213.

[77] Thomas Metzinger, *Being No One: The Self-Model Theory of Subjectivity* (Cambridge: MIT Press, 2004), 73.

[78] Graham Harman, "On Vicarious Causation," *Collapse* (2007), 2, 221.

Beauty, the Will to Power, and Life as Artwork

Aesthetico-Speculative Realism in Nietzsche and Whitehead

Theodor Leiber and Kirsten Voigt

University of Augsburg, Karlsruhe Institute of Technology

1 Introduction[1]

SPECULATIVE[2] PHILOSOPHY, AS IT is understood in this essay, or "descriptive generalisation,"[3] moves forward under the perspective of the whole—the observable and the non-observable; the measurable and the non-measurable; matter/energy and mind; object and subject; concept and intuition etc.—which is methodically most often excluded by the special sciences. Speculative philosophy works (more) on the basis of imagination and intuition without, however, neglecting the epistemological importance of conceptualisation and concept-based reflection. At the same time, speculative philosophy is not confined to metaphysics in a narrow sense of the term, namely to radically transcending (or apriorising) the phenomenological physical world. Instead, a moderate

---

[1] The authors would like to thank the referees for their very helpful comments. One of the authors (KV) would like to thank the Gerda Henkel Foundation, Düsseldorf (Germany) for a research grant on the aesthetic models of Friedrich Wilhelm Nietzsche and Joseph Beuys.

[2] Etymologically, *speculari* (from the Latin) means: to spy, or to look out for.

[3] Alfred North Whitehead, *Process and Reality: An Essay in Cosmology* (New York: The Free Press, 1978), 10.

realist stance is taken which comprises in the first place that real entities are not just given to us in a mode of (absolute) reality *per se*, i.e., without bilateral interaction between the perceiving and the perceived. Quite to the contrary, the real entities perceived and measured happen to be perceived and measured via and by other real processes which are thus (to a certain amount) co-constitutive and co-formative. That is, the distinction between the perceiving entities, perception processes and the perceived entities rests on the factual (though, *sub specie aeternitatis*, hypothetical) possibility of real processes (or processual entities).[4]

It will be shown that such a speculative realist point of view is adopted by both Alfred North Whitehead and Fried-rich Wilhelm Nietzsche.[5] On the one hand, they are both

---

[4] Thereby it is assumed that real entities are not absolutely stable but of gradually different material–energetic stability over time.

[5] It is neither the intention of this paper nor is it the place to put forward a detailed analysis of speculative realist approaches found in the current literature. In that sense we confine ourselves to a few remarks reflecting on considerations which have been presented by Graham Harman very recently in Graham Harman, "The Current State of Speculative Realism," *Speculations* (2013), 4, 22-28. Unlike Harman, we do not endorse Manuel De Landa's assertion and "grant reality full autonomy from the human mind, disregarding the difference between the observable and the unobservable." Manuel De Landa qtd. in Harman, "The Current State," 23. According to Harman all speculative realist philosophies reject correlationist positions, where "correlationism is the doctrine that we can only speak of the human/ world interplay not of human or world in their own right." Harman, "The Current State," 23. Neglecting for the moment the impression of vagueness concerning the terms world and human we agree with Harman (and Socrates) that we have to draw a "line of separation between reality and my knowledge of it." In that sense, speculative realism for Harman means that real objects are not directly accessible but only by (the relation of) "sensual translation," so that "inanimate objects fail to exhaust each other during collision just as human perception or knowledge of those objects fails to know them. Real objects do not encounter each other directly, but only encounter *sensual* objects, or images of real objects. All contact between real objects is indirect, mediated by sensual reality ... The real is precisely that which can never be perfectly translated." Harman, "The Current State," 26, 24-26, original emphasis. While we agree with most of that despite the perhaps too strong (Whiteheadian) accentuation of the similarities between the sensual and the non-sensual part of the world, we do not believe in things-in-themselves

rejecting any type of (strong) anti-realism because it would make a deep and, from an ontologically monistic point of view, insurmountable cut between our factual experiential life and our means of apprehending and valuing it.[6] On the other hand, Whitehead's and Nietzsche's philosophies are obviously in need of speculation because they oppose the doctrine of "vacuous actuality"[7] (i.e., reality without qualities); the trust in the power of language (natural and logical) to give adequate expression to feelings and thoughts; the (ontological) distinction of subject and object, and the often correlated *Substanz-Denken*; the sensualistic conception of perception (e.g., assuming an atomistic structure of the sensible outside world); naïve scientific realism (i.e., mistaking scientific abstractions and approximate models for comprehensive descriptions and explanations of reality as such); giving everyday experience and the lifeworld no distinct place of their own in relation to the scientific perspective. Moreover and above all, Whitehead and Nietzsche conceive aestheticist perspectives as constitutive for all judging and valuing, instead of having a merely regulative function.[8] In that sense it will be argued that Nietzsche's and Whitehead's philosophies imply rich concepts of beauty, conceive the world as a network of real, experiential processes which cannot be grasped by absolute dogmatic (non-hypothetical) epistemology, and interpret human life as (a work of) art.

Our analysis will also show that the two thinkers differ in some important respects which are relevant for the concepts

---

as Harman does.

[6] Of course, it seems possible to assume no real (experiential) processes at all. Such an assumption would imply a strong anti-realist stance, and thus either a strong idealism or radical constructivism. Counterarguments to such positions—which are not explicated here—would be based on considerations about conceptual and explanatory coherence and simplicity, and perhaps performative contradictions.

[7] Whitehead, *Process and Reality*, xiii.

[8] Covering the broad semantic spectrum of "aesthetics" ranging from the Greek "aisthesis" (sensory perception, feeling) to the modes of perception of (works of) art and emotional as well as cognitive reactions to it.

of beauty, culture and civilisation. In particular, a notion corresponding to Whitehead's important force counterbalancing the ubiquitous striving for intensity, namely "harmony,"[9] seems to be missing in Nietzsche's conception of the will(s) to power. The most prominent difference between Whitehead and Nietzsche, however, lies in their approach to eternal entities, in particular God. It is only in this context that Whitehead seems to adopt more of an idealist position which is neither shared by Nietzsche nor easily compatible with Whitehead's otherwise realist approach.

As a further basis of the considerations of this paper, we adopt the thesis that Whitehead delivers a metaphysically speculative—intuitive as well as conceptual—framework for Nietzsche's and, of course, his own basic perspectives.[10] This framework implies that our approach to the world is basically emotional (or aestheticist), that the meaning and purpose of all life, or of all sentient being, is to be creative, and that the fundamental creation is creative self-design and self-overcoming.[11]

---

[9] Alfred North Whitehead, *Adventures of Ideas* (New York: The Free Press, 1967), 252, 275.

[10] This is an interpretive extension of a proposal one can find in Forrest Wood, "Creativity: Whitehead and Nietzsche," *Southwest Philosophical Studies* (1983), 9:2, 49-59.

[11] It might be noted that Nietzsche seems to phenomenologically focus on the human being, while Whitehead's systematicity and explanatory approach is (much more) open to "selves" of various complexities and organisational levels. This does, however, not imply that there is no space for a Whiteheadian cosmological and physiological approach in Nietzsche since, e.g., his talk of "wills to power" is not categorically restricted to the forces humans (as particular species of animals and types of *nexus* of prehensions) are driven by. At the same time we do not share Whitehead's conception of building up the universe from bipolar sentient/non-sentient actual entities all the way down to the smallest (observable) ones.

2 Philosophical Methodology and Aesthetico-Speculative Realism

The three most important basic concepts of his "complete cosmology"[12] Whitehead calls "actual entities" or "actual occasions," "prehension," and "*nexus*."[13] Whitehead replaces the traditional terms of substance, soul or spirit by the concept of "actual entity": actual entities are receiving-sentient (valuing) organisms,[14] and they are "the final real things of which the world is made up," i.e., "there is no going behind actual entities to find anything more real."[15] "Prehensions" comprise all sorts of experiences of the world of "actual entities" and are characterised as bipolar, mental-physical "feelings." A Whiteheadian "*nexus* is a set of actual entities in the unity of the relatedness constituted by their prehensions of each other, or—what is the same thing conversely expressed—constituted by their objectifications in each other."[16]

By means of these basic concepts, Whitehead is attempting to "base philosophical thought upon the most concrete elements in our experience."[17] Together with the "ontological principle" that without actual entities there is no reason,[18] they comprise the basic elements of Whitehead's speculative pan-experientialist systems theory—and therefore of his speculative realism.

It is our assumption that Nietzsche's notions corresponding to Whitehead's "actual entities" and "societies"[19] of actual entities are the "wills to power"[20] and "useful 'under-wills'

---

[12] Whitehead, *Process and Reality*, xii.

[13] Ibid., 18.

[14] Ibid., 161.

[15] Ibid., 18.

[16] Ibid., 24.

[17] Ibid., 18.

[18] Ibid., 18, 19.

[19] Ibid., 34.

[20] "Only where life is, is there also will; but not will to life, instead—thus

or under-souls" since "our body is, after all, only a society constructed out of many souls."[21] Nietzsche describes "willing" as "something *complicated*," the ingredients of which are a plurality of sensations.[22] Moreover, for him, willing is an emotion but "in every act of will there is a commandeering thought,"[23] i.e., willing is a bipolar emotion. Such bipolarity of feelings is also typical for Whitehead's approach.

Whitehead's conception of actual entities, which are potentially influenced by all past occasions and potentially do influence all future occasions, also comprises the thesis that the whole of reality is empirically inexhaustible for any actual entity.[24] This corresponds to Whitehead's approach to perspectivism, which is of central importance also for Nietzsche who criticises the idea and conceptions of comprehensively lucid and transparent (philosophical) systems designed from a singular—the one and only—perspective.[25] In contraposition to such system philosophies, Nietzsche thinks that perspectivism is a fundamental aesthetic-epistemological condition of all living beings because all of them do have access only to specific sections of the world (although, very often but erroneously, they do take this for the whole world). According to Nietzsche we cannot get rid of perspectives: we are bound to a certain perspective and there is no absolute

I teach you—will to power." Friedrich Nietzsche, *Thus Spoke Zarathustra: A Book for All and None*, ed. Adrian del Caro and Robert B. Pippin (Cambridge: Cambridge University Press, 2006), 90. The Nietzschean "will to power" does not indicate an individual, egoistic will but the ongoing striving for self-design and self-overcoming.

[21] Friedrich Nietzsche, *Beyond Good and Evil: Prelude to a Philosophy of the Future*, ed. Rolf-Peter Horstmann and Judith Norman (Cambridge: Cambridge University Press, 2005), 19.

[22] Ibid., 19, original emphasis.

[23] Ibid., 18.

[24] Whitehead, *Process and Reality*, 18, 106.

[25] See Donald A. Crosby, "Two Perspectives on Metaphysical Perspectivism: Nietzsche and Whitehead," *The Pluralist* (2007), 2:3, 57–76. Such hypotheses of empirical inexhaustibility and perspectivism do have further far-reaching consequences, e.g., for (the limitations of) our understanding of the human psyche.

super-perspective achievable: "We cannot look around our corner: it is a hopeless curiosity to want to know what other kinds of intellects and perspectives there *might* be."[26]

According to Whitehead's speculative realism, each prehension process includes three action items: (a) the "'subject,' which is prehending, namely, the actual entity in which that prehension is a concrete element," (b) the "'datum' which is prehended" and (c) the "'subjective form' which is *how* that subject prehends that datum."[27] The prehension process is always mutual, a bilateral interaction (between a subject and a datum).[28]

Furthermore, there are different "species of subjective forms," that is different ways how a sensing subject may capture data, or different modes in which data may be detected: Whitehead mentions "emotions, valuations, purposes, adversions, aversions, consciousness, etc."[29] Accordingly, there are sentient detecting, evaluative, purpose-setting, conscious, or unconscious prehensions which set up a pluralistic ontology of types of subjects.[30]

Prehending systems of actual entities—such as living cells, brains, or people—are what Whitehead calls "societies," that is, they are *nexus* constituted by the networking of actual entities, which is realised by their mutual sentient prehending of each other. Actual occasions exist, i.e., they are generated, only

---

[26] Friedrich Nietzsche, *The Gay Science: With a Prelude in German Rhymes and an Appendix of Songs*, ed. Bernard Williams (Cambridge: Cambridge University Press, 2001), bk. 5, aph. 374, 239, original emphasis.

[27] Whitehead, *Process and Reality*, 23, original emphasis.

[28] Alfred North Whitehead, *Modes of Thought* (New York: The Free Press, 1968), 111.

[29] Whitehead, *Process and Reality*, 24.

[30] On the one hand, postulating these species of bipolar feelings sets Whitehead free from typical problems of mind-matter dualism(s) or emergence theories. On the other hand, Whitehead's assumptions will presumably not stand the empirical test of primordial physics (e.g., is it arguable that quarks are bipolar?). This in turn sets obvious limits to the force of his descriptive generalisation and shows that his cosmological approach is not so much different from Nietzsche's focus on the metaphysics of the will and the human perspective.

within the structures of such societies; they cannot be isolated in reality but only in the sense of a conceptual abstraction.[31] According to Whitehead as well as Nietzsche speculative metaphysics—which for an empirical realist implies speculative realism—is inevitable, i.e., epistemically unavoidable and methodically indispensable for several reasons. A prominent one is their mistrust in the power of language (natural and logical) to give adequate expression to feelings and thoughts (and, in particular, to the experience of works of art). In Whitehead's own words:

> But no language can be anything but elliptical, requiring a leap of the imagination to understand its meaning in its relevance to immediate experience. The position of metaphysics in the development of culture cannot be understood without remembering that no verbal statement is the adequate expression of a proposition.[32]

Nietzsche would have agreed with this—primarily because linguistic statements and, in particular, formal logical abstractions always remain semantically inadequate, i.e., non-exhaustive. Nietzsche says:

> The things we have words for are also the things we have already left behind. There is a grain of contempt in all speech. Language, it seems, was invented only for average, mediocre, communicable things. People vulgarise themselves when they speak a language.[33]

Thus, both Nietzsche and Whitehead believe in immediate

31 "But there are no single occasions, in the sense of isolated occasions. Actuality is through and through togetherness—togetherness of otherwise isolated eternal objects, and togetherness of all actual occasions." Alfred North Whitehead, *Science and the Modern World* (Glasgow: Fontana Books, 1975), 208. Also: Whitehead, *Process and Reality*, 11-12.

32 Whitehead, *Process and Reality*, 13, 12.

33 Friedrich Nietzsche, "Twilight of the Idols, or How to Philosophise with a Hammer" in *The Anti-Christ, Ecce Homo, Twilight of the Idols, and Other Writings*, ed. Aaaron Ridley and Judith Norman (Cambridge: Cambridge University Press, 2005), "Skirmishes of an Untimely Man," aph. 26, 205.

(intuitive) aesthetic experience which cannot be (completely) grasped by our conceptual capabilities.

Moreover, for both thinkers speculative metaphysics, or descriptive/imaginative generalisation is not just inevitable, but is in fact *the* veritable method of the search for and discovery of generalities:

> The true method of discovery is like the flight of an aeroplane. It starts from the ground of particular observation; it makes a flight in the thin air of imaginative generalisation; and it again lands for renewed observation rendered acute by rational interpretation … Metaphysical categories are not dogmatic statements of the obvious; they are tentative formulations of the ultimate generalities.[34]

Yet as the last two citations do already make obvious, there seems to be a main (meta-) epistemological difference between Nietzsche and Whitehead, which concerns the latter's striving for a comprehensive and coherent philosophical system. According to Whitehead "the true method of philosophical construction" consists in framing "a scheme of ideas, the best that one can, and unflinchingly to explore the interpretation of experience in terms of that scheme."[35] The design of the optimal scheme of ideas Whitehead conceived as "speculative philosophy," "a method productive of important knowledge."[36] Such speculative philosophy "is the endeavour to frame a coherent, logical, necessary system of general ideas in terms of which every element of our experience can be interpreted."[37] "Metaphysics" is for Whitehead thus "nothing but the description of the generalities which apply to all the details of practice."[38]

It is well known that Nietzsche's aphoristic style is one of the means for expressing his critical attitude towards systems

[34] Whitehead, *Process and Reality*, 5-8.

[35] Ibid., xiv.

[36] Ibid., 3.

[37] Ibid.

[38] Ibid., 13.

of generalities. However, since Whitehead believes only in approximations to such systems[39] and because Nietzsche, of course, uses concepts, and any concept transcends the immediate sensual presence of impressions, the difference between Whitehead and Nietzsche with respect to system-thinking is not so big (and surely not insurmountable).

According to Whitehead's conviction, the speculative perspectives, concepts and models are essentially justified by their hermeneutic interpretive applicability and adequacy.[40] Although Nietzsche most of the time formally rejects the ideas of comprehensiveness and systematicity,[41] because he takes the idea that the world is inexhaustible for us very seriously (this is Nietzsche's perspectivism), he would agree on Whitehead's hermeneutics. Especially because Nietzsche's hermeneutics is not conceived as a methodology specific to the humanities (*Geistes- und Kulturwissenschaften*) based on a sharp distinction between the humanities and the (natural) sciences. Quite to the contrary, his "experimental philosophy"[42] denies such a sharp distinction—in full agreement with Whitehead who also does not believe in distinguishing the two cultures.[43]

For Whitehead "philosophy is the criticism of abstractions which govern special modes of thought."[44] Thus, his philosophical core objective is to counteract (the epistemological dominance of) abstractions (in the sense of conceptual analytical classifications)[45] by means of (re-)specifications

---

[39] "No metaphysical system can hope entirely to satisfy these pragmatic tests. At the best such a system will remain only an approximation to the general truths which are sought." Whitehead, *Process and Reality*, 13.

[40] Whitehead, *Process and Reality*, 3.

[41] "I mistrust all systematisers and avoid them. The will to a system is a lack of integrity." Nietzsche, "Twilight of the Idols," "Arrows and Epigrams," aph. 26, 159.

[42] See Friedrich Kaulbach, *Nietzsches Idee einer Experimentalphilosophie* (Köln: Böhlau, 1980).

[43] See, e.g., Whitehead, *Science and the Modern World*.

[44] Whitehead, *Modes of Thought*, 48-49.

[45] Ibid., 15, 157.

of abstractions[46] and interpretive syntheses, in order to adequately grasp the systemic and quasi-holistic networks of the procedural and gradualistic nature of things. In particular, Whitehead thinks that "there is no groove of abstraction which is adequate for the comprehension of human life."[47] Such an attitude is fully shared by Nietzsche when he says that what "we have words for are also the things we have already left behind."[48]

Despite the systems-theoretic features of his philosophy, Whitehead (now even more obviously in full accordance with Nietzsche) suggests a phenomenological perspective:

> Philosophy can exclude nothing. Thus it should never start from systematisation. Its primary stage can be termed *assemblage* ... All that can be achieved is the emphasis on a few large-scale notions, together with attention to the variety of other ideas which arise in the display of those chosen for primary emphasis.[49]

In this sense, for Whitehead the "useful function of philosophy is to promote the most general systematisation of civilised thought,"[50] i.e., philosophy should promote a (more) comprehensive, holistic-systemic way of understanding. The thesis may be ventured that, irrespective of the systematic attitude and the goal of approaching and approximating a comprehensive system, this is definitely still in line with Nietzsche's views, e.g., when he says that "the honest naked goddess philosophy" is the "most truthful of all sciences."[51]

Nietzsche would also agree with Whitehead's view that the most basic prehensions and experiences show up in the mode

---

[46] Whitehead, *Process and Reality*, 15.

[47] Whitehead, *Science and the Modern World*, 233.

[48] Nietzsche, "Twilight of the Idols," "Skirmishes of an Untimely Man," aph. 26, 205.

[49] Whitehead, *Modes of Thought*, 2, original emphasis.

[50] Whitehead, *Process and Reality*, 17.

[51] Friedrich Nietzsche, "On the Uses and Disadvantages of History for Life" in *Untimely Meditations*, ed. Daniel Breazeale (Cambridge: Cambridge University Press, 1997), 5, 85.

of self-evidence or intuition. According to both Whitehead and Nietzsche, such basic experiential (self-)evidence "cannot be proved," i.e., it cannot be deduced analytically from "abstraction[s]."[52] Nietzsche tries even the scholastics to make his argument:

> This relation [between self-evident intuitions and concepts] may be very well expressed in the language of the scholastics by saying, the concepts are the *universalia post rem*, but music [i.e., intuition] gives the *universalia ante rem*, and the real world the *universalia in re*.[53]

Linguistically—within predicate logic—such intuitive prehending or experiencing can only be approximated. In that, philosophy is similar to poetry.[54] At the same time, however, Whitehead holds that the "clarity of intuition" is "limited, and it flickers," so that we cannot, in our understanding, refrain from language-based inference and from proofs "as tools for the extension of our imperfect self-evidence."[55]

Thus, in Whitehead philosophising, among other things, means to try to phenomenologically grasp the self-evident pre-conditions of all relationships of understanding (and

---

[52] Whitehead, *Modes of Thought*, 49.

[53] Friedrich Nietzsche, "The Birth of Tragedy Out of the Spirit of Music" in *Basic Writings of Nietzsche*, ed. Walter Kaufmann (New York: The Modern Library, 2000), sect. 16, 102-03.

[54] "Philosophy is either self-evident, or it is not philosophy. The attempts of any philosophical discourse should be to produce self-evidence. Of course it is impossible to achieve such aim … The aim of philosophy is sheer disclosure." Whitehead, *Modes of Thought*, 49. "In fact, self-evidence is understanding … Language halts behind intuition. The difficulty of philosophy is the expression of what is self-evident. Our understanding outruns the ordinary usages of words. Philosophy is akin to poetry. Philosophy is the endeavour to find a conventional phraseology for the vivid suggestiveness of the poet." Whitehead, *Modes of Thought*, 47, 49-50.

[55] Whitehead, *Modes of Thought*, 50. In particular, this is true for scientific methodology where abstractions (e.g., in the sense of approximate models) are unavoidable and indispensable for such restricted, factually non-holistic experiential beings as we are.

explaining).[56] According to him, this power "makes the content of the human mind manageable," "adds meaning to fragmentary details," "discloses disjunctions and conjunctions, consistencies and inconsistencies."[57] In a similar attitude Nietzsche identifies the epistemic basis of his aestheticism in immediate and reliable intuition: "We shall have gained much for the science of aesthetics, once we perceive not merely by logical inference, but with the immediate certainty of vision."[58]

3 Aesthetic Categories of Importance

Richard M. Millard has identified six "categories of importance" of Whitehead's process philosophy as "modes of aesthetic complementation":[59]

(1) Harmonious Individuality,
(2) Endurance,
(3) Novelty,
(4) Contrast,
(5) Depth,
(6) Vividness or Intensity.

We think that these six categories represent a model of an aesthetic epistemology which is also of relevance for (understanding) Nietzsche's philosophy.

For Whitehead, these categories correspond to his conception of actual entities continually striving for (more) intensity and mutual adaptation. These processual entities are of a certain endurance but there are no eternal (actual) substances. Of central importance is the category of novelty,

---

[56] Whitehead, *Modes of Thought*, 48-49.

[57] Ibid., 48.

[58] Nietzsche, "The Birth of Tragedy," sect. 1, 33.

[59] Richard M. Millard, "Whiteheads's Aesthetic Perspective," *Educational Theory* (1961), 11:4, 255-68, 258. Whitehead developed these categories in *Science and the Modern World* and *Religion in the Making*. Four of them became (minimal) conditions of existence of occasions, and "contrast" became one of the Categories of Existence.

which reflects the creative potentials of real processes. In summary, Whitehead's categories of importance of concrete experience or actual entities are the conditions of harmonised intensity, i.e., the conditions of (forever) intensifying aesthetic individuality, which is the real and justificational basis of all processes and activities in the universe.[60] Moreover, Whitehead's philosophy and epistemology are aesthetic-ontological from the outset, since the six categories of importance are the basics of an aestheticist realist epistemology starting from intuitive phenomena, which is fundamentally different from an epistemology that is erected on concept-based judgements:

> The metaphysical doctrine, here expounded, finds the foundations of the world in the aesthetic experience, rather than—as with Kant—in the cognitive and conceptive experience. All order is merely certain aspects of aesthetic order, and the moral order is merely certain aspects of aesthetic order. The actual world is the outcome of the aesthetic order. [61]

For the following reasons the above mentioned aesthetic categories of importance can also be ascribed to Nietzsche—with the (partial) exception of the first one, harmonious individuality. First of all, these categories are basic epistemological elements which are pragmatically unavoidable: e.g., any epistemology has to adopt some conception of endurance in time and contrast in the sea of chaos in order to deal with a universe of becoming. The concepts of novelty, depth and intensity are also basic for and present all over Nietzsche's writings—they are encountered in concepts such as, e.g., "will to power,"[62] "depth,"[63] and "self-overcoming."[64] In the end, even

[60] Maybe, according to Whitehead, this is even true for God.

[61] Alfred North Whitehead, *Religion in the Making* (New York: World Publishing Company/The New American Library, 1960/74), 101.

[62] E.g., Nietzsche, *The Gay Science*, bk. 5, aph. 349, 208.

[63] E.g., he speaks of "people of depth." Nietzsche, *The Gay Science*, bk. 3, aph. 256, 150.

[64] Nietzsche, *Thus Spoke Zarathustra*, 88ff. Friedrich Nietzsche, *Writings from*

"harmonious individuality"[65] could be ascribed to Nietzsche, although he might have resisted the literal notion of harmony. But without doubt the conception of structured, concrete individuals, or aesthetic individuality, is foundational for Nietzsche, e.g., when he explicates his understanding of an autonomous person.[66]

4 A Table of Phenomenological Values and the Outstanding Role of Beauty

The doctrine of the primacy of aesthetic categories, and particularly the dominance of beauty in the system of values are basic elements of both Nietzsche's and Whitehead's philosophy. Whitehead's (rather abstract) definition of beauty reads: "Beauty is the mutual adaptation of the several factors in an occasion of experience."[67]

On many occasions in his writings Whitehead makes it clear that underlying this statement is a concept of harmony, or, at least, optimality of mutual adaptation. At first glance, such an assumption would seem to be unacceptable for Nietzsche, because he adopts the Heraclitean idea that war, conflict or quarrel is the "father of all things." On closer inspection, however, the difference between the two authors is not so big: on the one hand, Whitehead, within his process philosophy, conceives harmony as the ongoing process of mutual adaptation of real events (instead of characterising a static state), and on the other hand, Nietzsche adopts the Heraclitean understanding of the world as an eternal becoming and perishing of individual entities—Nietzsche's "Eternal Recurrence of the Same":

---

the *Late Notebooks*, ed. Rüdiger Bittner (Cambridge: Cambridge University Press, 2003), 131, 138, 176, 228 et passim.

[65] Millard, "Whiteheads's Aesthetic Perspective," 258.

[66] See Volker Gerhardt, *Friedrich Nietzsche* (München: Beck, 1999), 207. See also the discussion of the phenomenological value of freedom below.

[67] Whitehead, *Adventures of Ideas*, 252.

Behold, we know what you teach: that all things recur eternally and we ourselves along with them; and that we have already been here times eternal and all things with us … I will return to this same and selfsame life, in what is greatest as well as in what is smallest, to once again teach the eternal recurrence of all things.[68]

But joy does not want heirs, not children—joy wants itself, wants eternity, wants recurrence, wants everything eternally the same.[69]

Yet one remaining—and crucial—difference is that while Whitehead relies on a developmental trans-human *telos* (which, in the end, cannot be understood as a completely innerworldly issue), Nietzsche radically denies such possibility when he is insulting any teleological scholasticism in philosophy. For him the only aims in the world are those that we generate and construct ourselves.

Whitehead's definition of beauty implies that it is more fundamental than any other type of value, because all occasions by their very nature of bipolarity and permanent bilateral interaction do realise mutual adaptations of the factors that constitute them. In this basic sense "the Universe is directed to the production of Beauty."[70] Moreover, for Whitehead the most general notion of beauty comprises almost all other types of value, which he conceives as types and gradations of beauty.[71]

Nietzsche mentions a number of features of the concept of beauty, thereby delivering an implicit definition: the "*Uebermensch*" is representative of the concept of perfect beauty, and beauty can only be recognised by "the most awakened souls."[72] For Nietzsche being a beautiful person means to live the attitude of superior serenity (e.g., without jealousy,

---

[68] Nietzsche, *Thus Spoke Zarathustra*, 178; see, e.g., also Nietzsche, *The Gay Science*, bk. 4, aph. 341, 194.

[69] Ibid., 262.

[70] Whitehead, *Adventures of Ideas*, 265.

[71] Millard, "Whiteheads's Aesthetic Perspective," 260.

[72] Nietzsche, *Thus Spoke Zarathustra*, 67, 72.

endowed with humour, etc.),[73] while we can find beauty only in self-overcoming and self-abandonment: "Where is beauty? Where I *must will* with my entire will; where I want to love and perish."[74] Thus, similar to Whitehead, Nietzsche thinks that beauty is *the* goal to be pursued by humans. However, we also immediately recognise that Whitehead's concept of beauty is of broader scope, and that Nietzsche's understanding is much more emphatically focused on self-overcoming—while Whitehead, in general, is content with mutual adaptation.

A further inspection of the phenomenological values Whitehead advocates makes it possible to specify in more detail the similarities and differences between Whitehead and Nietzsche. For that purpose we build on an analysis of Richard M. Millard who proposes to order the value types that Whitehead discusses[75] hierarchically according to "progressive aesthetic enrichment, individually and communally."[76] The corresponding list of phenomenological values reads: (1) minor beauty, (2) survival, (3) freedom, (4) moral goodness, (5) understanding, (6) holiness, (7) truth, (8) major beauty, (8a) adventure, (8b) civilisation, and (8c) peace.[77]

(1) Minor Beauty

Whitehead distinguishes major and minor types of beauty in correspondence to the ends aimed at: if the goal is only the avoidance of mutual inhibitions among the various prehensions—e.g., the absence of a painful clash, or vulgarity—we speak of "minor beauty." According to Whitehead, the minor form of beauty is a sort of pre-condition for the major form (which is one of the highest types of value realisable).

It must be assumed that Nietzsche would not differentiate "minor beauty" because the minimalist approach of mere

---

[73] Nietzsche, *Thus Spoke Zarathustra*, 72, 91–92.

[74] Ibid., 96.

[75] Predominantly in his *Adventures of Ideas*.

[76] Millard, "Whiteheads's Aesthetic Perspective," 260.

[77] Ibid.

avoidance of harm would be too unpassionate and unemphatic for him, in the sense that he would not distinguish between avoiding obstacles of beauty and actively striving for beauty.[78]

(2) Survival

For Whitehead the phenomenological value of survival corresponds to endurance as a category of importance and is accepted as a basic—though lower level—value. In contrast to Whitehead, Nietzsche would accept survival as a value only for the "last human beings," who are "blinking" contently, stuck in their pleasant habits[79]—but not for the *Uebermensch* striving for self-overcoming.

(3) Freedom

According to Whitehead, the value of freedom corresponds to novelty as a category of importance. For him, freedom is the indispensable core condition and "the supreme expression of individuality" above and beyond survival: "freshness, zest, and the extra keenness of intensity arise from it."[80]

In close agreement, for Nietzsche freedom does not exist as absolute trans-empirical freedom, but rather is an expression and means of complex forms of life that are capable of making evidence-based decisions and carrying out actions. In that sense, throughout his writings Nietzsche develops and advocates an ideal of a sovereign person with a free mind— thus positioning himself in the tradition of philosophical enlightenment since antiquity. Remarkably, according to him, such a concept of a (free) person is not conceivable without the set of virtues of antiquity (see, e.g., Aristotle) like honesty, truthfulness, courage, bravery, justice, wisdom and others.[81]

---

[78] However, it does not seem to be decidable whether minor beauty may be a tacit assumption of Nietzsche, or not.

[79] Nietzsche, *Thus Spoke Zarathustra*, 10.

[80] Whitehead, *Adventures of Ideas*, 258.

[81] See Gerhardt, *Friedrich Nietzsche*, 207.

In summary, for Nietzsche human freedom comprises self-determination, self-design and self-transcendence of a pro-active and creative person proper—thus meeting Whitehead's core condition of individuality.

(4) Moral Goodness

For both Whitehead and Nietzsche, moral values are instrumental rather than intrinsic or (metaphysically) objective, i.e., in the first place their obligation and reliability originate from their functionality. The reason for this is that moral values are derived from aesthetic ones because the most basic activities of our access to the world are valuing prehensions, or aesthetic preferences. In other words, the achievement of beauty in the case of Whitehead, or the fulfilment of the will(s) to power in the case of Nietzsche, imply aesthetic-pragmatic concepts of truth and goodness (in contradistinction to approaches which are solely based on conceptual judgements). Roughly speaking, true and good is what serves the aesthetic goals or complies with them. For Whitehead and Nietzsche when a statement is called true or a value is called morally good, this unavoidably implies that these epistemic and ethical judgements are not only in agreement with our (evidence-based) aesthetical preferences but originate from them.[82]

(5) Understanding (Wisdom)

For pragmatic process thinkers like Nietzsche and Whitehead, wisdom and understanding are not characterised by absolute (metaphysical) standards or very specific (cognitive) goals. Quite to the contrary, "wisdom" (as a process and not a state) is characterised as "persistent pursuit of the deeper understanding."[83] For both philosophers, "the fruit of wisdom

---

[82] For example, we first feel that a certain event is hurting us or hindering our development before we try to explicate (moral feelings) and (then possibly) define moral values corresponding to this experience.

[83] Whitehead, *Adventures of Ideas*, 47.

or understanding is not certainty but the opening up of new perspectives."[84] This is clear from the prominent status of creation, perspectivism, and self-design in their philosophies. Moreover, in both authors wisdom requires some amount of speculation. For Whitehead, wisdom emerges from the moral and rational reflection of (the options of) freedom so that the "whole determines what it wills to be, and thereby adjusts the relative importance of its own inherent flashes of spontaneity."[85] In a quite similar manner, Nietzsche makes it clear that with the insights of a critical and moderate constructivist—speculative—realism

> a culture is inaugurated that I venture to call a tragic culture. Its most important characteristic is that wisdom takes the place of science as the highest end—wisdom that, uninfluenced by the seductive distractions of the sciences, turns with unmoved eyes to a comprehensive view of the world, and seeks to grasp, with sympathetic feelings of love, the eternal suffering as its own.[86]

(6) Holiness

First of all, it must be clearly stated that Nietzsche's understanding of holiness—implicit, dialectic and ironic as it is—can only be conceived as a secularised one—since, according to him, God is dead (although his remnants are still there): "God is dead; but given the way people are, there may still for millennia be caves in which they show this shadow.—And we—we must still defeat his shadow as well!"[87] Therefore, it seems that holiness, in any non-ironic religious sense, does not designate a value for Nietzsche. However, in his discussion of the meaning we might give to our lives, Nietzsche maintains that such a meaning "ought to heighten our feeling of power

---

[84] Millard, "Whiteheads's Aesthetic Perspective," 261.

[85] Whitehead, *Adventures of Ideas*, 47.

[86] Friedrich Nietzsche, "The Birth of Tragedy," sect. 18, 112.

[87] Nietzsche, *The Gay Science*, bk. 3, aph. 108, 109.

and give us a sense of reverence for ourselves."[88]

This view is coherent with Whitehead's conception that "fundamental religious experience is a direct intuition of the unity of three concepts—the value of the individual for himself, of individuals for each other, and of the objective world as a community of value realising mutually interdependent individuals"[89]—which issues into a "concept of the rightness of things."[90] For Whitehead, "this is the intuition of holiness, the intuition of the sacred, which is at the foundation of all religion."[91] It is quite clear that this abstract aesthetic-ethical concept of religion is compatible even with a secularised approach to ethics like Nietzsche's.[92]

(7) Truth

In accordance with the type of speculative realism that is ascribed to Nietzsche and Whitehead here, they both maintain a relaxed attitude towards the concept of truth: they advocate a pragmatic, aesthetically creative and coherentist concept of truth (and meaning), and not an absolute, transcendent(al) correspondence-theoretic one. [93] Accordingly, both philosophers reject narrow verificationist concepts of truth. In Whitehead's own words, "Truth is the conformation of Appearance to Reality."[94] For him, it is clear that "Truth derives

---

[88] J. Thomas Howe, *Faithful to the Earth: Nietzsche and Whitehead on God and the Meaning of Human Life* (Oxford: Rowman and Littlefield, 2003), 78.

[89] Whitehead, *Religion in the Making*, 59.

[90] Ibid., 66.

[91] Whitehead, *Adventures of Ideas*, 342–43; Millard, "Whiteheads's Aesthetic Perspective," 262.

[92] At the same time, since it seems to be very difficult to interpret Whitehead's concept of God in a completely innerworldly manner, there remains a distinctive difference between the two authors in this respect.

[93] "We do not consider the falsity of a judgment as itself an objection to a judgment." Nietzsche, *Beyond Good and Evil*, 7. "It is more important that a proposition be interesting than that it be true." Whitehead, *Adventures of Ideas*, 244.

[94] Whitehead, *Adventures of Ideas*, 241, see also 250–51, 266. By the way, this

this self-justifying power from the services in the promotion of Beauty. Apart from Beauty, Truth is neither good, nor bad."[95] Further, "Beauty is a wider, and more fundamental, notion than Truth."[96] It is obvious that Nietzsche would have agreed with that, in particular because for him truth is a "play of interpretation" (Gianni Vattimo).[97] Nietzsche vehemently rejects the idea of truth as the most basic, absolute principle of metaphysics from which the categories of being may be deduced.

Moreover, in close accordance with Whitehead Nietzsche strongly opposes to treat truth and knowledge as a priority, because this would inevitably express contempt for all direct expressions of life, and because all human perception and recognition "merely slide[s] across the surface of things."[98]

> What, then, is truth? A mobile army of metaphors, metonymies, anthropomorphisms, in short a sum of human relations which have been subjected to poetic and rhetorical intensification, translation, and decoration, and which, after they have been in use for a long time, strike a people as firmly established, canonical, and binding; truths are illusions of which we have forgotten that they are illusions, metaphors which have become worn by frequent use and have lost all sensuous vigour, coins which, having lost their stamp, are now regarded as metal and no longer as coins.[99]

Furthermore, for Nietzsche truth must be redefined as experiential truth which denotes a conceptual abstractum subsuming all our perspectivist and interpretative relations

---

statement again corroborates Whitehead's realist position.

[95] Whitehead, *Adventures of Ideas*, 267.

[96] Ibid., 265.

[97] Wiebrecht Ries, *Nietzsche und seine ästhetische Philosophie des Lebens* (Tübingen: Francke, 2012), 14.

[98] Friedrich Nietzsche, "On Truth and Lying in a Non-Moral Sense" in *The Birth of Tragedy and Other Writings*, ed. Raymond Geuss and Ronald Speirs (Cambridge: Cambridge University Press, 1999), 1, 142.

[99] Ibid., 1, 146.

we may experience in the quarrel with other bearers of interpretation and agency.

(8) Major Beauty

According to Whitehead, "Major Beauty" is "the one aim which by its very nature is self-justifying" in the sense that all actual entities are striving for that process state of experiential (quasi-)perfection, which, of course, may be realised in uncounted individual variants.[100] The key to major beauty is "prehension of individuality," which "is the feeling of each objective factor as an individual 'It' with its own significance."[101] Nietzsche would certainly agree—if we were to replace "major beauty" by "fulfilment of the will(s) to power." This is quite obvious if we remind ourselves that Whitehead's idea of the process of experiential perfection is in close agreement with Nietzsche's idea of will(s) to power which, during their process of self-overcoming—momentarily and tentatively—achieve their (partial) empirical fulfilment. Consequently, for Whitehead,

> any part of experience can be beautiful. The teleology of the Universe is directed to the production of Beauty. Thus any system of things which in any wide sense is beautiful is to that extent justified in its existence.[102]

With the above mentioned replacement this passage is in full accordance with Nietzsche's aestheticism, which finds its expression in the statement that "it is only as an *aesthetic phenomenon* that existence and the world are eternally *justified*."[103]
Whitehead describes the major form of beauty as follows:

> This form presupposes the first form [i.e., minor beauty], and adds to it the condition that the conjunction in one synthesis of the various

---

[100] Whitehead, *Adventures of Ideas*, 266.

[101] Ibid., 262, original emphasis.

[102] Ibid., 265.

[103] Nietzsche, "The Birth of Tragedy," sect. 5, 52, original emphases.

prehensions introduces new contrasts of objective content ... the parts contribute to the massive feeling of the whole, and the whole contributes to the intensity of the feeling of the parts.[104]

According to Whitehead, such beauty can be described as "the perfection of Harmony."[105] However, major beauty, for Whitehead, is still a preliminary culmination of aesthetic values, which in turn gives rise to the highest values—adventure, civilisation, and peace.

Yet Nietzsche would agree with Whitehead's concept of major beauty only to a certain extent. In this context the (perspectivist and gradual) difference between the two philosophers is rooted in the incompatibility of Whitehead's concepts of harmony and teleology with Nietzsche's ideas of chaos and aimlessness (of life *per se*). For example, in contradistinction to Whitehead, Nietzsche believes that "the total character of the world ... is for all eternity chaos."[106] Moreover, while in Whitehead's cosmology a pragmatically perfect harmony of the whole universe is assumed to be achievable, in Nietzsche's existentialism the aesthetic perspective is a self-produced way out of absurdity, and it is the only one that is feasible (for us). In contrast to Nietzsche the escapist or healing function in Whitehead's system is realised by his understanding of eternal entities, teleology and God (which are empirically empty concepts for Nietzsche). At the same time, however, Nietzsche's superior serenity[107] can be related to Whitehead's harmony, since the serenity of a human individual, possibly an exemplar of the *Uebermensch*, can in fact be understood as a process of harmonisation of their will(s) to power in confrontation with other wills and interests.

---

[104] Whitehead, *Adventures of Ideas*, 252.

[105] Ibid., 252.

[106] Nietzsche, *The Gay Science*, bk. 3, aph. 109, 109.

[107] Nietzsche, *Thus Spoke Zarathustra*, 72, 91–92.

(8a) Adventure

According to Whitehead, because of the process character of all reality all valuable situations, including major beauty, are perishable (and all actual occasions will perish). However, in his view this also creates new possibilities for optimised fulfilment, for fuller beauty, i.e., occasions of adventure. For Whitehead, adventure is the general name for the value type of freedom and self-overcoming under the condition of (striving for) major beauty. Accordingly, adventure is constitutive for art, civilisation and peace.[108] Moreover, creative speculation is but one concretion or realisation mode of adventure.

These considerations are in complete compliance with Nietzsche's philosophy of life characterised by self-designing and self-overcoming which cannot be tackled or achieved without taking risk. Without doubt, the following statements by Whitehead could also have been written down by Nietzsche: "Without adventure civilisation is in full decay,"[109] and "Advance or Decadence are the only choices offered to mankind."[110] In accordance with that, Zarathustra, in the section "On Self-overcoming," says that "this secret life itself spoke to me: 'Behold,' it said, 'I am that *which must always overcome itself.* To be sure, you call it will to beget or drive to a purpose ....'"[111]

(8b) Civilisation

Whitehead's "general definition of civilisation" is "that a civilised society is exhibiting the five qualities of Truth, Beauty, Adventure, Art, Peace."[112] In other words, science and

---

[108] Whitehead, *Adventures of Ideas*, 271ff.

[109] Ibid., 279.

[110] Ibid., 274.

[111] Nietzsche, *Thus Spoke Zarathustra*, 89, original emphasis.

[112] Whitehead, *Adventures of Ideas*, 274. Based on what we have learned about the commonalities between Nietzsche and Whitehead, we can assume that Nietzsche would agree on Whitehead's concept of civilisation—with the

art, conceptual knowledge and aesthetics in combination with creative enhancement realised under peaceful conditions represent the pre-conditions of human civilisation. Although Nietzsche does not literally talk about civilisation, he certainly advocates a conception of a higher developed culture, the ingredients and basics of which are science and art based on an aesthetic access to and perspective of the world. We have already mentioned, however, that peace from Nietzsche's Heraclitean perspective is not as important as it is for Whitehead.

(8c) Peace

Whitehead says, "I choose the term 'Peace' for that Harmony of Harmonies which calms destructive turbulence and completes civilisation."[113] Peace "is broadening of feeling due to the emergence of some deep metaphysical insight, unverbalised and yet momentous in its coordination of values."[114] At first glance, this gives the impression that Whitehead advocates a rather transfigured or romanticised concept of peace. However, he further specifies that peace is "primarily a trust in the efficacy of Beauty. It is a sense that fineness of achievement is, as it were, a key unlocking treasures that the narrow nature of things would keep remote."[115] Still, up to that point it seems that Whitehead's understanding of peace is just harmonic—and therefore in contraposition to Nietzsche who again and again stressed (basically since "The Birth of Tragedy") that life is a permanent struggle and even war, an ongoing process of delimiting oneself at the expense of others. But then Whitehead adds that:

---

exception of "peace." In this respect, Nietzsche has much more affinity with the Heraclitean conception of *polemos* (controversy; quarrel; war) as the origin of reality.

[113] Whitehead, *Adventures of Ideas*, 285.

[114] Ibid., 285.

[115] Ibid., 285.

As soon as high consciousness is reached, the enjoyment of existence is entwined with pain, frustration, loss, tragedy. Amid the passing of so much beauty, so much heroism, so much daring, Peace is then the intuition of permanence. It keeps vivid the sensitiveness to tragedy; and it sees the tragedy as a living agent persuading the world to aim at fineness beyond the faded level of surrounding fact. Each tragedy is the disclosure of an ideal:—What might have been, and was not: What can be. The tragedy was not in vain.[116]

With such an existentialist statement, perhaps unexpectedly, Whitehead again very much closes up to Nietzsche. We have finally learned that Whitehead's "peace" does not denote a situation of harmonious harmony of harmonies, but unavoidably comprises a dialectics of the unavoidable interweaving of harmonic and tragic (real) events.

5 The Aesthetic Justification of Existence and Life as (a Work of) Art

Nietzsche's and Whitehead's conceptions of epistemic processes (broadly construed) are axiological—which for them means aesthetic in the first place—and realist from the outset and across all levels of reality processing or types of prehensions.[117] In other words, for them the basic values are unavoidably aesthetic values (and not moral or epistemic ones) because all constituents of reality (in whatever sense and of whatever level of constitutive complexity) originate from basic processes of mutual prehending and perceiving of actual occasions or wills to power, respectively. For both Whitehead and Nietzsche, there is no concrete or real experience without valuing because all experience, i.e., all actual relationships of any occasion or occurrence or event to any other occasion, concerns self-actualisation and happens as a type of "feeling."[118] Whitehead repeatedly stresses this point:

---

[116] Whitehead, *Adventures of Ideas*, 268.

[117] In particular, human valuing is a real empirical process (and not a non-scientific, purely subjective one).

[118] "Feeling ... as a synonym for 'actuality.'" Whitehead, *Religion in the Making*, 100.

Remembering the poetic rendering of our concrete experience, we see at once that the element of value, of being valuable, of having value, of being an end in itself, of being something which is for its own sake, must not be omitted in any account of an event as the most concrete actual something. 'Value' is the word I use for the intrinsic reality of an event. Value is an element which permeates through and through the poetic view of nature![119]

Value experience ... is the very essence of the universe. Existence, in its own nature, is the upholding of value intensity.[120]

An actual fact is a fact of aesthetic experience. All aesthetic experience is feeling arising out of the realisation of contrast under identity.[121]

Overall, for Whitehead the developmental *telos* (goal) of the universe is beauty and therefore striving for beauty—becoming or being beautiful—justifies existence.[122] However, Whitehead does not tie beauty to (mesoscopic) sensory perception; rather, he thinks that beauty "involves conformal feelings in self-actualisation, the individuality of every experimental occasion."[123] As a consequence, the general concept of art is by no means restricted to the fine arts but comprises art as "a way of life, a mode of existence, the goal of communal process."[124] According to Whitehead, art is the optimal refinement of nature, it is the optimised form of civilisation. Further, art heals and (somehow) transcends the finiteness of our lives. Thus, Whitehead holds that art, in its broadest sense, is civili-

---

[119] Whitehead, *Science and the Modern World*, 117.

[120] Whitehead, *Modes of Thought*, 111.

[121] Whitehead, *Religion in the Making*, 111.

[122] Whitehead, *Adventures of Ideas*, 265. In contradistinction to Nietzsche, Whitehead suggests that the aesthetic order (which by itself is the generative basis of the real world) "is derived from the immanence of God." Whitehead, *Religion in the Making*, 101, also 96.

[123] Millard, "Whiteheads's Aesthetic Perspective," 255.

[124] Ibid., 255.

sation, "for civilisation is nothing other than the unremitting aim at the major perfections of harmony."[125]

> [Art] exhibits for consciousness a finite fragment of human effort achieving its own perfection within its own limits. Thus the mere toil for the slavish purpose of prolonging life for more toil or for mere bodily gratification, is transformed into the conscious realisation of a self-contained end, timeless within time ... Thus Art heightens the sense of humanity.[126]

Art and science are core activities of an optimally developing human kind.[127] Since for Whitehead, however, beauty is more highly valued than truth, art is more highly valued than science. Art is the way actual entities like humans realise the ubiquitous striving for major beauty. Art is also the expression of "felt meaning" that cannot be expressed otherwise, and it culminates in the idea of *homo ludens*:

> Art expresses depths of felt meaning which cannot be formulated in any other way. The need for expression of these gives rise to ritual, dance, play, the primitive arts and finally the more developed arts. In its ability to crystallise, to bring to vivid individuality the range of human experiences with their deep emotional roots but divorced from necessity, lies the freedom and the therapeutic as well as the formative function of art.[128]

On the level of the original design of the world and the meaning of human life, Nietzsche also strongly advocates a priority of the artistic over the scientific when stating the following about the belief of science in its ability—by "using the thread of causality"—to reach out to the "deepest abysses

---

[125] Whitehead, *Adventures of Ideas*, 271.

[126] Ibid., 270-71.

[127] "Science and Art are the consciously determined pursuit of Truth and of Beauty." Whitehead, *Adventures of Ideas*, 272.

[128] Ibid., 348.

of being" which it might not only know but also correct: "This sublime metaphysical illusion accompanies science as an instinct and leads science again and again to its limits at which it must turn into *art*."[129] Moreover, Nietzsche also holds "that through art nature comes to language and thus life to its symbolic expression."[130] In the words of Volker Gerhardt, for Nietzsche this means that "the human being who despairs of his meaningless existence is hindered by art to give himself up. Viewed in isolation, human existence has no appeal and no value, but through art, it becomes 'possible and worth living.'"[131]

> Here, when the danger to his will is greatest, *art* approaches as a saving sorceress, expert at healing. She alone knows how to turn these nauseous thoughts about the horror or absurdity of existence into notions with which one can live: these are the *sublime* as the artistic taming of the horrible, and the *comic* as the artistic discharge of the nausea of absurdity.[132]

Moreover, Nietzsche interprets and idealises human life as a whole as a work of art: "Wild life brings out a fantastic variety of forms, in its vast production only obeys its own law and everything seems like a great play[133] to run."[134]

Furthermore, Nietzsche describes the "world as a work of art giving birth to itself,"[135] and Zarathustra unmistakably states: "Creating—that is the great redemption from suffering, and

---

[129] Nietzsche, "The Birth of Tragedy," sect. 15, 95-96, original emphasis.

[130] Gerhardt, *Friedrich Nietzsche*, 91, this and all subsequent translations are ours.

[131] Ibid., 85. Gerhardt is quoting Nietzsche, "The Birth of Tragedy," sect. 1, 35 here.

[132] Nietzsche, "The Birth of Tragedy," sect. 7, 60, original emphasis.

[133] In the aesthetic sense of "play(ing)" that has been introduced by Kant and Schiller.

[134] Gerhardt, *Friedrich Nietzsche*, 88.

[135] Friedrich Nietzsche, "Notebook 2, autumn 1885–autumn 1886" in *Writings from the Late Notebooks*, 2[114], 82.

life's becoming light."[136] In his later works Nietzsche explicates the idea that the dynamic expression and self-realisation of the wills to power ultimately can only be viewed according to the manner of a work of art. In that sense, that which gives unity to the processes we call world and life has to be considered art. This is how Nietzsche's early dictum that art is actually "the highest task and the truly metaphysical activity of this life"[137] has to be understood.[138]

6 Summary and Conclusions

Friedrich Nietzsche and Alfred North Whitehead have many philosophical subjects in common.[139] One of their very basic commonalities is the rejection of the idea that the world is composed of (eternally stable) substances. In contradistinction, their philosophies represent a *comprehensive processual view of the universe* and conceive centres of dynamicity as constituents of any empirically real process. These processual entities are the respective building blocks of the universe as centres of power, which are characterised by their creative mutability, activity and reactivity: Nietzsche introduces the wills to power while Whitehead declares actual occasions, or real prehending entities, as "the primary actual units of which the temporal world is composed."[140]

Both thinkers also "reject absolutism as a characteristic of philosophy."[141] A further attitude they share is their common starting point for any metaphysical speculation: it must commence—and prove its reliability—in our experience;

---

[136] Nietzsche, *Thus Spoke Zarathustra*, 66.

[137] Nietzsche, "The Birth of Tragedy," "Preface to Richard Wagner," 31-32.

[138] See Gerhardt, *Friedrich Nietzsche*, 88–89.

[139] These commonalities are not a consequence of direct influence since it seems to be a "fact that Whitehead's published writings give only scant evidence that he had read or even thought about Nietzsche." Howe, *Faithful to the Earth*, 8-9.

[140] Whitehead, *Religion in the Making*, 88.

[141] Wood, "Creativity: Whitehead and Nietzsche," 50.

this is what we have called their *speculative realism*. At the same time, they both disapprove of: the idea that language is an adequate expression of judgements; a faculty psychology; the subject-predicate form of statements; sensualist as well as extensionalist epistemologies. All of these rejections are reasons for why we are in need of rationally controlled speculation—controlled by checking its empirical adequacy and relevance as well as logical consistency and conceptual coherence. Concerning speculative realism it should be added that Whitehead's philosophy transports a gradually stronger realism or objectivism and a more harmonious optimism as regards (aesthetic) values: for him they are somehow intrinsic to the universe out there. However, Whitehead attempts an "imaginative construction" which "must have its origin in the generalisation of particular factors discerned in particular topics of human interest" [142] and conceives of speculative philosophy as an "experimental adventure."[143]

On a rather general level, Janusz Polanowski has already stated that the

> commonalities that link Whitehead's philosophy with Nietzsche's thinking about the world can be summed up in their mutual exaltation of novelty, complexity, creativity, multiplicity, and adventurousness, and at the same time their incontrovertible rejection of ontological duality, essentiality, finality, certainty, simplicity, and sterility.[144]

To this (rather extensive) list one may add the topics of epistemological gradualism and perspectivism—meaning that our understanding of the world comes and only functions in gradual terms, and that the world seems to be epistemically inexhaustible for humans and for other societies of prehensions of an appropriate organisational complexity.

[142] Whitehead, *Process and Reality*, 5.

[143] Ibid., 9.

[144] Janusz A. Polanowski, "Points of Connection in Whitehead's and Nietzsche's Metaphysics" in *Whitehead's Philosophy: Points of Connection*, ed. Janusz A. Polanowski and Donald W. Sherburne (New York: State University of New York Press, 2004), 144-45.

For Whitehead and Nietzsche, (sufficiently complex) aesthetic prehensions—perceptions, intuitions and judgements—are indispensable ingredients of the quality of (human or animal) life because they are the most basic activities of self-fulfilment and self-transcendence. Art, Whitehead says, "transforms the soul into the permanent realisation of values extending beyond its former self"[145]—a statement that could easily be ascribed to Nietzsche, since he believes that nature comes to language and life to its symbolic expression in (a work of) art, which is the stimulant of life. More than that, art is "a metaphysical supplement of the reality of nature, placed beside it for its overcoming."[146] In that sense, art inspires us to discover new ways of being in the world. It provides us with options and means for attaining experiences of greater contrast, depth and intensity. And it helps us to come to grips with absurdity and horror—to heal the absurdity of (human) life, in the case of Nietzsche without an external *telos* and guarantor.

Moreover, for both thinkers conducting one's life and doing philosophy are creative activities—leading one's life according to relevant standards of reflection and, more importantly, aesthetic values, generates a work of art. Among other things, this comprises, at least for Nietzsche, that we create our own values because only that way can we give meaning to our lives. Whitehead's view that *the universe is a creative advance* is compatible with Nietzsche's conception of continuously striving for a fulfilment of the will(s) to power, for the self-design and self-conquest of life—the most prominent symbol of which is the *Uebermensch*. Neither Nietzsche nor Whitehead claim (absolute) finality; for them, the creative process of the world is an ongoing one. At the same time, it must be made clear that the scope of the two approaches as well as their balancing of forces is somehow different.

Some of the few—though important—aspects their opinions differ on is Whitehead's fundamental and strong commitment

---

[145] Whitehead, *Science and the Modern World*, 240.

[146] Nietzsche, "The Birth of Tragedy," sect. 24, 114.

to philosophy as (metaphysical) system and his tendential (quasi-)transcendentalism[147] with respect to the concepts of God[148] and "eternal objects."[149] Concerning the systematicity of philosophy the two authors, however, do not differ so much since Whitehead conceives all systems as hypothetical in the first place. Yet, in contradistinction to Nietzsche Whitehead believes that God is foundationally important.[150] The main difference between Nietzsche and Whitehead in this respect can be illustrated by the following statements. Nietzsche says:

> The total character of the world, by contrast, is for all eternity chaos, not in the sense of a lack of necessity but of a lack of order, organisation, form, beauty, wisdom, and whatever else our aesthetic anthropomorphisms are called.[151]

And he continues that the "universe … is neither perfect, nor beautiful, nor noble, nor does it want to become any of these things."[152]

We suggest contrasting these quotes of Nietzsche with a fictitious statement that Whitehead could have uttered, which—in our opinion—is in complete accordance with his "complete cosmology":[153]

> The total character of the world, by contrast, is for all eternity beauty—harmony of harmonies—in the sense of the processual order, organisation, form, freedom, moral goodness, understanding, truth, adventure and civilisation (which, finally, are guaranteed by the immanence of God).

---

[147] See James Bradley, "Transcendentalism and Speculative Realism in Whitehead," *Process Studies* (1994), 23:3, 155-91.

[148] "The actual world is the outcome of the aesthetic order and the aesthetic order is derived from the immanence of God." Whitehead, *Religion in the Making*, 101.

[149] Whitehead, *Religion in the Making*, 40 et passim.

[150] Ibid., 115.

[151] Nietzsche, *The Gay Science*, bk. 3, aph. 109, 109.

[152] Ibid.

[153] Whitehead, *Process and Reality*, xii.

For Whitehead, the products of art, like all achievements of beauty, are enduring individualities which at least symbolise—or maybe even realise—a sort of transcendental immortality in a processual universe.[154] In other words, for him the universe-in-itself—as God's universe—is intrinsically striving for beauty and nobleness. However, even in Whitehead's view this universe is unavoidably tragic because of the presence of all those disharmonic elements and suffering.[155] While both authors share the conviction of the ambivalences and the tragic character of the universe, Nietzsche's existentialist and nihilist approach is conceivably different: coming to grips with the absurdity of human life is only possible—and strictly speaking: possible only to some extent—by our active anthropomorphic innerworldly intervention, i.e., by self-designing our lives under the framework condition of permanently striving for self-overcoming.[156] In that sense, Zarathustra teaches—and Whitehead would agree so far—that we must *"remain faithful to the earth."*[157] However, in contradistinction to Whitehead, Nietzsche's Zarathustra makes it very clear that one should "not believe those who speak ... of extraterrestrial hopes."[158]

To summarise, according to Whitehead the ultimate and only aim in itself of the (development of the) world is *beauty* and harmony, i.e., maximising individual experiential intensity while minimising the hindrance of other individual entities' intensities. In a similar vein, Nietzsche argues that *the only justification of human existence*—in the sense of self-design on the basis of the will(s) to power, and not just as self-conservation—*is the aesthetic one.*

---

[154] "A great civilisation interfused with Art presents the world to its members clothed in the Appearance of immortality." Whitehead, *Adventures of Ideas*, 364.

[155] Thus confronting Whitehead again with Leibniz's *theodicee* problem.

[156] But again, the difference is not so big, because Whitehead's rather abstract philosopher God lives in the background.

[157] Nietzsche, *Thus Spoke Zarathustra*, 6, original emphasis.

[158] Ibid.

Sellars Contra Deleuze
on Intuitive Knowledge

Matija Jelača

University of Pula

Tedge has haunted philosophy since
the beginning of philosophical
time.[1] It appeared under various guises, and took on many
different names. But its essence remained the same: it was
always supposed to be some kind of immediate knowledge
defined explicitly in opposition and as an alternative to conceptual knowledge. Depending on the general framework in
which it was invoked, it either proclaimed a *higher* form of
knowledge capable of attaining the absolute (rationalism),
or a more *basic/fundamental* kind of knowledge necessary to
ground all knowledge claims (empiricism).

[1] I am deeply indebted to Ray Brassier and Pete Wolfendale without whom
most of this would not even have been intuited. Apart from their ideas, I
am just as grateful for their continual support, encouragement, generosity
and patience. I would also like to thank the organisers of the *Aesthetics in
the 21st Century* conference for the opportunity to present my views in front
of such an esteemed audience, and all the participants for making it such
a memorable event. This version of the paper benefited immensely from
the discussions that followed my talk, especially the ones I had with Steven
Shaviro, Vijak Haddadi and Ridvan Askin. Finally, a special thanks is in order
to Ridvan for being such an attentive reader and discerning interlocutor.
The final version of this text is certainly much better for all his questions,
interventions, and suggestions.

Kant was the first to denounce the spectral nature of intuitive knowledge. But although Kant's critical injunction against its possibility, both in its rationalist ("thoughts without content are empty") and empiricist ("intuitions without concepts are blind") guises, certainly put the spectre on the defensive, it was by no means enough to vanquish it.[2] Kant's attack was followed by numerous others, but always with the exact same results: no sooner had one of its incarnations been laid to rest, the spectre would rise from the dead almost instantly, each time in a slightly different form. And to this very day, it continues to haunt us still.

Gilles Deleuze and Wilfrid Sellars, two major representatives of the continental and analytic philosophical traditions respectively, are the best testaments to the claim that the spectre of intuitive knowledge is pretty much alive and well on both sides of the philosophical divide. While the former developed his whole philosophical system around an incredibly rich and sophisticated (and all the more insidious for it!) account of intuitive knowledge, the latter devoted the greatest part of his philosophical adventure to sharpening the weapons necessary to haunt this spectre down and exorcise it in whichever form it takes. Confronting the two with regards to their opposing views on intuitive knowledge presents a perfect opportunity not just for testing their respective claims to knowledge, but also, and more importantly, for posing again the question of the nature and justification of knowledge, a question almost completely forgotten by recent trends in continental philosophy.

Ray Brassier, one of the very few contemporary continental philosophers unwilling to join in on this collective forgetting of the question of knowledge, expressed his perplexities about one particular variant of this trend:

I am very wary of "aesthetics": the term is contaminated by notions of "experience" that I find deeply problematic. I have no philosophy of

---

[2] Immanuel Kant, *Critique of Pure Reason*, trans. Paul Guyer and Allen W. Wood (Cambridge: Cambridge University Press, 1998), 193-94, A51/B75.

art worth speaking of. This is not to dismiss art's relevance for philosophy—far from it—but merely to express reservations about the kind of
philosophical aestheticism which seems to want to hold up "aesthetic
experience" as a new sort of cognitive paradigm wherein the Modern
(post-Cartesian) "rift" between knowing and feeling would be overcome.[3]

Although it has recently been taken up again by certain fac-
tions of contemporary continental philosophy, the tendency
that Brassier describes here is nothing new. In fact, it has a
long and noble heritage dating back all the way to the early
Romantics. Deleuze's critique of discursive reason and his
appeal to intuitive knowledge, on the one hand, coupled with
the strong alliance he has forged with art and aesthetics, on
the other, reveal him as a direct successor to the philosophical
legacy of early Romanticism. What better way to challenge
Deleuze's Romantic attempt at overcoming the dualism of
knowing and feeling than to contrast it with Sellars's rationalist upholding of its necessity and irreducibility?

This essay is divided into three parts. The first part attempts
to demonstrate that Deleuze was in fact a firm believer in
the powers of intuitive knowledge. To this end, I will present
Deleuze's accounts of three important notions that appeared
throughout his early work: the ideas of *mathesis universalis*,
Bergsonian intuition as a method, and the transcendent exercise of the faculties. The second part of the essay is devoted
to Sellars and attempts to show that his famous myth of the
given is nothing else than intuitive knowledge itself. Three
different accounts of this myth are presented, namely the
ones found in "Empiricism and the Philosophy of Mind,"[4]
"The Structure of Knowledge,"[5] and "The Carus Lectures of

---

3 Ray Brassier, "Against an Aesthetics of Noise," *Transitzone*, nY, http://ny-
web.be/transitzone/against-aesthetics-noise.html (accessed July 15, 2013).

4 Wilfrid Sellars, "Empiricism and the Philosophy of Mind" in *Science, Perception and Reality* (Atascadero: Ridgeview, 1991).

5 Wilfrid Sellars, "The Structure of Knowledge," http://www.ditext.com/
sellars/sk.html (accessed January 22, 2013). Published in: *Action, Knowledge
and Reality: Studies in Honor of Wilfrid Sellars*, ed. Hector-Neri Castañeda
(Indianapolis: Bobbs-Merrill, 1975), 295-347; originally presented as The

Wilfrid Sellars."[6] The third and final part concludes the essay by staging a confrontation between these two formidable opponents.

Deleuze: *Mathesis Universalis,* Intuition, Transcendental Empiricism

For Deleuze, "the world of representation" is not a philosopher's world.[7] It might be a scientist's world, it certainly is a technician's, politician's, journalist's, and bureaucrat's world, but the only engagement with it worthy of a philosopher's time is learning how to escape it. The main reasons for Deleuze's philosophical distrust in this world are neither new nor particularly original, and neither is his plan of escape. Possibly the clearest and most straightforward expression of Deleuze's views on this account can be found in his first published text on Bergson:

> One says that science gives us a knowledge of things, that it is therefore in a certain relation with them, and philosophy can renounce its rivalry with science, can leave things to science and present itself solely in a critical manner, as a reflection on this knowledge of things. On the contrary view, philosophy seeks to establish, or rather restore, *an other* relationship to things, and therefore *an other* knowledge, a knowledge and a relationship that precisely science hides from us, of which it deprives us, because it allows us only to conclude and to infer without ever presenting, giving to us the thing in itself.[8]

To understand this passage fully, it is best to supplement it

---

Matchette Foundation Lectures for 1971 at the University of Texas.

[6] Wilfrid Sellars, "Foundations for a Metaphysics of Pure Process: The Carus Lectures of Wilfrid Sellars," *The Monist* (1981), 64:1, 3-90.

[7] Gilles Deleuze, *Difference and Repetition*, trans. Paul Patton (New York: Columbia University Press, 1994), xix.

[8] Gilles Deleuze, "Bergson, 1859-1941" in *Desert Islands and Other Texts, 1953-1974*, ed. David Lapoujade, trans. Michael Taormina (New York: Semiotext(e), 2004), 23, original emphasis.

Speculations V

with another quote from one of Deleuze's earliest published writings, "Mathesis, Science and Philosophy":

> Scientific method is explanation. To explain is to account for a thing through something other than itself … At the other extreme, philosophical method is description in the widest sense of the word; it is that reflexive analysis whereby the sensible world is described as the representation of the cognizing subject—that is to say, here once again, it receives its status from something other than itself.[9]

Deleuze's argument is seductively simple: science and philosophy (of representation) give us a knowledge of things only through something other than the thing itself. Therefore, they cannot give us the knowledge of the thing itself. An other kind of knowledge is necessary in order to get us at the thing itself. Other to representational or mediated knowledge is immediate knowledge. Therefore, only immediate knowledge can give us knowledge of the thing itself. This is the general structure of Deleuze's argument against representational and in favour of intuitive knowledge. Depending on the context, the terms may vary, but its basic structure remains the same throughout Deleuze's entire opus.

To confirm this claim and dispel the possible objection that the quotes above come from Deleuze's early texts, which do not necessarily express his own views, it will suffice to take a closer look at one important and well known passage from *Difference and Repetition*, considered by many to be Deleuze's single most important philosophical work, and also the first book in which Deleuze expressly speaks in his own name. By the end of chapter one, entitled "Difference in Itself," Deleuze famously claims:

> We have contrasted representation with a different kind of formation. The elementary concepts of representation are the categories defined

---

9 Gilles Deleuze, "Mathesis, Science and Philosophy," trans. Robin Mackay, *Collapse* (2007), 3, 147. Deleuze's text was originally published as an introduction to Jean Malfatti de Montereggio's *Études sur la Mathèse ou anarchie et hiérarchie de la science* (Paris: Editions Du Griffon D'Or, 1946).

as the conditions of possible experience. These, however, are too general
or too large for the real. The net is so loose that the largest fish pass
through ... Everything changes once we determine the conditions of
real experience, which are not larger than the conditioned and which
differ in kind from the categories.[10]

It does not take much effort to notice the similarity with the
previous argument: representation can give us knowledge of
the real only through the categories. Categories are by definition general, while the real is singular. Therefore, representation cannot give us knowledge of the real. An other kind of
knowledge is necessary. Other to general concepts are singular
concepts, and only the latter can give us knowledge of the real.

Deleuze, then, has staged pretty much the same argument
against representation that he has staged in favour of immediate knowledge from his earliest writings up to *Difference
and Repetition*. Let us briefly analyse the structure of this
argument. It consists of two parts: the first, critical part lays
the basis for the second, constructive part. Although it might
be interesting to question the critical part of the argument,
it will be best to leave that aside for now and focus instead
on its constructive part, which is much more important for
my present purpose.

Deleuze's conclusion of the critical part of the argument
presents the first premise of the second, constructive part: in
order to get at the knowledge of the thing itself/the real, an
other kind of knowledge is necessary. This other knowledge
is supposed to be immediate and to consist of the creation
and application of some kind of singular concepts, concepts
appropriate to the thing itself/the real. In order to learn more
about this *other knowledge*, it is necessary to return to the texts
mentioned above.

Although it was one of Deleuze's earliest published writings, later explicitly disowned by him along everything else
published before 1953, "Mathesis, Science and Philosophy"
might very well be the most revealing text by Deleuze when

---

[10] Deleuze, *Difference and Repetition*, 68.

it comes to the question of what this *other knowledge* is supposed to be. The short answer would be *mathesis universalis*. But then, what is *mathesis universalis*? According to Deleuze, the opposition of science and philosophy has opened up a fundamental dualism within knowledge, the Cartesian dualism between *res extensa* and *res cogitans*.[11] *Mathesis universalis* (universal knowledge or universal science) names the desire to overcome this dualism and accomplish a "unity of knowledge."[12] This unity is "the unity of life itself": "Life is the unity of the soul as the idea of the body and of the body as the extension of the soul."[13] Accordingly, "mathesis deploys itself at the level of life, of living man: *it is first and foremost a thinking of incarnation and of individuality*."[14] But how does *mathesis* attain this knowledge of incarnation and individuality? As we have seen, both science and philosophy reduce the sensible object to an object of thought. In order to overcome this duality of the object of thought and the sensible object, the method of *mathesis* must reduce "this object of thought back to the sensible, quantity to quality."[15] It achieves this through the deployment of the *symbol*, which presents precisely "a sensible object as the incarnation of an object of thought," this sensible object being "the very incarnation of knowledge."[16] And finally, "the symbol is the identity, the *encounter* of the sensible object and the object of thought. The sensible object is called symbol, and the object of thought, losing all scientific signification, is a hieroglyph or a cipher. In their identity, they form the concept."[17]

Without getting into all the details that a complete account of this text would require, this short and condensed exposition

---

[11] Deleuze, "Mathesis, Science and Philosophy," 142.

[12] Ibid., 142.

[13] Ibid., 143.

[14] Ibid. my emphasis.

[15] Ibid., 150.

[16] Ibid.

[17] Ibid., 150-51.

of only a few of its aspects is more than enough to clearly show that *mathesis universalis* indeed is Deleuze's *other knowledge*. Defined as a knowledge of incarnation and individuality, *mathesis universalis* responds perfectly to our earlier description of Deleuze's *other knowledge* as an immediate knowledge of the thing itself. Furthermore, this text provides a clue as to how this singular knowledge might be possible: by way of concepts formed through the deployment of symbols.

In his various writings on Bergson, this *other knowledge* figures under the name of *intuition*. In "Bergson, 1859-1941," Deleuze explicitly pits intuition against science: contrary to science, which "allows us only to conclude and to infer without ever presenting, giving to us the thing in itself," it is "in and through intuition that something is presented, is given in person, instead of being inferred from something else and concluded."[18] But, in Deleuze's reading of Bergson, intuition is not to be understood in the ordinary sense of the word. That is, intuition is "neither a feeling, an inspiration, nor a disorderly sympathy, but a fully developed method, one of the most fully developed methods in philosophy," a method capable of establishing philosophy as an "absolutely 'precise' discipline, as precise in *its* field, as capable of being prolonged and transmitted as science itself is."[19] A question immediately springs to mind, one that Deleuze certainly acknowledges: "How is intuition—which primarily denotes an immediate knowledge (*connaissance*)—capable of forming a method, once it is accepted that the method essentially involves one or several mediations?"[20] As an answer to this question, Deleuze first states that although Bergson often does present intuition "as a simple act," this simplicity "does not exclude a qualitative and virtual multiplicity," following which he formulates "three different sorts of acts that determine the rules" of intuition as a method: "The first concerns the

---

[18] Deleuze, "Bergson, 1859-1941," 23.

[19] Gilles Deleuze, *Bergsonism*, trans. Hugh Tomlinson and Barbara Habberjam (New York: Zone Books 1991), 13-14, original emphasis.

[20] Ibid., 13-14.

stating and creating of problems; the second, the discovery of genuine differences in kind; the third, the apprehension of real time."[21] The most interesting aspect is addressed in the second rule, which presents intuition as a method that "rediscovers the true differences in kind or articulations of the real."[22] The most concise account of this crucial aspect of intuition as a method is to be found in Deleuze's text "Bergson's Conception of Difference":

> Intuition suggests itself as a method of difference or division: to divide whatever is composite into two tendencies. This method is something other than a spatial analysis, more than a description of experience, and less (so it seems) than a transcendental analysis. It reaches the conditions of the given, but these conditions are tendency-subjects, which are themselves given in a certain way: they are lived. What is more, they are at once the pure and the lived, the living and the lived, the absolute and the lived. What is essential here is that this ground is *experienced*, and we know how much Bergson insisted on the empirical character of the *élan vital*. Thus it is not the conditions of all possible experience that must be reached, but the conditions of real experience. Schelling had already proposed this aim and defined philosophy as a superior empiricism: this formulation also applies to Bergsonism. These conditions can and must be grasped in an intuition precisely because they are the conditions of real experience, because they are not broader than what is conditioned, because the concept they form is identical to its object ... Reason must reach all the way to the individual, the genuine concept all the way to the thing, and comprehension all the way to "this."[23]

The first thing to note with regard to this quote is that it un-equivocally reveals that, despite being a method, and therefore involving various mediations, intuition still remains an es-

---

[21] Deleuze, *Bergsonism*, 13-14.

[22] Ibid., 21.

[23] Gilles Deleuze, "Bergson's Conception of Difference" in *Desert Islands and Other Texts 1953-1974*, ed. David Lapoujade, trans. Michael Taormina (New York: Semiotext(e), 2004), 35-36.

sentially immediate faculty. Let us summarise: as a method of difference and division, that is, a method capable of dividing the composites into two tendencies, intuition is able to reach the conditions of the given or real experience. These conditions are variously named by Deleuze "tendency-subjects," "pure," "the living," "the absolute" and "the ground." Deleuze's claim that these conditions "can and must be grasped in intuition" simply reiterates his previous claims that these conditions are "themselves given in a certain way," "lived" and "experienced." Therefore, proclaiming it to be a method in no way excludes the immediacy of intuition. As Deleuze puts it himself: "Intuition has become method, or rather method has been reconciled with the immediate."[24] Secondly, this quote confirms once more that for Deleuze the aim of philosophy is the knowledge of the thing itself or the individual, and that this knowledge is attainable by constructing a singular or "unique" concept "identical to its object."[25] Finally, the quote above reveals not only that Deleuze's philosophical project as explicated in *Difference and Repetition* is best read as a continuation of Bergson's own project, but also in which respects Deleuze departs from it. To demonstrate both these claims, it is necessary to turn our attention to *Difference and Repetition* itself.

With regard to the first claim, some of the most important passages in *Difference and Repetition* are stated in virtually the exact same terms as those found in the quote above. One well-known passage in particular stands out in this respect:

> Empiricism truly becomes transcendental, and aesthetics an apodictic discipline, only when we apprehend directly in the sensible that which can only be sensed, the very being of the sensible: difference, potential difference and difference in intensity as the reason behind qualitative diversity. It is in difference that movement is produced as an "effect," that phenomena flash their meaning like signs. The intense world of differences, in which we find the reason behind qualities and the being of the sensible, is precisely the object of a superior empiricism. This

---

[24] Deleuze, *Bergsonism*, 32.
[25] Deleuze, "Bergson's Conception of Difference," 36.

empiricism teaches us a strange "reason," that of the multiple, chaos and difference (nomadic distributions, crowned anarchies).[26]

If we add to this quote the already cited claim from the ending of the first chapter of *Difference and Repetition* that philosophy should search for the conditions of real experience, and not merely possible experience, it becomes quite obvious that Deleuze makes in his own name virtually the very same claims as those he attributes to Bergson in the passage quoted above from "Bergson's Conception of Difference." What, then, does Deleuze retain from Bergson? First and foremost, Deleuze clearly has not relinquished Bergson's belief in the power of intuition to immediately apprehend the conditions of real experience: "Empiricism truly becomes transcendental, and aesthetics an apodictic discipline, only when *we apprehend directly* in the sensible that which can only be sensed" (my emphasis). Likewise, Deleuze retains the idea that intuition is a method of difference, i.e., that which intuition directly apprehends is *difference*: "that which can only be sensed," or "the very being of the sensible" is "difference, potential difference and difference in intensity," or simply "the intense world of differences." It is in this world of differences that

we must find the lived reality of a sub-representative domain. If it is true that representation has identity as its element and similarity as its unit of measure, then pure presence such as it appears in the simulacrum has the 'disparate' as its unit of measure—in other words, always a difference of difference as its immediate element.[27]

Add to this Deleuze's earlier equation of "the immediate" with the "sub-representative"[28] and there can be no more doubt: for Deleuze, "the intense world of differences" or "sub-representative domain" is "a pure presence," "a lived reality," or simply "the immediate."

---

[26] Deleuze, *Difference and Repetition*, 56-57.

[27] Ibid., 69.

[28] Ibid., 56.

Let us now address the second question: in which respect does Deleuze depart from Bergson? The passage from "Bergson's Conception of Difference" quoted earlier is of great assistance here. In a seemingly offhand remark at the beginning of the passage, Deleuze makes the following claim: intuition as a method is "more than a description of experience, *and less (so it seems) than a transcendental analysis*" (my emphasis). It is my contention that Deleuze's account of the transcendent or superior exercise of the faculties as presented in *Difference and Repetition*'s central chapter "The Image of Thought" is precisely the *transcendental* version of Bergson's intuition as a method that Deleuze invokes in this quote. In order to confirm this claim, let me briefly outline the basic contours of Deleuze's account of the transcendent exercise of the faculties.

Deleuze famously states, "Something in the world forces us to think. This something is an object not of recognition but of a fundamental *encounter*."[29] The first characteristic of the object of this encounter is "that it can only be sensed."[30] Following this, Deleuze variously refers to "that which can only be sensed" as "the sign," "the being of the sensible," "that by which the given is given" and the "*sentiendum*."[31] Furthermore, it is important to highlight that this object of the encounter is "imperceptible (*insensible*) from the point of view of an empirical exercise of the senses in which sensibility grasps only that which could also be grasped by other faculties, and is related within the context of a common sense to an object which also must be apprehended by other faculties."[32] Contrary to its empirical exercise thus defined, "sensibility, in the presence of that which can only be sensed (and is at the same time imperceptible) finds itself before its own limit, the sign, and raises itself to the level of a transcendent exercise:

---

[29] Deleuze, *Difference and Repetition*, 139, original emphasis.

[30] Ibid., 139.

[31] Ibid., 139-40.

[32] Ibid., 140.

to the 'nth' power."[33] Once sensibility has been raised to its transcendent exercise by its encounter with the *sentiendum*, it "forces memory to remember the *memorandum*, that which can only be recalled,"[34] thereby raising memory to a transcendent exercise of its own. Finally, memory in its turn

> forces thought to grasp that which can only be thought, the *cogitandum* or *noeteon*, the Essence: not the intelligible, for this is still no more than the mode in which we think that which might be something other than thought, but the being of the intelligible as though this were both the final power of thought and the unthinkable.[35]

According to Deleuze, what is revealed by this "transcendent, disjointed or superior exercise of the faculties" is precisely their "transcendental form."[36] For, in order to avoid tracing the transcendental form of the faculties from their empirical exercise, as Kant does, Deleuze claims that

> each faculty must be borne to the extreme point of its dissolution, at which it falls prey to triple violence: the violence of that which forces it to be exercised, of that which it is forced to grasp and which it alone is able to grasp, yet also that of the ungraspable (from the point of view of its empirical exercise).[37]

It is at this point that each faculty "discovers its own unique passion,"[38] or its transcendental form.

As I have emphasised, thought always begins with an encounter with the *sentiendum*. But what is this paradoxical element that can only be sensed yet is imperceptible at the same time? This element which forces sensibility to its transcendent exercise is

---

[33] Deleuze, *Difference and Repetition*, 140.

[34] Ibid., 141.

[35] Ibid.

[36] Ibid., 143.

[37] Ibid.

[38] Ibid.

intensity, understood as pure difference in itself, as that which is at once both imperceptible for empirical sensibility which grasps intensity only already covered or mediated by the quality to which it gives rise, and at the same time that which can be perceived only from the point of view of a transcendental sensibility which apprehends it immediately in the encounter.[39]

Thus, for Deleuze, thought always begins with an immediate apprehension of difference in itself. Deleuze could hardly be any more explicit about his belief in the idea of intuitive knowledge. The notion of the transcendent exercise of the faculties represents nothing less than Deleuze's attempt to give a properly transcendental account of this age-old philosophical ideal.

One last remark is in order. It might be objected that I am equivocating by eliding the distinction between thought and knowledge. As the objection might go, not only does Deleuze take over the Kantian distinction between thought and knowledge, but he is also expressly critical of the notion of "knowledge" throughout the book. This is, of course, true. But it is also quite obvious that "thought" in *Difference and Repetition* has almost the exact same function as "*mathesis universalis*" and "an other knowledge" have in his earlier texts. If the account given above of the transcendent exercise of the faculties were not enough by itself, this claim could be further reinforced by highlighting the fact that on various occasions throughout the book, Deleuze explicitly invokes both "an esoteric knowledge"[40] and "*mathesis universalis*"[41] itself. To establish even stronger ties between Deleuze's earlier texts and *Difference and Repetition* in this regard let me quote from the preface of the book:

> Empiricism is by no means a reaction against concepts, nor a simple appeal to lived experience. On the contrary, it undertakes the most

---

[39] Deleuze, *Difference and Repetition*, 144.

[40] Ibid., 15, 242.

[41] Ibid., 181, 190, 199.

insane creation of concepts ever seen or heard. Empiricism is a mysticism and a mathematicism of concepts, but precisely one which treats the concept as object of an encounter, as a here-and-now, or rather as an Erewhon from which emerge inexhaustibly ever new, differently distributed "heres" and "nows."[42]

Similar to his earlier work, Deleuze here explicitly invokes the creation of concepts identical to their objects as the goal of philosophy. Furthermore, his identification of empiricism with "a mysticism and a mathematicism of concepts" further encourages the conclusion that "transcendental empiricism" itself is, for Deleuze, just another name for *mathesis universalis* or intuition as a method.

Sellars: The Myth of The Given

Around the same time as Gilles Deleuze was invoking the mythical powers of *mathesis universalis*, Bergsonian intuition, and transcendental empiricism, Wilfrid Sellars was waging his lifelong battle against "the myth of the given" on the other side of the Atlantic. By no means was Sellars the first, nor will he be the last philosopher to face this mythical creature in an open field of battle. But he may very well be its most tenacious opponent to date. What made Sellars's attack on the myth of the given so powerful was his recognition of its highly protean nature. As he famously states at the very beginning of "Empiricism and the Philosophy of Mind,"

Many things have been said to be "given": sense contents, material objects, universals, propositions, real connections, first principles, even givenness itself. And there is, indeed, a certain way of construing the situations which philosophers analyze in these terms which can be said to be the framework of givenness. This framework has been a common feature of most of the major systems of philosophy, including, to use a Kantian turn of phrase, both "dogmatic rationalism" and "skeptical empiricism." It has, indeed, been so pervasive that few, if any,

---

[42] Deleuze, *Difference and Repetition*, xx.

philosophers have been altogether free of it; certainly not Kant, and, I would argue, not even Hegel, that great foe of "immediacy." Often what is attacked under its name are only specific varieties of "given." Intuited first principles and synthetic necessary connections were the first to come under attack. And many who today attack "the whole idea of givenness"—and they are an increasing number—are really only attacking sense data … If, however, I begin my argument with an attack on sense-datum theories, it is only as a first step in a general critique of the entire framework of givenness.[43]

Sellars clearly realises that the various instances of the given are only different instantiations of the same general framework of givenness. He also realises that if we are to have any success in vanquishing this myth once and for all, it will be necessary to formulate a general critique of this entire framework of givenness. Unfortunately, due to the nature of Sellars's philosophising, heavily oriented as it was towards specific debates with his contemporaries, Sellars himself never presented either a systematic account of the framework of givenness, or the announced general critique of it. What he did leave behind, though, was a whole host of specific attacks on various different varieties of the given. Although all of these various critiques of different forms of the given were presented by way of debates with his analytic peers, the passage quoted above clearly shows that Sellars's intended target was much wider in scope. In light of this, our later attempt at a Sellarsian critique of the Deleuzian "given" should seem a little less unlikely than it probably appears at first glance. However, if we are to stage this confrontation, it will first be necessary to briefly outline Sellars's account of the myth of the given and his main arguments for rejecting it. And it will be paramount to do so in terms general enough so that this confrontation does not turn into a missed encounter. Three texts will be of particular assistance to us with regard to this task: "Empiricism and the Philosophy of Mind," "The Structure of Knowledge," and "Foundations for a Metaphysics of Pure Process: The Carus Lectures of Wilfrid Sellars."

---

43 Sellars, "Empiricism and the Philosophy of Mind," 127.

Let us start with "Empiricism and the Philosophy of Mind" (EPM). Of the various different formulations of the myth of the given, the one found in chapter eight, entitled "Does Empirical Knowledge Have a Foundation?," in many ways the central chapter of the book, is definitely the most appropriate for our present purposes:

> The idea that observation "strictly and properly so-called" is constituted by certain self-authenticating nonverbal episodes, the authority of which is transmitted to verbal and quasi-verbal performances when these performances are made "in conformity with the semantical rules of the language," is, of course, the heart of the Myth of the Given. For the *given*, in epistemological tradition, is what is *taken* by these self-authenticating episodes. These "takings" are, so to speak, the unmoved movers of empirical knowledge, "knowings in presence" which are presupposed by all other knowledge, both the knowledge of general truths and the knowledge "in absence" of other particular matters of fact. Such is the framework in which traditional empiricism makes its characteristic claim that the perceptually given is the foundation of empirical knowledge.[44]

First and foremost, this passage reveals which specific version of the given is under attack, not just in this chapter, but in the book as a whole: it is, of course, the given as conceived by traditional empiricism. Secondly, the passage possibly presents the most concise account provided by Sellars of the empiricist given. To summarise, the empiricist given consists in taking certain self-authenticating nonverbal episodes given in perception as the foundation of empirical knowledge, and by extension as presupposed by all knowledge. Clearly, the key term here is "self-authenticating nonverbal episodes." What Sellars denies is neither that these "observings are *inner* episodes, nor that *strictly speaking* they are *nonverbal* episodes."[45] Contrary to ill-informed popular belief, Sellars is not a reductionist, and especially not with regard to notions like "inner episodes," "impressions," or "immediate experi-

---

[44] Sellars, "Empiricism and the Philosophy of Mind," 169-70.

[45] Ibid., 170, original emphasis.

ence." In fact, the later parts of EPM are explicitly devoted to devising an account of these very notions. What Sellars does deny, though, is the idea that these episodes are to be taken as *self-authenticating*, that is, that they have *epistemic* authority or the status of *knowledge* solely in virtue of their being perceptually *given*. This is the crucial point of Sellars's critique of the given.

The main reasons for Sellars's denial of the given thus construed is to be found in his famous definition of knowledge:

> The essential point is that in characterizing an episode or a state as that of *knowing*, we are not giving an empirical description of that episode or state; we are placing it in the logical space of reasons, of justifying and being able to justify what one says.[46]

Add to this Sellars's earlier denial that there is "any awareness of logical space prior to, or independent of, the acquisition of a language,"[47] and the main contours of his argument slowly begin to emerge. If awareness of the logical space of reasons is impossible without the acquisition of a language, and if to know something is to place it in the logical space of reasons, then it follows that only that which is linguistically structured can lay claim to the status of knowledge.[48] Finally, insofar as what is perceptually given is not linguistically structured, it obviously cannot lay claim to the status of knowledge.

In order to present Sellars's argument in its entirety, though, it will be necessary to return once more to his formulation of the myth of the given. Let us recall: the claim made by traditional empiricism was not only that what is perceptually given is self-authenticating, but also, and just as importantly, that it can serve as a foundation of empirical knowledge,

---

[46] Sellars, "Empiricism and the Philosophy of Mind," 169.

[47] Ibid., 162.

[48] Or as Robert Brandom famously put it: "only what is propositionally contentful and conceptually articulated can serve as (and stand in need) of justification, and so ground or constitute knowledge." Robert Brandom, "Study Guide" in Wilfrid Sellars, *Empiricism and the Philosophy of Mind* (Cambridge: Harvard University Press, 1997), 122.

and by extension all knowledge. The first thing to note with regard to this claim, and as Sellars emphasises himself, is that by rejecting it, Sellars does not imply "that empirical knowledge has *no* foundation."[49] On the contrary: "There is clearly *some* point to the picture of human knowledge as resting on a level of propositions—observation reports—which do not rest on other propositions in the same way as other propositions rest on them."[50] In other words, by rejecting the myth of the given, Sellars does not reject the idea that inferential judgments are grounded in some way on non-inferential judgments. His notion of "observation report" is precisely this kind of non-inferential judgment. But, on the other hand, Sellars does insist "that the metaphor of 'foundation' is misleading in that it keeps us from seeing that if there is a logical dimension in which other empirical propositions rest on observation reports, there is another logical dimension in which the latter rest on the former."[51] Without giving a complete account of Sellars's term "observation reports," the following will have to suffice for our present purposes: according to Sellars, even the simplest observation report like "this is green" implies "that one can have the concept of green only by having a whole battery of concepts of which it is one element."[52] Moreover, "there is an important sense in which one has *no* concept pertaining to the observable properties of physical objects in Space and Time unless one has them all—and, indeed ... a great deal more besides."[53]

Returning to Sellars's suspicion of the metaphor of "foundation," his beautifully written concluding remarks on this topic will also be the best possible way to conclude this short presentation of his views on the myth of the given as presented in EPM:

---

[49] Sellars, "Empiricism and the Philosophy of Mind," 170.

[50] Ibid., original emphasis.

[51] Ibid.

[52] Ibid., 148

[53] Ibid.

Above all, the picture is misleading because of its static character. One seems forced to choose between the picture of an elephant which rests on a tortoise (What supports the tortoise?) and the picture of a great Hegelian serpent of knowledge with its tail in its mouth (Where does it begin?). Neither will do. For empirical knowledge, like its sophisticated extension, science, is rational, not because it has a *foundation* but because it is a self-correcting enterprise which can put *any* claim in jeopardy, though not *all* at once.[54]

If making a knowledge claim consists of placing it in the logical space of reasons, then any and every such claim can never be safe from challenge, and therefore cannot serve as the firm ground of knowledge as a whole. But by the same token, if this is the only kind of knowledge available to us—by refuting the myth of the given, Sellars believes he has sufficiently demonstrated this—then there is no way to challenge this framework as a whole. The only thing there is *is* a slow, arduous, hazardous, and never-ending process of testing each and every claim put forth. This is the inglorious venture of rational knowledge.

Let us now move on to Sellars's second text under consideration here, "The Structure of Knowledge."[55] Interestingly enough, neither the notion of "the given," nor that of "the myth of the given" are to be found in these lectures; at least not explicitly. But it is precisely because of this terminological peculiarity that this text is of particular interest. For while Sellars may not invoke the given explicitly, it is quite obvious that what he is in fact discussing is precisely another version of the myth of the given. And what makes this particular account of the myth especially interesting for our present purposes is the fact that Sellars here explicitly invokes "intuitive knowledge," thereby unequivocally confirming that the myth of the given indeed refers to this age-old notion.

The third and final lecture of the series, entitled "Epistemic Principles," is crucial in this regard. After briefly conveying

---

54 Sellars, "Empiricism and the Philosophy of Mind," 170, original emphasis.
55 Sellars, "The Structure of Knowledge."

the traditional arguments for the necessity of non-inferential judgments, Sellars goes on to state,

> We are clearly in the neighbourhood of what has been called the "self-evident," the "self-certifying," in short, of "intuitive knowledge." It is in this neighbourhood that we find what has come to be called the *foundational* picture of human knowledge. According to this picture, beliefs which have inferential reasonableness ultimately rely for their authority on a stratum of beliefs which are, in some sense, self-certifying.[56]

By using here almost the exact same terms to refer to intuitive knowledge ("self-evident" and "self-certifying"), as when referring to the given in EPM ("self-authenticating"), this passage clearly demonstrates that "the myth of the given" and "intuitive knowledge" are virtually synonymous for Sellars. Likewise, by being almost identical to the discussions of the myth of the given in EPM, it surely dispels any possible doubts left. But only a few paragraphs later, an even more interesting passage appears:

> Now many philosophers who have endorsed a concept of intuitive knowledge are clearly committed to the position that there is a level of *cognition* more basic than *believing*. This more basic level would consist of a sub-conceptual—where "sub-conceptual" is far from being used as a pejorative term—awareness of certain facts. In terms of the framework sketched in the preceding two lectures, there would be a level of cognition more basic than *thinkings* or tokenings of sentences in Mentalese—more basic, in fact, than symbolic activity, literal *or* analogical. It would be a level of cognition unmediated by concepts; indeed it would be the very *source of* concepts in some such way as described by traditional theories of abstraction. It would be "direct apprehension" of facts; their "direct presence" to the mind.[57]

Sellars here clearly presents a somewhat different version of the myth of the given to the one provided in EPM. But

---

[56] Sellars, "The Structure of Knowledge," lecture 3, section 3, paragraph 14.

[57] Ibid., lecture 3, section 5, paragraph 21, original emphases.

there is little doubt that it still is the same mythical creature we have learned to recognise so very well. Here again the claim is that there is some kind of non-conceptual and non-inferential knowledge that has the status of knowledge simply by virtue of being directly present, apprehended, or given to the mind. Given that this kind of knowledge essentially depends on the idea of "direct apprehension," Sellars asks, how is this notion to be understood? To begin to answer this question, Sellars notes that "'apprehend', like 'see' is, *in its ordinary sense*, an achievement word."[58] This clearly implies that the act of apprehending might not be successful, that is, that it might occur without anything being apprehended. The consequences of this seemingly simple observation are spelled out in the next paragraph:

> Many who use the metaphor "to see" in intellectual contexts overlook the fact that in its literal sense "seeing" is a term for a successful conceptual activity which contrasts with "seeming to see." No piling on of additional metaphors (e.g., "grasping," which implies an object grasped) can blunt this fact. Now the distinction between *seeing* and merely *seeming to see* implies a criterion. To rely on the metaphors of "apprehending" or "presence of the object" is to obscure the need of criteria for distinguishing between "knowing" and "seeming to know," which ultimately define what it means to speak of knowledge as a *correct* or well-founded *thinking* that something is the case.[59]

To put it in the simplest possible terms, *knowledge* necessarily implies some criteria by which it is to be distinguished from *ostensible knowledge*. Therefore, invocations of direct apprehension, which obviate this simple fact, cannot lay claim to the status of knowledge. Finally, Sellars concludes:

> In short, I suspect that the notion of a non-conceptual "direct apprehension" of a "fact" provides a merely verbal solution to our problem. The regress is stopped by an *ad hoc* regress-stopper. Indeed, the very

---

[58] Sellars, "The Structure of Knowledge," lecture 3, section 5, paragraph 23, original emphasis.

[59] Ibid., lecture 3, section 5, paragraph 24, original emphases.

metaphors which promised the sought-for foundation contain within themselves a dialectical moment which takes us beyond them.[60]

The last sentence is worth highlighting. Instead of providing a non-conceptual foundation for conceptual knowledge, as they are supposed to do, metaphors of direct apprehending, grasping, seeing and the like, allow us to arrive at the exact opposite conclusion: if something is to lay claim to the status of knowledge, there has to be an explicit (or implicit) criterion by which this claim is to be adjudicated.

To conclude this second part of my essay, let me briefly address one last account of the myth of the given, the one presented by Sellars in his Carus Lectures.[61] In the first lecture of the series, given under the title "The Lever of Archimedes," Sellars states this:

> If a person is directly aware of an item which has categorial status C, then the person is aware of it *as* having categorial status C.

> This principle is, perhaps, the most basic form of what I have castigated as "The Myth of the Given" ... *To reject the Myth of the Given is to reject the idea that the categorial structure of the world—if it has a categorial structure—imposes itself on the mind as a seal imposes an image on melted wax.*[62]

Thus, "the most basic form" of the myth of the given consists in the idea that the "*categorial structure of the world*" is in some way directly available or given to the mind. To understand why this might be problematic for Sellars, we have to take a look at his conception of the categories. In Sellars's functionalist-nominalist Kantian interpretation, categories are defined as "the most generic functional classifications of the elements

---

[60] Sellars, "Empiricism and the Philosophy of Mind," lecture 3, section 5, paragraph 25.

[61] Sellars, "Foundations for a Metaphysics of Pure Process."

[62] Ibid., 11-12, original emphasis.

of judgments."[63] This definition of the categories makes it obvious that, for Sellars, the categorial structure of the world is not something that can be simply read off of the world. On the contrary, we can arrive at the categorial structure of the world only as a result of that long, slow, and arduous self-correcting rational enterprise described earlier. This might in fact be one of the most important lessons to be learned from Sellars: knowledge of the world is indeed possible; but it will most certainly not come by some miraculous insight. Hard work is still our best bet.

Sellars Contra Deleuze: Normativity versus Creativity

Now that we have assembled all their weapons, let us follow these two formidable opponents onto the field of battle. The stakes of this confrontation are high indeed! Nothing less than their respective claims to knowledge are on the line, possibly even the nature of knowledge itself. But before we let them engage each other in battle, one last effort is in order. If we are to confront these two great philosophers in their guises of major representatives of two opposing philosophical camps, some common ground has to be found upon which this confrontation is to be staged. The problem of universals might very well be just what we are looking for. For it could be argued that both Sellars and Deleuze fashioned their re-spective philosophies in general, and accounts of knowledge in particular, precisely in response to this ancient and well-travelled philosophical problem.

Traditionally, three types of answers were given to the ques-tion of the existence of universals. Platonic realism affirmed it, nominalism denied it, and conceptualism (or idealism) acknowledged the existence of universals but merely as concepts or ideas in the mind. While Deleuze could arguably be classified in the first, realist camp, Sellars is to be situated

---

[63] Wilfrid Sellars, "Toward a Theory of the Categories" in *Kant's Transcendental Metaphysics*, ed. Jeffrey F. Sicha (Atascadero: Ridgeview Publishing, 2002), 329.

firmly in the second, nominalist one.[64] Let us start once more with Deleuze.

As Deleuze, following Nietzsche, famously stated, the overturning (or reversal) of Platonism is the principal task of modern philosophy.[65] Deleuze's solution to the problem of universals, and possibly even his philosophy as a whole, is best read in light of this often repeated pronouncement of his. The first thing to note in this regard is that this operation of overturning is not to be confused with a simple denial of Platonism. Quite the contrary, "that this overturning should conserve many Platonic characteristics is not only inevitable but desirable."[66] Therefore, in order to understand Deleuze's stated ambition to overturn Platonism it is necessary to determine which aspects of Plato's system Deleuze retains, and in what form, and which ones he discards.

It could be argued that Plato's whole philosophical enterprise is a response to the problem of universals. And his solution is very well known. To put it in the simplest possible terms, in order to account for the existence of universals, Plato found it necessary to postulate an Other world: beyond the sensible world of appearances (individuals, becoming, images, copies, simulacra, differences) existing in time, there is an intelligible world of essences (Universals, Being, Forms, Ideas, the One) outside of time. The task of philosophy, then, is to think this Other world. In order to accomplish this, Plato also had to postulate an Other kind of knowledge: beyond the discursive intellect capable of providing knowledge of the sensible world, there is an intuitive intellect capable of immediately apprehending the intelligible world.

Interestingly enough, Deleuze's overturning of Platonism retains virtually all of Plato's dualisms listed above. But it does

---

[64] With regard to Deleuze's solution to the problem of universals, I am following Pete Wolfendale's account provided in his paper "Ariadne's Thread: Temporality, Modality, and Individuation in Deleuze's Metaphysics," http://deontologistics.files.wordpress.com/2011/03/deleuze-mmu.pdf, (accessed July 15, 2013).

[65] Deleuze, *Difference and Repetition*, 58.

[66] Ibid.

so with the intent to abolish the fundamental Platonic dualism of the sensible world of appearances and the intelligible world of essences. For Deleuze, there simply is no Other world: the world we live in is the only world there is. And, as Deleuze and Guattari put it, "it may be that believing in this world, in this life, becomes our most difficult task today."[67] In order to accomplish this difficult task, Deleuze recruits the help of a whole host of figures from the entire history of philosophy. Arguably, Immanuel Kant is the most important of these. For as the one who discovered "the prodigious domain of the transcendental," Kant is hailed by Deleuze as the "analogue of a great explorer—not of another world, but of the upper and lower reaches of this one."[68] It is Kant's discovery of the transcendental that allows Deleuze to solve the problem of universals. Ideas (or universals) do exist, but not as eternal essences in an Other world; rather, they are to be conceived of as the conditions of experience to be found in the lower reaches of this world. But contrary to Kant, who conceived of the transcendental in epistemological terms, that is, as conditions of *possible* experience, Deleuze famously reconceives the transcendental in ontological terms, that is, as conditions of *real* experience.

Deleuze's world therefore truly is a reversed version of Plato's dualist universe. While Deleuze retains Plato's dualism of the intelligible and the sensible he, instead of opposing them as two distinct worlds, conceives of them as two complementary aspects of this world. The intelligible domain of Ideas is to be conceived as the condition of the sensible domain of real experience. In a similar inversion and contrary to Plato, for whom the intelligible world is to be thought in terms of the One and the Same, and the sensible world in terms of the multiple and the different, the intelligible realm of Deleuze's world is populated by Ideas defined as differential multiplicities, which are then to be actualised in the sen-

---

[67] Gilles Deleuze and Félix Guattari, *What is Philosophy?*, trans. Hugh Tomlinson and Graham Burchill (New York: Columbia University Press, 1994), 75.

[68] Deleuze, *Difference and Repetition*, 135.

sible realm as self-identical individuals. Furthermore and again contra Plato, for whom only the intelligible world of essences is real, Deleuze draws on Duns Scotus's doctrine of the univocity of being in order to affirm the reality of both the intelligible and the sensible domains. "Being is said in a single and same sense of everything of which it is said, but that of which it is said differs: it is said of difference itself."[69] Finally, if the overturning of Platonism is to be complete, Deleuze has to find a principle of immanence which will allow him to demonstrate that the intelligible and the sensible indeed are to be conceived as two domains of the same world. Contrary to Plato's relegation of time to the sensible world of appearances, and the upholding of the eternal nature of the intelligible world of essences, Deleuze affirms precisely time as *the* unifying principle. These are the basic contours of Deleuze's ontology.

In order to think this world, Deleuze will, once again, follow in Plato's footsteps. If we are to think the immediate unity of the intelligible and sensible, discursive reason with all its mediations simply will not do. What is needed is an other knowledge capable of going beyond the sensible. But this time, contrary to Plato, this *beyond* is not situated up and above this world, but down and below in its lower reaches. Thought is to apprehend directly the intelligible, the being of the sensible or the conditions of real experience. As we have seen in the first part of this essay, thought begins with an encounter with the *sentiendum* (the being of the sensible, or that which can only be sensed), and proceeds to think the *cogitandum* (the being of the intelligible, or that which can only be thought). Interestingly enough, in his quest for this other knowledge, Deleuze will once again find an unlikely ally in Kant. For it is precisely Kant's account of the sublime that Deleuze takes as a model for his account of the transcendent exercise of the faculties.

The consequences of Deleuze's overturning of Platonism for philosophy were revolutionary indeed. Ever since Plato

---

[69] Deleuze, *Difference and Repetition*, 36.

and up until Kant's Copernican or epistemological turn, metaphysics was proverbially considered to be the queen of all sciences. After almost two centuries of various attempts in the wake of Kant to disprove its possibility, Deleuze was one of the first contemporary philosophers to give back to metaphysics the pride of place it deserves. But in Deleuze's world of overturned Platonism, metaphysics will find itself allied with the most unlikely of allies. In contrast to both Plato's denial of the reality of the sensible realm, on the one hand, and Kant's denial of the reality of the intelligible realm, on the other, Deleuze's affirmation of the univocity of being, affirming as it does the reality of both the sensible and the intelligible domains, breeds a new philosophical alliance between metaphysics and aesthetics. In this regard, Deleuze's famous pronouncement on aesthetics, castigating Kant and his transcendental conditions of possibility for introducing the familiar schism between the two senses of the term, is of a particular significance:

> No wonder, then, that aesthetics should be divided into two irreducible domains: that of the theory of the sensible which captures only the real's conformity with possible experience; and that of the theory of the beautiful, which deals with the reality of the real in so far as it is reflected. Everything changes once we determine the conditions of real experience, which are not larger than the conditioned and which differ in kind from the categories: the two senses of the aesthetic become one, to the point where the being of the sensible reveals itself in the work of art, while at the same time the work of art appears as experimentation.[70]

This quote expands on the already cited claim made by Deleuze: "Empiricism truly becomes transcendental, and aesthetics an apodictic discipline, only when we apprehend directly in the sensible that which can only be sensed, the very being *of* the sensible."[71] Whether we want to call Deleuze's philosophy an aesthetical metaphysics or a metaphysical aesthetics, it

---

[70] Deleuze, *Difference and Repetition*, 68.

[71] Ibid., 56-57, original emphasis.

is quite obvious that for Deleuze aesthetics and metaphysics are virtually interchangeable terms. But what the first quote also reveals is the importance that Deleuze attributes to art. Add to this Deleuze's earlier equation of the work of art with transcendental empiricism or the science of the sensible,[72] and it becomes clear that Deleuze has forged an equally strong bond between art and philosophy itself. Never since the early Romantics has there been such a grand alliance of aesthetics and metaphysics on the one hand, and art and philosophy on the other.

Let us now turn to Sellars. There is little doubt that Sellars was a scientific realist. As he famously put it in EPM, "in the dimension of describing and explaining the world, science is the measure of all things, of what is that it is, and of what is not that it is not."[73] But Sellars's commitment to scientific realism is to be interpreted in terms of his deeper commitment to naturalism. To be is to exist in nature, nature being understood here as the spatiotemporal causal domain. Science is the measure of all things simply because it has proven itself time and again as the best and most reliable way for exploring this spatiotemporal causal realm. Sellars's nominalism, in turn, follows from his naturalism. Being causally impotent, universals or abstract entities cannot be said to exist in any meaningful way. Individuals are all there is.[74]

It might seem tempting to read Sellars as a reductive or even, as some have done, an eliminative materialist. But nothing could be further from the truth. If there is one thing Sellars was always unequivocal about, it is his insistence that the greatest challenge facing modern philosophy today is how "to take both man and science seriously."[75] The clash of the scientific and manifest images of man in the world is to be

---

[72] Ibid., 56.

[73] Sellars, "Empiricism and the Philosophy of Mind," 173.

[74] I am here following Willem A. deVries' characterisation of Sellars as presented in his study *Wilfrid Sellars* (Chesham: Acumen, 2005).

[75] Wilfrid Sellars, *Science and Metaphysics* (Atascadero: Ridgeview, 1967), 1.

resolved not by reducing one to the other, or by eliminating one altogether, but by fusing these two images into one stereoscopic vision.[76] If philosophy is to meet this challenge, it is imperative to acknowledge both the authority of the scientific image over the *natural space of causes* (the order of being, or the real order), as well as the authority of the manifest image over the *normative space of reasons* (the order of knowing, or the conceptual order). Defining the nature of the complicated relationship between the *natural* and the *normative* has been *the* central problem of Sellars's entire philosophical enterprise.

Sellars's response to this predicament is ingenious to say the least. The normative space of reasons is to be understood as *causally reducible*, but *logically (conceptually) irreducible* to the natural space of causes.[77] Insofar as conceptual thought or the logical space of reasons has a material substrate from which it arises, there is nothing, in principle, preventing the natural sciences from exploring it. This is why, for Sellars, the normative is *causally* reducible to the natural. On the other hand, insofar as the space of reasons is essentially *normative* in character there is nothing, in principle, that the natural sciences can teach us about it. Given that they are empirical, descriptive and concerned with what *is* the case, natural sciences cannot by definition provide an account of the transcendental, the prescriptive and what *ought to be* the case. This is why, for Sellars, the normative is *logically (conceptually) irreducible* to the natural.

There is another sense in which the normative can be said to be ineliminable. Following Kant, Sellars defines thought as essentially conceptual, that is, as a rule-governed activity. The rules governing thought, as Pete Wolfendale puts it, are to be conceived as "the fundamental norms of rationality—those norms by which we are bound simply in virtue of making claims at all, or those norms that provide the conditions of

---

[76] See Wilfrid Sellars, "Philosophy and the Scientific Image of Man" in *Science, Perception and Reality* (Atascadero: Ridgeview, 1991), 4-5.

[77] Cf. James O'Shea, *Wilfrid Sellars: Naturalism with a Normative Turn* (Cambridge: Polity Press, 2007), 21.

the possibility of rationality itself."[78] Insofar as the natural sciences are essentially rational, they are bound by these same fundamental norms of rationality. This is why, for Sellars, the normative is to be construed not only as irreducible to, but as constitutive of the transcendental conditions of empirical knowledge that the sciences provide of the natural domain.

In claiming that the norms of reasoning are to be construed as the transcendental conditions of knowledge of the natural world, Sellars clearly sides with Kant. But on the other hand, in upholding that the knowledge which the natural sciences attain is a knowledge not of appearances, but of the real order or the in-itself, Sellars obviously rejects Kant's injunction against the possibility of such a knowledge. By the same token, Sellars certainly does not shy away from affirming the possibility of metaphysics. Yet, once again siding with Kant, Sellars clearly believed that if metaphysics is to be anything more than a flight of fancy, it needs to be coupled with epistemology. Or as Ray Brassier puts it: "just as epistemology without metaphysics is empty, metaphysics without epistemology is blind."[79]

The time for confrontation has finally come. Let us start it by foregrounding the single most important conviction that Deleuze and Sellars both share: they both firmly believe not just in the possibility, but the necessity of metaphysics—if philosophy is to be anything at all, it has to be a metaphysics. To describe and explain the fundamental structure of the world has always been and always will be the ultimate goal of philosophical thinking. But with regards to answering the question of how philosophy is to achieve this formidable goal, Deleuze and Sellars could not be further apart from one another.

---

[78] Pete Wolfendale, "Essay on Transcendental Realism," http://deontologistics.files.wordpress.com/2010/05/essay-on-transcendental-realism.pdf, 38 (accessed July 15, 2013).

[79] Ray Brassier, "Concepts and Objects" in *The Speculative Turn: Continental Materialism and Realism*, ed. Levi Bryant, Nick Srnicek, and Graham Harman (Melbourne: Re.press, 2011), 49.

Deleuze's epistemology, insofar as he can be said to have one, follows from his ontology. In his attempt to overturn Platonism, Deleuze affirms a one world ontology. This world is the only world there is. Yet Deleuze retains Plato's distinction of the sensible and the intelligible. Only this time, these distinct realms are to be conceived as two aspects of this world: the intelligible, universal, virtual, transcendental Ideas constituting its lower reaches, and the sensible, singular, actual, and empirical individuals the upper ones. If we are to know this world, Deleuze insists, conceptual, representational knowledge will not do. An other knowledge is necessary, a knowledge supposedly capable of apprehending directly the intelligible Ideas, but also of creating the concepts identical to the sensible individuals. These two dimensions of knowledge, the intuitive and the creative, are not to be conceived as distinct, but as two sides of the same coin, or two aspects of a single principle governing thought. Once again, Deleuze's account of thought follows from his account of being. In line with his affirmation of the univocity of being, Deleuze believes that if we are to affirm the being of thought, being has to be said of thought in the same sense in which it is said of everything else. And, as is well known, the sense of being, for Deleuze, is productive or creative difference. This is why Deleuze affirms that "to think is to create."[80] Finally, following the early Romantics, Deleuze finds the model for this other knowledge in aesthetic experience (for its intuitive aspect) on the one hand, and artistic practice (for its creative aspect) on the other. By the same token, Deleuze will proclaim aesthetics to be the greatest ally of metaphysics, and art that of philosophy.

Sellars, on the other hand, unequivocally upholds the distinction between epistemology and ontology. But this distinction itself is to be conceived in epistemological, and not ontological terms.[81] By construing thought as a rule-governed,

---

[80] Deleuze, *Difference and Repetition*, 135.

[81] For a much more detailed and precise account of this aspect of Sellars's philosophy, see Daniel Sacilotto's paper "Realism and Representation: On the Ontological Turn," *Speculations* (2013), 4, 53-62.

normative activity, Sellars is able to affirm both the epistemological difference and ontological indifference of thought
from being. Insofar as it is an *activity*, that is, something that
we *do* and not something that *is*, thought, strictly speaking,
has no being. But by the same token, precisely because it is
an *activity*, it is not to be conceived as something otherworldy
or supernatural, but as firmly rooted in this world and in
the order of natural causality. Therefore, and in contrast to
Deleuze's program, Sellars clearly shows that upholding the
distinction between being and thought need not imply a commitment to an ontological dualism of some sort. That is, the
difference between thought and being is not an ontological
but an epistemological difference. Sellars's ontological commitment to naturalism and scientific realism follows from
his epistemological commitment to the distinction between
being construed as the natural space of causes, and thought
construed as the normative space of reasons. To be, for Sellars, is to be causally efficacious, and thus only a naturalism
willing to take seriously the advances of the natural sciences
can explore the natural space of causes. Yet, if this naturalism is to provide a complete account of this world, it has to
acknowledge its normative dimension, that is, the specificity
of the normative space of reasons. Sellars's philosophy indeed
is a "naturalism with a normative turn."[82]

Deleuze and Sellars both affirm the univocity of being. And
they both attempt to devise an account of thought that would
not go against this basic ontological principle. For Deleuze,
this means that if the distinction between being and thought
is not to be construed as an ontological dualism, thought is to
be said in the same sense as that in which being is said, that
is, as creative difference. But by construing thought purely in
ontological terms, Deleuze collapses the very distinction he
is trying to explain, making it thereby unintelligible. By the
same token, Deleuze's failure to acknowledge the specificity
of thought in its difference from being leaves him without a
proper epistemology, making it thereby impossible for him to

---

[82] O'Shea, *Wilfrid Sellars*, 3.

justify his ontology. Finally, by erasing the difference between being and thought, Deleuze might have escaped the need to construe thought as an ontologically distinct domain, but he has accomplished this at a steep price indeed, the price being nothing less than idealism. Ironically enough, Deleuze's attempt to overturn Platonism ends up affirming Plato's worst idealist excesses.

In order to provide an account of thought that does not violate the principle of the univocity of being, Sellars takes the exact opposite route to the one travelled by Deleuze. For Sellars, thought is expressly *not* to be construed in ontological terms. If we are to avoid the dangers of collapsing the distinction between being and thought on the one hand, and of turning it into an ontological dualism on the other, it is imperative to conceive thought both in its *difference from* but also in its *relation to* being. As we have seen, Sellars achieves this by conceiving thought in normative terms, as a rule-governed activity. Thought is at the same time different from (logically irreducible to) and in relation to (causally reducible to) being. By securing the rights of thought in its distinction from being, Sellars simultaneously secures the rights of being from the idealist incursions of thought. This way, Sellars is able to uphold a decidedly realist ontology. Finally, insofar as the normative space of reasons can be construed in transcendental terms, as consisting of the very conditions of the possibility of rationality, Sellars's ontology can be said to be a properly transcendental realism.

Let us conclude. Ultimately, the confrontation between Deleuze and Sellars revolves around their contrasting views on *normativity*. While Sellars's entire philosophical edifice is built upon his normative conception of thought and knowledge, Deleuze's philosophical adventure is best described as an attempt to escape the norm-bound world of judgment and representation. In fact, Deleuze's quest for an other knowledge is nothing but such an attempt. But what Deleuze fails to realise, and what Sellars makes so perfectly clear, is that the choice to leave the normative space of reasons is not ours to make in the first place. To reiterate once again

Wolfendale's pronouncement: insofar as we make any claims at all, we are bound by the fundamental norms of rationality, the very norms that provide the conditions of the possibility of rationality itself. Unless one is willing to leave behind the claim to rationality itself, there simply is no way out of the normative space of reasons.

Not Kant, Not Now
Another Sublime

Claire Colebrook

Pennsylvania State University

I

IT STARTED CLEARLY ENOUGH, PER-haps: speculative realism announced itself handily with a collective voice, in the form of a conference and then an edited collection.[1] Unlike other movements that are not quite unified or even vaguely coherent (postmodernism, post-structuralism, new historicism, thing theory), speculative realism seemed to gain in focus as it gained numbers. There are differences voiced among the party faithful, and it might not be entirely accurate to align speculative realism with object-oriented ontology *tout court*, but there is one thing that can be said for certain: speculative realism and deconstruction are not the same thing.[2] I would justify this claim (even if it might

[1] The inaugural conference took place at Goldsmiths, University of London in 2007 the transcript of which can be found in Ray Brassier, Iain Hamilton Grant, Graham Harman, and Quentin Meillassoux, "Speculative Realism," *Collapse* (2007), 3, 307-449. This first collective outing was followed by a far broader volume in 2011, *The Speculative Turn: Continental Materialism and Realism*, ed. Levi Bryant, Nick Srnicek, and Graham Harman (Melbourne: Re.press, 2011).

[2] Focusing on the following quotation from *Of Grammatology* Peter Gratton argues that *nothing* can be referred to in full presence but only as mediated through the temporality of difference: "there have never been anything but

seem not to require any such justification) by way of three points. First, if we take the term "speculative realism" seriously then its embedded claim goes against two Derridean strategies: the critique of speculation and the deconstruction of realism. In his discussion of Lacanian psychoanalysis, the very possibility of speculation, of surveying a scene and then accounting for its possibility, must leave out of consideration the point of view from which that scene is viewed.[3] One can purvey a field only by way of an already established distance. What is left out of play is the *mise-en-scène*, or distribution, that enables speculation (or what Jacques Derrida refers to as the "scene of writing"). The economy of this visual sense of speculation is therefore exorbitant: it cannot be the case that one takes account of a scene and then emerges with a greater degree of insight, for there must have been (already and without retrieval) some spending of force that enabled the relation of speculator to scene to unfold. Deconstruction would be anti-speculative. Second, once one ties speculation to realism things only get worse: speculation or the stepping outside of the given in order to account for the real must necessarily be distanced from the real that is its supposed end. For Derrida, empiricism or any attempt to close the gap and find a proximity with *what is* has always been metaphysics' most spontaneous gesture:

> the profundity of the empiricist intention must be recognized beneath the naiveté of certain of its historical expressions. It is the dream of a purely *heterological* thought at its source. A *pure* thought of *pure* difference. *Empiricism* is its philosophical name, its metaphysical pretension

---

supplements, substitutive significations which could only come forth in a chain of differential references, the 'real' supervening, and being added only while taking on meaning from a trace and from an invocation of the supplement, etc." Peter Gratton, "Post-Deconstructive Realism: It's About Time," *Speculations* (2013), 4, 84. My argument is slightly different; all the features that we use to describe textual mediation—such as dispersal, unthinking automaticity and decaying matter—are at the heart of anything we deem to be a thing.

3 Jacques Derrida, *The Post-Card: From Socrates to Freud and Beyond*, trans. Alan Bass (Chicago: University of Chicago Press, 1987).

or modesty. We say *dream* because it must vanish *at daybreak*, as soon as language awakens.[4]

If speculation claims to be realist then it loses the recognition of the difference, distinction and unfolding of our relation to what is. From a deconstructive point of view what this, in turn, yields is a diminished responsibility: it is because there is no direct access to the real, and because any speculation is necessarily unable to give an account of itself and its possibility, that any of our decisions are ultimately undecidable. Any decision we make emerges from this undecidability and is necessarily haunted by the sacrifice of not following the other potential decisions.

Third, speculative realism relies on a certain diagnosis of deconstruction and post-Kantianism in order to make its own claims. The Kantian Copernican turn rejects the project of speculation that would step beyond the limits of finite human understanding: to know is to be given what is other than oneself, and therefore requires a relation to the known. Knowledge is essentially, and not just contingently, finite. Our knowledge is always *our* knowledge, and the only claims we can make that are not subject to the contingencies of finite knowledge are drawn from the conditions of our knowing.

Deconstruction, for all its rejection of foundations and transcendental conditions is, nevertheless, an acceptance of finitude and conditions; there can only be *quasi*-transcendentals precisely because any condition that we posit for knowledge (such as language, trace, the subject, culture or history) is itself given after the event of the differential dispersal that makes knowing and experiencing possible. It might seem that the epitome of this deconstructive abandonment of speculative thought that would go beyond the given could be found in the more literary versions of deconstruction, such as Paul de Man. Derrida, at least, thought that the abandonment of foundational or speculative knowledge would open to a future

---

4 Jacques Derrida, *Writing and Difference*, trans. Alan Bass (Chicago: University of Chicago Press, 1978), 151, original emphasis.

beyond any of the calculations and conditions of the present. But no such dimension seems present in de Man's work, and if one can charge deconstruction with limiting thought to its conditions then de Man's emphasis on tropes would seem to limit his use of the term "materiality" to a linguistic materiality. I want to argue that this is not the case, and my counter narrative would go like this: Derrida increasingly turns to a more Kantian or hyper-Kantian conception of the future, where the very differential condition of language generates a promise beyond any actualised context. When *matter* is conceptualised after deconstruction it is either as that which the text gestures towards but can never comprehend; *or*, as in speculative realism, matter is that which ought to be our concern once we have rid ourselves of deconstructive bad conscience. I would argue that there is another text and another matter: not matter as outside the text, but text as matter and text as dead. All the features that we have used to differentiate text from matter and things (such that texts operate in a viral manner, repeated beyond their point of genesis, without comprehension, without intent, circulating and having force without sense)—all the rogue features of texts mark what we think of as things, just as texts *are things*. This is the great de Manian deconstructive claim: a text is a *thing*. We may read the text as a living presence, as the opening onto a world of sense, soul, meaning, contexts and relations—but the text itself is an inscribed and finite thing. By the same token, if we strive to be purely literary and see the text as nothing more than text, if we strive to rid ourselves of the illusion that texts open out or gesture towards presence we are once again creating yet one more narrative and one more relation that becomes the relation of all relations: all we are given is text—the rogue detachment and dispersal of matter—and yet all we do is *read*, positing a real that is, in itself, a presence as such free from all our projections:

the relationship and the distinction between literature and philosophy cannot be made in terms of a distinction between aesthetic and epistemological categories. All philosophy is condemned, to the extent that it is dependent on figuration, to be literary and, as the depository of this very problem, all literature is to some extent philosophical.[5]

I would argue that it does no one any good either to save deconstructive mediation or to return to the matter that deconstruction vanquished. I would suggest that what has been expelled from deconstruction for the sake of realism—the literary or textual deconstruction that was tied to de Man and rejected in favour of a philosophical and futural deconstruction—offers a more radical materialism. That is, realism, the real and reality are effects of what de Man referred to as materiality; that materiality is textual, rhetorical and literary not because it is tied to some form of human construction or speech but because it is dispersal that effects a relation between interior and exterior, before and after, real and ideal.

II

The uses of the term "matter," since deconstruction, have tended to be increasingly semiotic or—worse perhaps—performative. For Judith Butler, "matter" is that which gives itself in terms of effects; her materialism is certainly not a form of realism:

> materiality will be rethought as power's most productive effect. And there will be no way to understand "gender" as a cultural construct which is imposed upon the surface of matter, understood either as the body or its given sex. Rather, once sex itself is understood in its normativity, the materiality of the body will not be thinkable apart from the materialization of that regulatory norm. "Sex" is thus not simply what one has or a static description of what one is: it will be one of the norms by which the "one" becomes viable at all, that which qualifies a body for life within the domain of cultural intelligibility. At stake in such a reformulation of the materiality of bodies will be the following: (1) the recasting of the matter of bodies as the effect of a dynamic of power, such that the matter of bodies will be indis-

---

[5] Paul de Man, *Aesthetic Ideology*, ed. Andrzej Warminski (Minneapolis: University of Minnesota Press, 1996), 50.

sociable from the regulatory norms that govern their materialization and the signification of those material effects; (2) the understanding of performativity not as the act by which a subject brings into being what she/he names, but, rather, as that reiterative power of discourse to produce the phenomena that it regulates and constrains; (3) the construal of "sex" no longer as a bodily given on which the construct of gender is artificially imposed, but as a cultural norm which governs the materialization of bodies; (4) a rethinking of the process by which a bodily norm is assumed, appropriated, taken on as not, strictly speaking, undergone *by a subject*, but rather that the subject, the speaking "I," is formed by virtue of having gone through such a process of assuming a sex; and (5) a linking of this process of "assuming" a sex with the question of identification...[6]

Butler is by no means coterminous with deconstruction, and certainly not deconstruction of the de Man mode. However, one might say that if the various new materialisms have any force, it is at least in large part because deconstruction had the effect, after phenomenology, of problematizing any supposed or posited "outside" to the forces or powers of textuality, and that Butler was one of the most formidable voices in negotiating the problem such a suspension of any simple matter would have for feminist politics that could not be purely constructive, or anti-materialist in any simple sense. The self-proclaimed new materialisms that have followed Butler and post-structuralism have not sought to turn back to matter so much as see matter as more dynamic than any theory of cultural construction or linguistic mediation would allow.[7] That said, it might be worth noting—despite interconnections—that there is a difference between the self-presentation of new materialism and the claims of speculative realism or

---

[6] Judith Butler, *Bodies That Matter: On the Discursive Limits of "Sex"* (London: Routledge, 1993), 2-3, original emphasis.

[7] *New Materialisms: Ontology, Agency, and Politics*, ed. Diana Coole and Samantha Frost (Durham: Duke University Press, 2010); *Material Feminisms*, ed. Stacey Alaimo and Susan Hekman (Bloomington: Indiana University Press, 2008); Rick Dolphijn and Iris van der Tuin, *New Materialism: Interviews and Cartographies* (Michigan: Open Humanities Press, 2012).

object-oriented ontology. To a great extent the latter has not had all that much to say about sexual politics, and certainly not about feminist sexual politics.

For the new materialists, matter thought in this new dynamic mode allows for a re-theorisation of the body and sexual identity, thereby avoiding some naïve appeal to sexual essence, while nevertheless allowing for material forces as tendencies irreducible to the norms, regulations and performances that marked Butler's account. By contrast, most of the force of object-oriented ontology has—as the name indicates—relied upon exiting from the concerns of identity, gender and subject formation, even to the point of having less to do with questions of biology and more with the forces of the non-living. Not surprisingly, while materialism gets a great deal of attention in feminist and queer scholarship, the same cannot be said about object-oriented ontology, even if—as Timothy Morton claims—OOO will render everything essentially queer.[8] One explanation might be that objects are not sexed, and do not have political identities. The harder end of the OOO spectrum does not have that much to say about humans, so ignoring the woman question (if there is one) is hardly a glaring or guilty omission. So if deconstruction allows OOO to have purchase by acting as a foil against which a post-linguistic, post-correlationist position might be articulated, and if deconstruction itself always spoke of the real—if at all—in terms of matter (which is how the real is given), then perhaps the clearest mark of a divide between the two critical tendencies comes from the critical voices directed against Meillassoux in *The Speculative Turn* including objections from Peter Hallward, Adrian Johnston, Alberto Toscano and Martin Hägglund. Despite the complexity of the respective objections and their differences, the overall problem is still one of conditions, or the problem of insisting on a real *without* falling back into some mode of condition: how, Toscano argues, can Meillassoux really be materialist, if speculative reason remains sovereign? Johnston, similarly,

---

[8] Timothy Morton, "Queer Ecology," PMLA (2010), 125:2, 273-82.

argues that there is an inconsistency between the aim for *absolute* contingency and "real empirical data," while Peter Hallward's critique focuses on the inability for speculation to detail the conditions of genuine political thought.[9] What all these objections share, though they are by no means aligned with Derrida or deconstruction, is nevertheless some insistence that thinking bears a relation to the world, and that this relation is problematic.

For Martin Hägglund (and in the more recent essay by Peter Gratton) there is a problem with the insistence on contingency, and this problem lies in the very *condition* for thinking the contingent. In order for there to be contingency there must be the ongoing destruction of any possible framing order, ground, essence, schema or transcendental horizon; but it is just that process of the ever-new of contingency that *must* be temporal. There can only be the new or the absolutely ungrounded if what has preceded has been destroyed, or at the very least if what has preceded cannot in any way be seen as the condition for what comes after: "since there can be no contingency without the succession of time, which entails irreversible destruction and rules out the possibility of resurrection a priori."[10] Such a thought of the contingent, or the radically new and unfounded, is therefore within a frame of temporal synthesis that—for Hägglund—is not subjective, precisely because any supposed subject would itself be effected from a synthesis or tracing that is the condition for both grounds, and the un-grounding required by contingency. (I actually do not think this objection to Meillassoux is cogent: could one not imagine change and destruction as contingent; could there not be an absence of change, an absence of coming into being and passing away?)

---

9 Alberto Toscano, "Against Speculation, or, A Critique of the Critique of Critique: A Remark on Quentin Meillassoux's *After Finitude* (After Colletti)" in *The Speculative Turn*, 91; Adrian Johnston, "Hume's Revenge: À Dieu, Meillassoux?" in *The Speculative Turn*, 112; Peter Hallward "Anything is Possible: A Reading of Quentin Meillassoux's *After Finitude*" in *The Speculative Turn*, 139.

10 Martin Hägglund, "Radical Atheist Materialism: A Critique of Meillassoux," in *The Speculative Turn*, 116.

If Butler and her emphasis on a materiality given through relations of power, norms, possible identity and *what counts as mattering* cannot be seen as exhaustive of deconstruction and post-structuralism (for there are *other* deconstructions that aim to think a materiality that is not appropriately spoken of in terms of normativity *or temporality*, which for de Man is what comes "after" tropes, after an inscriptive marking out of before and after), then even less can we identify Hägglund's critique with what Derrida or deconstruction *would* say in response to an ontology without humans, knowledge, conditions, or transcendental inquiry. So here is a genealogy that I would like to outline primarily also as a gnoseology and nosology: deconstruction begins with an anarchic, counter-ethical and radically material conception of the trace. It is anarchic precisely because it is not some transcendental condition of time so much as that which can only be occluded when thought of as temporal, as some prior condition from the point of view of human knowing. Such a trace is also counter-ethical because it is not spatial, not thinkable in terms of ethos or that which would be the condition for our "world" lived as here and now. In short, the deconstructive trace is *not* a condition precisely because the thought of conditions is always dependent upon a before and after, which would place the condition as a ground. If Hägglund replies to Meillassoux that the thought of an utterly contingent and non-cognitive, non-human object of thought already presupposes temporality and therefore the trace, this is because Hägglund has defined the trace via a conditional logic: the trace is that which marks out the sequence through which something like a contingency that is destructive of the given might be thought. But this prompts two questions: is it not legitimate to ask about contingency as such, as that which *can be thought* and not a contingency which can only be known *as thought* (as traced out, temporalized and therefore after a conditioning trace?) Second, is it possible to think the trace as a radical materiality that is itself contingent and not rendered into some form of condition for matter? Here is where we return to genealogy, gnoseology, and nosology: genealogically, let us posit an early deconstruction—a thought of the trace that would not be some type of condition for thinking—that was then domesticated by a series of philosophical manoeuvers that justified, legitimated and rendered rigorously unavoidable a concept of trace as condition. Deconstruction would then have been divided from itself, set at war with itself: one mode would be a properly transcendental form of inquiry in which phenomenology's conception of the grounds of knowledge as ultimately temporal would then require a thought of the constitution of time, which in turn could not be located *in* the human subject, but might include material processes such as writing, language systems, technological extensions of the living body and so on. It is this Derrida and this deconstruction—a rigorous, responsible and ethical Derrida—who is defended against notions of play, and is aligned with an inescapable philosophy of temporality. There would be a direct line from Husserl's inquiry into the conditions of appearing and the absolute character of the transcendental subject, to Heidegger's critique of all vulgar modes of clock time that did not confront the time of appearing and disclosing, to Derrida's insistence that any thought of time is always already vulgar, and dependent upon a prior field of inscription. It would follow, then, that a logic of the conditions of time would yield an ethics of the future; and this, indeed, is precisely where deconstruction started to develop in its ethical mode. Any present or now is only possible because of a retained past and an anticipated future—and so the now is never fully present to itself. Any decision undertaken in the now—because of its traces of the past—cannot command or control a future: the future is necessarily open. On the one hand, this seems to heighten responsibility, precisely because I may undertake a decision with the best of intentions but there will always be an anarchic force that takes the decision into territory and potentiality beyond my command. On the other hand, this very undecidability that enables and demands a genuine decision (because the future cannot be known or calculated) promises a future that is not ours and that may come to us as a gift in the form of a democracy or justice "to come." We are at once compelled to make a decision, and yet given the thought and promise of that which may—for all our limits—arrive beyond the decision no decision could be ethical or closed. One can see the ways in which here a certain relation between time and knowledge yields a healing future: our decisions—our modes of knowing—are never fully our own but are marked by traces that will make our future never reducible to the limits of our now. Thought's calculative, and even speculative faculty (or the power to determine the future from the present) has as its condition the very means of its own cure. The contingency that will cure us from our calculative command of the future, and our attempts to master non-human reality, is thought's own contingency. The future is unknowable and open because any *thought* of the future and any decision of the future are invaded by traces that will be incalculable.

The open future is a future of open justice and open democracy: those forces of "democracy" and "justice" that cannot be contained by the very thought that is their partial author. It is not surprising that this deconstruction of decisions, promise and an open future has come under fire from a certain sobering recollection of materialism. There has been both the environmental criticism of David Wood that questions the ethics of an open future in a time when human decisions have contracted rather than expanded both justice and promise, and several attempts to think outside human futures by way of the concept of the anthropocene.[11] It is not surprising that some writers originally associated with deconstruction, such as Timothy Morton, have—by way of writing on ecology—started to shift towards speculative realism. From the speculative realist point of view there is an even more profound criticism than that which has been generated from environmental philosophy; the thought of time, far from being that which takes us back to conditions and demands something like a transcendental logic, should

---

[11] David Wood, "On Being Haunted by the Future," *Research in Phenomenology* (2006), 36:1, 274-98; see also the special issue of *Oxford Literary Review* (2012), 34:2, ed. Timothy Clark.

annihilate the primacy of thinking, conditions and a contingency that would be a contingency *of the trace*. That is, whereas an ethical deconstruction introduces undecidability into the very possibility of a decision, because decisions are traced and made possible by inscriptive systems, speculative realism wants to think a far more material contingency.

If it is possible to make statements about a time before humans and life—and Meillassoux demonstrates that we do in fact do this—then we already acknowledge that we can think of that which is unconditioned by the rules of thinking, unconditioned by the logic of conditions. Either, then, we take the now common move of aligning deconstruction with textualism and a dependency on human inscriptive systems and move on to a post-deconstructive materialism, *or* we argue that deconstruction was neither human nor textual and that concepts such as "trace" actually referred to real and material processes outside of the human altogether. The trace could be aligned either with a Darwinism of proliferating living difference, or a proto-neuro-materialism of dynamic networks without centre. One saves Derrida, smuggles him back into heaven, by reading him as neo-Darwinist or proto-neural.[12] The last thing one would want to do would be to ask about the *other* deconstruction—the deconstruction of literary play and rhetoric. For those who would defend deconstruction against speculative realism, such as Hägglund, contingency is a temporal notion and is therefore dependent on the trace that allows the thought of a destructiveness to emerge—for destruction is always destruction *of* some presence and is therefore traced out, marked, synthesised and cannot be said to *be*. For those who would want to smuggle Derrida back into heaven, deconstruction's "writing" or "text" were neither linguistic nor literary; rather, those features that were consigned to the linguistic—such as the capacity to operate beyond intent—were the very same that marked evolving and dynamic *life*. It would seem then that the present's series of

---

[12] Colin Nazhone Milburn, "Monsters in Eden: Darwin and Derrida," *MLN* (2003), 118:3, 603-21; Ellen Spolsky, "Darwin and Derrida: Cognitive Literary Theory as a Species of Post-Structuralism," *Poetics Today* (2002), 23:1, 43-62.

proclaimed new, radical or speculative materialisms merely repeats an already offered but never fully acknowledged material deconstruction. It is not surprising, then, that Hägglund finds himself constantly berating Derrideans for betraying the properly godless nature of deconstruction: just because our immanent conditions of experience leave us without any full presence and only the marks and traces *from which* presence would be posited, this does not mean that we can then legitimately argue from the non-presence of this world to some transcendent divinity. The failure for the given world to secure an exhaustive account of presence—the absence of all knowable grounds—does not only not entail some non-worldly other, but positively precludes any form of theism. The problem with materialism, for Hägglund at least, and those Derrideans who are not keen to argue for Derrida as an object-oriented ontologist *avant la lettre*, is that matter is something that cannot be thought without some form of immateriality or absence. *Either* matter operates as yet one more posited metaphysical ground from which all relations would be generated, in which case the thinking of matter is unethical and irresponsible unless it includes some consideration of the *mise en scène* through which matter is given *as matter* (which is why Judith Butler will play on matter as verb, and how something comes *to matter*). *Or*, matter needs to be defined in the same way as one might use terms such as "writing," "trace," "différance," or "plasticity":[13] these terms at once seem to refer to actual things within the world, but are also non-things insofar as they might be thought less as nouns and more as markers or place-holders for an attempt to think about that which can never be given precisely because it is the disturbing, destructive and disinterring movement through which any givenness or thing is possible. When Graham Harman writes about things as withholding themselves then the thing, far from being a materiality or foundation from which the world and relations might be explained, becomes

[13] Catherine Malabou, *Plasticity at the Dusk of Writing: Dialectic, Destruction, Deconstruction*, trans. Carolyn Shread (New York: Columbia University Press, 2010).

a quasi-transcendental: "a" way of thinking the generation of the world and relations, while also being given as something already worldly and effected from relations. It seems then that what is at stake between deconstruction and speculative realism is the "quasi" nature of the transcendental: either we posit the thing, matter or the real as the inhuman condition from which thinking emerges (in which case ethics might consist of a "turn" to the inhuman and aesthetics would be less about formal conditions and more about objects), *or* we maintain some form of deconstructive ethical responsibility by declaring that any thing, matter or real is always given *as real to us*, with the "us" also bound up with the processes of givenness that can never be mastered.

I would suggest, though, that we reject this seeming excluded middle of either proclaiming the real to be that which can be thought as such, or a deconstructive ethics of necessary impossibility. Another form of deconstruction that was set aside in favour of an ethical deconstruction was generated precisely through an institutional binary set up between a Derrida who was genuinely concerned with an (impossible) relation to the ethical other, and a Paul de Man whose theorisation of materiality bore neither the mediated caveats of Derridean deconstruction nor the affirmative exit strategy from the human that appears to be offered by speculative realism. De Man's was a deconstruction of rhetoric, tropes *and* a marking out of aesthetic ideology: not ideology as what we think, but the ideology that something like *thinking* is what characterises time and reading.

III

In all its varied forms, perhaps speculative realism can at least be defined against what it is not: Kantian correlationism. If it is the case that the only world we can know is given through the synthesising forms of the subject, then it follows that aesthetics would not be about the beautiful as such, nor sensation as such, but the givenness of sensation, and the beautiful harmony that is felt when the subject is once again drawn back to the forming power that they contribute to the world. If correlationism has dominated knowledge claims well beyond Kant—carrying over to all forms of social construction and even pragmatic relativisms that abandon any claims to knowledge beyond our own vocabularies—then correlationism has been just as powerful in ethics/politics and aesthetics. Because we cannot know things in themselves there can be no moral law or political imperative that would provide a foundation for action; but for this very reason we are required to give a law to ourselves, and this law—because self-constituted—cannot legislate *over* other selves.[14] I cannot claim to know better, cannot claim authority or expertise or any form of exceptionalism: that which I choose as a law should therefore be a law that would be chosen by any subject whatever. Not only does this lead to the dominant tradition of liberal theory—where a just society allows maximal free deliberation and decision without any imposition of the good—it also dominates most forms of what passes for poststructuralist ethics. If Derrida can claim that deconstruction *is justice*, this is precisely because of the heightened responsibility that follows from undecidability: because no ground offers itself outside the play of differences, any decision proceeds only from itself and can only appeal to a justice to come rather than any given or intuitable justice.[15]

Even though I would argue against Deleuzian philosophy as akin to any form of ethical Kantianism (and the political work of Manuel de Landa and John Protevi grounded in materialism would certainly be counter-Kantian)[16] a more general celebration of Deleuzian "becoming" and self-creation would be in line with a Kantian tradition that allows the self to be nothing other than its own act of free self-constitution, forming a style of its own without submission to any tran-

---

[14] Onora O'Neill, *Constructions of Reason: Explorations of Kant's Practical Philosophy* (Cambridge: Cambridge University Press, 1989).

[15] Elisabeth Weber, "Deconstruction is Justice," *SubStance* (2005), 34:1, 38-43.

[16] Manuel De Landa, *A New Philosophy of Society: Assemblage Theory and Social Complexity* (London: Continuum, 2006); John Protevi, *Political Affect: Connecting the Social and the Somatic* (Minneapolis: University of Minnesota Press, 2009).

scendent authority. It is not that easy to find a space outside the liberalism and anti-foundationalism that follow from Kantian correlationism, but there was at least—before speculative realism—the Aristotelian claim to communitarianism, with more substantive and culturally embedded conceptions of the good life. However, it is in aesthetic theory, practice and criticism that the Kantian heritage seems, to me at least, to be indomitable. Modernist formalism has been *the* default norm in aesthetics since Kant, and truly defines—again—what passes for post-structuralist aesthetics. If it is the case that the world is given through mediating systems—whether those differentiating structures be transcendental or cultural—then the value of art would lie in allowing us once again to feel the form we give to the world. This is why what came to be known as "theory" worked in tandem with modernist aesthetics: all art is self-reflexive, not about content but about the ways in which content is given. Again, we can think of Derrida, for whom literature is democratic in its capacity to "say anything" precisely because what is said is detached from voice and reference; it is in the literary texts that the word is given *as word*.[17] More recently we can think of the vogue for Giorgio Agamben's work and his celebration of poetic language as rendering communication and reference inoperative, thereby disclosing *that there is language*.[18] In all cases—ranging from liberalism to modernist formalism and postmodern irony and meta-fiction—Kantian correlationism leads to anti-foundationalism, which in turn leads to the imperative for self-reflexivity. All art is directed less towards what is said or presented, and more towards the mode or style of articulation. This is so much so that in high modernism *form is content*, and in high postmodernism all art becomes quotation—the repetition of the already given structures through which the world is given, never the world as such.

---

[17] Derek Attridge, *The Singularity of Literature* (London: Routledge, 2004).

[18] Colby Dickinson, "The Poetic Atheology of Giorgio Agamben: Defining the Scission between Poetry and Philosophy," *Mosaic: A Journal for the Interdisciplinary Study of Literature* (2012), 45:1, 203-17.

Graham Harman, noting the many philosophical differences and disputes that mark speculative realism, nevertheless argues that what follows from anti-correlationism is an insistence that we recognise the autonomy of art objects—such as poems. He astutely notes that this places the implications of object-oriented ontology close to American New Criticism, in which the poem is not a mere epiphenomenon that might allow us to grasp either reference, feeling, political force or something equally communicable or translatable. Harman ups the ante by arguing that it is not only poems that possess this autonomy: all verbal or visual objects (science textbooks and diagrams as much as poems and canvases) are distinct beings that *by virtue of being* cannot be reduced to the relation they bear to us. Harman's second claim for distinction is the being of the poem itself; whereas New Criticism (and probably the practice of criticism since the New Criticism) defines the poem organically as more than a collection of discrete parts, Harman does not want to concede that understanding a poem requires a study of its internal relations. You can, Harman insists, add a few more chapters to *Don Quixote* or a few more lines to *King Lear*, and you still have other aspects of the whole that are not necessarily altered. They might be altered, but not necessarily. It follows that Harman will only feel even more hostile to later critical developments, such as New Historicism, in which the poem or art object loses its detachment from the world and instead becomes an aspect of one grand circulating system. Harman wants to grant a genuine force to the thing—*any thing* including the art object, which (contra Cleanth Brooks) does not have a special autonomy and (contra the seemingly object-oriented thing theory) has an autonomy that goes beyond its capacity to unsettle us: "The problem that thing theory seems to share with the New Historicism lies in the assumption that 'the real' has no other function than to accompany the human agent and mold or disrupt it from time to time."[19] Harman also notes the extent to which deconstruction and the attention

---

[19] Graham Harman, "The Well-Wrought Broken Hammer: Object-Oriented Literary Criticism," *New Literary History* (2012), 43:2,193.

to the trace and difference preclude any commitment to a reality outside systems of reference; just because we cannot have full presentation of things in themselves does not mean we should abandon realism *tout court*. Harman argues that Derrida "thinks that all ontological realism automatically entails an epistemological realism according to which direct access to the world is possible."[20]

In the remainder of this essay I want to conclude by making two claims, one critical and another (I hope) positively destructive. The first is to look at how Harman spells out the implications of object-oriented ontology for literary criticism—which would not be a method that followed on from realism, precisely because *realism* would always be committed to the difference between whatever reading strategy we adopted and the reality towards which any method would be directed: "What object-oriented philosophy hopes to offer is not a method, but a *counter*method. Instead of dissolving a text upward into its readings or downward into its cultural elements, we should focus on how it resists such dissolution."[21] That is: it is the nature of things *as things* to be different and distinct from us. This means that for Harman there can be no privileged aesthetic autonomy—all verbal and visual objects have a force that operates beyond our world and our constituted relations. We can imagine real forces creating real changes that have *nothing* to do with human knowledge, even if they may (or may not) eventually have implications for our human and inhuman world. The cosmos acts and reacts largely without concern for us, and without our noticing it. In this respect, and Harman does not deny this, the Kantian "in-itself" remains, but the difference of the in-itself and the relations *from* the in-itself are not the privileged domain of human experience. Two forces—such as a weather system and a colony of bats—can come into relation, but there would also be a force in either of those terms not exhausted by the event of their encounter.

---

[20] Harman, "The Well-Wrought Broken Hammer," 198.

[21] Ibid., 200.

Here is my critical point: is this conclusion really anti-Kantian, or more importantly, anti-correlationist, both in the objections it states to already practiced modes of criticism, and in its conclusion? I would suggest not. Let us say that there is an acceptance of the Kantian in-itself but that the importance for aesthetics would be the refusal of any subjective distinction granted to the relation *to* the in-itself. Even if we accept that one should not fetishise proper names, and even if we accept that philosophy is about problems rather than the authority of signatures, we can see "Kant" as a way of thinking about distance, relations and the given. Harman's objection to aesthetic autonomy claims that all things—not just art objects—are, *by virtue of being things* not only given to us, but also have a force that exceeds the relation they bear to us and all other things. But is this not—as Heidegger's reading of Kant would have it—just what Kant achieves in his insistence on the givenness of the thing: in being given the thing is at one and the same time relational (for us) *and* non-relational? The practice that would follow from Harman's conclusion seems to be no different from (subjective formalist) business as usual. There are art objects that have a relative autonomy, and then there are those same objects as actualised in the many modes of reading as a form of relation. There would be no privileged relation, so one could not grant a specific meaning to a work based on an author's statement, an account of the text's genesis, or on the basis of a specific literary critical tradition. On the one hand, I would want to applaud and grant as distinct and revolutionary Harman's claim for decontextualisation:

> In contrast to the endless recent exhortations to "Contextualize, contextualize, contextualize!" all the preceding suggestions involve ways of decontextualizing works, whether through examining how they absorb and resist their conditions of production, or by showing that they are to some extent autonomous even from their own properties.[22]

---

[22] Harman, "The Well-Wrought Broken Hammer," 202.

"Autonomous even from their own properties": this, I would argue, is exactly what deconstruction in its Derridean form entails, and is still thoroughly in line with Kantianism and formalism. We know a thing as given through its properties, but that neither exhausts the thing's being nor its capacity for producing other relations. From here it follows, as Derrida insisted in his debate on context with Searle: if I can read or apprehend what you say, what you do, or even what you present to me as being a thing, then this is because our capacity to speak and experience in common (or our capacity to say that something *is*) already tears every event and presence from any putative "own" context.[23] To see something *as something*, as having a proper identity, is to already mark out in the thing that which would be repeatable beyond the present.

In his work on Husserl and the formal sciences, Derrida describes this process of meaning, being and truth in a manner that is captured by Harman's notion of that which exists "autonomous even from [its] own properties": if we can say something true about the world, then we make a claim for its presence beyond our own context, beyond any of the structures through which truth has been constituted. We may only know what is true via constituted sense and tradition, but once constituted, truth *in its meaning or being* transcends any local context.[24] If Derrida grants a special status to the literary text, which he does, this is because of a certain realist materialism: the condition for any text to exist through time is that it take on some material support—printing, painting, digitalised media—and for that very reason a text can only operate within a context (or be a constituted thing) if it can be repeated and transported across other contexts. This is why deconstruction, as a reading practice, attended less to the author or a text's emergence, and more to the capacity of the text to operate quasi-autonomously: attention to the

---

[23] Jacques Derrida, *Limited Inc.*, trans. Samuel Weber (Evanston: Northwestern University Press, 1988).

[24] Jacques Derrida, *Edmund Husserl's The Origin of Geometry: An Introduction*, trans. John P. Leavey (Lincoln: University of Nebraska Press, 1977).

inscription or matter that allows a text (or any thing) to exist through time, and therefore to have force beyond any present. There is, however, an element in deconstruction that is far less Kantian than this commitment to the autonomy of a text (or any thing) and this lies in just the two dimensions that Harman objects to in new criticism. So to conclude my critical point I would say that Harman's position remains Kantian insofar as the condition for correlation—that something be given *to us*—is that it bear some autonomy alongside the relations of being given. This is true of any thing, and it is why Kantian aesthetics stresses an attention to the conditions through which we intuit what is not ourselves, with sublimity being the feeling of that which is inassimilable to our relational powers. But here is where Harman's criticism starts to bite, for it seems as though sublimity—or the feeling of the limits of our cognition—narrows the potential for art and politics. Do we value art or experience simply for its disturbance of *our* limits, in which case we are left with the goal of self-reflexivity: art makes us aware of the distance and mediation of all knowing. Is politics nothing more than liberal self-critique, where a certain not-knowing yields a chastening humility, but nothing positive or genuinely destructive?

It is just this problem—of relations beyond us that are not reducible to the force they present to us by way of disturbance—that should take us beyond Kant and Derridean deconstruction. Where might resources be found?

First, I would offer Leibniz as the other (counter-Kantian) tradition that did not yield an aesthetic theory: any thing (and things go all the way down, such that my body is a thing, composed of other things including cells, organs, memories, scars and weaknesses) is related to everything else *but in its own way*. For Leibniz this means that my body—to be my body—bears a relation to everything, including the crossing of the Rubicon by Caesar and Adam's eating of the fruit of the tree of knowledge. To quote Deleuze, "In short, every possible monad is defined by a certain number of preindividual singularities, and is thus compossible with all the monads whose singularities converge with its own, and incompossible with those whose singularities imply divergence or nonprolongation."[25] My world and relations of my body are distinct from the worlds (or perceptions) of the things that make up my body: my heart beats to its own world, perceiving the various events that compose my metabolism. For Leibniz it is God, and God only, who apprehends all relations fully and completely; all other things have a dim awareness, various degrees of clarity and distinction and confusion of all the other things that make up the infinite. If we do not have Leibniz's God as the perceiver of all perceivers then we are left with infinite series of diverging relations; everything perceives the infinite, but perceives or unfolds the infinite from its own point of view. If there were a God, then all these relatively clear perceptions of the truth of the whole would be composed in a coherent unity. One would not just exclude the illogical (A and not-A), but also the incompossible: Adam either sins or does not sin, and the entire world that follows from one of these paths follows a series of choices resulting in the best possible totality. The Leibnizian universe is ultimately compossible in its multiplicity. However, without God and the guarantee of the harmony of the whole, we would not just have a baroque aesthetic where every perception expressive of the universe contributes to a contrapuntal unity, but there would be incompossible and diverging worlds. There would be no principle that excluded a world where—for example—Cathy really does love Heathcliff and where Cathy really does despise Heathcliff. If this is so then the reading of a literary text (or any thing) takes part in a sublime *unfolding* in which the detachment of the text from a single privileged context ultimately results in the proliferation of relations. Commenting on Jorge Luis-Borges's godless Leibnizian aesthetic, Deleuze writes:

> It is clear why Borges invokes the Chinese philosopher rather than Leibniz. He wanted ... to have God pass into existence all incompossible

[25] Gilles Deleuze, *The Fold: Leibniz and the Baroque*, trans. Tom Conley (London: Continuum, 2006), 72.

worlds at once instead of choosing one of them, the best. And probably it would be globally possible, since incompossibility is an original relation, distinct from impossibility or contradiction.[26]

This is a different mode of sublimity, where the non-given extends to infinity and bears its own force of relations. And this makes a key difference to how we think first about the art object and then things as such. Harman says that we can alter the character of the fool in *King Lear* but the character of King Lear remains the same, and that is true—possibly—only if we have a knowledge of King Lear that is clear and distinct. How do we know what alterations to a literary text would or would not change another part? We can make a claim for the ongoing sameness of King Lear *if and only if* we think of an immaterial or ideal object that remains the same through time regardless of inscription. Harman's argument requires us to think of an ideal or non-relational sameness of the thing—in this case the essential sameness of *King Lear* that is immune to minor variation—whereas a Leibnizian sublime prompts us to recognise that the smallest details of the thing (such as the difference between a comma and a semi-colon) would generate a thousand or more textual series. The positing of an ideal sameness to a text does have a pragmatic or operational value, and this mode of reading is what allows us to attribute constant functions to scientific objects. But literary reading is sublime in its practice because it entertains all the infinites that would unfold from the seemingly insignificant minutiae of textual matter.

It does not matter whether I read Einstein's theory of relativity on paper or on screen, or in German or French, because the truth of theory transcends its material inscription: we know the principles of physics, geometry and logic independently of the inscriptive process that brings them to our knowledge. We could say the same about literary knowledge—and people do indeed grant a truth to fictions, such that Sherlock Holmes lives on Baker Street and that Tony Soprano lives in New

---

[26] Deleuze, *The Fold*, 71.

Jersey. But it is the nature of literary objects (and art objects) to indicate a certain resistance or non-ideality (or what Paul de Man referred to as materiality) that cannot be willed away, unless we posit some "meaning" that would remain the same through time without relation to material inscription.

When we talk about scientific things, we grant them a distinction from their material inscription; but it is the nature of literary or aesthetic reading to keep everything in relation. We think some aspect of a text has no bearing on the central theme—that Hamlet is Hamlet regardless of what Rosencrantz and Guildenstern say to each other, and that the very minor mention of Robinson Crusoe's wife at the end of Defoe's novel could be deleted without altering the novel as a whole: but then Tom Stoppard writes *Rosencrantz and Guildenstern are Dead* and J. M Coetzee writes *Foe*. Hamlet's indecision—if there is such an ideal thing that goes through time to be read and re-read—and the very sense of Crusoe as an autonomous individual (which are both aspects of the text) change in nature when another element is attended to. We may read *Wuthering Heights* for two hundred years focusing on Cathy and Heathcliff, and we may feel quite confident that they exist as such, as fictional characters not alterable by accidental marks in the text; but then we look to the character of Nelly and framed relation and suddenly Cathy is not Cathy any more. Here is the problem with aesthetic objects: they are radically material. No matter what we do in terms of isolation of their elements—ranging from the sense of events to single words to characters—those projections of meaning are distinct from the material object. It would be unscientific to attend to the binding, colours, penmanship and erasures of a mathematical manuscript, but even though we can read *The Prelude* or *The Four Zoas* in a reprinted poetry anthology, the material object can always open up new relations, rendering what we thought to be merely material and irrelevant into a part that (following Leibniz) opens an entirely divergent whole.

We *could* read all texts as literary texts, as material objects that *remain* beyond all reading and explication; we could read all texts as scientific, as referring to what would be true and the same beyond articulation. These two possibilities of reading indicate two ways of thinking relations: one in which (as in literary texts) the object is what it is, and has its own force to produce relations that cannot be exhausted by reading and explication, and another in which we see the text as detached and irrelevant with a truth of relations that we posit as being real regardless of articulation. The former entails Deleuze's reading of a Leibniz without God: there is a relativism, but it is not a relativism *to us*, because everything bears its relations to everything else, offering not the relativism of truth, but the truth of the relative.[27]

I would conclude by advocating—as genuinely materialist, object-oriented *and* wildly speculative—the deconstruction of Paul de Man. Here, it is a question of spelling out the implications of what we mean by text. For Derrida text does increasingly come to refer to the inextricably intertwined location of any presence in a network of difference, such that anything that we posit as having being can always be repeated into the future, opening a justice to come. To perceive something *as something* is to grant it an identity or property that exceeds the present, and therefore exceeds any already given actuality. This repeatability is what Derrida refers to as the "opening to infinity," which relies on text for its inauguration, but exceeds its textual support. To read a text and grant it sense is therefore at once to posit what would be readable for any other subject, in any other context, thus opening the idea of context in general or *truth*. For de Man by contrast there is a quite different, material, inhuman non-relational understanding of text: to read a literary text is *not* to aim for some intended sense to come, but to attend to the detached deadness beyond intentionality:

> The language of the poets therefore in no way partakes of mimesis, reflection, or even perception, in the sense that would allow a link between sense experience and understanding, between perception

---

[27] Deleuze, *The Fold*, 23.

151

and apperception. Realism postulates a phenomenalism of experience which is here being denied or ignored. Kant's looking at the world just as one sees it ("wie man ihn sieht") is an absolute radical formalism that entertains no notion of reference or semiosis.[28]

There is a deconstruction that radicalises correlation: to perceive a thing, as a thing, is to posit what it would be beyond its present sense, and this opens an infinite future. But there is also a deconstruction, de Manian deconstruction, that places a bet (and one that we always lose) on thinking the text just as it is, and then—from that non-meaning, inert, contingent and given matter (that is neither substance nor sense)—consider what it might be to look at nature with such a blank eye. *This* sublime is one that we might refer to as geological and Leibnizian, precisely because the striving of the reading or viewing eye is not that of comprehension that would include nature within our ordering gaze, but destruction: what might a thing be if no longer perceived by us, as ours, as intending a presence. For de Man there is *another* Kant, closer to Leibniz, in which the affect of the sublime (a *sense* but not a sensation of being overwhelmed) leads to what he refers to as architectonic, in which—far from feeling empathy and connectedness—something like a construction that would be amenable to a pure calculus emerges. To see in this manner is *not* to see into the life of things, but just to see; to see nature as architectonic, *as a building*, is to see it as a construction. (This is not a social, divine or ideal construction, just the elements that are put together):

the eye, left to itself, entirely ignores understanding; it only notices appearances (it is *Augenschein*) without any awareness of a dichotomy between illusion and reality—a dichotomy which belongs to teleological and not to aesthetic judgment. In other words, the transformation of nature into a building, the transformation of sky and ocean into vault and floor is not a trope. The passage is entirely void of any substitutive exchange, of any negotiated economy, between nature and mind; it is

---

[28] De Man, *Aesthetic Ideology*, 128.

free of any facing or defacing of the natural world ... The dynamics of the sublime mark the moment when the infinite is frozen into the materiality of stone, when no pathos, anxiety, or sympathy is conceivable; it is, indeed, the moment of a-pathos, anxiety, or apathy, as the complete loss of the symbolic.[29]

The aesthetic or poetic—the text—is not living, mindful, but *figural*; for we are presented with a construction of elements. How would we read if we imagine the text not as that which is given to us, opening our world, but as bearing its own world, as though it were left behind, after humans, in our wake and no longer signed by us?

IV

For all its talk of realism and things, very little has been said about sex in this world of new speculations, and yet this blind-spot helps to explain the lack of impact and attention with regard to the literary and aesthetics. Here I would want to mark a decisive difference between sex and sexes: there are sexes—or differences in kind, genders—because of sex. Sex, following a principle of life, might be defined as a coming into relation in which the force of each term exceeds the will, interest or maintenance of the relatively stable terms given through the relation. An organism may require sustenance, but when the pleasure or sensation of consumption takes over from the will or needs of the organism something like sex occurs. It is, if you like, architectonic or entirely devoid of teleology—a random assembling. The human species has extended itself through technology, consumption, production and reproduction but when those processes take on a life of their own we have reached and surpassed the sexual threshold. There are genders—men and women—because there is sex, and not vice versa. This fundamental Freudian principle is counter-Kantian (or Kantian in de Man's sense), Leibnizian, sublime, aesthetic and ultimately realist in the

---

[29] De Man, *Aesthetic Ideology*, 127.

most speculative of senses. It commands us not to begin explanation from constituted things—but it also precludes us from dissolving things, terms, rigidities or points—back into some flourishing and transcendental principle of life. Instead, we are left with detached and wild—anarchic—forces that generate rogue relations that have no concern for the maintenance of identity.

Here we can think of reading *not* as the manoeuver of contextualisation, where texts are returned to their point of genesis, *nor*—as some strands of post-structuralism suggest—opening texts to a radically proliferating and generative future (or a meaning to come). Instead we might read each element as *destructive* of the terms with which it is coupled. If two organisms are coupled and the relation is sexual, then what occurs is irreducible to the will, interest, maintenance and life of each. And this is because in a world without Kant, without God, without humans and without spirit (or let us say without *future*) we would have forces without internal relations, where coming into relation would be at once creative of new terms but also destructive of the plane from which forces were generated. The earth, or life as we know it, has at once destroyed itself, but also created new strata—has at once generated what has come to be known as the anthropocene, while at the same time annihilating various ecosystems.

Here, then is how we might read sexually, materially and with a nod to an inhuman sublime: the sublime would be sexual if the encounter with what cannot be assimilated or comprehended were not to draw back to the subject, but to destroy subjective coherence, and would be material if what were given were robbed of sense. It would, further, be realist in a speculative sense if it were presented *not* as that which would be given as meaningful for us, as furthering our world but—following a godless Leibnizianism—as a matter that generated relations beyond our sense. We can think of the material sublime as at once sexual—there are relations that have diverging effects that exceed those of any will and life—and that it is nevertheless this sexuality of the real, this autonomy of force, that generates the thing-like nature of figures (such as gender), and art objects. Look at the way, just to take one example, images, phrases and art objects circulate: I would suggest that it is more and more the case that things, figures, characters, anthems, motifs and other fragments of what we might like to think of as art or meaning have their own worlds, open their own relations. Our sense of them as meaningful is, to use de Man's terminology, aesthetic ideology: and nowhere is this more so than with gender. The figure of gender—woman as natural, caring, nurturing, fruitful, goddess—seems to be generative, seems to be ours and meaningful. Yet it is precisely the figural power of gender that operates without us, like a repetition compulsion, usually at those moments when thinking and connection is what is most required. Consider for example how the figure of woman operates in Cormac McCarthy's *The Road*. Audaciously envisioning what it might be to witness the world's end—where "world" stands for the world of meaning, ethics, coherence and human benevolence—a father and son journey through a wasteland of violence and destruction, haunted by memories of the boy's mother, whose life and moral beauty signify all that has been lost.[30] The novel's conclusion avoids any confrontation with the dead-end of the species, and can be read as a fantasy of redemption in a mode of true post-apocalyptic therapy: after the end of the world there will be a brief period of mourning, and yet the figure of that lost plenitude—woman—will return at the end of *The Road* to carry the child into a new future. Far from McCarthy accidentally falling back into the trope of gender in order to avoid the more destructive architectonic of sex, we might note a certain recalcitrance or resistance to a genuinely material sublime of which McCarthy is just one of far too many instances. We read and see this over and over again: rather than look at things as things—as detached, void of sense and operating without us—figures intervene to create the lure of sense.

---

[30] David R. Jarraway, "'Becoming-Woman:' Masculine 'Emergency' After 9/11 in Cormac McCarthy," *Canadian Review of American Studies* (2012), 42:1, 49-64.

More positively, I would argue that certain manoeuvers in contemporary art production are better thought in these materially sublime/Leibnizian/De Manian terms: as trying to write as if humanity were absent, as though a world could be opened from a grain of sand. There is a long tradition of a poetry of the object that runs counter to the Kantian sublime, whereby the resistance of the world would intensify the human striving for sense. In the powerful writing of Deryn Rees-Jones it is as though the separation of other worlds is at once silencing and intrusive, yielding questions that are also projections:

Slugs

Each night the slugs have found a way of getting in.
They slip through cracks, inhabiting corners,
edging up table-legs, walls, or chairs.
With their slug etiquette, slug gestures,
are they silently dreaming of lettuces, hostas?
Do they elegise greenhouses, commune with their dead?
Or fantasize brethren on distant planets?
What mistakes do they make, and how will they tell us?
Do we ask their forgiveness? Do they imagine us saved?
Of their psychobiographies will I ever be sure?
Occipital horns conduct in the darkness.
They know nothing of envy, nothing of blame.
In the gastropod inchings of their midnight séances,
the slow rehearsals of molluscular dance,
they're themselves absolutely, beyond imitation.
And their silvery cast offs Isadora's
just at the moment in the silvery moonlight
when she sheds her scarves to a million stars.[31]

The poem's conclusion is at once abandonment—"they're themselves absolutely, beyond imitation"—alongside ironic concession; for all the striving to see what is absolutely itself,

---

[31] Deryn Rees-Jones, *Burying the Wren* (Bridgend: Seren, 2013), 32.

the poem recalls the highly contingent reference to the dancer Isadora Duncan—who died when her scarf caught itself in the back wheel of a car: the accoutrements of art intrude, operate, kill—and yet for all that we anthropomorphise. The slug's silvery trail becomes both a human dance, which in turn opens to the cosmos and "a million stars." The poem is at once self-annihilation—the slugs in their sluggy world—and failure, with the final return to the humanisation of the inhuman, and then the rendering cosmic of that human-mollusk dance. The truth of the relative.

Speculative Aesthetics
and Object-Oriented Inquiry (OOI)

N. Katherine Hayles

Duke University

HROUGHOUT THE LONG AND varied tradition of aesthetics, one premise has always, implicitly or explicitly, remained unquestioned: that aesthetics has at its centre human perception. Indeed, this idea is embedded even in the etymology of the term, which derives from the Greek *aisthetikos*, meaning "esthetic, sensitive, sentient," in turn derived from *aisthanomai*, meaning "I perceive, feel, sense." To this premise, speculative realism issues a strong challenge. It endorses the idea that the centrality of the human should be displaced in favour of what Graham Harman calls an object-oriented philosophy,[1] an approach in which everything—humans, nonhuman biological creatures, inanimate objects, imaginary concepts—exists equally without privileging any viewpoint, especially the human, as the defining perspective for the others.[2]

---

[1] Harman's ideas were taken up by Levi Bryant, among others, who named the field object-oriented ontology (OOO), which designation Harman has retrospectively used to describe his work. Hereafter the field will be referred to as OOO.

[2] Graham Harman, *Tool-Being: Heidegger and the Metaphysics of Objects* (New York: Open Court, 2002), 2, 16 et passim.

This position immediately poses problems for aesthetic theory. Virtually all aesthetic theories to date, whether they ground the aesthetic experience in objective qualities, as William Hogarth and Edmund Burke maintained, in cultural influences, as André Malraux argued, or as a "counter-environment" designed to break cultural preconceptions, as Marshall McLuhan suggested, rely on the centrality of human sense experience. Even Eli Siegel, the American philosopher who in 1941 founded the Aesthetic Realism movement that maintained reality itself is aesthetic, relied on human perception when he argued that art, self and the world are all interconnected and constitute an aesthetic oneness.[3] What would it mean, then, to imagine an aesthetics in which the human is decentred and inanimate objects, incapable of sense perceptions as we understand them, are included in aesthetic experience?

One approach would be to define speculative aesthetics as the aesthetic techniques employed by speculative realism, for example, the wildly heterogeneous lists that populate the works of Bruno Latour and Graham Harman. In this case, however, speculative aesthetics could safely be relegated to a subset of rhetorical theory, and much of its explosive potential would be defused. A better approach would be to engage the ideas and arguments of speculative realism and extend them into the aesthetic regime. This is the strategy taken by Graham Harman in "Aesthetics as First Philosophy," in which he notes commonalities between Levinas's and his own approach.[4] The essential move here is to identify aesthetics with "enjoyment" (Levinas's term) or "allure" (Harman's) so that the sensual qualities of objects in which other objects "bathe" is understood as an essentially aesthetic response. Thus aesthetics is generalised so that it applies not only to humans but to all objects, including inanimate ones.

---

[3] Eli Siegel, *Self and World: An Explanation of Aesthetic Realism* (New York: Definition Press, 1981).

[4] Graham Harman, "Aesthetics as First Philosophy: Levinas and the Non-Human," *Naked Punch* (2007), 9, www.nakedpunch.com/articles/147 (accessed July 1, 2013).

A problem with this approach is that we have no idea of what this "enjoyment" might consist; for instance, in Harman's example of the cotton and the flame, what is the nature of the aesthetic "allure" each experiences in the other? An aesthetics based on this approach would, except for humans, be devoid of content, beyond the abstract conception of an object's "allure" for another. Moreover, this approach ties speculative aesthetics too tightly to speculative realism, constraining its expansive potential. My preferred approach, for which I argue here, is to put speculative aesthetics into conversation with speculative realism but without granting that speculative realist principles can contain all of the possibilities to which speculative aesthetics can rightfully lay claim. To flesh out this approach, I propose a concomitant methodology that I call object-oriented inquiry (OOI), which is indebted to OOO but also diverges from it in significant ways.

To develop this approach, I take as my tutor texts two works that partially overlap and partially diverge, namely Vilém Flusser's *Vampyroteuthis Infernalis*, a treatise on the vampire squid, and Ian Bogost's *Alien Phenomenology: What It's Like to Be a Thing*.[5] Whereas Bogost takes Harman's version of speculative realism as his main inspiration, Flusser, writing his treatise in 1981, follows a method that could never draw assent from Harman or Bogost, because it involves projecting the human imagination into the nonhuman other and thus, far from trying to escape anthropomorphism, revels in it, although in a complex fashion that both reinforces and undermines it simultaneously. Bogost, for his part, tries faithfully to follow speculative realism's precepts, but in the process develops a methodology that undermines at least part of its ideas. These deviations, however, are consistent with (and an important inspiration for) OOI.

First let us explore Flusser's method. Here I must immediately interject a qualification. At the time Flusser was writ-

---

[5] Vilém Flusser, *Vilém Flusser's Brazilian Vampyroteuthis Infernalis*, trans. Rodrigo Maltex Novaes (Dresden: Atropos Press, 2011); Ian Bogost, *Alien Phenomenology, or What It's Like to Be a Thing* (Minneapolis: University of Minnesota Press, 2012).

ing, very little was known about the vampire squid, a species that lives in the deep ocean at about 3,000 feet underwater. Since then, robotic submarines and ultra-sensitive cameras capable of recording images with almost no light have been developed, and biologists now can give a much more detailed account of the organism's anatomy and behaviours. It would be easy to dismiss Flusser because of the assumptions he makes that have subsequently been shown not to be the case. For example, in correspondence he carried on while writing this manuscript, he describes the organism achieving a diameter up to 20 meters.[6] In fact, however, the species that biologists recognise as *Vampyroteuthis infernalis* is doing good to achieve a diameter of 20 *centimetres*—a hundred-fold difference in size that makes Flusser's description of the creature as "violent" and "ferocious" difficult to credit. I am at a loss to explain this discrepancy, short of suspecting that he somehow confused the giant squid (or its close cousin, the Humboldt squid), which can grow to that immense size, with its much more diminutive cousin. Moreover, many aspects of his descriptions of the vampire squid's behaviours are clearly over-determined by its name—the vampire squid from hell—and this lends his interpretations an exaggerated romanticism not justified by the creature's behaviours in themselves. Whatever mistakes Flusser made, however, are for my purposes more or less beside the point. What interests me here is his methodology and the claims that he makes for it. If the method has merit—and I believe it does—then it can make an important contribution, even if Flusser is mistaken about certain particulars.

Working from what he thinks he knows about Vampyroteuthis, Flusser constructs a binary relation with the human; Vampyroteuthis is the human inverted, as in a mirror. The purpose is two-fold: to understand Vampyroteuthis through the ways in which he encounters the world, and to use these discoveries to reveal the Vampyroteuthis hidden or repressed

---

6 Flusser, *Brazilian Vampyroteuthis Infernalis*, 137.

within human culture.[7] Obviously, there is an agenda here that goes beyond reconstructing the worldview of the creature, and this may explain why Flusser wants him to be seen as one of the top predators in his aqueous environment, making him parallel to humans as top terrestrial predators. He is unapologetic about drawing these parallels, writing that he studies,

> the zoology of cephalopods not because I am able to assume an objective point of view in relation to them but, on the contrary, in order to consider them as part of the vital tide that drags me along with it. I intend to understand them in order to orient myself in my world. Science is interesting precisely because it relates to me ... an entirely objective science would be uninteresting, inhuman ... the present essay demands that we give up the ideal of objectivity in favour of other intersubjective scientific methods.[8]

The vampire squid, like other molluscs, uses the foot to grasp and to suck in water. The brain is arranged circularly surrounding the foot, which is also the mouth. These facts lead Flusser to the following comparison:

> When we erected our body, we freed our eyes for the horizon and our hands for grasping objects. When Cephalopods erected themselves, their perception, locomotion and attack organs were relocated toward the ground, surrounded the mouth, and came into direct contact with the brain that surrounds the mouth.[9]

He characterises these two postures towards the world as rational and passionate, respectively: "For man, knowing is a gesture that advances against the world, an active gesture," while for Vampyroteuthis, "the world for him is an opposite pole that has to be sucked in passionately."[10] He is "sexually

---

[7] I follow Flusser's usage in referring to the organism as "he" rather than "it."

[8] Flusser, *Brazilian Vampyroteuthis Infernalis*, 38.

[9] Ibid., 39.

[10] Ibid., 74.

excited by the world," making him "a passionate transcendent subject," which Flusser identifies with "the Devil."[11] In a move reminiscent of Lakoff and Johnson (whom he does not cite),[12] he argues that the creature's psychology can be inferred from his biology: "When the mouth and anus find themselves in the same organ, the foot, and when the two find themselves near the brain, the mouth and anus are cerebralized and the brain is sexualized."[13]

Some of Flusser's most interesting conjectures concern Vampyroteuthian culture and art, and here we see the pay-off for his projective method. Noting that "every attempt to limit mentality to the human species is doomed to failure," he does not doubt that the creature has a rich inner life.[14] Without verbal language, Vampyroteuthis communicates in part through the play of colours on his skin, made possible by the internal activation of chromatophores, which he uses to attract mates. Therefore "his language's syntax ... is the logic of sex."[15] Living in a fluid medium, he is unable to construct durable stable objects, only fleeting ephemeral phenomena like the sepia ink cloud that he models into shapes as protection from predators. In his philosophy, consequently, "there cannot be for him an immutable form. He is not Platonic, he is organismic. It is not philosophical contemplation, but philosophical vertigo and its posture."[16] "From this point of view," Flusser concludes, "the only material for information storage that is worthy of trust is the egg," that is, genetic information storage. This is in sharp contrast to humans, who as Flusser rightly observes, construct their history by manipulating objects and imprinting them with information. While humans "trust the permanence of objects," Vampyro-

---

[11] Flusser, *Brazilian Vampyroteuthis Infernalis*, 77.

[12] George Lakoff and Mark Johnson, *Metaphors We Live By*, 2nd ed. (Chicago: University of Chicago Press, 2003).

[13] Flusser, *Brazilian Vampyroteuthis Infernalis*, 57.

[14] Ibid., 48.

[15] Ibid., 85.

[16] Ibid., 79.

teuthis "seeks his immortality in the other," the seduction and camouflage that enables him to attract mates. "In sum," Flusser concludes, "it effectively comes down to two different types of art."[17] The comparison suggests that OOO may harbour an unrecognised anthropomorphic bias at its centre, namely the fascination with objects that is, if not a uniquely human trait, nevertheless far more prominent in humans than in any other species.

The human struggle to "inform" objects, that is, to imprint them with information, has gone on for millennia and has strongly influenced every field of human endeavour. To Flusser, this struggle is essentially aesthetic:

> Human art is not, as the well-meaning bourgeoisie would have us believe, the fabrication of 'beautiful' objects. Human art is the gesture through which man imprints his experience upon the object of his vocation in order to realize himself in it, to immortalize himself in it. Every object that is informed is therefore a 'work of art,' be it a mathematical equation, political institution, or symphony.[18]

For Vampyroteuthis, art is not the creation of objects but the seduction of the other: "That is why when he creates, Vampyroteuthis does not experience the resistance of the object but the resistance of the other."[19] Since the species sometimes attacks and eats its mate, it is necessary to seduce the other through "deliberate deception, artifice and lies." "He seeks his immortality by means of violence exerted on the other. To him, science and politics are nothing but stratagems, nothing but traps."[20]

In Flusser's view, the "communication revolution" (by which he means primarily television, but which is even truer of the Web)

---

[17] Flusser, *Brazilian Vampyroteuthis Infernalis*, 106.

[18] Ibid., 108.

[19] Ibid., 109.

[20] Ibid., 111.

consists of a diversion of the existential interest stagnating in objects back toward the other. Our communicational structures are being fundamentally transformed, in the sense of becoming constituted by ephemeral and transient media that allow the other to be informed without the need of objects. It is as if humanity, after a multi-millennial turn through the objective world, has now reencountered the vampyroteuthian path.[21]

Even as the two species come closer into alignment, however, the long struggle with objects has left a permanent mark on human culture and biology. We can never become like Vampyroteuthis, Flusser maintains, but we can recognise that he lurks in the depths of the human, even as the human is the repressed side of his culture and art.

Meditating on the evolution of communication technologies, Flusser suggests that the "informing" process has moved from objects to tools as they become more sophisticated. "The writer becomes toolmaker," he remarks, a proposition that now seems prescient given contemporary works of electronic literature generated by algorithmic processes in which the writer creates the code (that is, makes the tool) and then the tool creates the textual output.[22] A case in point is Mark Marino's essay "Reading *exquisite_code*: Critical Code Studies of Literature," in which he virtually ignores the "finished" novel and concentrates almost exclusively on the live coding sessions and algorithmic processes that created it.[23] In Flusser's view, "this inflationary tide of devalued objects leads to a disinterest in objects ... Society's interest is increasingly diverted from objects towards information, which however is inaccessible

---

[21] Flusser, *Brazilian Vampyroteuthis Infernalis*, 114. For an excellent treatment of Flusser's view of media in this text, see Melody Jue, "Reframing Photography through the Vampire Squid in Vilém Flusser's Vampyroteuthis Infernalis," unpublished ms.

[22] Ibid., 113.

[23] Mark Marino, "Reading *exquisite_code*: Critical Code Studies of Literature," in *Comparative Textual Media: Transforming the Humanities in the Postprint Era*, ed. N. Katherine Hayles and Jessica Pressman (Minneapolis: University of Minnesota Press, 2013), 283-310.

to consumers. It is stored in the memory of apparatus and is transmitted, diluted, not only by gadgets, but also and above all else by the ephemeral channels of mass communication."[24]

Although Flusser (or anyone else) might have arrived at these insights without knowing anything about *Vampyroteuthis infernalis*, the path through the comparison has resulted in de-naturalising human presuppositions, enabling a critical stance towards assumptions about aesthetics, along with much else. In summary, the method here has been to extrapolate from a base of scientific evidence (Flusser says that "the present fable is more or less informed by biology"),[25] using human imaginative projections to understand the alien creature not only in biological terms but in terms of its own phenomenological experience of the world. Moreover, for Flusser, it is precisely because of the mirror relation between the human and the Vampyroteuthis that these projections can succeed. This implies a double gesture of using the biologist's knowledge but also going beyond it into what can be known only because of the deeply shared relationship: thus "the present fable hopes to be able to exorcise Vampyroteuthis, and to make him emerge alive."[26]

On some points, Ian Bogost would agree with Flusser. For example, Flusser writes that "we must liberate ourselves above all from a model according to which existence is the meeting of a 'transcendental' subject (a mind) with objects; of a 'self' with a 'world.' According to this model, for example, knowledge would be the meeting between the one-who-knows with what-is-to-be known."[27] This strongly resonates with Bogost's pronouncement that "The philosophical subject must cease to be limited to humans and things that influence humans. Instead it must become *everything*, full stop."[28] Yet Bogost would certainly be uneasy with Flusser's "intersubjective

---

[24] Flusser, *Brazilian Vampyroteuthis Infernalis*, 114.

[25] Ibid., 123.

[26] Ibid., 124.

[27] Ibid., 71.

[28] Bogost, *Alien Phenomenology*, 10, original emphasis.

scientific methods," especially his determination to construct the Vampyroteuthis as the romanticised mirror "other" to the human, because it still leaves intact the human as an essential reference point.

Bogost's rejection of a human-centric position is evident in his comments on Thomas Nagel's famous essay, "What Is It Like to be a Bat?"[29] He emphatically endorses the distinction Nagel draws between experiencing one's species-hood from the inside and inferring it from scientific evidence about a creature's sense perceptions and behaviours. Here we might think of a similar distinction that Pierre Bourdieu draws between a tribal people's habitus, the structures that organise their way of being in the world, and the inferences that an anthropologist may draw from observing their behaviours.[30] For the people, the patterns that inform the layout of their villages, the architecture of their buildings, and their behaviours as they enact traditional ways of doing things, are not necessarily ever consciously considered; rather, they are absorbed unconsciously as the right and proper ways to live. Once abstracted into an anthropologist's calendar, diagrams, and mythic structures, the habitus ceases to be a way of living and instead becomes an abstraction, a different kind of knowledge altogether. Similarly, what it is like to know about a bat is altogether different than what it is like to *be* a bat.

The question of what kinds of knowledge are accessible to us is central both to Bogost's argument and Harman's OOO. Following Harman, Bogost accepts that "all objects recede interminably into themselves," which implies that putting things "at the center of a new metaphysics also requires us to admit that they do not exist just for us."[31] Determined to avoid an anthropomorphic perspective and granting that we can never know objects in themselves, Bogost is nevertheless powerfully drawn to say something about objects in them-

29 Thomas Nagel, "What Is It Like to Be a Bat?" *The Philosophical Review* (1974), 83:4, 435-50.

30 Pierre Bourdieu, *Outline of a Theory of Practice* (Cambridge: Cambridge University Press, 1977).

31 Bogost, *Alien Phenomenology*, 10.

selves. But how is this possible if objects always withdraw? Harman solves this problem by distinguishing between an object's sensual qualities (its "allure") and its essence; similarly, Bogost's solution is to emphasise that anything we can say about objects from an evidentiary basis is a "caricature," a representation "in which the one is drawn into the distorted impressions of the other."[32] Quoting Harman, he identifies such a representation as a metaphor: "It's a move that solves Nagel's puzzle: we never understand the alien experience, we only ever reach for it metaphorically."[33] From here he goes on to develop "metaphorism" as his method of choice, deploying

> metaphor itself as a way to grasp alien objects' perceptions of one another. Metaphorism offers a method for alien phenomenology that grasps at the way objects bask metaphorically in each others' 'notes' [Harman's name for the sensual attributes of an object] by means of metaphor itself, rather than describing the effects of such interactions on the objects. It offers a critical process for characterizing object perceptions.[34]

Where I begin to depart from Bogost and Harman is on the issue of how objects manifest themselves. Whereas they emphasise an object's allure, the attraction it emanates for other objects, more important in my experience is the resistance objects offer to human manipulation and understanding. During my days as a scientist, my experiences included such resistances on an everyday basis, from using spectrum analysis to identify an element to determining the composition of chemicals in a solution. Andrew Pickering writes eloquently about the importance of resistance in *The Mangle of Practice*, where the "mangle" is the cyclic process of a human prodding and probing a nonhuman object to answer some question.[35] The object responds by resisting the human's inquiry, in a continuing

---

[32] Bogost, *Alien Phenomenology*, 64.

[33] Ibid., 66.

[34] Ibid., 67. Whether this ploy satisfactorily resolves the issue is a moot question, as the following discussion makes clear.

[35] Andrew Pickering, *The Mangle of Practice: Time, Agency, and Science* (Chicago: University of Chicago Press, 1995).

dialectic in which the resistance forces the questions to be modified, and the modified questions uncover new forms of resistance. One could see this as the creative complement to Heidegger's present-to-hand versus ready-to-hand. Here it is not the moment the hammer breaks that brings it into our awareness, but rather the continually transforming and morphing resistance that leads to expanding and deepening knowledge. Resistance is crucial because, although objects cannot tell us what they are, they can tell us what they are not. Resistance enables us to distinguish a rock from a tree, a Higgs boson from a quark. The difference between resistance and acquiescence is that acquiescence is always metaphoric, whereas resistance is decisive: "Whatever I am, I'm not *that*," an object can respond to human probing. This distinction between positive and negative knowledge suggests that our knowledge of objects is always relative to other objects rather than to an object's essence in itself, although negative answers do allow for increasingly fine distinctions. That this process has no necessary end coincides with Harman's contention that an object's reserve can never be exhausted. At times, Harman seems to recognise the importance of an object's resistance, as in this passage from *The Quadruple Object*:

> A real object has no closer link with its own real qualities than with the sensual qualities that one would never dream of ascribing to it … a real object is real and has a definite character, but its essence is first produced from the outside through causal interactions.[36]

"From the outside" here can be interpreted to mean precisely the kind of probing that is part of the mangle of practice.

Yet a significant difference emerges here as well, for Harman refuses to quantify the extent to which a real object withdraws, maintaining that it withdraws infinitely. According to him, then, there can never be an increase in knowledge; we can never know more or less about a given object. This seems to me contradicted by scientific, technical, and engineer-

---

[36] Graham Harman, *The Quadruple Object* (Winchester: Zero, 2011), 106.

ing knowledge, as well as by everyday experience. Moreover, Harman also resists what he calls "scientific naturalism," maintaining that it seeks to "undermine" objects by reducing them to their elementary components, such as sub-atomic particles.[37] I think this fear is greatly exaggerated, as most scientists recognise there are emergent effects that appear at different levels of organisation. Effects not noticeable at the molecular level, for example, may appear at the cellular level; effects not noticeable at the cellular level may appear at the level of the organism, and so on. Few scientists believe that reductionist strategies can succeed in explaining everything.

Like Harman, Bogost also argues that "scientific naturalism," which he matches up with social relativism, is deeply flawed. The case against social relativism is straightforward: it is rejected because it explains events "through the machinations of human society—particularly the complex, evolutionary forms of culture and language."[38] With "scientific naturalism," however, the case is far from clear, and indeed is seemingly contradicted in Bogost's wonderful account of the Foveon-equipped Sigma DP digital image sensor, which draws deeply on scientific and engineering knowledge. Bogost is interested in the differences between how the human eye perceives in situations of low light intensity and how the digital image sensor perceives. In exploring these differences, he importantly opens the possibility that an object-oriented approach can be fleshed out through meticulous accounts of how nonhuman objects experience the world—or to put it in more general terms, the ways nonhuman objects have of being in the world.

As mentioned earlier, Bogost is careful to say that his account is a caricature rather than an accurate representation, which is forbidden by the idea that objects withdraw infinitely from one another.[39] The choice of terms, which he takes over from Harman, is significant: a caricature differs from a portrait or

---

[37] Harman, *The Quadruple Object*, 13-18.

[38] Bogost, *Alien Phenomenology*, 13.

[39] Ibid., 13, 65-66.

photograph precisely because it exaggerates selected features, in this way making clear that the object is represented in a distorted fashion, and that embodied in this distortion is a certain perspective. As noted earlier, he also refers to such accounts as "metaphors." To his credit, he recognises that anthropocentrism may be unavoidable:

> we can find evidence for our speculations on perception … even if we are only ever able to characterize the resulting experiences as metaphors bound to human correlates … the answer to correlationism is not the rejection of any correlate but the acknowledgement of endless ones, all self-absorbed, observed by givenness rather than turpitude.[40]

Expanding on this idea, I note that what is often called the "human perspective" is not singular but multiple, not only because of differences in language and cultures, but even more importantly, because the devices humans have invented to expand their sensory and perceptual ranges create a wide variety of different perspectives, from optical microscopes to particle accelerators, radiocarbon dating to seismic detectors. If we accept Bogost's proposition that "the answer to correlationism is not the rejection of any correlate but the acknowledgement of endless ones," then humans as a species have developed ways to access far more perspectives than any other species.

Notwithstanding his allegiance to OOO, Bogost shows that an object-oriented account can be developed from an evidentiary basis. Otherwise, what possibilities are there for the development of OOO, assuming that one is not a philosopher? One can imagine that philosophers will continue to argue about what constitutes OOO, modifying or contesting the framework, but for robust development and dissemination beyond the relatively narrow boundaries of speculative philosophy, there have to be ways to apply OOO that move beyond ontological questions to epistemological, social, cultural and political issues. It is precisely this task that OOI undertakes by building

---

[40] Bogost, *Alien Phenomenology*, 78.

bridges between evidentiary accounts of objects that emerge from the resistances and engagements they offer to human inquiry, and imaginative projections into what these imply for a given object's way of being in the world.

How might this methodology work? First, one needs a substantial body of knowledge, usually gained from scientific, technical, or engineering sources. Then one extrapolates into perceptions or world views, speculating about how that object encounters the world. Implicit in this procedure is an assumption that scientists, technicians and engineers take so deeply for granted that it is not an assumption so much as a presupposition. To exist in the world, every object that does so must have a certain internal coherence; otherwise, it could not endure for even a nanosecond. This is obvious in the case of biological organisms, winnowed through evolutionary dynamics. But it is also true of all real objects, from the tensile strength of their components to the stabilisations of the atomic orbits that hold them together. Because of this coherence, it is possible to develop accounts that have causal and predictive efficacy. This does not mean, however, that such accounts have exhausted (or can ever exhaust) all of an object's way of being in the world.

Indeed, part of my attraction to speculative realism is its insistence that objects resist us knowing them completely, withdrawing their essence in an infinite regress while still sending out their "alluring" sensual qualities. I made a not unrelated distinction when I wrote about the difference between physicality and materiality.[41] Physicality in my understanding is similar to an object's essence; potentially infinite, it is unknowable in its totality. What we can know, however, are the physical qualities that present themselves to us, which I designated as materiality. What distinguishes my position from that of Harman and Bogost, however, is that for me objects do not passively present their qualities; rather, humans *attend* to certain qualities in specific contexts

---

[41] N. Katherine Hayles, *My Mother Was a Computer: Digital Subjects and Literary Texts* (Chicago: University of Chicago Press, 2005), 103-04.

for motivated reasons. The same is true of a lion hunting a gazelle or an instrument perceiving the number encoded in an RFID (Radio Frequency Identification) tag.[42] Qualities are *never* perceived in their totality but only within the frameworks and contexts that define the relation of one object to another. This is why I am sympathetic to Jane Bennett's argument in *Vibrant Matter: A Political Ecology of Things* that relationality has to be part of the picture, for it is through relations that one object senses the specific parts of another object's "allure" germane for the first object's purposes and contexts.[43]

Does this mean that relations are confined to human perceptions, or even more narrowly to human consciousness? Definitely not! Steven Shaviro, in a 2011 conference paper entitled "Panpsychism and/or Eliminativism," argues that "if we accept that thought (or feeling or experience) need not be conscious, then we might well be led to abandon the demarcation between mind and matter altogether ... I propose that [panpsychism] gives us a good way to avoid the problematic baggage both of consciousness and of phenomenological intentionality."[44] He goes on to clarify that even if "everything is mindful, or has a mind ... this does not necessarily entail that everything is 'given' or 'manifested' to a mind."[45] Relations between objects need not and certainly do not imply that conscious thought is necessary for relationality. Conscious thought for humans represents only a small part of their processing of information from the environment, and for nonhuman objects such as the expert systems and RFID tags mentioned above, conscious thought does not operate at all.[46]

---

42 For a discussion of how RFID tags work and their cultural implications, see my "RFID: Human Agency and Meaning in Information-Intensive Environments," *Theory, Culture and Society* (2009), 26:2-3, 1-24.

43 Jane Bennett, *Vibrant Matter: A Political Ecology of Things* (Durham: Duke University Press, 2010).

44 Steven Shaviro, "Panpsychism and/or Eliminativism," The Pinocchio Theory, www.shaviro.com/Blog/p=1012 (accessed July 1, 2013).

45 Shaviro, "Panpsychism and/or Eliminativism," 7.

46 This argument is developed more fully in my book *How We Think: Digital Media and Contemporary Technogenesis* (Chicago: University of Chicago Press, 2012), 85-122.

Nevertheless, these objects enter into relations with other objects and have their own ways of parsing another object's qualities, encountering them (and sometimes acting upon them) within their own contexts and frameworks.

What speculative realism can learn from these accounts is an awareness that, despite an objects' withdrawal, it *is* possible to say a great deal about a real object's real qualities. What it can teach is that these accounts are always partial representations of an object's materiality rather than an accurate representation of the object in itself, and for entirely different reasons that a correlationist account would give. Over and above these lessons to and from speculative realism, there are other contributions that speculative aesthetics can make. Here Flusser is useful, for he is very clear on this issue: his "intersubjective scientific methods," although originating in a biological basis of fact, go far beyond them by using his human imagination to project what art, culture, and language analogues would be for the Vampyroteuthis. If he sometimes blurs the line between metaphor (or analogy) and biological fact, and if he also has a strong bias toward constructing Vampyroteuthis as the romanticised "other" to the human, he nevertheless achieves provocative interpretations that reveal by contrast assumptions that would otherwise remain opaque, such as our fascination with objects as durable substrates that can be "informed" by humans and thereby serve as a kind of immortality. By imaginatively projecting Vampyroteuthis's art and culture, he enables us to see our own more clearly.

In *Vibrant Matter*, Bennett explicitly connects the human capacity to project imaginatively into other entities with aesthetics: she wants to use "arguments and other rhetorical means to induce in human bodies an aesthetic-affective openness to material vitality."[47] Not surprisingly, in her recent essay "Systems and Things: A Response to Graham Harman and Timothy Morton," she argues for a stronger role for relationality, pointing out that there may be "no need" to choose objects or their relations. "The project, then, would

---

47 Bennett, *Vibrant Matter*, x.

be to make both objects and relations the periodic forms of theoretical attention."[48]

The issue of relationality is crucial, as the exchange in *The Speculative Turn* between Shaviro ("The Actual Volcano") and Harman ("Response to Shaviro") illustrates.[49] In this exchange, I find myself more persuaded by Shaviro than Harman. I am confused by Harman's assertion in *The Quadruple Object* and elsewhere that relations between objects can themselves become objects, and that relations can also be encapsulated within objects. In this case, what exactly is the difference between a relation and an object, if everything can be converted to (or already is) an object? Moreover, although Harman distinguishes between different categories of relations in his development of the four-fold object, within these categories he tends to refer to "relations" as undifferentiated black boxes. His criticism of holistic philosophies clearly shows this tendency. In his "Response to Shaviro," he sharply criticises Whitehead's view that everything is relational by arguing that "if an object could be identified with its current relations, then there is no reason why anything would ever change," as objects would then have their reserves exhausted by the infinite web of relations in which they are caught.[50] To have change, he asserts, new relations would have to emerge, but how would these relations develop if everything is already connected? To me, this makes no sense. According to Shaviro, Whitehead does assert that "every actual entity is present in every other actual entity," but with the important qualification that this is so only "if we allow for degrees of relevance, and for negligible relevance."[51] For example, if we ask how a dust storm on Mars would affect the online issue in which this

---

[48] Jane Bennett, "Systems and Things: A Response to Graham Harman and Timothy Morton," *New Literary History* (2012), 43, 225-33, especially 227.

[49] See Levi Bryant, Nick Srnicek, and Graham Harman, eds., *The Speculative Turn: Continental Materialism and Realism* (Melbourne: Re.press, 2011).

[50] Harman, "Response to Shaviro," 295.

[51] Shaviro, "The Actual Volcano," 287.

essay appears, we would, according to Whitehead, conclude that it has "negligible relevance."

My own view is that relations exist within systems, and the organisation of components within a system determines what relations it will have. Of course, the boundaries of systems are often fuzzy; they overlap and transform, not to mention that human perspectives determine what counts as a system boundary. Nevertheless, the dynamics of systems are clearly of different kinds. The effect of encapsulating relations within objects, as Harman does, is to mask the system's dynamics and make it difficult to think about the dynamics at all. The black boxing of relations obliterates the specificity of how complex systems work. In chaotic, complex, and complex adaptive systems, multiple recursive feedback loops make such systems extraordinarily sensitive to small perturbations; something as small as the proverbial flapping of a butterfly's wing can have cascading large-scale ripple effects. Change does not require, as Harman seems to think, the emergence of new kinds of relations; all it requires are systemic organisations that tend toward instability rather than stability. The more interconnected such a system is, the more liable it is to constant change, rather than an absence of change. A clear distinction between objects and relations would help to make complex dynamics visible and ensure that the reserves intrinsic to objects are strongly correlated to the kinds of relations in which they engage.

Putting relations back into the picture empowers the OOI methodology of imaginative projection into nonhuman others as a theoretical possibility for speculative aesthetics that is either forbidden (in Harman's case) or under-theorised (in Bogost's argument). This leads to a strong paradox: human imagination is the best way, and perhaps the only way, to move beyond anthropocentrism into a more nuanced understanding of the world as comprised of a multitude of world views, including those of other biological organisms, human-made artefacts, and inanimate objects. Bennett makes a similar point:

Maybe it's worth running the risks associated with anthropomorphiz-ing (superstition, the divinization of nature, romanticism) because it, oddly enough, works against anthropocentrism: a chord is struck between a person and thinking, and I am no longer above or outside a nonhuman 'environment.'[52]

Empowering the role that human imagination plays in al-lowing us to go beyond anthropocentrism poses another challenge to OOO. Even if this is heresy within the frame-work of speculative realism, one could argue that humans, among all the objects and species that exist on earth, can imaginatively project themselves into the worldviews of other objects along a greater spectrum of qualities than most other objects can do. We know that many other species are capable of constructing mental models of how others think and perceive. The evidence is especially strong in the case of other primates, but one could also include such computer programs as expert systems and inference engines, includ-ing those constructed to create narratives. Nevertheless, one could concede that humans exceed all these in the scope and variety of imaginative projections. Does this then mean that human specialness must be reinstated after all? Along with the speculative realists and fellow travellers such as Timo-thy Morton, I agree that humans need to be more humble about their abilities and more receptive toward the abilities of what Bennett calls "lively matter" to act in the world. The conundrum can be resolved by recognising that humans *need* this ability more than most objects because they are more inclined to think of themselves as special. In effect, the ability of humans to imaginatively project themselves into other objects' experience of the world is *necessary* to combat the anthropocentrism and narcissism for which the human species is notorious. Without it, we would be in worse straits than we are; it is the silver lining that enables us to overcome the biases of specialness and reach out to understand other objects by analogy, although never (as Nagel, Harman and

---

[52] Bennett, *Vibrant Matter*, 120.

Bogost point out) in the terms that the objects themselves experience. Perhaps this is what Bogost means by his enigmatic pronouncement, italicised for emphasis: "*all things equally exist, yet they do not exist equally.*"[53]

What does all this mean for speculative aesthetics? I started with the observation that human perception has always been central to aesthetics and noted the strong challenge that speculative realism poses to that assumption. I ended by arguing that the way to escape anthropocentrism is precisely through an imaginative projection into the worldviews of other objects and beings, based on evidence about their ways of being in the world, although with the important caveat that these are analogies and should not be mistaken for an object's own experience.

If speculative realism is modified in these arguments, so is aesthetics. The traditional division in aesthetics between those who hold that aesthetics is grounded in the object's own qualities, and those who locate it in human perception, is in a certain sense fused into a single approach which holds that the object's own qualities are expressed through the evidentiary bases, and that these are apprehended by human imagination and perception to create analogue projections of an object's world view. At the same time, aesthetics is separated from its traditional basis in beauty and re-located in the endeavour to recognise that every real object possesses—or even more strongly, *has a right to*—its own experience of the world, including biological, animate, and inanimate objects.

This approach, I conclude, has a strong claim to be called speculative aesthetics. Influenced by speculative realism, it does not slavishly follow its precepts but uses speculative realism's best insights to re-define the aesthetic mission. What I have staged in this essay is a kind of Zen tennis match between speculative realism and speculative aesthetics, in which the two are positioned less as antagonists than as partners, each helping the other to perform at a higher level. Seen in this light, speculative aesthetics is not so much a derivative

---

[53] Bogost, *Alien Phenomenology*, 11.

from speculative realism as a complementary perspective based in the methodology of OOI, potently suited to a post-human world in which other species, objects, and artificial intelligences compete and cooperate to fashion the dynamic environments in which we all live.

Actual Qualities of Imaginative Things
Notes towards an Object-Oriented Literary Theory[1]

Jon Cogburn and Mark Allan Ohm

Louisiana State University

W̲HEN CONSIDERED AGAINST the context of dominant twentieth century meta-philosophical tropes, speculative realism might appear first and foremost as an attempt to move away from *textualism*, the view that we must understand reality in terms of linguistic categories. While such a view is perhaps today most associated with deconstructionism's 1980s heyday, it is actually a perennial temptation, arguably going back to Plato's Socrates. Simply put, since philosophical discourse takes place via language it is *very* easy for one's bad philosophy of language to leak out and corrupt one's metaphysics.

Consider, for example, a representative passage by Robert Brandom.

> A complementary order of semantic explanation, by contrast, begins with what discursive practitioners actually *do*, that is, with the practical discursive process of rectifying and amplifying their commitments. It seeks to make the notion of objective modal relations intelligible in terms of this process, via pragmatically mediated semantic relations.[2]

---

[1] With apologies to Gilbert Sorrentino, *Imaginative Qualities of Actual Things* (London: Dalkey Archive Press, 2000).

[2] Robert Brandom, *Between Saying and Doing: Towards Analytic Pragmatism*

Brandom justifies this by claiming that metaphysical posits such as "facts" and "objective modal relations" are "reciprocally sense dependent" upon linguistic entities such as "propositions" and "pragmatically mediated semantic relations." Reciprocal sense dependence means that concepts of one domain are parasitic on concepts in the other domain. Thus, we are forced to understand reality in terms of linguistic categories.

We applaud Brandom's non-caginess about this. However, as students of H.P. Lovecraft we of course find this mystifying. If Lovecraft is successful, then one *can* use language to express an inexpressible reality. His entire corpus is to some extent an extended meditation on this very problematic. Assuming that his stories are not nonsense, it follows that (pace textualism) our linguistic, mental, and worldly concepts do *not* a threefold cord make.[3]

Even though few defend textualism as explicitly as Brandom or 1980s deconstructionists, one might argue that something like a plurality of contemporary analytic and continental philosophy simply makes no sense unless something like textualism is understood as being presupposed. Certainly, speculative realism (and Lovecraft for that matter) irritates many academic philosophers because if it ends up being successful much of the point might be robbed from textualist philosophies. In our Whig histories of speculative realism and object-oriented ontology (Sections I through III below) we make clear the precise nature of this threat.

But articulating a general Lovecraftian ontology is not sufficient for defeating textualism. One must also articulate a regional ontology of texts themselves. Barring this, one

---

(Oxford: Oxford University Press, 2008), 195, original emphasis.

[3] In "Expressing the Inexpressible" Jon Cogburn and Neal Hebert discuss this issue with respect to horror fantasy novels and fantasy role playing. In *Weird Realism* Graham Harman discusses the same issues, arguing that Lovecraft's approach is not inextricably tied to horror. See Jon Cogburn and Neal Hebert, "Expressing the Inexpressible" in *Dungeons and Dragons and Philosophy*, ed. Jon Cogburn and Mark Silcox (Chicago: Open Court, 2012), 133–50, and Graham Harman, *Weird Realism: Lovecraft and Philosophy* (Washington: Zero Books, 2012).

could at best be accused of a radical dualism between text and world. Perhaps more importantly, it is our hope that a non-textualist ontology of texts might once and for all block the infiltration from bad philosophy of language to bad metaphysics. While such a project is a lifetime's labour, we hope that the suggestions that follow (in Sections IV through VIII) are enough to begin damming the seepage. If so, then from this point forward we could confidently declare metaphysics first philosophy, epistemology second, and the epistemology of linguistic understanding finally a distant third (though no less interesting for all that).

I. The Speculative Turn

Besides a deep fondness for Lovecraft, perhaps the only non-trivial belief held in common by the original four speculative realists (Ray Brassier, Iain Hamilton Grant, Graham Harman, and Quentin Meillassoux) is the Hegelian conviction that metaphysics buries its own undertakers. In *After Finitude* Meillassoux argued trenchantly that the phenomenological tradition had, through Martin Heidegger and the French philosophers of the 60s, degenerated into a naïve neo-Kantianism only plausible to those who have forgotten the lessons of the period between Kant and Hegel. Meillassoux coined the term "correlationism" (of which textualism is just one example) to name the neo-Kantian thesis that one cannot think being without simultaneously thinking of a subject cognising being. If true, correlationism prohibits us from claiming knowledge, or (in stronger forms) even talking meaningfully, of a reality independent of human minds cognising it.

Rather than discuss the speculative realist critique of correlationism,[4] we concern ourselves here with very briefly

---

[4] For an explanation of how correlationism implodes from within, see Quentin Meillassoux, *After Finitude: An Essay on the Necessity of Contingency*, trans. Ray Brassier (London: Continuum, 2006) as well as Graham Priest, *Beyond the Limits of Thought* (Oxford: Oxford University Press, 2003). For an account of the history which had to be forgotten for correlationism to rise to the level of philosophical common sense, see Frederick Beiser, *The*

explaining how the position came to seem inevitable in continental philosophy.

First step. In *Heidegger Explained* Harman traces the genesis of contemporary continental philosophy to Heidegger's 1919 emergency war lectures, translated now as *Towards the Definition of Philosophy*.[5] At a crucial point in the first lecture series, Heidegger argues that even when we are presented with a completely novel object we never see it as mere object, but rather immediately perceive possible uses for it, even if we do not know the proper uses. Decades later Heidegger returned to this theme first in the lecture series that formed the rough draft of *Being and Time* (i.e. *History of the Concept of Time*), and then in *Being and Time* itself as the famed tool analysis.[6] On the standard reading of this,[7] Heidegger's main

---

Fate of Reason: German Philosophy from Kant to Fichte (Cambridge: Harvard University Press, 1993) and Frederick Beiser, *German Idealism: The Struggle Against Subjectivism, 1781-1801* (Cambridge: Harvard University Press, 2008). For an interpretation of Hegel understood correctly as both responding to the issues raised by Beiser and Priest and as (sadly, pace Beiser's own *Hegel*—see Frederick Beiser, *Hegel* (London: Routledge, 2005)) defending metaphysical positions still worth taking seriously, see Robert Stern, *Hegelian Metaphysics* (Oxford: Oxford University Press, 2009). In light of all this material, one can characterise speculative realism precisely in terms of two theses: (1) the "back to Kant" movements that birthed analytic and continental philosophy (Marburg and Southwest schools, respectively) resulted in the unwitting twentieth century triumph of academic Fichteanism, and (2) this is a bad thing. On Robert Brandom's Fichteanism, see Paul Franks, "From Quine to Hegel: Naturalism, Anti-Realism, and Maimon's Question *Quid Facti*" in *German Idealism: Contemporary Perspectives*, ed. Espen Hammer (London: Routledge, 2007), 50-69. For relevant material on Brandom and the *quid facti*, see Jon Cogburn, "Review of Robert Brandom's *Reason in Philosophy*," *The Journal of Value Inquiry* (2011), 45, 465-76, and Jon Cogburn, "Critical Notice of Robert Brandom's *Between Saying and Doing: Towards an Analytic Pragmatism*," *Philosophical Books* (2010), 51:3, 160-74.

⁵ Graham Harman, *Heidegger Explained* (Chicago: Open Court, 2007). Martin Heidegger, *Towards the Definition of Philosophy* (London: Continuum, 2008).

⁶ Martin Heidegger, *History of the Concept of Time: Prolegomena*, trans. Theodore Kisiel (Bloomington: Indiana University Press, 2009). Martin Heidegger, *Being and Time*, trans. Joan Stambaugh (Albany: State University of New York Press, 2010).

⁷ In Section III below, we discuss (and endorse!) Harman's critique of this traditional interpretation.

point is an anti-reductionist one. The world in which we find ourselves is first and foremost full of alethic and deontic modalities, that is, replete (respectively) with possibilities and permissibilities. And these permissibilities only make sense relative to a teleological realm ordered by a rich set of referential relations. The podium refers to the papers that one ought to set upon it. The papers refer to the audience to whom they ought to be read, etc. etc. For Heidegger, we never experience objects merely as bare objects, nor as bundles of static properties, but rather first and foremost in terms of these normative modes.[8]

Good enough thus far. But then the second step concerns how Heidegger uses this bit of phenomenology to critique the philosophical tradition. For the orthodox Heideggerian, the phenomenological primacy of proprieties (the relational, teleological realm of alethic and deontic modalities) shades into a critique of explanations that try to reduce such proprieties to a realm of "objectively present" (non-modal, non-teleological) things that just are what they are in themselves. Heidegger thus sought to set on its head the standard model of metaphysical or scientific reduction that would try to reduce the proprietary to a non-modal realm. Rather, Heidegger suggests in *Being and Time*, this actually works in reverse. Supposedly foundational ("originary") things such as Platonic forms or Aristotelian or Cartesian matter are actually themselves "founded," arrived at by a process of abstraction where we take everyday objects and try to intellectualise away from all of the modal, normative proprieties that relate them to their broader world.

---

[8] One might attribute this point to Kant originally, as it is one take on his quip that intuitions without concepts are blind. By attributing to Kant the view that concepts are first and foremost inferential proprieties, Jonathan Bennett, *Kant's Analytic* (Cambridge: Cambridge University Press, 1966) and Robert Brandom, *Reason in Philosophy: Animating Ideas* (Cambridge: Harvard University Press, 2009) both come close to doing so. However, Mark Okrent, "On Layer Cakes," http://www.bates.edu/philosophy/files/2010/07/onlayer.pdf (accessed January 8, 2013) shows that what is distinctive about Heidegger in this context is that the proprieties fundamentally concern the appropriateness of acting in certain ways, and that properly linguistic inferential propriety is founded on this.

Understanding speculative realism and object-oriented ontology requires grasping precisely how one can accept all of the above and still not fall prey to the correlationist equivocation of being with being for us. As Harman shows in *Tool-Being*, correlationism only follows from Heidegger's critique if one maintains a traditional conception of the way human and non-human reality is divided.[9] That is, correlationism only follows from Heidegger's critique if one thinks (on the one hand) that a non-human world would have to be something like that described in Descartes' metaphysical physics, and (on the other hand) that the modal and valuative dimension of reality must be a function of the human mind. It is only then that the idea that Cartesian objects are metaphysically founded on a more originary modal world would entail that we can have no concept of a human-independent reality. Paradoxically then, the supposed correlationist overcoming of the Cartesian distinction between mind and reality only gets off the ground if one maintains a naïve (Cartesian!) view of that very distinction.[10] If anything is constitutive of speculative realism it is a willingness to actually take the anti-Cartesian journey suggested by Heidegger, but upon which he never really managed to himself embark.

---

[9] Graham Harman, *Tool-Being: Heidegger and the Metaphysics of Objects* (Chicago: Open Court, 2002).

[10] Again, we see speculative realism overcoming the Fichtean consensus: (1) one of the many ways in which correlationism required forgetting the lessons of the period between Kant and Hegel involves the forgetting of Schelling's *Naturphilosophie*, which can be understood as reacting to precisely this dialectic. See Iain Hamilton Grant, *Philosophies of Nature after Schelling* (London: Bloomsbury Academic, 2008). (2) The anti-correlationist must also respond to the Berkeley-Fichte conceivability argument (first articulated in George Berkeley, *Three Dialogues Between Hylas and Philanous* (New York: Penguin Classics, 1988)) to the conclusion that to be is to be conceived. Reactions vary on this score, Meillassoux and Priest (op. cit.) take the argument to be valid, yet to paradoxically explode, since the person making it must transcend the very limits of conceivability entailed by the argument. Whereas Graham Harman, in *Quentin Meillassoux: Philosophy in the Making* (Edinburgh: University of Edinburgh Press, 2011), and Jon Cogburn, in "Moore's Paradox as an Argument Against Anti-Realism" in *The Realism-Antirealism Debate in the Age of Alternative Logic*, ed. Shahid Rahman, Giuseppe Primiero, and Mathieu Marion (Heidelberg: Springer, 2011) take the argument to be simply invalid.

But it is not enough to just refuse to take this third step in the Heideggerian route to correlationism; speculative realism is speculative precisely because all of the philosophers involved have taken up the task of articulating accounts of reality at variance with the correlationist's Cartesian account of mind and world.

II. Object-Oriented Ontology

Object-oriented ontologists such as Ian Bogost, Levi Bryant, Graham Harman, Tristan Garcia, Timothy Morton, and the authors of this paper get properly underway via another layer of critique, which can be seen as complementary to the Heideggerian phenomenological critique of objective presence. Heidegger's initial critique naturally lends itself to the critique of attempts to reduce or explain away various aspects of human reality such as art, mind, language, and morality in terms of a supposedly more fundamental realm of objectively present objects. Harman calls such reductive explanatory strategies "undermining," and notes that they all involve a philosophical degradation of objects.[11]

> The first critical response to objects asserts that they are not funda-
> mental. All of the dogs, candles, and snowflakes we observe are built
> of something more basic, and this deeper reality is the proper subject
> matter for philosophy. As the surf pounded the shores of Anatolia,
> Thales proposed water as the first principle of everything. Later came
> Anaximenes, for whom air rather than water was the root of the world.
> It is slightly more complicated with Empedocles, for whom things are
> composed not of one but of four separate elements: air, earth, fire, and
> water, joined and divorced through the forces of love and hate. And

---

[11] See the discussion of undermining and overmining in Graham Harman, *The Quadruple Object* (Washington: Zero Books, 2011), the meditation on reductionism throughout Graham Harman, *Prince of Networks: Bruno Latour and Metaphysics* (Melbourne: Re.press, 2009), as well as the discussion of "more than things" and "less than things" in Tristan Garcia, *Form and Object: A Treatise on Things*, trans. Mark Allan Ohm and Jon Cogburn (Edinburgh: Edinburgh University Press, 2014).

finally with Democritus, atoms of different shapes and sizes serve as the root element of all larger things. In present-day materialism one speaks instead of quarks or infinitesimal strings. In all such cases, the critical method is the same: what seems at first like an autonomous object is really just a motley aggregate built of smaller pieces. Only what is basic can be real.[12]

Rejecting the explanatory presumption of undermining is old hat to many philosophers working in both continental and analytic anti-reductionist traditions, and is part of traditional phenomenology preserved by most speculative realists.

Object-oriented ontologists are distinct in endorsing a parallel critique of what Harman calls "overmining," which Harman and Garcia take to be the mirror image of undermining. Here is Harman again:

A different way of dismissing objects as the chief *dramatis personae* of philosophy is to reduce them upward rather than downward. Instead of saying that objects are too shallow to be real, it is said that they are too deep. On this view the object is a useless hypothesis, a *je ne sais quoi* in the bad sense. Rather than being undermined from beneath, the object is overmined from above. On this view, objects are important only insofar as they are manifested to the mind, or are part of some concrete event that affects other objects as well.[13]

If the pre-Socratics are the patron saints of undermining, then the British Empiricists, with their attempt to see objects as mere bundles of perceptible properties, are the patron saints of overmining. Much contemporary continental philosophy can only be seen as heir of this tradition, as overmining occurs whenever the nineteenth century "hermeneutics of suspicion" (e.g. Nietzsche, Marx, Freud) are married to phenomenology[14] in attempts to explain aspects of non-human

---

[12] Harman, *The Quadruple Object*, 8.

[13] Ibid., 10-11.

[14] Given the level of caricature, it pains us to admit this, but Luc Ferry and Alain Renaut, *French Philosophy of the Sixties: An Essay on Antihumanism*, trans.

reality such as atoms, quarks, numbers, and divinities in terms of relational networks such as discursive practices, social norms, class struggles, Freudian mechanisms, power, phallo-logocentrism, etc. etc. etc. Thus, object-oriented ontology is a natural outgrowth of the speculative realist critique of correlationism. Overmining explanations are almost always instances of correlationism in action, tying the very being of some putatively non-human phenomenon to provincial human practices.

Let us be absolutely clear here. The object-oriented ontologist is *not* urging people to stop providing undermining and overmining explanations. Nor is she saying that such explanations never yield important truths about objects. Successful undermining explanations tell us about the behaviour of objects' constituents and how these relate to the behaviour of the object. Successful overmining explanations tell us much about how objects relate to other objects, including human ones. The epistemic project of object-oriented ontology concerns how and when such explanations are successful, and when they wrongly shade into reductionism. The militant anti-reductionism of the object-oriented ontologists is not merely epistemic though. The metaphysical task is to characterise objects such that it is a part of their being to resist complete characterisation by undermining and overmining.

<hr>

Mary H. S. Cattani (Amherst: University of Massachusetts Press, 1990) had a point. It is impossible to really understand the *soixante-huitard* philosophers unless you at least initially apply the formula "= (late Heidegger + some combination of Nietzsche, Freud, and Marx)."

III. Three Ontologies[15]

Harman's "A Fresh Look at *Zuhandenheit*," republished in *Towards Speculative Realism*, can be seen as the first cast of the die that would lead to the object-oriented wing of speculative realism.[16] The main idea, developed at length in *Tool-Being*, is that the standard account of Heidegger's tool analysis (presented in Section I above) contains two related mistakes. While explaining how speculative realism rose out of the ashes of phenomenology we touched on the first mistake. This was the Cartesian error of seeing the valuative, modal,

---

[15] Ontologies do not *really* individuate well enough to be so cleanly counted. In particular, we consider here neither Adrian Johnston's recent speculative labours in the service of a new materialism (the view is still being developed, though see footnote 23 for citations to important work), nor the Simondonian/Deleuzian metaphysical tradition. The latter *clearly* overlaps with various currents of object-oriented philosophy in essential ways: (1) the Simondonian/Deleuzian distinction between non-individuated/virtual and individuated/actual is replicated in the capacity metaphysics approach to object-oriented philosophy, (2) John Protevi's Deleuzian explanatory mode of getting "above and below the subject" (and the object!) in Chapters I and II of *Political Affect* (Minneapolis: University of Minnesota Press, 2009) has resonances with Garcia's differential model of objects, (3) a possible regress facing Simondon and Deleuze about the role of the seed/singularity with respect to individuation has similarities with a general issue about causation raised by Harman (albeit, biting the bullet with respect to the regress would arguably involve rejecting process ontology, and hence rejecting a central part of the Simondon/Deleuze project). For a preliminary discussion of this latter point, tying it to Harman's work, see Jon Cogburn, "Review of *Gilbert Simondon: Being and Technology*, by Arne De Boever, Alex Murray, Jon Roffe, and Ashley Woodward, eds. (Edinburgh: Edinburgh University Press, 2012)," *Notre Dame Philosophical Reviews*, (2014), 07/28, n.pag., as well as Jon Cogburn and Graham Bounds, "Vicarious Causation as Generalized Affection," in preparation. For a sustained discussion of Harman's philosophy in light of Simondon's, see Miguel Penas López's essay in this volume.

[16] Dialectical and temporal progress sometimes diverge. Note that Harman's "A Fresh Look at *Zuhandenheit*" was written in 1999 while speculative realism did not exist until 2007! Still, the authors of this paper are not alone in having been first moved by the fervour around Meillassoux's critique of correlationism and then experiencing Harman's radical reading of Heidegger as the decisive next step. Graham Harman, "A Fresh Look at *Zuhandenheit*" in *Towards Speculative Realism: Essays and Lectures* (Washington: Zero Books, 2010), 44–66.

relational world as somehow constituted by human beings. Harman shows how, in the context of Heidegger scholarship, this has often been articulated by taking Heidegger's pragmatist anti-representationalism as exhausting the entirety of the tool analysis.

For Heidegger, humans have a prelinguistic[17] understanding of the valuative, modal, and relational properties of objects which is actually grounded in our ability to appreciate the appropriate and inappropriate uses of objects. Then, for the Heideggerian philosopher of mind and language, linguistic and conceptual understanding is parasitic on this prior understanding. This is a radical inversion of the Cartesian, representationalist philosophy of mind, and has deep and complicated ties to the sense in which objective presence is understood privatively by Heidegger.

The tendency then, among many Heidegger scholars, is to take this pragmatist philosophy of mind not to be a consequence of the tool analysis, but rather to exhaust the entirety of the tool analysis.[18] Here *Zuhandenheit*, or "readiness to

---

[17] Far, far too many commentators (paradigmatically Robert Brandom, *Tales of the Mighty Dead: Historical Essays in the Metaphysics of Intentionality* (Cambridge: Harvard University Press, 2002)), try to foist an even more radical Cartesianism on Heidegger by claiming that for Heidegger understanding cannot be prelinguistic. This is a non-starter though. It is uncharitable both since the view itself is so implausible and because it only works as Heidegger exegesis via misunderstanding the German word *"Rede."* See Okrent, "On Layer Cakes" for a definitive rebuttal on both counts.

[18] Strangely, even though their interpretations contradict, we think that Mark Okrent, *Heidegger's Pragmatism* (Ithaca: Cornell University Press, 1991) has equal validity as a useful interpretation of Heidegger as does Harman's account. It seems overwhelmingly clear to us (as it does to Herman Philipse, *Heidegger's Philosophy of Being: A Critical Interpretation* (Princeton: Princeton University Press, 1998)) that Heidegger contradicts himself over and over again on these very issues, and (here we depart from Philipse) that Okrent and Harman present the two most philosophically fruitful consistifications of Heidegger's *oeuvre*. The most plausible and interesting Heidegger that experienced a great turn in thought is Okrent's. The most plausible Heidegger that articulates one great idea is Harman's. Though Okrent's Heidegger is indispensable for the philosophy of mind, at the end of the day we do agree with Harman that the pragmatism must be seen as one instance of a broader metaphysical reality.

hand," simply is the modal serviceability of objects in the world for human manipulation and *Vorhandenheit*, "objective presence," is the function of humans' thinking of such objects as abstracted from their serviceability.

Harman examines the notion of privativity in Heidegger and argues that the pragmatist analysis is radically incomplete. First, the pragmatist reading ignores the fact that human practical engagement with the world is equally privative! When I pre-linguistically understand the Tupperware container in terms of the uses to which it should be put, I am equally abstracting away from all sorts of properties of the container. Harman shows that Heidegger's discussion of "withdrawal" applies both to the way (some) practical, modal properties disappear when we intellectualise *and* to the properties that disappear when we take something as something via practical comportment.

Harman's second point, the genesis of his speculative realist break from correlationist anthropocentrism, is that there is nothing unique about human beings in this regard. Just as another human might isolate a distinct set of properties of the container from those that become manifest when I interact with it, so too would a dog, match, ray of light, and neutrino. For all of these things too, the container presents a different face, actualising different properties as others withdraw.

The key point here is that Harman is not trying to undermine Heideggerian theories of perception and understanding. His point is that the *Zuhandenheit/Vorhandenheit* reversal is not merely a model of understanding, but a model of the interaction of any two objects. In this manner one can (and should) be a non-correlationist phenomenologist.[19]

---

[19] Just as correlationism only arose by forgetting the proper lessons of post-Fichtean German Idealism, contemporary phenomenology only came to mirror logical positivism's anti-metaphysical stance by forgetting the tradition of Austrian phenomenology. For a discussion, see Raphaël Millière, "Metaphysics Today and Tomorrow," trans. Mark Allan Ohm, Workshop on Contemporary Metaphysics and Ontology at the École Normale Supérieure, http://atmoc. files.wordpress.com/2012/06/milliere_metaphysics_today_and_tomorrow1. pdf (accessed January 8, 2013).

Speculations V

Harman's guerrilla reading of Heidegger naturally suggests a picture of objects in themselves as capacities (in *The
Democracy of Objects*, called by Levi Bryant "virtual proper
beings") that are actualised in causal engagement with other
objects.[20] Undermining and overmining are avoided by giving a non-reductionist account of "ontological emergence,"
as Cogburn and Silcox do in "The Emergence of Emergence:
Computability and Ontology."[21] Cogburn and Silcox characterise genuinely ontological emergence as happening when
there is no algorithm for detecting instances of the properties that emerge upon an object's interactions with others.[22]

Though capacity metaphysics[23] versions of object-oriented
ontology were developed in reaction to his insights into Heidegger and Bruno Latour, it is clear from Harman's recent
work that he himself would reject the views of Bryant, Cogburn,
and Silcox. In 2005's *Guerrilla Metaphysics* and elsewhere[24]

[20] Levi Bryant, *The Democracy of Objects* (Ann Arbor: Open Humanities
Press, 2011).

[21] Jon Cogburn and Mark Silcox, "The Emergence of Emergence: Computability and Ontology," *American Philosophical Quarterly* (2011), 48:1, 63–74.

[22] Though the theory presented in "The Emergence of Emergence: Computability Theory and Ontology" is motivated by Harman's *Tool-Being*, it is built
on some of Cogburn and Silcox's earlier work. See Jon Cogburn and Mark
Silcox, "Computing Machinery and Emergence," *Minds and Machines* (2005),
15:1, 73–89, and Jon Cogburn and Mark Silcox, "Computability Theory and
Literary Competence," *The British Journal of Aesthetics* (2006), 46:5, 369–86.

[23] Just as we have recruited Graham Priest as a possibly unwilling speculative
realist, we should note that Nancy Cartwright, *Nature's Capacities and their
Measurements* (Oxford: Oxford University Press, 1994) should henceforth
be taken as a key departure point for the capacity metaphysics approach to
object-oriented ontology. In particular, those who wish to defend the approach
from a Harmanian or Garcian critique will need to avail themselves of the
debates surrounding Cartwright's justly canonical text. We are encouraged and
excited by Adrian Johnston's recent interventions with respect to Cartwright.
See Adrian Johnston, "Second Natures in Dappled Worlds: John McDowell,
Nancy Cartwright, and Hegelian-Lacanian Materialism," *Umbr(a): A Journal
of the Unconscious* (2011), 71–91, and Adrian Johnston, "Points of Forced Freedom: Eleven (More) Theses on Materialism," *Speculations* (2013), 4, 91–98.

[24] Graham Harman, *Guerrilla Metaphysics: Phenomenology and the Carpentry of
Things* (Chicago: Open Court, 2005). See also especially essays eight and nine
from *Towards Speculative Realism*, as well as the entirety of *The Quadruple Object*.

Harman presents a novel reading of Edmund Husserl just as significant as his earlier take on Heidegger. Harman begins with Husserl's insight that we do not perceive objects as mere bundles of qualities. Then, analogously to his externalisation of Heidegger, Harman goes on to argue that objects themselves are not mere bundles of qualities for each other. And for Harman these sensual objects are not something that is created merely when humans and the world interact, but when any two real objects interact. Put together with his account of Heidegger, this yields Harman's fourfold ontology, where things split across two axes into real and sensual objects and real and sensual properties.[25]

So, minimally, Harman would hold that capacity metaphysics neglects the impact that Husserl's insight has for anti-correlationists. But, in addition, Harman would likely see such approaches as instances of undermining and overmining,[26]

---

[25] This is a little misleading, as Harman's sensual objects do a great deal of work with respect to the vicarious causation problematic, and this is independent of his reading of Husserl. See Jon Cogburn and Graham Bounds, "Vicarious Causation as Generalized Affection," which understands Harman's relation to the "affection argument" (with scheme-content problems one of the two engines of German Idealism) analogously to his relation with Heidegger. For Harman, an affection problem arises whenever any two objects interact, and the regress of sensual objects is the solution to this problem. So a real theoretical virtue of sensual objects is that they both answer to Husserl's worry and the generalised affection argument.

[26] This is clear from Harman's discussion of Garcia in Graham Harman, "Object-Oriented France: The Philosophy of Tristan Garcia," *continent.* (2012), 2:1, 6–21. We should note that we find this criticism to be *prima facie* compelling, and hope that it does not undermine the aspects of capacity metaphysics that we use throughout this paper (our picture of a text as an engine that creates interpretation is clearly to interpret texts as capacities). We think that the basic picture does not fall prey to Harman's critique because we have attempted to state it in a way consistent with the regressive model of causality bruited in footnote 15. To be clear though, we are not certain exactly how this all will ultimately pan out. In addition, we still have reservations about Harman's full four-fold metaphysics. One could interpret Husserl as just arguing that one directly perceives an object's *individuality*, understood as a property of the object, not a new kind of object to be distinguished from the real one. Of course if trope theory is the correct metaphysics, then the property instance ("abstract particular") might be an object of sorts, but again the object's individuality would be no different from its colour or mass in

since the virtual proper being of an object is still determined by its capacity to actualise in different ways in response to different objects. Consider his analogous comments on materialism.

> [According to the materialist, the] tiny bulk of the atom may be viewed as a substrate for unifying all of its qualities, but this very substrate is taken to be nothing more than a certain set of palpable qualities such as hardness and resistance. In other words, there is no need to regard the atom as an object at all … In this way, materialism both undermines *and* overmines objects by treating them as ultimate elements that are actually nothing but sets of qualities.[27]

One could, even without appeal to Harman's reading of Husserl, make exactly this comment with respect to capacity metaphysics generally.

Very recently, in *Form and Object*, Tristan Garcia has presented a radically novel third approach to object-oriented ontology, one which, pace Harman, actually *defines* the objectivity of an object in terms of its active resistance to undermining and overmining. For Garcia an object just is the difference between that which composes that object and that which the object composes (including relations into which the object enters).[28]

These three approaches (Bryant, Cogburn, and Silcox's capacity metaphysics, Harman's fourfold, and Garcia's differential model) are all instances of what might be called pure ontology, in that they characterise the properties of any object whatsoever. But they readily lend themselves to regional

---

this respect. This being said, it is not clear to us if abstract particulars (or the property of individuality more abstractly conceived) will do the work of solving the problem of vicarious causation.

[27] Harman, *The Quadruple Object*, 14, original emphasis.

[28] For Garcia's own take on his divergences from Harman, see Tristan Garcia, "Crossing Ways of Thinking: On Graham Harman's System and My Own," trans. Mark Allan Ohm, *Parrhesia* (2013), 16, 14–25, and Harman's response: Graham Harman, "Tristan Garcia and the Thing-in-itself," *Parrhesia* (2013), 16, 26–34.

ontology, where specific kinds of objects are characterised in terms of how the properties of the pure ontology are manifested and affected by the kinds in question.[29] After adding the category of intensity to his initial differential model, in Book II of *Form and Object*, Garcia provides uniformly illuminating regional ontologies of over a dozen such things, including time, art, value, adolescence, and death. Cogburn and Silcox actually developed their view while working on the ontologies of games. In works such as *Alien Phenomenology, Or What it is Like to be a Thing* Ian Bogost has built on his expertise with video games to develop a much finer grained regional ontology.[30] Timothy Morton has done likewise with respect to the ontology of the environment in works such as *Realist Magic*.[31]

The fecundity of object-oriented ontology for regional ontology is why there have been as of this writing dozens of conferences and meetings devoted to a wide panoply of applications, including architecture, visual arts, communication studies, technology studies, and environmental studies. All such investigations explore what a given kind of object must be like given that objects in general are as articulated by object-oriented ontology. Indeed, such is the task of this paper with respect to texts.

Some of the initial ideas concerning texts as engines to generate thought experiments were presented by Cogburn and Silcox in the paper "Against Brain-in-a-Vatism."[32] While this

---

[29] There is actually an important philosophical point here. For the object-oriented ontologist, the pure ontology cannot itself overmine. As a result, regional ontology will always have a kind of autonomy.

[30] Ian Bogost, *Alien Phenomenology, Or What It Is Like to Be a Thing* (Minneapolis: University of Minnesota Press, 2012).

[31] Timothy Morton, *Realist Magic: Objects, Ontology, Causality* (Ann Arbor: Open Humanities Press, 2013). Our impression is that we owe to Morton the insight that for object-oriented ontologists all objects are both aesthetic and interpreters (a view we characterise in Section VI below), but this impression comes merely from reading various internet blogs, so we are not at all certain that it is correct.

[32] Jon Cogburn and Mark Silcox, "Against Brain-in-a-Vatism: On the Value of Virtual Reality," *Philosophy & Technology* (November 2013), n.pag.

was in context of their broader project of thinking through a capacity metaphysics with respect to games, we do not think that the theory is committed to the aspects of that view that Harman would find problematic. Moreover, the fact that we are now able to directly motivate the view in terms of how textual objects actively resist their own undermining and overmining strongly suggests a provisional affinity with Garcia's metaphysics. We should note here that although we do not discuss in this paper the extent to which the mechanics of Harman's fourfold are needed for a full account of the textuality of a text, such a discussion (as well as engagement with Garcia's own writings about art and representation) will prove fruitful for the further articulation of an object-oriented literary theory.

IV. Text as Object

Until very recently nearly every literature major in the United States was subjected to a "theory" class where students worked through a text such as Terry Eagleton's *Literary Theory: An Introduction*.[33] Assignments invariably involved writing different interpretations of random texts according to whatever hermeneutic of suspicion was being covered at the time: Freudianism, Marxism, Structuralism, Deconstructionism, etc. Now that "theory's empire" has begun a period of decline in literary study, the benefit of hindsight reveals what was lost during its ascent.

Simply put, such approaches systematically robbed their practitioners of the ability to say anything illuminating about specific texts. This is because the central idea of theory was to mine the hermeneutics of suspicion so as to give critics general procedures to unmask "what is really going on" in any given text. But when applied to works of art the effect is too often that of wearing blue tinted glasses and then saying that everything is blue, or evidence of class struggle, the will

---

[33] Terry Eagleton, *Literary Theory: An Introduction*, Anniversary Edition (Minneapolis: University of Minnesota Press, 2008).

to power, castration anxiety, the failure of the metaphysics of presence, phallo-logocentrism, etc. etc. etc. And what really happened is that one too often either cherry picked works that could easily be read in terms of one's hermeneutics, or one ignored everything about a work that did not validate the story. The end result is that there are no longer any textual objects, but rather just an encompassing inter-textuality equally present in Dr. Seuss and the Constitution of the United States. In the wake of such depredations, theory has largely been abandoned altogether, and textual objects are now usually reduced to their relative historical, cultural, sociological, empirical contexts, conditions of production, reception, or the correlation between the biography of the author and text à la Sainte-Beuve.

Again, there is nothing wrong with interpreting a literary text using one's favourite hermeneutics of suspicion or (post-theoretical) social science. What is wrong is identifying texts as mere vehicles for such a priori application of theory and social science. With all we have said above, it should be clear that this is the very pinnacle of overmining, and that there is a very clear sense in which the autonomy of the textual object has been attacked. When texts are overmined nothing can be learned from them, since the philosophy undergirding the critical method always already provides all of the answers. And perhaps the very pinnacle of perversity in this regard is Stanley Fish's "reader response criticism," which is the apotheosis of theory obliterating practice. If, as Fish claims, the individual artworks themselves have no meaning whatsoever, then there is no hope of anyone learning deep truths articulated in the artworks. Never in the history of thought has necessity so shamelessly been trumpeted as virtue.[34]

---

[34] For an account of what is right about Fish, see the discussion in Cogburn and Silcox, "Computability Theory and Literary Competence." We should probably also mention "post-modern" literary criticism of the type associated with John Fiske. For a proper excoriation of this tendency as well as the Frankfurt School type Marxist approaches that Fiske was attacking, see Noël Carroll, *A Philosophy of Mass Art* (Oxford: Oxford University Press, 2008). Carroll shows that both approaches uncritically rely on a very implausible neo-Kantian account of judgments of taste.

Speculations V

Contrast Fish's nihilism with the traditional view, coming out of nineteenth century literary realism (and naturalism), that texts (even fictional ones) represent the actual world. Whatever its other problems, this view respects the autonomy of the text at least in the sense that it respects the fact that part of why we study texts, *even fictional ones*, is to learn about the actual world. Though we do not seek to revive literary realism (or naturalism), it will be clear from what we go on to say that we do think that this is the most important test case for a hermeneutics that avoids overmining and undermining. Can one's hermeneutics make sense of the actual truth of fictional texts?

Given the discussion in the recent anthology *Theory's Empire*, one would expect to be able to appeal to the analytic philosophy of art for some kind of material support in the war against overmining, but this is certainly not so with respect to our desiderata of understanding truth in fiction.[35] That is, contemporary analytic philosophy of fiction, which (if taken to exhaust what one might say about texts) overmines just as badly as does traditional theory and contemporary post-theoretic historicism.

Prior to the mid-seventies the issue of truth from fiction was a going concern, with giants such as Monroe Beardsley and Morris Weitz proposing mechanisms by which one could infer actual truths from fictional texts. However, after Mary Sirridge critiqued these views in her canonical article "Truth from Fiction?" the issue disappeared.[36] Indeed, Sirridge's arguments make it very doubtful that use of linguistic-turn standbys such as entailment, presupposition, and meta-languages could be of even minimal help in elucidating the way a good reader might infer actual truths from fictional texts.

Since Sirridge's paper, analytic philosophers have followed continental hermeneuts of suspicion and largely given up on

---

[35] Daphne Patai and Will H. Corral, eds., *Theory's Empire: An Anthology of Dissent* (New York: Columbia University Press, 2005).

[36] Mary Sirridge, "Truth from Fiction?," *Philosophy and Phenomenological Research* (1975), 35:4, 453-71.

198

the task of understanding truth in fiction, instead focusing on three main issues: (1) discerning a semantics for fiction that might aid metaphysical programs that take certain putatively non-fictional objects (e.g. numbers) to be ficta,[37] (2) trying to understand the extent to which we are irrational when reacting emotionally to fiction,[38] and (3) trying to discern the extent to which moral properties of artworks are relevant to their aesthetic properties.[39] These are important tasks. But for our purposes what is interesting is that, as with theory's empire, one can read thousands of pages about these debates and have no idea that actual truth in fiction ever even existed as a philosophical concern.

It is clear that a text is overmined in all three cases: (1) when (with continental aestheticians) one simply interprets it according to a priori hermeneutic principles, (2) (with post-theory historicists) one is only concerned with facets of the text's historico-cultural milieu, and (3) (with analytic aestheticians) when one only examines texts to the extent that they provide test cases for broader philosophical debates such as the three from the previous paragraph.

Undermining is a bit more complicated on this score. For nobody, as far as we know, thinks that textual meaning can be derived from the *material* composition of the texts. But then what would it be to undermine a text? In this regard, it is important to realise that undermining can happen whenever putatively intrinsic properties are put forward as providing a total explanation of an object. From this perspective we take it that the relevant textual properties are the representational ones. This is a bit confusing because representation is a relation between a medium and the represented world. However,

---

[37] For a great overview of how extant theories of fiction contribute to metaphysical debates about fictionalism, see Joseph Dartez, *Ficta as Mentalia: Surveying Theories of Fiction in Search of Plausible Ontology* (Louisiana State University Electronic Thesis & Dissertation Collection, 2009).

[38] See Eva Dadlez, *What's Hecuba to Him: Fictional Events and Actual Emotions* (University Park: Pennsylvania State University Press, 1997).

[39] For the most recent word on these debates, see Berys Gaut, *Art, Emotion, and Ethics* (Oxford: Oxford University Press, 2009).

this worry disappears once one realises that what the text represents in some sense depends solely upon the text, and is thus intrinsic. What is non-intrinsic then is whether the text's representation successfully represents the actual world. Thus, the canonical undermining strategy with regard to a text is the view that all of the modal and valuative properties of the text can be derived from its representational purport. In analytical philosophy one might understand this purport along the lines of David Lewis, as the set of possible worlds where the text is true.[40] This is approximately fine as far as it goes.[41] The problem occurs if one thinks that such representational properties are, to use the Heideggerian term, "originary."

Two immediate problems. First, as Graham Priest convincingly both argues and shows in *Towards Non-Being: The Logic and Metaphysics of Intentionality*, fiction does not just represent non-actual but possible entities, but also impossible entities.[42] Thus, the representational purport of a text cannot be identified with a set of *possible* worlds. Second, texts do not just represent what is the case, but give us guidance concerning what ought to be the case. Unless one can explicate the normative facts being represented, it is not clear how one could derive such

[40] David Lewis, "Truth in Fiction," *American Philosophical Quarterly* (1978), 15:1, 37–46.

[41] See Ruth Ronen, *Possible Worlds in Literary Theory* (Cambridge: Cambridge University Press, 1994) for a wonderful application of Lewis's ideas to literary theory. We should note here that Lewis's own view is slightly more complicated than what we have presented above, as for Lewis the story has to also be told as true in the worlds in question. This actually causes serious problems in determining what the proper set of possible worlds is for a work where the proper understanding of the text requires recognising distance between author and narrator.

[42] Graham Priest, *Towards Non-Being: The Logic and Metaphysics of Intentionality* (Oxford: Oxford University Press, 2007). In the appendix to Chapter 6, "Sylvan's Box," Priest actually tells a story that contains a metaphysical impossibility. It is important to realise that such worries are in no way "non-mimetic," as they represent impossible states of affairs. One should note that Priest also argues that certain true contradictions are not just possible, but actual. In *Beyond the Limits of Thought*, some of these concern the limits of representation. Such cases are also clearly mimetic though, when one paradoxically represents the non-representable, one is still successfully representing.

instructions from the mere set of possible worlds consistent with the factual propositions of the text.

The deepest problem for textual undermining is in fact the one articulated by Heidegger. Representation itself is not originary, but is rather founded upon a complex set of modal and normative phenomena. In his essay on truth, reprinted in *Basic Writings*, Heidegger considers the face on a given unit of currency.[43] With such cases humans naturally possess the ability to recognise that the face represents a real human. This is fine as far as it goes, but the mistake happens when this naturalness leads us to treat representation as an ultimate explainer of normative phenomena such as truth. Again, it is fine to say with the representationalist that P is true just in case the state of affairs that P represents is actual. But Heidegger notes that then knowing that P is true will require knowing both what state of affairs P represents and knowing that this state of affairs is actual. But then the ability to determine that states of affairs are actual is in some sense prior to the ability to know that a sentence is true. This prior ability is what Heidegger tries to articulate with his theory of truth as unconcealedness.

Let us return to the representational purport of individual words. Knowing what "money" represents requires knowing the representation of "money," which requires being conversant with the proprieties regarding how money ought to be treated. So the meaning of "money" cannot be like pieces of string connecting the representation to all of the bits of money in the world, or even *all possible worlds*. Instead, we only have a word for "money" because money already has normative force in the actual world. We are only able to use the word "money" correctly because of our sensitivity to this normative force.[44]

---

[43] Martin Heidegger, *Basic Writings*, ed. David Farrell Krell (New York: Harper Perennial, 2008).

[44] We should note that the application of this key Heideggerian insight to representational accounts of mind and language was independently made by Ludwig Wittgenstein, *The Brown and Blue Books* (Mineola: Dover Books, 1965) and Wilfrid Sellars, *Empiricism and the Philosophy of Mind* (Cambridge:

This is not a mere terminological quibble! The ideologies that support textual undermining have real world consequences, perhaps most notably with respect to legal reasoning and our approach to religious texts. For the former, note that constitutional originalists absurdly hold that the representational purport of a document written hundreds of years ago could be sufficient to adjudicate issues such as how powerful a weapon individuals should be able to purchase or what kinds of software innovations are copyrightable. Taking representation to be originary is almost always a necessary step in not realising the sense in which textual meaning is often underdetermined.[45] Contrariwise, once one realises that representation itself is founded on a background of modal proprieties, one realises that normative reality can change (minimally in the sense that radically novel kinds of objects such as video games bring new norms with them) and that as a result representational purport will not always clearly apply in novel situations.

The textual underminer is probably best represented in our culture by the biblical literalist, who is most concerned with claiming that the actual world is a member of the set of possible worlds consistent with the Bible. This is unfortunate for all sorts of reasons, mostly because biblical literalism brings with it so many other pernicious beliefs and actions. Consider literalist's beliefs with respect to the text itself. Biblical literalists typically believe that the Bible is consistent and that Moses wrote the Pentateuch and Jesus's disciples wrote the gospels. Or consider historical beliefs unrelated to the composition of the text, such as the belief that in the early Roman Empire people had to travel to areas where they did not work in order to register for a tax census. Or consider false, legalistic approaches to morality of the very type condemned by Jesus and Saint Paul. If one thinks of the Bible as a list of propositions that simply mirror the facts that make

Harvard University Press, 1997).

[45] On this point, see Mark Wilson, "Predicate Meets Property," *The Philosophical Review* (1982), 91:4, 549–89.

them true, then one is much more likely to think of moral reality as representable by such a finite set of propositions.

The moral rot of textual undermining is actually an instance of a broader spiritual psychosis. The problem is that representations are accorded magical powers. But then believers accord magical powers to their own representations of reality. Massive weirdness results, for example people who think that the primary spiritual fact about humans is whether or not they accept a history of the world that includes the resurrection. This makes no sense; it is as if the state of one's soul depended upon whether one believes that the Gettysburg Address was delivered on a Thursday.

V. Truth in Fiction

The object-oriented ontologist is correct, and we desperately need an understanding of what texts must be like such that they resist their own undermining and overmining. Since texts are linguistic, they are clearly representational. But they are more than that. They do not just tell us what reality is like; they give us guidance. And (as we will argue) sometimes in order to guide us to a truer conception of reality the texts must misrepresent that very reality. Likewise, since texts are socio-cultural entities, they are clearly interpretable by hermeneutic strategies devised by humans. But again, they are more than that, for there are surprises in individual texts either at variance with or simply not covered by hermeneutic strategies.

If one had a good theory of the actual truth of fictional texts, then one could easily thread the Scylla and Charybdis of undermining and overmining. For since the work is fictional, its truth cannot be explained by the actual world being an element of the set of possible worlds determined by its representational purport. Since the work is true, it cannot be explained away as mere symptom of class struggle, castration anxiety, the metaphysics of presence (or the overcoming thereof), power, etc.

Speculations V

Breaking from the representationalist paradigm requires taking care in exactly how the problem of truth is formulated. First, we should not define truth *tout court*, because the end result of this would probably be just that the vast majority of (if not all) texts end up being simply false. Instead we will define the extent to which a text is true. Moreover, we must define this with respect to some subject matter. For example, a science fiction novel can be very true psychologically while being nonsense with respect to the laws of physics, or (as was often the case in bad 1950s science fiction) the reverse. Second, we should not (as Cogburn and Silcox do in "Against Brain-in-a-Vatism") define the truth of a text in overly representational terms. It should be *a consequence of* our definition that someone reading a true text will end up having more of the relevant kinds of linguistically assertible true beliefs. Posing the definition in terms of true beliefs would both fail to capture key ways that texts can be true, but also draw us back into a pre-Heideggerian naivety where representational media are treated as originary. So with these caveats we put forward the following:

> X is true (false) with respect to subject area Y to the extent that imaginatively complicit readers of X will,
> all else being equal and as a result of reading X,
> better (worse) partake in reality normative with respect to Y.

This is a mouthful. What might it mean to say that a novel is psychologically true to the extent that all else being equal one who reads it better partakes in reality normative with respect to psychology? To partake well in psychological normative reality is to be more likely to do the things involving psychological reality that one ought to do. So a novel is psychologically true to the extent that, all else being equal, reading it helps one develop virtue with respect to the things that psychology attempts to treat.[46]

46 Clinical psychology in general makes a hash of this, as it misconstrues the normative nature of things like "mental health." When psychologists address this issue they tend to (as in the new DSM) equate mental health

And "having true beliefs" is, albeit important, just one such virtue. Thus, while we agree with Mary Sirridge that people imaginatively complicit in *The Scarlet Letter* are more likely to arrive at the ethical and psychological insight that "unacknowledged guilt leads to perdition, whereas expiated guilt leads to salvation," we also think that the book helps a sympathetic reader's general pre-linguistic attunement to ethical reality.[47] Being non-judgmental goes far, far beyond what kind of sentences one is likely to utter and extends into every facet of one's behaviour towards others. The properly complicit reader of *The Scarlet Letter* is better attuned to reality normative with respect to how we treat people.

Now to illustrate actual falsity of fictional texts, let us consider Ayn Rand's *Atlas Shrugged*. The book is false with respect to economics, because it can only overcome a reader's imaginative resistance if she accepts that all of a modern, industrialised society's large scale infrastructure could be privately financed.

The false beliefs are not limited to possible worlds! Rand's fictional character Nathaniel Taggart is based on the actual James J. Hill, who ran the Great Northern Railway. As a result of this, fans make much of the fact that (in common with Taggart's fictional company) the Great Northern was supposedly privately financed and did not receive land grants. But this is not correct, since the Great Northern was actually the second renaming of the Minnesota and Pacific Railway, which was a public railroad formed out of massive land grants and millions of (and this is nominal!) dollars' subsidy. While Hill did privately finance the purchase of this in a fire-sale, the idea that anyone could actually build such a railroad without land grants and other public inducements is dangerous lunacy.[48]

---

with the ability to function well in one's society. As if all societies nurtured health in equal amounts.

[47] See Sirridge, "Truth from Fiction?" and Nathaniel Hawthorne, *The Scarlet Letter* (Mineola: Dover Publications, 1994).

[48] I should note that there are plenty of reflective libertarian fans of Ayn Rand who do not have this economic belief. I cannot imagine Roderick

Of course, having false economic beliefs is just one way that one can be out of synch with normative reality with respect to economics. And one can be out of synch with any other layer of reality as well: moral, mathematical, historical, metaphysical, psychological, etc. But we think our examples here are enough to illuminate the definition.

In the next section we suggest a theory of how texts manage to embody the properties isolated by our truth definition. But first we must clarify two points, the second of which illustrates our ontological need. First, one might think that our definition, as well as our blithe discussion of "normative reality," completely precludes any concessions to relativism. Are we committed to a text just having one truth for everyone? No we are not. Our picture of true texts is that they are engines for helping people partake in normative reality, including developing relevant true beliefs. But this is consistent with normative reality being multi-faceted and with different people discerning different true beliefs from the same texts. Indeed, part of what makes a great work great is that it remains a productive truth engine through reinterpretations motivated by historical changes and cultural differences. The analogy we would like to suggest here is to what direct reference theorists such as Alva Noë have to say about differences in perception.[49] A dog's sense of smell is quite different from that of a boy, but this does not mean that a boy and his dog are not both directly perceiving smell properties that actually exist in the world. Likewise, if I get radically different truths from a text than from the same reader of that text thirty years ago, that does not mean that we have not both discerned truths.

Long, who himself sometimes engages in libertarian critiques of large scale infrastructure, asserting it. This kind of libertarian would note that of course one cannot be a railroad tycoon without corruptly harnessing the resources of the state with respect to funding, eminent domain, and help in co-opting and crushing labour movements, but so much the worse for railroad tycoons. We are not endorsing this train of thought (and in fact both quite like passenger rail), rather just noting this so that the above is not read as putting forward a comic-book version of contemporary libertarianism.

[49] Alva Noë, *Action in Perception* (Cambridge: MIT Press, 2006).

Our second issue provides even more motivation. Suppose that Timothy Leary et. al. were right all along about LSD, and that it really does grant mystical insight into reality. Then suppose that someone has laced my copy of Justin Bieber's ghost-written memoir (published when he was 16) *First Step 2 Forever*[50] with enough of the drug that when I read it I absorb it through my fingers, I get fantastically high. After I come down I am a better person.

It might look like our definition of truth in fiction would entail that Bieber's drug laced memoir is ethically true. But this is not correct, because my ethical transformation did not come about as a result of *reading* the wretched book, which is required by the definition. But, to be fair, this just pushes the problem back. What is it about reading that allows books to have such an outsized effect on us? This then is what Sirridge's question now becomes, what is it about true (false) texts that makes it the case that reading *qua* reading better (worse) aligns us with normative reality? Without an answer to this question we are no closer to our goal than when we began.

VI. Interpretation as Thought Experiment

When skilled fiction writers such as Stephen King describe their craft, they almost invariably describe it in a strangely passive manner.[51] The process stereotypically works like this. King wakes up in the middle of the night with some very vivid scene impressing on him, and then stays up until morning trying to figure out how that scene fits into a plausible evolution. In doing this he will determine a setting and central problem. His phenomenology then is that there is a fact of the matter about how the setting will evolve in response to the problem. His primary job at this point is just to get the facts of the evolution correct. During writing he is often surprised by what his characters end up doing.

---

[50] Justin Bieber, *First Step 2 Forever: My Story* (New York: HarperCollins, 2012).

[51] Stephen King, *On Writing: A Memoir of the Craft*, Tenth Anniversary Edition (New York: Scribner, 2008).

Importantly, it is not just that the initial set-up is a gift of the muse. Plot is also something writers experience as an external object with its own autonomy. The writer's attentiveness to the muse regarding plot is attentiveness to how the set-up really would plausibly evolve, were the set-up incarnate in the actual world. A good book must first and foremost get both of these things (set-up and plot) correct. And this is our central claim concerning how texts paradigmatically put readers in accord with normative reality.

Let us return to Mary Sirridge, whose critical intervention had the unintended effect of largely killing off the debate surrounding the actual truth of fictional texts. Interestingly, Sirridge is clear at the end of the article that she does not think that the failure of linguistic turn mainstays means that fictions cannot teach us about the actual world:

> works of fiction are by no means alone in not being able to serve as direct evidence about the actual world. Cooked-up counterexamples may defeat proposed criteria meant to apply to kinds of things in the actual world. Thought experiments are often used to clarify hypotheses and to do them in. Counterfactual analysis is often used to support the corresponding positive claim. No one supposes that the "facts" adduced in these cases are genuine—in fact, they are usually so chosen that we can assume that certain things are unproblematically true, as we could not in actual life ... We seem to have no satisfactory explanation of how these methods work epistemologically.[52]

In defence of the cognitive status of thought experiments, Sirridge notes that they "form one of the mainstays of philosophical thinking." Eva Dadlez follows Sirridge here,[53] persuasively arguing that if one takes thought experiments in ethics to have *any* positive epistemic weight, then one cannot gainsay the positive epistemic weight of fiction.

However, attending to writers such as King shows that the issue is considerably more general than just thought experi-

---

[52] Sirridge, "Truth from Fiction?," 470-71.

[53] Dadlez, *What's Hecuba to Him.*

ments in ethics. For all thought experiments have the same structure as interpretations of fictional works. First there is a set-up, which will often involve physical impossibilities such as frictionless planes. Then the system evolves. Centrally, scientists are interested in the way in which the actual world would evolve, were the set-up incarnated, even in cases when the set-up is physically impossible in some respect.[54]

Consider, for example, the clear null-interpretation of Johannes Kepler's *Somnium*. The set-up for the experiment is a young man transported to the moon by demons. The evolution concerns what he would experience. In the evolution the young man floats slowly down to the moon's surface and must breathe through a sponge. In addition, even though the moon is orbiting the earth, from the moon he sees the earth moving across the sky. So even though the set-up was impossible (in the 1620s), the evolution of the impossible system did tell us three important things about the actual world: (1) that the moon has less gravity than earth, (2) that gravity is related to atmosphere, and (3) that people on the orbiting Earth would see the stationary sun as moving across the sky.

Here is an interesting thing. Though it is a classic thought experiment motivating the Copernican revolution, Carl Sagan and Isaac Asimov have called it the first science fiction novel. This is because, like Stephen King, most authors view novels as machines for generating thought experiments. The author

---

[54] In this context we should cite Lewis's later claim that "fiction might serve as a means for the discovery of modal truth" (David Lewis, "Postscripts to 'Truth in Fiction'" in *Philosophical Papers I* (Oxford: Oxford University Press, 1983), 278, albeit keep in mind all of the caveats we offer in this section. Also one should consider the argument in Tobias Klauk, "Thought Experiments in Literature" in *Counterfactual Thinking/Counterfactual Writing*, ed. Dorothee Birke, Michael Butter, and Tilmann Köppe (Berlin: DeGruyter, 2011), 30-44. Klauk argues that fiction should not be explicated in terms of thought experiments, because thought experiments in science and philosophy are characterised by (a) imagining a scenario, (b) considering whether and how the scenario answers the question, and (c) using the answer to the question. But Klauk is only able to make his argument because he does not consider questions like "what is reality like?" or "how should one be?" and does not count the transformation of oneself with respect to normative reality as a possible use of the answer.

is the first interpreter, working through a set-up and, (if the novel is true), correctly describes the evolution. In writing the novel, she typically attempts to use language to create a machine that will convey this first interpretation to the reader. Of course: (1) as we will discuss below, the machine will get away from the author, yielding interpretations that she never foresaw, interpretations that may be better than the null-interpretation the author was aiming to build a machine to develop, (2) the set-up/evolution pair of an interpretation generated by a text-machine is typically recursive, containing stories inside of stories, where parts of earlier set-ups and evolutions become incorporated into contained set-ups and evolutions. *All* postmodern, and much modern, writing builds off of these two properties. The fact that in standard novels the author's intent concerning what kind of thought experiment should be generated is not decisive can lead a good author to design texts where the intent of the author is actually to produce a text-machine radically under-determined (leaving it very unclear which thought experiment should be produced) or over-determined (producing inconsistent thought experiments) with respect to the interpretations. The fact that set-up/evolution is recursive in the way at which we have gestured is part of what allows authors to produce text-machines that yield so-called "meta-fictional" interpretations, where the text should be interpreted as commenting on itself in some way.[55]

Let us also note that contra Lewis, interpretations of true fictions do not describe mere possibilia, but rather *actual* possibilia, as the plot describes the way the actual world would plausibly evolve if such a set-up were incarnate.[56] And related

---

[55] The connection between recursivity, self-reflection, and paradoxes is formally complicated. It should be unproblematic that fiction is expressively rich enough to do the relevant work. For a great discussion tying these themes convincingly to recent continental philosophy, see Paul Livingston, *The Politics of Logic: Badiou, Wittgenstein, and the Consequences of Formalism* (London: Routledge, 2012). Priest's *Beyond the Limits of Thought* is also extraordinarily helpful in thinking about meta-fiction.

[56] The metaphysical task involved in differentiating mere possibility from

to this, we should note that our use of "interpretation" is liberal here. We do not mean to just note what literature professors produce when writing articles. In our theory, there is no reason to go through yet another linguistic epicycle when producing an interpretation. *Any* imaginatively complicit reader of fiction is producing an interpretation while reading, an interpretation produced via sensitivity to the (true or false) window into counterfactual reality produced for her by the text-machine. This happens even if she is completely lost to herself while reading. Perhaps she can later articulate, expand, and alter the interpretation while discussing the novel with friends. But the text-machine generates interpretations (again, these are merely recursively nested set-up/evolution pairs) for anyone reading it, even if that person is constitutively unable to talk about the text.[57]

So here we have a general ontology of stories, which are machines producing recursively nested set-up/evolution pairs, the proper teleology of which is to get people in accord with some aspect of normative reality. The proper interpretations of many such stories, in science and literature, have set-ups that are impossible in some respect. But in discerning facts about how the actual world would plausibly evolve if that impossibility were incarnate we align ourselves with normative reality. In science this alignment is usually constituted by the ability to better design and predict the evolution of closed environments. In life, the abilities paradigmatically involve the extent to which we are able to craft worthwhile lives.

---

actual possibility is horrendous. See Laura Schroeter, "Two-Dimensional Semantics" in *Stanford Encyclopedia of Philosophy*, ed. Edward N. Zalta (Winter 2012 Edition), http://plato.stanford.edu/archives/win2012/entries/two-dimensional-semantics/ (accessed January 13, 2014). We should also note that much more philosophy of science is needed to account for the objectivity of our judgments concerning whether a plot really does describe the way the world would evolve or not. We do not think that these reduce to mere intuitions, as with the way one might think of an ethical thought experiment.

[57] These abilities do come apart in certain types of aphasia, where people cannot talk but can still read and via behaviour it is clear that they understand what has been read. A surprising amount of philosophy and aesthetics cannot accommodate even the *possible* existence of such people.

Let us not make too much of these differences though. There is no *metaphysical* difference in kind between a physics textbook and a novel. Both allow readers to grasp, within margins of error, how the actual world would evolve after set-ups that are often impossible. This being said, there are obviously other differences between the two, most notably the norms involving form and content, or rather the connection between those formal properties of the text relevant to a given interpretation (and by "content" we mean to solely reference our understanding of interpretation) and those formal properties that are not so relevant. In physics, the connection is treated much more loosely in the sense that two different accounts of the same thought experiment might be expressed in radically different ways. In literature, (for reasons articulated by Nelson Goodman in a discussion of plagiarism and also earlier by Cleanth Brooks) this is not possible.[58] We read literature with openness to the idea that what now seems contingently formal might in fact play a key role in articulating the content of the work according to some other interpretation. With poetry, form and content are even more inseparable. Mathematics is a weird hybrid of natural science and poetry. The basic descriptions of the mathematical structures themselves are treated like natural science descriptions, where form and content are loosely related. But with respect to proofs establishing properties of those structures, form is highly relevant to questions of individuation. Philosophy is, perhaps, even weirder in the norms employed with regard to separating form from content. In philosophy we typically take our own intuitions concerning abstract matters to be guided merely by content. But recent experimental philosophy has shown that this is not typically the case. Differences in wording can produce radically different intuitions about basic issues in ethics such as whether one can believe an act to be right without being motivated to do that act.[59]

---

[58] Cleanth Brooks, *The Well Wrought Urn* (New York: Harcourt, Brace, & World, 1947); Nelson Goodman, *Languages of Art* (Indianapolis: Hackett, 1976).

[59] See, for example, Derek Leben, "Cognitive Neuroscience and Moral

Much more needs to be said on this issue, and doing so will, we think, show not only what is unique about fiction *qua* fiction, but also provide the ground for arguing that fictional narrative is the originary concept, with other types only arrived at by operating on the norms in various respects involving the relations to formal properties of the text and the content summoned in interpretation. For example, consider how one might also argue that a norm constitutive of reading a text as fiction is that the circumstances of its production can be relevant to its proper interpretation.[60] To the extent that this is plausible for fiction, one might be able to see its falsehood for other literary genres as a consequence of the reading norms involving the relation between form and content (or rather content relevant form and content irrelevant form). For one can only translate a physics thought experiment into a radically different form without loss of content if the circumstances in which the physics thought experiment were thought up are taken to be irrelevant.

Much clearer examples can be given with respect to scientific modelling; it is usually very clear which properties of physical models are content irrelevant. Say that I build the planets in my model out of styrofoam when, for the purposes of providing the relevant window into counterfactual reality, I would have lost nothing by using rubber balls. If there is anything to Nelson Goodman and Cleanth Brooks's canonical arguments, they show that part of what is distinctive about aesthetic objects (and this holds when, as the object-oriented philosopher takes to be fundamental, one looks at the natural world itself from an aesthetic point of view) is

---

Decision-Making," *Neuroethics* (2011), 4, 163-74. For an extended and provocative meditation on the relation between style and content, see Harman's *Weird Realism*.

[60] Our departure from the New Critics on "the intentional fallacy" might render our view more Garcian than Harmanian, though the emphasis on texts as machines that generate interpretations has the most in common with the capacity metaphysics view. Again, we do not think that this implicates it in the problems for capacity metaphysics that Harman isolates, but of course we might be mistaken here. In this context we would love to see how a fourfold hermeneutics differs from our own.

that such distinctions are always provisional. With respect to some interpretation, using rubber rather than styrofoam makes all the difference in the world. But this interpretation too will neglect some formal features as irrelevant. For the object-oriented ontologist who follows Harman's reading of Heidegger, reality just is inexhaustible in this very way, the way that Goodman articulates with respect to paintings.

Let us restate this with an exclamation point. For an object-oriented philosopher, the property of aesthetic objects isolated by Goodman and Brooks is in general a property of all objects! The Husserlian "scientific world-view" involves pretending that this is not the case in order to better predict things. And this is why for the object-oriented philosopher, as opposed to the naturalist underminer, one can say that fictions are engines that generate recursively structured set-up/evolutions, and that physics is a species of fiction.

But objects in and of themselves are aesthetic. And even in physics this has to be allowed for. As Mark Steiner has shown with respect to mathematical parts of modelling, what seemed to be contingently formal at one time can end up years later being shown to have empirical import.[61] For physics to do what it does, one must be able to relax the regulative ideal that nature herself separates the content relevant and content irrelevant form of objects. These are separated in acts of interpretation that objects engender whenever they interact with one another, acts which never exhaust the reality of the interpreted objects.

VII. Objections and Explications

Here we want to consider three possible objections as a way to be clearer both about what we have said as well as how one might further develop the view. First, what we have described in terms of set-up and evolution might seem only to describe

---

[61] Mark Steiner, *The Applicability of Mathematics as Philosophical Problem* (Cambridge: Harvard University Press, 2002).

very conventional, mimetic literature. [62] In particular, while we have allowed impossible set-ups, our doctrine that true fictions yield correct interpretations that get the evolution correct (in the sense of describing what the actual world would do were the set-up incarnate) seems to entail that novels which yield interpretations with improbable and impossible evolutions are one and all false. But, do not many books succeed precisely because they flaunt these? At one end, books such as Laurence Sterne's *Tristram Shandy*,[63] a good narrative can evolve in implausible ways. At the other end lay much experimental fiction.

This is not actually correct though. First, our definition of the actual truth and falsity of fictional texts only concerns truth or falsity with respect to some subject matter. So a physically false interpretation might nonetheless be psychologically true, and even *in virtue of* the fact that the evolution of the text is physically impossible. Second, actual reality is improbable and true fiction must teach this. For a quotidian example, note the incredibly low prior probability of the exact performance of a set of one hundred coins that you just tossed. For less quotidian examples, note that if Graham Priest is correct, then the actual world is in fact logically contradictory. In this respect, remember that the recursive nature of the set-up/evolution pair entails that part of the evolution can be set-up for new evolution. This not only allows meta-fiction, but makes sense of the full draw of writers such as Lovecraft. Lovecraft does

---

[62] We thank the reviewers of *Speculations* for this objection as well as some of the examples we use. For a great discussion of how the unnatural *does* place constraints on theories of fiction, see Jan Alber, Stefan Iversen, Henrik Skov Nielsen, and Brian Richardson, "Unnatural Narratives, Unnatural Narratology: Beyond Mimetic Models," *Narrative* (2010),18:2, 113-36. The article focuses on three sources of the unnatural: storyworlds, minds, and acts of narration. It would take us too far afield here to consider each of these in depth, but we think enough is said above to show how our theory of fictions (as machines that generate recursively stacked set-up/evolutions with the teleology of bringing the reader into alignment with normative reality) can explain the mechanisms at work in the texts discussed in the article.

[63] Laurence Sterne, *The Life and Opinions of Tristram Shandy, Gentleman*, Oxford World's Classics (Oxford: Oxford University Press, 2009).

not only create a text which is an engine for interpretations that grant us sensitivity to what would actually happen were an impossible set-up incarnate. When you read Lovecraft in the dark of night you also wonder if anything like those set-ups are actual. Maybe reality itself contains horrifyingly indescribable things that are impossible with respect to any human conceptual scheme. In this sense, the best fantastical writing forces us to be deeper two-dimensionalists about the set-up itself, not just what would actually follow.

That is, one would only think that the holdovers from mimeticism in our theory tell against unnatural fiction to the extent that one is a naturalist about reality. But we think that unnatural fiction truly teaches that reality itself is not natural.

Surely there will be a remainder of fiction that does not fit well with our theory. To address this, let us define a technical term here, "Carrollism,"[64] which construes philosophies of art as in the business of providing necessary and sufficient conditions, and then uses experimental art to argue against all such purported philosophies. This is a mug's game though, just because artists are so good at self-consciously creating art that counter-exemplifies philosophical definitions. And there is no reason for philosophers to play along. Instead of providing necessary and sufficient conditions for various concepts, the philosopher of art should rather be providing relevant genetically necessary conditions for the practices in question. For example, instead of trying to ascertain the extent to which cruelty works in the definition of "humour," we should see if the practice of humour would be possible in a world without cruelty. Our claim is analogous with respect to fiction. A world without textual machines that produce reader sensitivity to recursively nested set-up/evolution pairs would be a world without fiction.

---

[64] See Noël Carroll, *Philosophy of Art* (London: Routledge 1999) for a book structured around this very conceit. It is still an excellent book though, because Carroll only plays the game with respect to trying to define "art," and half of the book himself making sense of the relevant concepts (form, representation, etc.) independently of the definition of art.

This does not mean that everything we call "fiction" automatically must fit our theory. However, to the extent that an aesthetic theory is complete, it must be the case that the genetically necessary conditions for the practice are such that anything that does not satisfy the conditions and is also an instance of the *explanandum* (e.g. experimental fiction that does not do what we have alleged) is parasitic on work that does. So, for example, while mimeticism is not necessary for artistic painting, non-mimetic paintings must be understood parasitically with respect to mimetic ones, and in fact could not exist as an autonomous practice. That is non-mimetic painting must best be thought either as really mimetic (as most abstract expressionists actually described their work) or in some sense making a comment upon a tradition founded in mimetic art.[65]

A second criticism is that our focus on thought experiments leads to a narrowly scientistic view. If all that matters with respect to truth or falsity in a certain respect is that the actual world really would evolve in that respect were the set-up manifest, then is not this just to view truth or falsity in terms of the scientific virtue of predictive value? We do not think that this is the case. Intuition pumps in ethics, and philosophy general, do work as narratives in the way we have suggested. However, there is something correct about the worry. Interpretations can be morally true only to the extent that they are affectively engaging, and it should be clear that a theory of what makes a text affectively engaging will have to use resources far beyond those marshalled by us thus far with respect to a text's correct interpretation. And, moreover, having the correct affective states in certain contexts is a paradigm way that we are in accord with normative reality. So one would need to say much more about how thought experiments achieve this. This leads to our third criticism.

---

[65] One of Danto's most powerful late period essays (Arthur Danto, "Art and Meaning" in *Theories of Art Today*, ed. Noël Carroll (Madison: University of Wisconsin Press, 2000)) makes a surprisingly powerful independent argument for this claim with respect to all art.

Finally, we have said nothing at all about the tropes via which literature does much of its work (e.g. allegory, antanaclasis, irony, metaphor, metonymy, synecdoche) nor about narrative voice in itself or as opposed to other voicings relevant to the text.

We agree that this would be a problem if anything we have said undermines good theories about how these tropes work. We do not think that this is the case. But this is not enough, one's basic theory of actual truth of fictional texts and ontology of fiction should in addition shed lights on these very tropes. In this respect, we confess a kind of Simondonian[66] hope here. Just as Gilbert Simondon modelled physical, vital, psychic, and collective objects in terms of various types of individuating processes, our intuition is that characteristic modes of treating content relevant and content irrelevant form is involved in all of these tropes. For example, for metaphor to work, the connection of a predicate to a subject must be understood to be *both* irrelevant (human beings are not firecrackers) and essential. One must prize apart form and content in distinct ways in the same interpretation so that the sentence is both false and true.

A less speculative example might be from narratology, where different takes on narrators reliably yield different interpretations in exactly the sense we mean. One who wrongly (albeit at the author's later drunken insistence) identifies the narrator and author of Jack Kerouac's *On the Road* is likely to read the book as a how-to manual for beatnik kicks. But once one realises that the book was the sixth time he had rewritten the material and that it was exhaustively rewritten multiple times, one starts to see how much distance there is between narrator and author. And once one realises how fallible the narrator is in every respect then the novel is far more satirical and much sadder. These different interpretations are non-linguistically experienced by most fair minded readers of the text, the

---

[66] For an excellent overview, see Arne De Boever, Alex Murray, Jon Roffe, and Ashley Woodward, eds., *Gilbert Simondon: Being and Technology* (Edinburgh: Edinburgh University Press, 2012).

first when the book is read in high school, the second when returned to decades later. People who read it decades later and do not separate narrator from author are likely to see the book as simply obnoxious. While these different interpretations are experienced viscerally while reading the text, they can all be made explicit in terms of the thought experiment machinery of recursively nested set-up/evolutions. Of course the explications themselves will involve affectively weighted language (e.g. "then Dean Moriarity once again showed how pathologically selfish he is by. . ."). But only a philosophical naturalist would take anything we have said to preclude this.

The furthest end of our Simondonian hope would be to characterise different stances towards the narrator entirely in terms of how the reader differentiates content relevant form from content irrelevant form. But we must add a caveat; we do *not* think that one could do this entirely in terms of formal properties of a text. This would fail for the same reasons Sirridge showed traditional approaches to the actual truth of fictional texts failed. Moreover, one cannot even begin to characterise the formal content of a text without *already having* begun to attribute content to it. This is similar to the way that formal properties of paintings are partly a result of what is depicted, for example in the unpainted lines of sight of the people or animals in the picture. This too is another way that form and content do not clearly separate with respect to aesthetic objects.[67]

VIII. Necessary Fictions

Kurt Vonnegut's *Slaughterhouse Five* contains a discussion of *The Gospel from Outer Space*, written by fictitious author Kilgore Trout:

> The flaw in the Christ stories, said the visitor from outer space, was that Christ, who didn't look like much, was actually the Son of the Most

[67] McDowell's *Mind and World* (Cambridge: Harvard University Press, 1996) is to some extent an extended meditation on just this problematic, which (as noted earlier) was one of the engines moving forward German Idealism.

Powerful Being in the Universe. Readers understood that, so, when they came to the crucifixion, they naturally thought, and Rosewater read out loud again:

Oh, boy—they sure picked the wrong guy to lynch that time!

And that thought had a brother: "There are right people to lynch." Who? People not well connected. So it goes.[68]

While this is certainly right as part of an explanation for why Christians have often been so horribly cruel to one another and to non-Christians, it is not clear to us that the space alien really gets the new Gospel correct.

The visitor from outer space made a gift to Earth of a new Gospel. In it, Jesus really was a nobody, and a pain in the neck to a lot of people with better connections than he had. He still got to say all the lovely and puzzling things he said in the other Gospels.

So the people amused themselves one day by nailing him to a cross and planting the cross in the ground. There couldn't possibly be any repercussions, the lynchers thought.

The reader would have to think that, too, since the new Gospel hammered home again and again what a nobody Jesus was.

And then, just before the nobody died, the heavens opened up, and there was thunder and lightning. The voice of God came crashing down. He told the people that he was adopting the bum as his son giving him the full powers and privileges of The Son of the Creator of the Universe throughout all eternity. God said this: From this moment on, He will punish horribly anybody who torments a bum who has no connections![69]

By our account there is some truth to the space alien's interpretation, as one who shares it is all else being equal more likely to treat bums who have no connections better. But we think not as true as the correct interpretation of the gospel stories. For one whose kindness is based in fear of horrible punishment is not as in accord with normative reality as much as one whose kindness is not so grounded.

---

[68] Kurt Vonnegut, *Slaughterhouse Five* (New York: Dial Press, 1999), 94.

[69] Ibid., 94-95.

In this context, consider Reinhold Niehbur's favourite Bible passage, Ephesians 4:32: "And be ye kind one to another, tender-hearted, forgiving one another, even as God for Christ's sake hath forgiven you."[70] To Niehbur, all of the Bible leads a reader to be in accord with the norm expressed in this one sentence. But, pace Vonnegut's space alien gospel, how might this work in the actual Bible?

Following others, we interpret it this way.[71] There is initially an impossible set-up, a real creature somehow creating reality. This creature, despite all appearances to the contrary, assures us that her kingdom is coming, a kingdom just as impossible, where the suffering of innocents is somehow redeemed. Then there is an evolution. A central trope of the story is that this impossible being has no idea how to respond to the wickedness of her creation, for example actually acting surprised when witnessing the aftermath of the first murder. By her understanding of humans, the best thing one could hope for would be for one's offspring to thrive, and she promises this over and over again to various people. But most of her interventions leave things even more messed up than before, and after throwing a temper tantrum at the much suffering Job, she decides it is better to largely leave us to our own devices. But then she does just one more thing, sending a son who tells us things that we do not want to hear and acts in ways at variance with the political and religious powers of the time, and so we torture and kill him. Then, even though this impossible being possesses the power to destroy us, and even though it is clear that she regards the wellbeing of one's offspring as among the greatest goods, she does not get revenge for what we have done to her offspring. In fact her son successfully petitions for our forgiveness from the very instrument of

---

[70] Justin R. Hawkins, "Reinhold Niehbur's One Scripture Passage," *Fare Forward: A Christian Review of Ideas* (2013), http://www.patheos.com/blogs/fareforward/2013/03/reinhold-niebuhrs-one-scripture-passage/(accessed September 24, 2013).

[71] Our reading of the Old Testament is from Jack Miles, *God: A Biography* (New York: Vintage, 1996).

his torture. This is of a piece with the very messages that got him killed in the first place.

One might argue that a fiction correctly interpreted in this manner is not only true, but also necessary. Necessary in two respects. First, the transcendent nature of God and the kingdom of heaven might be such that it is disastrously misleading to think that we could talk about either except as impossible beings. To think that one can have any inkling of how this could be the best possible world, or for that matter even a minimally acceptable one, is to warp one's soul. Voltaire's *Candide* was right about this, and as a result the kingdom of heaven must be approached as an impossibility for which one nonetheless hopes.[72] While the impossibility of the set-up might thus be necessitated by great mystery, we hope that we have said enough to dispel any deep mystery about how we achieve a description of it. Frictionless planes and point masses are likewise impossible entities, but nonetheless unavoidable.

This points to the second way in which one might take religious texts to be necessary fictions, not the sense in which God and the kingdom of heaven are necessarily fictional, but in the sense that they are also indispensable for the Bible to be true. Imagine if one were to do to the whole Bible what Thomas Jefferson attempted with the Gospels, assiduously removing all mention of the impossible. Call this the Jefferson Bible. Would such a book be just as true as the text that involved impossible set-ups? In logic we might express this question by asking whether the Bible we have is a conservative extension of our imagined Jefferson Bible. We would like to argue that it is not.

In the standard Bible, God is presented as deserving the highest praise and also powerful enough to create and destroy worlds. Then humans do to her the worst thing one can do to someone. They kill her child. Yet she does not destroy the world, but rather forgives humanity.

---

[72] Voltaire, *Candide*, trans. François-Marie Arouet (Mineola: Dover Publications, 1991).

If this is a true story it is because reading it in the Bible brings one more into conformity with the normative reality expressed in Ephesians 4:32. It, combined with worship of the very God the Bible attempts to describe, will lead the person to be forgiving and more hopeful.

We are *not* saying that only Christians are forgiving and hopeful. Rather, we are merely noting that if the Jefferson Bible is not as good as the actual Bible at engendering forgiveness and hope, then the Jefferson Bible is not as morally true as the actual one. The Bible's God is very much like a friction-less plane in that her power and praiseworthiness are taken to be infinite limits of qualities (such as relative smoothness in the case of friction) that we do perceive. To say that such a being herself responds with forgiveness to the worst offense one can commit is to affirm in the strongest possible manner the praiseworthiness of forgiveness and love.

This kind of thing is, we suspect, a core facet of all good fiction. Could a non-fictional book be just as psychologically, anthropologically, and ethically true as *Huckleberry Finn*? If not, then the fiction is necessary in exactly the way we have suggested the Bible might be.

There is a final sense in which one might argue fictions to be necessary.[73] If we return to the kind of pragmatist account of understanding that Okrent gets from Heidegger, then we see that the essential thought is that thinking is grounded in a certain sort of behavioural sensitivity to normative coun-terfactual facets of reality, facets concerning what ought to be the case if something were actually to be.

Consider Heidegger's hammer. Grasping the hammer requires not representing it in some Cartesian medium, but rather an understanding of its appropriate uses, which (according to Okrent) does not require language. However, this behavioural sensitivity will involve different things one *could* do with the hammer that one has not actually done. And with our account of true fictions, a true narrative is one that correctly limns the counterfactual facts about the actual world. This is

---

[73] We would like to thank Ridvan Askin for pushing us on this point.

consistent with Harman's guerrilla Heidegger, because the nail and neutrino also have their own interpretations of the Hammer, which is itself an inexhaustible reservoir of being.

But note that counterfactuals are already in a sense fictional since they concern states of affairs that are not actual. Many true stories about what the actually existing hammer would do involve states of affairs that will never actually come to be and new future objects that will never exist. It is true that one could use this hammer to build a birdhouse that one never does actually build.

Thus, if Okrent's Heidegger is correct (again, interpreted as one instance of the broader theory of being Harman finds), then fictions are necessary in a more originary sense than what we have claimed with respect to Mark Twain. The good writer's ability to discern what would really happen were some set-up incarnate is just a development of an ability that is fundamental to all cognition. Non-fictional, true propositions only get their content because the concepts involved can occur in true fictions. But then fictions themselves are genetically necessary in the very strongest sense. One could not have non-fiction without also having fiction.[74]

---

[74] We would like to first and foremost thank Ridvan Askin for an extended e-mail correspondence. Somewhere between one-fourth and one-third of the above was developed in reaction to Askin's gentle Socratic prodding. We would also like to thank Askin and Paul Ennis for their similarly helpful detailed comments on the first full draft. In addition several people provided helpful input at various stages, in particular: Graham Bounds, Levi Bryant, Emily Beck Cogburn, Tristan Garcia, Graham Harman, Raphaël Millière, John Protevi, Duncan Richter, Jeff Roland, Mark Silcox, Jordan Skinner, Jazz Salo, Dawn Suiter, and Bradley Woods.

Speculative Experiments
What if Simondon and Harman Individuate Together?

Miguel Penas López

Universitat Autònoma de Barcelona
Université Toulouse II-Le Mirail

THERE ARE SOME QUESTIONS THAT have persisted throughout the history of philosophy, and they remain with us. These questions constitute the business of philosophers, a business that does not fit very well in our present market-based economy because questions cannot be sold. We can only try to answer them, which leads to new questions. This is what *philo*sophy does: to bear the tension of questions and the distance of answers. Putting it simply, one of these persistent questions is whether the intrinsic nature of reality is static or dynamic, whether we can isolate in it immutable traits or encounter nothing but perpetual change and transience. In scholarly expositions of pre-Socratic thought, Parmenides and Heraclitus are usually taken as representatives of these two positions: while Parmenides is seen as the champion of immutable being who denounces the illusion of non-being, Heraclitus has been known as the philosopher of change who cannot bathe in the same river twice. However, such exposition perhaps presents but a superficial understanding of ancient thought. Hermeneuticians have taught us that both Heraclitus and Parmenides were trying to name the same thing—being—in an age in which this verb was not limited to the copular function we expect it to perform today.[1] Since then, the question about the nature of being and change has solidified into the metaphysical problem of substance, where substance means the enduring features of an entity—or, more precisely, it means those entities or realities which do not need others as a support in order to exist—whereas properties are those features that change over time. Another commonplace in scholarly expositions is to attribute this doctrine to Aristotle, mainly due to the translation of the Aristotelian concept of "first *ousia*" as substance or essence. This translation can be seen as one of the most harmful ones in the history of philosophy, because it meant a loss of richness of the Aristotelian concept that has conditioned the whole metaphysical tradition.

In recent years, this dispute regarding objects, individuals and substances on the one hand, and processes, flux and becoming on the other has become one of the most interesting disputes in continental philosophy. Closely related to this is the question concerning the suitability of relational ontology. The presence of this dispute within the domain of speculative realism counts as further evidence of the heterogeneous character of this movement: in the original group, Graham Harman represents the object-oriented pole whereas Ian Hamilton Grant defends an ontogenetic and dynamic approach in his Schellingian philosophy of nature.[2] As we will see, Harman also maintains a long-term debate with other processualist and relational thinkers close to speculative realism such as Steven Shaviro. In the present article, I want to address this issue through an analysis of the encounter between Harman's object-oriented philosophy and Gilbert Simondon's philosophy of individuation with one main purpose in sight: trying to overcome the mistake that we have

[1] See Felipe Martínez Marzoa, *Historia de la Filosofía*, 2 vols (Madrid: Istmo, 1994), especially 13-26 and 32-58.

[2] See the transcript of the London *Speculative Realism* workshop where the term was coined to designate the common features of four different philosophical proposals: Ray Brassier, Ian Hamilton Grant, Graham Harman, and Quentin Meillassoux, "Speculative Realism," *Collapse* (2007), 3, 306-449.

already seen at work in the scholarly expositions of Greek thought. This mistake, which is revamped in the current debate, is the belief that processes and objects, individuation and the individual, cannot be thought together (as it can be noted, I do not make a difference between Harman's concept of "object" and Simondon's concept of "individual"). Since all objects have their particular process of individuation, why should an object-oriented philosophy have a problem with offering a philosophical account of it? Likewise, since all processes of individuation produce individuals with their particular haecceity, why should a process philosophy have an interest in denying it?

At the core of Harman's philosophy is a defence of the unity and autonomy of objects with regard to their history, their components, and their relations. Hence, objects of all kinds and sizes, be they physical, social or fictional, become the principal actors of metaphysics, and Harman critiques two kinds of philosophical strategies in which this pre-eminence of objects is denied: undermining objects and overmining them. In the first case, "objects are a mere surface effect of some deeper force."[3] There are several ways of undermining objects: reductionism, monism, philosophies of the pre-individual, and process philosophy. In the second case, objects are dissolved in external relations. Here, we also find different ways of overmining objects. One of them is empiricism, in which there is no object but a "bundle of qualities."[4] Another is what Quentin Meillassoux calls "correlationism," a concept that denotes all post-Kantian philosophies, whether modern or postmodern, where objects can only be thought in primordial correlation to some human sphere, be it the subject, *Dasein*, textual dependence, or social relations of power. Harman distinguishes a variant of correlationism: in "relationism," the human sphere is no longer privileged, but the existence of some intrinsic substratum of objects outside their relations, with presence in, or effects on other

---

[3] Graham Harman, *The Quadruple Object* (Winchester: Zero, 2011), 6.

[4] Ibid., 11.

objects is denied. In short, Harman denounces that both the underminers and the overminers "skip the intermediate layer of autonomous objects that are both actually individual and also autonomous from all perception."[5]

In several places, Harman rejects Simondon's philosophy as undermining objects.[6] Along with Henri Bergson and Gilles Deleuze, Simondon is grouped with those anti-object-oriented ontologies that try to overcome the centrality of being or substance in traditional metaphysics by way of positing a primordial flux or becoming; more specifically, Simondon is considered, as is Manuel DeLanda, a moderate monist who believes in a "heterogeneous yet continuous" pre-individual reality.[7] In doing so, Harman forgets that Simondon, marking a difference with Bergson (one of his principal influences), privileges the discontinuous over the continuous.[8] What is more, Harman claims that the "philosophies of the so-called 'pre-individual' treat the world as a semi-articulate lump arbitrarily carved into pieces by the human intellect," suggesting an anti-realist flavour in these philosophies, which is totally inadequate, at least in Simondon's case.[9] In asking if there is a place for Simondon's philosophy in speculative realism, I try

---

[5] Harman, *The Quadruple Object*, 15.

[6] See, for instance, Harman, *The Quadruple Object*; Graham Harman, "On the Undermining of Objects: Grant, Bruno, and Radical Philosophy" in *The Speculative Turn: Continental Materialism and Realism*, ed. Levi Bryant, Nick Srnicek, and Graham Harman (Melbourne: Re.press, 2010), 21-40; Graham Harman, "Response to Shaviro" in *The Speculative Turn*, 291-303; and Graham Harman, *Prince of Networks: Bruno Latour and Metaphysics* (Melbourne: Re.press, 2009).

[7] Harman, *The Quadruple Object*, 9.

[8] This touches on a complex question that cannot be elaborated here. One of the principal reasons why Simondon is interested in quantum mechanics, to which he devotes a chapter in his major book, lies in that he saw in it a possibility of overcoming the opposition between the continuous and the discontinuous. It is in light of quantum physics that Simondon articulates the different modes of individuation (physical, biological, psychical-collective) as discontinuous but not detached. See Gilbert Simondon, *L'individuation à la lumière des notions de forme et d'information* (Grenoble: Éditions Jérôme Millon, 2005), 99-153.

[9] Graham Harman, "The Road to Objects," *continent.* (2011), 3:1, 172.

to show that the ontogenetic concepts coined by Simondon to give account of the processes of individuation of physical, biological, psycho-social, and technical individuals, lead to a metaphysical realism, a realism of relations. While Harman does not include Simondon in his critique of Alfred North Whitehead's and Bruno Latour's relational ontology, I claim that Simondon's own relational ontology can help us clarify this dispute about the nature of relations and (though this may sound strange) show that Harman's position is not all that far from Simondon's motto "relation has value of being."[10]

So far, I have identified three issues concerning the status of the individual that are closely related in Simondon's philosophy: the question of processes, that of relations, and that of realism. In what follows, I show that Harman's rejection of Simondon's ontology (or, more precisely, ontogenetic perspective) is too rash and not entirely fair. In the process, Simondon and Harman emerge as figures quite different from new contestants in an old metaphysical battle to become, to an extent, bizarre allies with respect to some of the questions they ask, and the answers they give. It would be wrong to say that Simondon denies the individuality of objects as his research on individuation precisely seeks an explanation of objects' individuality or haecceity. Here we find that both Simondon's philosophy and object-oriented philosophy face the same question: how can we explain the individuality of objects? The starting point of Simondon's philosophy is to reject the idea that this explanation can be found either in the individuals already formed or in a pre-existent individuation principle; it can only be found in their process of individuation, and this explains why Simondon severely criticises the two main ways in which traditional metaphysics has approached individuals, namely hylomorphism and substantialism. Although Harman's radical defence of the subterranean life of objects, according to which they are withdrawn even with respect to their history, differs from Simondon's statement, we may begin to wonder why object-oriented philosophy is not interested in the process of the genesis of objects.

---

[10] Simondon, *L'individuation*, 62, this and all subsequent translations are mine.

Before addressing the key points of Simondon's philosophy, we must keep in sight that Simondon and Harman share a common goal: to overcome the anthropocentric view dominant in most of modern and postmodern philosophy. In modernity, philosophy was somehow reduced from the love of wisdom to the obsessive necessity of human self-knowledge. Thus, its favourite topic was, and still mostly is, the "basic rift" between human and world (subjectivism), as well as the ways whereby the human constructs the world (idealism) or accesses it (epistemological realism). Even if the self is understood in a formal and universal way and not as the empirical self, this still counts as a form of idealism, just an objectivist or transcendental one. The strategies followed by Simondon and Harman in pursuit of their goals are quite different, and we will have the opportunity to analyse their respective strength and weakness below. Simondon's philosophy eludes the epistemological opposition between subject and object as being the starting point of philosophy by way of raising a more primary ontological question, i.e., the question about the genesis of both the subject and the object. This ontogenetical inquiry strips the subject and its relation with the world of all ontological privilege. On the other hand, Harman looks for the metaphysical framework of every object, which makes it possible to put all kinds of objects on equal footing. Instead of a basic rift between humans and objects, Harman's philosophy points out a general rift between objects.

Harman has lucidly stated that this question links directly with aesthetics.[11] The reduction of aesthetics to a reflection or theory of art is further evidence of the anthropocentric slant of modernity, because it means to understand aesthetics as the discipline of the sensible or perceptual relations held by human beings, with special attention to the conditions that make beauty appear in these relations. Harman opens the door to recover, in a panpsychist direction, the etymological sense of aesthetics as a "general theory of sensations or perceptions":

[11] See Graham Harman, "On Vicarious Causation," *Collapse* (2007), 2, 187-221.

intentionality is regarded by almost everyone as a narrowly human feature. If this depiction were correct, sensual objects would be confined to a metaphysics of human perception, with no place in an ontology designed to address plastic and sand dunes no less than humans. This confinement of sensuality to the human kingdom must be refused. Intentionality is not a special human property at all, but an ontological feature of objects in general.[12]

As we can see, for Harman, the sensual problem is not confined to human beings, but is present in every relation between two real objects. This relation means the construction of a third real object which is an intentional object formed by the real object that is perceiving (thus absorbed in "sincerity") and the sensual object that is perceived. Inasmuch as this is a problem common to every object, the primary question of aesthetics becomes that of panpsychism: is it true that all objects, even physical ones, have a mind that allows them to perceive and feel? Harman does not like to treat the issue in these terms because he does not want to ascribe the same mental properties present in human beings to every object and he has proposed the interesting concept of "polypsychism" instead.[13] For now, we can leave this issue here; the related question about the possibility of access to real objects will be addressed right below.

---

[12] Harman, "On Vicarious Causation," 205. This quotation gestures towards what I think is the most interesting prospect in carrying on with the phenomenological path; phenomenology should not be limited to a phenomenology of consciousness, but must take into account an a-subjective and non-conscious phenomenology of stones, tornadoes, plants, or any thing whatsoever.

[13] On Harman and panpsychism, see Harman, *The Quadruple Object*, 118-23 and Graham Harman, "Zero-Person and the Psyche" in *Mind that Abides: Panpsychism in the New Millenium*, ed. David Skrbina (Amsterdam: John Benjamins, 2009), 253-82, which in my view is one of his best essays. Although I appreciate Harman's proposition of a plurality of minds, I do not share his worries about the term "panpsychism," because the mind (even in the case of the human one) has not to be necessarily understood *prima facie* in a rationalist, conscious, or reflective way, but can be understood in an affective or sensitive mode (eventually shared by all entities).

Simondon forces philosophy to seek the explanation of the haecceity of individuals not in an abstract principle—substance, matter, form—but in the materiality of their real, effective and unique process of individuation.[14] But what kind of movement can do this? Is it possible to gain an epistemological access to the various processes of individuation? If not, what is the nature of the task Simondon assigns to philosophy?[15] These questions allow us to further explore the links that can be established between Simondon, speculative realism, and aesthetics. In my view, the main division between the different proposals made under the heading "speculative realism" is not that between the processualists and the object-oriented camp, but between those who think that we can gain access to the real and those who do not. While all of them agree on rejecting the human-centred philosophy dominant in most of modern and postmodern thinking, and while all of them contest the privilege held by epistemology over ontology, they disagree on whether absolute reality is knowable or not. Meillassoux, for one, subtly avoids a return to dogmatic, pre-critical metaphysics without renouncing absolute statements: for him, there is no necessary entity or principle; only contingency is necessary.[16] Harman, on the other hand, contends that no access is possible to the always withdrawn real object. Any contact or relation with a real object is but a caricature of it; all that we can do is *allude* to the real. In this debate, Simondon is clearly aligned with Harman, since Simondon says that

we cannot, in the usual sense of the term, *know individuation*; we can only individuate, individuate ourselves, and individuate within ourselves ...

---

[14] See Simondon, *L'individuation*, 158-59. Although Simondon explicitly rejects the doctrine of materialism, his philosophy could be linked to the current developments known as "new materialisms."

[15] Simodon is quite assertive in stating the task of philosophy, "philosophical thinking being that which is driven by an implicit or explicit search for ontogenesis in all orders of reality." See Simondon, *L'individuation*, 229.

[16] See Quentin Meillassoux, *Après la finitude: Essai sur la nécessité de la contingence* (Paris: Seuil, 2006).

The individuation of the real that is exterior to the subject is grasped by the subject through the analogical individuation of knowledge within the subject; but it is *through the individuation of knowledge*, and not through knowledge alone, that the individuation of non-subject beings is grasped.[17]

So both Harman and Simondon try to develop a non-epistemological realism while differing on what the real that has to be grasped is. Even if the real is not knowable, we can speculate about its nature; that is the jovial message of speculative realism for me, and philosophy always needs joviality. At this point in time, I think that Simondon's analogical theory of access to objects' individuation is more developed than Harman's theory of allure. Simondon holds that all individuals are "result and agent" of a process of individuation; we, as subjects, have our own individuation, but we cannot enter, live or know other individuals' individuation.[18] In his already famous example of the production of a brick, Simondon states that even the slave who makes the brick cannot know the individuation of the brick;[19] to do that, "one would need to penetrate into the mould itself" while the clay progresses inside it.[20] However, what we can do is grasp the individuation of other beings *by analogy* with our own individuation. In Simondon, analogy does not mean a mere resemblance between structures or beings, but an identity of operations. He tries to develop a general theory of operations, called allagmatic, which would be the complement to the knowledge

---

[17] Simondon, *L'individuation*, 36, original emphasis.

[18] Ibid., 191.

[19] Simondon makes this statement in the context of his harsh critique of hylomorphism as an intellectual reflection of the psycho-social reality of ancient Greece where the master does not enter the factory to see how the slave *makes* the brick or, needless to say, to even make the brick himself: "the technical operation that *imposes a form onto a passive and indeterminate matter* [i.e., understood in terms of hylomorphism] ... is essentially the operation commanded by the free man and executed by the slave." Simondon, *L'individuation*, 51, original emphasis.

[20] Ibid., 46.

of structures provided by the special sciences.[21] The key point is that Simondon postulates the existence of a mutual reciprocity between the operations and the structures that both result from these operations and sustain them, between the processes of genesis and the object, the individuation and the individual. Simondon looks for a comprehensive theory that allows him to think together the individual, its genesis and its becoming.

The differences between Harman's theory of allure and Simondon's analogical theory touch directly on questions of aesthetics in the sense advocated by Harman. They also show the divergences between these two philosophers on what the real that has to be grasped is. The concept of allure is the place where Harman poses the issue of access to real objects; allure means "the separation between a sensual object and its quality."[22] The possibility of severing the sensual object from its qualities through *allusion* is considered the only way to access, though indirectly, the real object. Since every object, not only human beings, translate real objects into sensual ones, Harman grants this possibility to all kinds of objects, including inanimate ones. Simondon's analogical theory in turn does not address the issue of access to objects, but to their individuation. This access cannot be direct, and here Simondon and Harman agree, as I mention earlier. What we can do, according to Simondon, is to become aware of the operations whereby our own individuation is developed and, due to the identity of operations proposed by the analogical theory, this makes it possible to grasp the individuation of other beings. However, we can suppose that this awareness is limited to human beings, so in principle Simondon does not unfold the possibility of panpsychism as Harman does.

As a first step towards a philosophical account of ontogenesis, Simondon introduces a speculative hypothesis about pre-individual reality, i.e., the state of being from which the

---

[21] See the interesting appendix entitled "Allagmatique" in Simondon, *L'individuation*, 559-66.

[22] Harman, "On Vicarious Causation," 215.

individual comes into existence. Individuation means the formation of the individual from pre-individual reality, but its result is not only the individual but also its associated milieu; it is the totality formed by the individual and its milieu which makes new individuations possible (which are called "individualisations"). Thus, in order to explain the genesis of the individual and its subsequent individualisations, Simondon establishes that being is something more than the individual.[23] This is what Harman cannot accept, and the central point of contention is the concept of pre-individual reality. Before embracing or rejecting this concept, we must ask what, precisely, it denotes and what role it plays in the genesis of objects.

Drawing on physics, especially on thermodynamics, Simondon characterises pre-individual reality as the coexistence of heterogeneous orders of magnitude that do not communicate. This diversity—Simondon calls it *disparation*—has a potential. In this context, potential does not mean a hidden, not-yet-present feature, but a real capacity for transformation. The modern concept of potential energy marks a difference with classical conceptions of potency; becoming is not conceived as a mere unfolding from beings-in-potency to beings-in-action, inasmuch as individuals are not preformed or contained in any way in pre-individual reality. In a first energetic approach to pre-individual reality, Simondon takes from thermodynamics the notion of metastable equilibrium as a condition of possibility for individuation. While hylomorphism forgets these energetic conditions which make possible the acquisition of form by matter, it would also be wrong to take them as a sufficient condition for individuation. In addition to the material conditions (matter capable of receiving a form, e.g., the clay previously homogenised and purified by the slave) and the energetic ones (metastable equilibrium) of individuation, Simondon postulates the necessity of an evental condition: the appearance of a singularity. A process of individuation begins when communication between the different orders

---

23 Simondon, *L'individuation*, 63.

of magnitude is established through a singularity, which according to Simondon is the "beginning of the individual" and "is preserved in it."[24] After the formation of the individual, we cannot explain its successive transformations by understanding it in isolation, which is why Simondon states that the individual has a complement of being, a pre-individual reality associated with it.

The problem with understanding Simondon's philosophy is that, despite the centrality of the concept of pre-individual reality, he offers several approaches to it that are to some degree inconsistent. Focusing on this issue will help us clarify why Harman rejects Simondon's philosophy. For Harman, philosophies of the pre-individual, and, broadly speaking, all processualist philosophies must be rejected because they dissolve objects in "a semi-liquid, holistic quasi-lump."[25] Although I have depicted Harman's reading of Simondon as too rash, his criticism does rest on textual evidence. In trying to characterise pre-individual reality, Simondon claims that he is an heir to pre-Socratic thought:

> we might call *nature* this pre-individual reality that is carried by the individual, trying to find in the word nature the meaning that pre-Socratic philosophers attributed to it: ... nature is *reality of the possible*, under the species of this *apeiron* from which, according to Anaximander, every individuated form emerges.[26]

But as Isabelle Stengers reminds us in an article that is rather critical of Simondon, there is more to him than this pre-Socratic stance.[27] Simondon can also be seen as "a thinker of the sciences in the most demanding sense" when he poses the problem of the heterogeneity of orders of magnitude which

---

[24] Simondon, *L'individuation*, 97.

[25] Harman, "The Road to Objects," 172.

[26] Simondon, *L'individuation*, 305, original emphasis.

[27] Isabelle Stengers, "Pour une mise à l'aventure de la transduction" in *Simondon*, ed. Pascal Chabot (Paris: Vrin, 2002), 137-59.

constitute pre-individual reality.[28] This heterogeneity cannot be thought as "a semi-liquid, holistic quasi-lump," or through a substantialist or a predicative logic because it is a pure state of *disparation*. If Simondon recovers the concept of *apeiron* as "reality of the possible," this is because the heterogeneity of pre-individual reality makes individuation (energetically) possible. Harman's reading could be maintained if Simondon had stopped his research on individuation at this point. But Simondon adds that "individuation is thus presented as one of the possibilities of the becoming of being, that meets *certain defined conditions*."[29] What are these defined conditions? Here Simondon gives an answer to one of the main questions posed by an object-oriented philosophy, i.e., what defines an object as an autonomous entity? Of course, Harman has the right to reject Simondon's solution, but not to claim that Simondon eludes the question. A singularity—"the beginning of the individual"—is an interstitial reality which can solve in a unique way the problem posed by the heterogeneity of orders of magnitude. The individual performs a work of compatibilisation, and it exists to the extent that it gives *signification* to what until then was only disparity. This work is what characterises the haecceity of every object. It might even be called its identity. In any case, this identity is not conceived as some immutable traits of an underlying substance, but as an *activity* of mediation. Moving from the first energetic perspective to an informational one, Simondon conceives of it as a process of in-formation that he calls "transduction." Hence, ontogenesis, information, transduction, and individuation are different terms for the same process: the genesis of the individual and its associated milieu, the activity or operation of information, the transduction of a singularity in a metastable field. As we will see below, Simondon

---

[28] Stengers, "Pour une mise à l'aventure de la transduction," 153.

[29] Simondon, *L'individuation*, 64, my emphasis. It must be clarified that "being" is used by Simondon as equivalent to pre-individual reality before individuation (first phase of being). After individuation, it is equivalent to the totality formed by the individual and its associated milieu (second phase of being).

considers that both classical hylomorphism and the modern theory of information, as well as cybernetics, fail to grasp this process because they only take into account either its extreme terms (form-matter) or the message to be sent between them (signal), forgetting how these extremes can relate. Only then can the "defined conditions" of individuation announced by Simondon be understood.

I have tried to show that Simondon's mere use of the adjective "pre-individual" should not lead us to reject his philosophy from an object-oriented point of view. Let me propose a criterion for the meaning of the concept: speaking of pre-individual reality only makes sense in relation to the creation or development of a *new* individual, and there is nothing that forbids objects to be the pre-individual reality of a new object. But why should we keep the concept of "pre-individual reality"? My point is that what matters in pre-individual reality is not the presence of individuals. This is so for two reasons: firstly, an ontology that is limited to the statement that "there are individuals" cannot account for the productive potential of reality, since the potential of pre-individual reality lies not in the presence of individuals, but in the existence of a heterogeneity, of a diversity. Without differences, there can be no change, as thermodynamics readily shows. Secondly, though it is possible to take a frozen photograph of reality, and to hold that there are individuals with some intrinsic and hidden properties, we cannot explain the transformations these individuals undergo without taking into account their associated milieu. To take my favourite example: a seed is an individual with its own properties, with its haecceity, as Simondon repeatedly emphasises, and it has some powers which condition what it can become. But, appropriating Latour for our purposes, we must say that the seed needs allies in order to become a plant, namely water and light. The seed is a singularity in which a communication is established between the cosmic order of solar energy and the molecular order of the mineral salts contained in the soil water.[30] We can see that the photons of light and the mineral salts that are part of the pre-individual reality of the plant are themselves individuals. So pre-individual reality is not a reality mysteriously characterised as non-individual, but the very reality from which individuals emerge and that which makes their becoming possible. Even if we accept the plant as an autonomous object that persists over time and possesses a withdrawn reality that makes it be *this* plant, there are two questions haunting my reading of Harman's object-oriented philosophy: how is the genesis of the plant explained? Once the plant is already individuated, how can we explain its successive transformations without appealing to a reality outside the plant? There seems to be a lack of interest in these questions. I appreciate Harman's efforts to grant dignity to all kinds of objects after four centuries dominated by the *res cogitans*, the transcendental subject, conscience, *Dasein*, the exegesis of texts, and the critique of human institutions: in a word, by the delusion of a human-centred universe in which all objects revolve around the all so special human being. But there is a line beyond which this dignity can become a new delusion of manic omnipotence. Every object needs other realities in order to exist and to persist through time. It seems as if object-oriented philosophy must be complemented with a process-oriented philosophy, just as process philosophy must make space for enduring objects.

So far, I have argued for the pertinence of the concept of "pre-individual reality" for explaining the emergence and development of individuals. This explanation needs to be developed further. Despite the importance previously granted to differences in order to explain change, it would be as vain to say that "there are differences and that's all" as it would be to say that "there are individuals." We need an explanation of the mechanisms by which differences create individuals (i.e., of the creativity of becoming). If Simondon rejects the idea that hylomorphism can give us such an explanation, this is not only due to its abstract consideration of an active form

---

[30] See Simondon, *L'individuation*, 34-35n12.

and a passive, formless matter, but also because it forgets the operation of mediation whereby the energy system that comprises both form and matter is established.[31] The same holds for the modern theory of information, in which information is confused with the signal to be sent. This theory focuses on the optimum conditions of transmission: the signal must be regular and predictable in order to avoid confusion with the noise. Thus, it does not take into account the conditions that make the signal be *significative* for a receiver. To do that, the signal must be confronted with the structure of the receiver, and Simondon points out the two extremes in which there is no information: if the signal is totally coincident with the structure of the receiver, there is only an "outer iteration of an inner reality";[32] if there is a total disparity between the signal and the structure, the former cannot be effectively integrated in the functionality of the latter. Between these two extremes, there can be information, which is neither a form nor a signal sent or stored in a medium, but a *structuring activity* or operation. To sum up, "the signals must meet some previous forms in relation to which they are significatives in order to be received; *the signification is relational*."[33]

Here we arrive at the core of Simondon's philosophy: his defence of the necessity of relational ontology. By contrast, Harman completely rejects this necessity and he has radicalised this issue to the point of asserting that the fundamental metaphysical distinction must be sought in the difference between objects and their relations. But I think that Harman is aiming at the wrong target when he dismisses the philoso-

---

[31] See Simondon, *L'individuation*, 45-48.

[32] Ibid., 223.

[33] Ibid., 223. Simondon makes these statements in the context of his reading of information theory and cybernetics. They nevertheless are also related to aesthetics in the narrow sense of the discipline as regards artistic creation and experimentation. Artworks are not a signal stored in a painting or a sculpture, nor are they a signal sent to the spectator. The aesthetic experience can only emerge in the *specific relation* between the structure of the artwork and that of the spectator. Thus, the question of beauty (or any other aesthetic feature) cannot be posed in objective terms, but only in relational ones.

phies of Whitehead and Latour as "relational ontology." In my view, what Harman rejects is actually not relational ontology, but holism. We can approach the subtleties of this issue via the debate Harman and Shaviro stage in *The Speculative Turn*. Following Whitehead, Shaviro, in "The Actual Volcano: Whitehead, Harman, and the Problem of Relations," takes for granted the connection between relations and processes or becoming.[34] The source of novelty is the way in which every actual entity makes its prehensions or selections. This private sphere of actual entities constitutes their "singularity of aesthetic self-enjoyment."[35] But they also have a public sphere by which "every actual entity is present in every other actual entity."[36] In his response, Harman identifies this latter statement as the basic proposition of relational ontology and denies that it can provide us with an explanation of change. [37] Harman's argument is clear: if we dissolve every actual entity in the network of its interconnected relations, then there is no underlying reality of entities which can actually change. All we have is a perpetual perishing of cinematic networks, "an endless series of frozen statues, which give the illusion of continuous alteration as we flip through them as if through those novelty card decks that allow children to watch moving cartoons."[38] Thus, Harman can make his lapidary claim that "the only way to account for becoming is with a *non*-relational ontology," and he does not give much credit to what has been called process-relational ontology.[39]

Simondon can help us show that Harman is misidentifying his enemy and that he may find his ally against holism in a relational thinker such as Simondon. The connection between relations and becoming is clear in Simondon: encounters

---

[34] Steven Shaviro, "The Actual Volcano: Whitehead, Harman, and the Problem of Relations" in *The Speculative Turn*, 279-90.

[35] Ibid., 284.

[36] Whitehead qtd. in Ibid., 287.

[37] Harman, "Response to Shaviro," 291-303.

[38] Ibid., 300.

[39] Ibid., 293, original emphasis.

and relations between objects are the sources of individuation processes by which new objects come into existence. As we have seen, what characterises these new objects is the relational activity whereby they establish communication between the heterogeneous—and discontinuous—orders of magnitude of their pre-individual reality. The possibility of change resides not in Harman's mysterious non-relational and non-potential "reserves for change" but precisely in the creative activity by which individuals establish relations in an always novel way.[40] Hence, Simondon does not dissolve objects in their effects or in their presence in other objects; he does not assert that the being of objects resides in the network of their external relations, but rather that objects are an activity of relation. In other words, Simondon does not state that objects are the relations they have, but that objects *are* relations:

> Attempting to characterise the individual in itself or in relation to other realities amounts to making it the term of a relation, a relation with itself or with another reality; however, we must find a point of view from which we can grasp the individual as an activity of the relation, not as a term of this relation; properly speaking, the individual is not in relation with itself or with other realities; it is the being *of* the relation, and not a being *in* relation, because the relation is an intense operation, an active centre.[41]

French language gives Simondon the possibility of making a fundamental distinction between *rapport* and *relation*.[42] *Rapport* is an external relationship that does not result in the genesis of a new individual; a *relation* is a necessary condition for the emergence of an individual. It is in this sense that relations have an ontological value and this is what, I think, can properly be called a relational ontology. Such an ontology does not fall into the trap of the "house of

---

[40] Harman, "Response to Shaviro," 299.

[41] Simondon, *L'individuation*, 62-63, original emphasis.

[42] See Ibid., 68.

mirrors" denounced by Harman in his discussion of other relational thinkers such as Whitehead.[43] If we focus only on objects, and not on the relations between them that give rise to ontogenetic processes, we can explain neither the origin of objects nor their individuality. Simondon's distinction between *rapport* and *relation* cannot properly be understood by identifying it with the traditional distinction between internal and external relations. Since Simondon conceives of the individual as having a complement of being (the associated milieu), the categories of interior and exterior do not adequately express its relational activity. An individual is a place of communication; therefore, a relation is a movement from the outside to the inside which constitutes and sustains the individual, an operation which produces a structure. Due to the reciprocity between structures and operations, there is also a movement from the inside to the outside: the previously formed structures condition and make possible new relations. What, then, defines the external relationships with regard to relations? We can say that they are contingent for the individual because it does not need them in order to exist; these relationships do not constitute the singular activity that the individual consists of.

Harman also sees that these points are crucial for assessing the suitability of relational ontology. Despite claiming that the basic metaphysical opposition is that between objects and relations, he may in fact be pointing to a relational ontology in the sense advocated here when he writes that "although all objects are made up of relations between component objects, it is not necessarily the case that all objects enter into larger components in turn."[44] What is more, Harman himself depicts an inflationary universe of genetic relations when he emphasises that "*any relation immediately generates a new object.*"[45] The crucial question is: which ontological status should we attribute to these relations between component

---

43 Harman qtd. in Shaviro, "The Actual Volcano," 283.

44 Harman, "The Road to Objects," 177.

45 Harman, *The Quadruple Object*, 117, original emphasis.

objects? Harman makes a distinction similar to Simondon's, which can help us understand what he means by "relation." In an almost Simondonian paragraph, he holds that

> by speaking of relations on the interior of a thing, I mean something quite different: the assembly of actors on the inside of any black box that enable it to exist. For lack of a better term, we might call these "domestic" relations to avoid confusion with the internal relations that deserve to be expelled from view. I hold that there is an absolute distinction between the domestic relations that a thing needs to some extent in order to exist, and the external alliances that it does not need.[46]

So what is the point of discord with Simondon? The answer comes on the heels of the passage quoted above: "But the actor itself cannot be identified with either. An object cannot be exhausted by a set of alliances. But neither is it exhausted by a summary of its pieces, since any genuine object will be an emergent reality over and above its components."[47] We should note that Harman now takes a direction opposite to that taken earlier in his rejection of relational ontology: before it was identified with holism; now it is identified with reductionism (since Harman regards relations as a mere summary of the pieces of an object). This is precisely the mistake that Simondon wants to avoid, because it would deny relations ontological value. While both Simondon and Harman explicitly reject reductionism as well as holism as inadequate ways of explaining the haecceity of the individual, Simondon thinks of relations as something "over and above" the components of objects.[48] These components can have external relationships while they remain without genuine communication; they can be combined, stacked, or composed; but they are not truly articulated until a relation is established between them by a new individual. This is the difference between reductionism and relational ontology, and

---

[46] Harman, *Prince of Networks*, 135.

[47] Ibid.

[48] See, for instance, Simondon, *L'individuation*, 224-27.

the classical joke about reductionism serves to illustrate it: try to put the chemical components of a human being in a jar, and wait for the human being to appear. You will get a mass, maybe articulated to some extent at the chemical level, but never a human being. A genetic relation has to be established between the components: the human being, as every object, is "result and agent" of this relation, a creative activity which is the source of the novelty of becoming.

There is yet another point of divergence between Harman's and Simondon's conceptions of relation. When Harman points out that every relation generates a new object, he means something very different from what we find in Simondon's relational theory. As we have seen above, what Harman contends is that a relation between two real objects creates a third *intentional* real object. But he does not explain how the genesis of *non-intentional* real objects is produced, and this is exactly the metaphysical issue that Simondon's philosophy of individuation tries to develop.[49]

Before concluding, I want to address briefly the respective strength and weakness of the paths followed by Simondon and Harman in order to overcome anthropocentrism. Simondon's research shows that in paying attention to the ontogenetic processes whereby individuals come into existence, we cannot establish a substantial difference between the various regimes of individuation, namely physical, biological and psychical-collective. However, this does not imply reducing all these regimes to a monistic ontology without discontinuities. What we find in Simondon's philosophy is, on the contrary, one of the most astonishing developments of a pluralist ontology, which is based on a detailed analysis and a thorough knowledge of the special sciences devoted to each of these regimes.

---

[49] It must be clarified that Simondon tries to explain the genesis of objects in general, so he is not limited to non-intentional objects. My emphasis on these is only due to the fact that in my view Harman's philosophy does not address their genesis. It could be argued that, inasmuch as Harman grants intentionality to all objects, this distinction is not so relevant. However, according to Harman the always withdrawn reality of objects must be defined regardless of their relations or intentionality, and I contend that the genesis of this reality is what Harman does not explain.

Yet we may regret that Simondon did not push further the struggle against the ontological gap usually supposed to exist between the animate and the inanimate world. Thus, unlike Whitehead's concept of "sentience," Simondon restricts his concept of "affectivity" to living beings. On the other hand, Harman's interest in the basic metaphysical framework of the world can perhaps better help us develop a flat ontology in which no object enjoys a special ontological privilege, and where all relations between objects are on equal footing. In this sense, we must celebrate Harman's statement that "aesthetics becomes first philosophy."[50] However, although Harman's general metaphysics tries to depict an inflationary world of countless objects thus advocating a deeply pluralistic ontology, we may also regret the lack in such an object-oriented philosophy of the detailed analysis of atoms, bricks, or protozoa that we find in Simondon's work. If Harman and Simondon can be brought to individuate together, this should result in an ontogenetic theory of the plurality of objects, wherein the aesthetic concept of affectivity would be part of its basic ontological vocabulary.

It has not been my intention to restage the metaphysical battle between objects and processes, or between objects and relations in this paper. What I have tried to do is to show how a careful reading of Simondon's philosophy can help us overcome such oppositions. In my view, Simondon and Harman can both be considered philosophers of emergence who celebrate the radical novelty present in the irreducible individuality of every object. While Harman is more interested in showing the emergent features of objects that forbid reducing them to any other reality, be it their components or their external relations, Simondon tries to shed light on the processes of individuation, on the ontogenetic relations that give existence to emergent units and individuals. Which is the source of the individuality of objects? Which work do objects perform in order to be what they are? According to Simondon, the individual is a place of problem-solving. It ex-

---

[50] Harman, "On Vicarious Causation," 221.

ists because it manages to solve in a unique way the problem posed by the heterogeneity of those realities among which it establishes a communication. It perishes when it is no longer able to solve this problem. The relation or resolution that constitutes the being of the individual is not a mere composition or abstraction, but the creation of a new dimension not contained in any of its components. This is why an individual cannot be reduced to anything else. Simondon allows us to think reality as a process and a product at the same time, and he does so through a metaphysical realism in which relation means creation.[51]

[51] This essay is an extended version of the paper I delivered at the *Aesthetics in the 21st Century* conference in Basel in 2012. I would like to thank the University of Basel's Department of English for the wonderful hosting of the event and for the opportunity to participate in it. I want to thank also those present in the audience for the warm reception of my paper, with extra special thanks due to Graham Harman and N. Katherine Hayles for their encouraging words concerning the ideas developed here. I am very grateful to the editors of this special issue for their extremely careful editing. They were very helpful in improving this extended version. Last but not least, I want to show my gratitude to my *compañera*, Ana Manzano, for having accompanied me, both physically and emotionally, to Basel.

Part 2: The Theory of Art

Greenberg, Duchamp, and the Next Avant-Garde

Graham Harman

American University in Cairo

I N CLEMENT GREENBERG AND MAR-
cel Duchamp we have two of the
pivotal figures in the twentieth
century arts. Yet they seem to stand in complete opposition,
so that the reputation of Duchamp rises as that of Greenberg
falls, and vice versa. Greenberg is viewed as the champion of
formalism, of artworks sealed off from their socio-political
surroundings and even from the private intentions of the
artist. Greenberg held that Duchamp was simply "not a good
artist," and that his devotees (including the highly regarded
Joseph Beuys) were "also not especially good artists."[1] From
the late 1940s through the early 1960s, Greenberg's critical
views marched step-by-step with the progressive advance of
the artistic avant-garde, in the eclipse of Paris by New York,
and the triumph of Jackson Pollock and the so-called "post-
painterly abstraction" of Kenneth Noland and Jules Olitski.
Since that time, Greenberg and his preferred styles have fallen
into disfavour, while in the words of one observer "the reputation and work of Marcel Duchamp ... [have] surpassed those

---

[1] Clement Greenberg, *Late Writings* (Minneapolis: University of Minnesota Press, 2003), 221.

of Picasso in the eyes of art historians, artists, and Duchamp's admirers alike."[2]

Over the past decade, there has been a growing sense that Greenberg is becoming readable once again, while Duchamp's legacy was perhaps on the verge of becoming overexploited. My hope is that by re-examining Greenberg's complaints about Duchamp, by weighing the strengths and weaknesses of those complaints, we might gain a fresh sense of what avenues might still be open to art criticism and perhaps to the arts themselves.

1. Greenberg's Critique of Duchamp

From the dawn of his career in 1939 through May 1968, Clement Greenberg published a total of 333 essays, articles, and reviews. As far as I can determine, all of this written output contains just two references to Marcel Duchamp. In January 1943 there is a passing reference to some pieces by Duchamp in Peggy Guggenheim's new gallery, which Greenberg felt were unsuccessfully displayed.[3] Almost a quarter century later, in April 1967, Greenberg tells us that minimalism commits itself to the third dimension because this is where art intersects with non-art, and he credits Duchamp and the Dadaists with this discovery.[4] Just two references in twenty-eight years; that is all.

But beginning with Greenberg's May 1968 lecture in Sydney, published the following year, Duchamp becomes a more central opponent. Though the references become only slightly more numerous, they become more vehemently negative, as well as more central to Greenberg's defence of his own aesthetic views. The tables had turned. Greenberg was now an intellectual exile rather than a king, while Duchamp had been

---

[2] Gavin Parkinson, *The Duchamp Book* (London: Tate Publishing, 2008), 6.

[3] Clement Greenberg, *The Collected Essays and Criticism: Perceptions and Judgments, 1939-1944*, vol. 1, ed. John O'Brian (Chicago: University of Chicago Press, 1986), 141.

[4] Clement Greenberg, *The Collected Essays and Criticism: Modernism with a Vengeance, 1957-1969*, vol. 4, ed. John O'Brian (Chicago: University of Chicago Press, 1993), 253.

retroactively anointed as the heroic forerunner of more recent artistic trends. Let us look briefly at each of these references, so as to prepare for a more general discussion.

In the Sydney lecture of May '68, Duchamp is criticised twice for attempting to transcend the untranscendable difference in quality between good art and bad art. The first instance condemns not just Duchamp, but a large portion of the art of 1968:

> Things that purport to be art do not function, do not exist, as art until they are experienced through taste. Until then they exist only as empirical phenomena, as aesthetically arbitrary objects or facts. These, precisely, are what a lot of contemporary art gets taken for, and what any artists want their works to be taken for—in the hope, periodically renewed since Marcel Duchamp first acted on it fifty-odd years ago, that by dint of evading the reach of taste while yet remaining in the context of art, certain kinds of contrivances will achieve unique existence and value. So far this hope has proved illusory.[5]

Later in the Sydney lecture, Greenberg expands on this notion.[6] No one in the arts, he says, had ever questioned the difference between high-quality and low-quality art until the emergence of the "popular" avant-garde, by which he means Dada and Duchamp. The inherent difficulty of high artistic taste and production was replaced by the difficulty of accepting an ostensibly non-artistic phenomenon as an artwork. Greenberg offers a sarcastic list of real or imagined pseudo-artworks produced by the Duchampian pop avant-garde:

> The idea of the difficult is evoked by a row of boxes, by a mere rod, by a pile of litter, by projects for Cyclopean landscape architecture, by the plan for a trench dug in a straight line for hundreds of miles, by a half-open door, by the cross-section of a mountain, by stating imaginary relations between real points in real places, by a blank wall, and so forth.[7]

---

[5] Greenberg, *The Collected Essays and Criticism: Modernism with a Vengeance*, 293.

[6] Ibid., 301-03.

[7] Ibid., 302.

Greenberg concludes: "In this context the Milky Way might be offered as a work of art too. The trouble with the Milky Way, however, is that, as *art*, it is banal."[8] In the 1968 Sydney lecture, then, Duchamp is presented as someone who evades questions of aesthetic quality and replaces them with the claim that any arbitrarily designated object can be an artwork. This interpretation of Duchamp is not surprising and not inaccurate.

In Greenberg's 1971 essay "Counter-Avant-Garde,"[9] the critique of Duchamp becomes harsher and more intricate. In Western art, Greenberg says, there had always been a small number of innovators who also led the way in terms of aesthetic quality. Beginning in the 1860s, there was increasing distance between advanced art and official taste. Advanced art began to challenge that taste to such a degree as to cause a certain amount of shock—important new art actually became *scandalous* with Manet, the impressionists, Cézanne, the Fauves, and cubism. In each case the scandal wore off after some time, though the underlying aesthetic challenge of the avant-garde remained. But the challenge and the scandal came to be mistaken for one another. With the Italian futurists, "innovation and advancedness began to look more and more like ... categorical means to artistic significance apart from aesthetic quality."[10] With Duchamp, this avant-gardeness was replaced by a full blown avant-gardei*sm.* As Greenberg sees it,

in a few short years after 1912, [Duchamp] laid down the precedents for everything that advanced-advanced art has done in the fifty-odd years since ... [He] locked advanced-advanced art into what has amounted to hardly more than elaborations, variations on, and recapitulations of his original ideas.[11]

---

[8] Greenberg, *The Collected Essays and Criticism: Modernism with a Vengeance*, 303.

[9] Clement Greenberg, "Counter-Avant-Garde," *Art International* (1971), 15, 16-19. Reprinted in *Marcel Duchamp in Perspective*, ed. Joseph Masheck (Englewood Cliffs: Prentice-Hall, 1975), 122-23.

[10] Greenberg, *Late Writings*, 6.

[11] Ibid., 7.

These are strong words, given the near-total absence of Duchamp from Greenberg's writings until the latter was almost sixty years old. And what was the core of Duchamp's vision, now credited by Greenberg with setting the agenda for advanced-advanced art as of 1971? That agenda is that

> the shocking, the scandalizing, the mystifying and confounding, became embraced as ends in themselves and no longer regretted as initial side effects of artistic newness that would wear off with familiarity. Now these side effects were to be built in. The first bewildered reaction to innovative art was to be the sole and appropriate one.[12]

More than this, the shock and scandal in question were no longer aesthetic as it was with great avant-garde art, but came solely from the extra-aesthetic realm: "Duchamp's first readymades, his bicycle wheel, his bottle rack, and later on his urinal, were not at all new in configuration; they startled when first seen only because they were presented in a fine-art context, which is a purely cultural and social, not an aesthetic or artistic context."[13] The point became not to violate the aesthetic standards of the recent avant-garde in order to create progress in taste, but to violate social decorum.

There are a few other points to consider. Duchamp always took pride in an art that appealed to the mind rather than the eye, against what he dismissively called "retinal art."[14] But for Greenberg, this excess of *thinking* is precisely the death of art. In other words, avant-gardism of Duchamp's type involves too much conscious choice. The artist performs a series of easy cognitive stunts that fail to outrun their conception; the artist is no longer surprised by what the artwork discovers: "Conscious volition, deliberateness, plays a principal part in avant-gardist art: that is, resorting to ingenuity instead of inspiration, contrivance instead of creation, 'fancy' instead of "imagination"; in effect, to the known rather than the

---

[12] Greenberg, *Late Writings*, 7.

[13] Ibid., 12.

[14] Parkinson, *The Duchamp Book*, 6.

unknown."[15] The new becomes a consciously available set of external gestures rather than the object of unremitting struggle. As a result, "the exceptional enterprise of artistic innovation, by being converted into an affair of standardised categories, of a set of 'looks,' is put within reach of uninspired calculation."[16] Yet aesthetics ought to be a matter of surprise rather than of shock, of difficult grappling with something slightly beyond our grasp rather than the transparent mastery of a clever subversive concept. As Greenberg later put it, mathematical demonstrations become boring when repeated, and so too do the "demonstrations" of Duchamp as to the arbitrariness of what counts as an art object. By contrast, "that's not the way it is with more substantial art, good and bad: that kind of art you have to experience over and over again in order to keep on *knowing* it."[17]

A related notion is that avant-gardism thinks it can overturn the entire history of art with a single transgressive gesture, whereas for Greenberg art advances by mastering the best art of the past and adapting it in some relevant way:

> Maybe the most constant topic of avant-gardist rhetoric is the claim made with each new phase of avant-garde, or seeming avant-garde, art that the past is now being finally closed out and a radical mutation in the nature of art is taking place after which art will no longer behave as it has heretofore.[18]

Attempts to shock and overturn art from the outside have replaced challenges to taste from within the established tradition. But for Greenberg, surprise must always occur inside a given context: "new and surprising ways of satisfying in art have always been connected closely with immediately previous ways ... There have been no great vaults 'forward,' no innovations out of the blue, no ruptures of continuity in the

---

[15] Greenberg, *Late Writings*, 7.

[16] Ibid., 8.

[17] Ibid., 82.

[18] Ibid., 9.

high art of the past—nor have any such been witnessed in our day."[19] As he would claim five years later in his Bennington Seminars, "Duchamp had hardly grasped what real cubism was about"[20]—namely, the flattening-out of the picture plane as opposed to the deepening illusion of pictorial depth since the Italian Renaissance. For Greenberg this is evident from the rather traditional perspectival elements in Duchamp's own quasi-cubist painting efforts, before he gave up painting and turned to the bicycle wheel and other readymades. Instead, Greenberg holds, Duchamp mistakenly believed that the force of cubism lay in its difficulty and shock value.

This leads us to the final and perhaps most important aspect of Greenberg's anti-Duchampian views. Though it might seem surprising at first, Greenberg is adamant in treating both Duchamp and surrealism as forms of "academic art." There are two kinds of academic artist, Greenberg holds. The first is able to recognise the new avant-garde trends of the present day but follows them in a watered-down, nonthreatening form. Greenberg offers the example of Paul-Albert Besnard, whose vulgarised if imaginative variant of impressionism in the 1880s "outsold Sisley and Pissarro, to their grief, and became better known too, in the short term."[21] The second kind, far more common, "is one who is puzzled [by the new trends], and who therefore orients his art to expectations formed by an earlier phase of art."[22] Duchamp was a half-hearted early devotee of Cézanne and the Fauves, but was simply unable to grasp the new aesthetic standards generated by cubism, and misinterpreted cubism as nothing more than a shock and a scandal to previous standards rather than as a style with inherent aesthetic merit. For this reason, Greenberg holds, Duchamp can be taken seriously as an interesting cultural

---

[19] Greenberg, *Late Writings*, 15.

[20] Ibid., 81.

[21] Clement Greenberg, *Homemade Esthetics: Observations on Art* (Oxford: Oxford University Press, 1999), 87.

[22] Greenberg, *Late Writings*, 15.

figure, but not as an artist per se.[23] Dada, surrealism, pop art, and minimalism mark a gradual relaxing of aesthetic standards, with everything boiling down to how severely one can shock the previous expectations of what counts as art.

But we have not yet heard Greenberg's most powerful definition of academic art, from another important Sydney lecture given in 1979:

> Academicization isn't a matter of academies—there were academies long before academicization and before the nineteenth century. Academicism consists in *the tendency to take the medium of an art too much for granted*. It results in blurring: words become imprecise, color gets muffled, the physical sources of sound become too much dissembled.[24]

Up through the 1920s and even 1930s, academic art tended to be blatantly academic, defended by official academies and conventional taste while disdained by a relatively small modernist elite. But Greenberg holds that with surrealism, the heir of Dada, we see a form of academic art that is cannily disguised as cutting-edge modernism.

As early as his pioneering essay "Avant-Garde and Kitsch" in 1939, Greenberg wrote that "Picasso, Braque, Mondrian, Miró, Kandinsky, Brancusi, even Klee, Matisse, and Cézanne derive their chief inspiration from the medium they work in,"[25] but added in a dismissive footnote that "the chief concern of a painter like Dali is to represent the processes and concepts of his consciousness, not the processes of his medium."[26] For all the shock value of Dalí's flaming giraffes and skinny-legged towering elephants, his art is focused on shocking literary content, and in Greenberg's view we have reached a stage in the history of visual art in which literary content is just a non-artistic distraction. In this respect, surrealism and Dada are simply two sides of the same academic coin. Surrealism

---

[23] Greenberg, *Late Writings*, 153-54.

[24] Ibid., 28, my emphasis.

[25] Greenberg, *The Collected Essays and Criticism: Perceptions and Judgments*, 9.

[26] Ibid.

takes its medium too much for granted by replacing drawing room portraits with wild fantasies of hallucinogenic entities. Meanwhile, Dada takes its medium too much for granted by giving up on the project of transforming it from within, and challenges it only with shocking gestures from the outside.

There are other details to Greenberg's critique of Duchamp, other scathing and witty remarks, but already we have encountered the core principles of this critique, of which there are perhaps six:

1. Duchamp rejects quality as an aesthetic standard.

2. He treats the shock value of advanced art not as an unfortunate side effect that wears off over time, but as the central purpose of art.

3. He shocks established standards not by internal aesthetic means, but by transgressing everyday social decorum: displaying urinals, breasts, or the spread-out naked body of a murdered woman in a fine art context that will be predictably horrified by such gestures.

4. He privileges thinking in art, turning artworks into transparent concepts to an excessive degree.

5. He overestimates the radical break his work makes with the past.

6. Though he thinks himself to be the pinnacle of artist advancement, Duchamp is actually an academic artist who takes the medium of art too much for granted, despairs of being able to innovate from within, and is thus led into a sort of juvenile sabotage through shocking affronts to the fine arts gallery context.

This six-point list is perhaps more interesting if we reverse it into Greenberg's own positive aesthetic program:

1. Art is always a matter of high and low aesthetic quality.

2. Shock value is merely a temporary symptom of advanced art, never its central purpose.

3. Important art is characterised by aesthetic challenge rather than extra-aesthetic shock.

4. Art is a matter of taste rather than of thinking, and taste must always struggle to refine and improve itself in contact with the art object.

5. Important art builds on the past rather than breaking radically with it.

6. Art should not be academic, meaning that it should not take its medium for granted. This final principle entails that art reflects a constant struggle to reinvent its form.

Stated differently, art avoids academicism when its content manages to *reflect* or *embody* the possibilities of its medium, rather than presenting content as an isolated figure whose ground or medium can be taken for granted. This is why Greenberg increasingly celebrated painting that announced the flatness of canvas, why cubism was for him the greatest school of art in the twentieth century, and why he experienced such rapture over synthetic cubist collage as a way of negotiating the dangers of cubism's possible two-dimensional deadlock.[27] The content of cubism, for Greenberg, reflected and mastered the highest possibilities of its medium at that point in history. In other words, despite his concern with the flatness of the canvas, there is a sense in which Greenberg is primarily interested in *depth*: in making the invisible deep conditions of any medium somehow visible in the content of the art.

---

[27] Greenberg, *The Collected Essays and Criticism: Modernism with a Vengeance*, 61-66.

2. Non-Relational Philosophy

This links Greenberg closely with two key figures in the twentieth century humanities. One is the Canadian media theorist Marshall McLuhan, famous for his statements that "the medium is the message" and that "the content or message of any particular medium has about as much importance as the stenciling on the casing of an atomic bomb."[28] In other words, we waste our time when we argue about the good or bad content of television shows, since the real work is done by the invisible changes in the structure of consciousness brought about by television regardless of what high- or low-quality content it might possess. If we translate Greenberg into McLuhanian terms, then "the content of any painting has about as much importance as the stenciling on the casing of an atomic bomb." All political activism in art, all literary anecdote and inspirational messaging, fades before the purely formal consideration of how the medium itself is made to shine forth in the content.

But perhaps an even more important link is with Martin Heidegger, the heavyweight champion of twentieth century philosophy, in my view still unmatched by any figure of equal stature since. Is not Heidegger's entire philosophical breakthrough a premonition of what McLuhan and Greenberg formulated much later? The phenomenology of Edmund Husserl asked us to suspend judgment about any hidden reasons in nature for things to happen as they do, and to focus instead on the patient description of phenomena in consciousness, in all their subtlety. Heidegger's great breakthrough came when he first noted that usually we *do not* encounter entities as present in consciousness. This is already an artificial special case that occurs most often in the *breakdown* of entities. As long as your heart and lungs are healthy and working effectively, as long as the highway is not buckled by earthquakes, as long as the hammer and screwdriver are working in your hands rather

---

[28] The longer quotation comes from the famous 1969 *Playboy* interview in Marshall McLuhan, *Essential McLuhan*, ed. Eric McLuhan and Frank Zingrone (London: Routledge, 1997), 222-60.

than shattering into tiny pieces, they tend not to be noticed. While phenomena in the mind are *present* or *present-at-hand*, entities themselves are *ready-to-hand* for Heidegger, remaining invisible as they work towards various purposes.

Even this standard way of reading Heidegger turns out to be too superficial. He is not just giving us a difference between conscious perception and theory on the one hand and unconscious practical action on the other. Notice that even praxis reduces things to figures, since my use of a chair or hammer reduces it, oversimplifies it by interacting with only a small number of its vast range of qualities. The lesson from Heidegger is not that conscious awareness is the site of figure and unconscious praxis is the site of ground. Instead, the hidden ground is the thing itself, which is reduced, caricatured, or distorted by *any* relation we might have with it, whether theoretical or practical. And moreover, this is not just a special fact about human beings, but is typical even of inanimate relations. But for the moment there is no need to defend an unorthodox reading of Heidegger, since even the most orthodox reading already makes the point we need: what is visibly present in the world appears only against a hidden background from which it draws nourishment. In this sense, Heidegger's critique of presence in the history of philosophy can be viewed as another critique of "academic art": art that consists in the tendency to take its medium too much for granted, in Greenberg's powerful definition. In similar fashion, "academic philosophy" for Heidegger would be the kind that treats being as something that can be exhausted in some form of *presence*.

Yet there is a funny thing about this celebration of the deep background medium in Heidegger, McLuhan, and Greenberg. In all three cases, the depth turns out to be utterly sterile, incapable of generating anything new. Let us start with the clearest case, that of McLuhan. For McLuhan, the dominant medium in any situation is so deeply buried that there is no way to address it in direct cognitive terms. But not only can we not look at the medium directly—since any attempt to explain the effects of television or the internet will always fall short of the awesome depths of these media—the medium itself cannot even change without some impetus from the outside. As far as I am aware, McLuhan only allows for two ways that media can change. There is reversal through overheating, or retrieval through the work of artists. Reversal occurs when, for example, the speed and convenience of cars reverses into the slowness and inconvenience of traffic jams. Notice that this is not because cars themselves have changed, but only because their apparently superficial features (such as their shiny metallic bulk) became unmanageable due to the vast quantitative increase in the number of cars. What causes one medium to flip into another is not the deep aspect of a medium, but its more secondary and frivolous features.

As for retrieval, this happens for McLuhan when some current cliché or obsolete medium is given new life and made credible again. When vinyl LP records go from obsolete technology outstripped by compact discs to the newly revered medium of connoisseurs who despise the cold and sterile sound of CDs, we have a case of retrieval. But primarily, McLuhan thinks this is the work of *artists*. It is artists who transform banal visible figures by situating them in some sort of enlivening background medium that breathes new life into them. The crucial point for us here is as follows. For McLuhan, background media are more important than any of their content. Yet precisely because these media are *so* deep, *so* inaccessible to conscious contact, they are incapable of transformation. Such transformation can occur only at the most superficial layer of media—whether it be their peripheral features in the case of overheating and reversal, or the level of dead surface content in the case of the artist who retrieves some past medium as the content of a new one.

In Heidegger's philosophy the same point also holds, whatever the appearances to the contrary. There are admittedly some passages in Heidegger, especially in the later writings, when he treats humans as if we could only passively await the sending of new epochs of being. But in fact, the implicit problem faced by Heidegger is that since his objects withdraw so deeply from one another, they are unable to make contact precisely *because* they are deep. If they make contact, it is only through their most superficial outer layer. If I am injured by a hammer or virus, it is not because they assault the very core of my personality, but only because they exploit minor features of my being: such as a sensitive thumb or a few accidental cuts in the skin. Heidegger's depth is so deep that everything must happen on the surface, though he does not realise this as clearly as McLuhan does.

Even Greenberg admits that the content of painting is not unimportant. At times he calls it the site of inspiration: Picasso's painting is not just about a relation between the image and the flat picture surface of the canvas, but also about a guitar or horse or face of a woman. Yet this remains merely a placeholder in Greenberg's writing; he concedes the point without developing further what the role of sheer *content* might be in art. His primary concern remains the way that the content of the medium reflects the very structure of the medium: famously, in his case, the flatness of the picture plane. And though Greenberg freely admitted that this was a transient historical constraint not binding for all eras, he wrote so little about non-contemporary art that we can only speculate as to the principles he would have used to distinguish good from bad Renaissance perspectival art, or good from bad twenty-first century installation art.

3. Art and Relations

It is well known that Greenberg was an opinionated man, capable of swift and harsh judgments; for this reason it can be tempting to dismiss him as cranky and arrogant, his views not worth taking seriously. But this would be a mistake. Greenberg's dismissal of artists we might happen to like is based on his adoption of certain underlying aesthetic principles, and it is better to reflect on and possibly challenge those principles than to condemn Greenberg for being their messenger.

There was no more vehement defender of modernism than Greenberg, who viewed the modern not as a break with the past, but as an attempt to maintain the *quality* of the past by preventing its degeneration into a series of mechanically re-peated academic gestures. His definition of the academic, we have seen, is "art that takes its medium too much for granted," and we have linked this claim with certain insights in the media theory of McLuhan and the philosophy of Heidegger.[29] If academic art is the kind that takes its medium too much for granted, we can understand why Greenberg objected to Dalí and other surrealists as academic. There seems to be no innovation as to medium in the case of surrealist painting. Indeed, Greenberg thinks the surrealists deliberately retained the realist and perspectival conventions of academic paint-ing in order to keep everyone's focus on the startling *content* of their works. Though it may seem difficult to call Dalí an "academic artist" with a straight face, the charge is under-standable if we accept Greenberg's definition of the academic.

But with Duchamp, it seems almost impossible to use this designation. We have seen that Greenberg actually makes six separate critiques of Duchamp, with academicism being only one of them. The others were Duchamp's apparent rejection of quality as a standard, his overestimation of the value of shock in art, his tendency to shock not through aesthetic means but through breaches of social expectation, his overreliance on transparent concepts rather than the uncertainty of aes-thetic struggle and surprise, and finally his excessive claims of breaking radically with the past. But let us focus on the "academicism" charge. Dalí can easily (if controversially) be treated as an academic artist simply on the basis of Greenberg's definition of the term: academic art as insufficiently aware of its medium. In Duchamp's case a more oblique argument is needed, given that Duchamp is widely considered as the shining example of someone who challenges our expecta-tions of what an artistic medium should be.

Greenberg's point seems to be that Duchamp was so deeply academic in outlook (to judge from his insufficiently brilliant early efforts at fauvism and cubism) that he became frustrated by his limitations and misinterpreted cubism as primarily a

---

[29] Greenberg, *Late Writings*, 28.

brazen shock to societal expectations. He then tried to outdo even the cubists in this respect by exhibiting the most banal objects as if they were artworks: a bicycle wheel, a bottle rack, a urinal. In other words, the sole choice for Duchamp is one between academic art and provocative gestures, and Duchamp wrongly thought he was following Picasso and all other modernists in pursuing a dazzling career of provocative gestures. This explains Greenberg's other complaints about Duchamp as well. For once art is conceived merely as a shocking gesture, then quality as a standard of measurement no longer matters. New and provocative concepts of what might count as an artwork replace patient aesthetic struggle within a set of plausible ground rules. And finally, by putting ever more ironic quotation marks around the artistic enterprise than anyone before him, Duchamp might easily think of himself as making the most radical break with the history of art.

Surrealism and Dada will forever be linked in the history of art, and the two movements do share some overlapping membership, the use of humorous or incongruous titles for their works, and the deployment of irreverent public personalities. But from a Greenbergian standpoint, they actually work in contrary directions, like two scientists performing experiments with opposite controls. Dalí adopts the already banal conventions of three-dimensional illusionistic oil painting, all the better to let the strangeness of the content shine through. Duchamp works in reverse, choosing the most utterly banal content, all the better to shock our expectations about what might count as an artistic medium. If the two artists had not performed these respective controls, the result would have been massive confusion. Imagine that Dalí had painted his classics *The Ghost of Vermeer of Delft Which Can Also Be Used as a Table* or *Gala and "The Angelus" of Millet Preceding the Imminent Arrival of the Conic Anamorphoses*, not in what Greenberg calls academic illusionistic style, but broken up into planes in the manner of high analytic cubism.

Such a chaos of innovation would surprise the viewer from too many directions at once. It is hardly accidental that Picasso and Braque chose such simple subject matter for their cubist masterpieces—*Violin and Candlestick, Fruitdish and Glass, Portrait of Daniel-Henry Kahnweiler*—since these banal themes enable our undivided attention to innovations in technique. Likewise, Duchamp's readymades would have tangled things too badly if he had chosen to display not simple and recognisable everyday objects, but more complicated, esoteric, or ambiguous things. In any case, we can conclude from this that neither Dalí nor Duchamp can plausibly be treated as an academic artist. Dalí does not "take his medium for granted," but *deliberately suspends* innovation of medium in order to open up innovation of subject matter. Meanwhile Duchamp, at least in his readymade pieces, neither takes his medium for granted nor suspends innovation of it, but innovates his media to such a degree that Greenberg can view them only as shocks to fine art decorum, as in his followers' use of

> a row of boxes … a mere rod … a pile of litter … projects for Cyclopean landscape architecture … the plan for a trench dug in a straight line for hundreds of miles … a half-open door … the cross-section of a mountain … stating imaginary relations between real points in real places … a blank wall, and so forth.[30]

Such strategies can reach the point of academic banality as much as any other, and perhaps the arts in 2014 have long since reached that point. But there is no reason to assume that no distinctions of quality are possible within the medium-stretching genres of recent art, that such art really flouts gradations in quality in any sweeping sense, or that it exists solely to provide shocks to social decorum. We should also consider Greenberg's uneven track record as a predictor of greatness. For while he deserves much credit for his early defence of Jackson Pollock, it is by no means clear that history will join him in preferring Gottlieb, Morris, Noland, and Olitski to surrealism, Duchamp, Warhol, and Beuys. In fact, the opposite now seems more likely.

A Greenberg foe might say that he simply uses the term

---

[30] Greenberg, *The Collected Essays and Criticism: Modernism with a Vengeance*, 302.

"academic" for anything that he happens not to like. But this would not be quite fair; Greenberg's critical vocabulary is more versatile than that. For instance, another famous target of Greenberg's harshness is Wassily Kandinsky. A month after the Russian artist's December 1944 death in liberated Paris, Greenberg offered a dismissal of Kandinsky's career that was cold and brazen, but also rather fascinating. It would be difficult to describe a late-blooming innovator like Kandinsky as an "academic artist," and Greenberg does not try to do so. Instead, he classifies Kandinsky as a "provincial" artist. His obituary review opens as follows:

> There are two sorts of provincialism in art. The exponent of one is the artist, academic or otherwise, who works in an outmoded style or in a vein disregarded by the metropolitan center—Paris, Rome, or Athens. The other sort of provincialism is that of the artist—generally from an outlying country—who in all earnest and admiration devotes himself to the style being currently developed in the metropolitan center, yet fails in one way or another really to understand what it is about … The Russian, Wassily Kandinsky, [was a provincial of this latter sort].[31]

For Greenberg, the provincial Kandinsky was no naïve simpleton, but a quick-witted observer of advanced art:

> Like many a newcomer to a situation, seeing it from the outside and thus more completely, Kandinsky was very quick to perceive one of the most basic implications of the revolution cubism had effected in Western painting. Pictorial art was at last able to free itself completely from the object—the eidetic image—and take for its sole positive matter the sensuous facts of its own medium, reducing itself to a question … of non-figurative shapes and colors. Painting would become like music, an art contained in its own form and thus capable of infinitely more variety than before.[32]

---

[31] Clement Greenberg, *The Collected Essays and Criticism: Arrogant Purpose, 1945-1949,* vol. 2, ed. John O'Brian (Chicago: University of Chicago Press, 1986), 3-4.

[32] Ibid., 4.

But in this way, Kandinsky repeats Duchamp's supposed error of thinking he can make a clean break with the history of art. Greenberg makes other objections that seem even more decisive for his verdict on Kandinsky, who in his view "for a relatively short time was a great painter," namely in his earlier period.[33] Greenberg's biggest complaint is that Kandinsky was too focused on the *abstraction* of cubism while missing a more important aspect of that style. As he puts it in the same obituary review:

> [Kandinsky] rejected what to my mind is a prior and perhaps even more essential achievement of avant-garde art than its deliverance of painting from representation: its recapture of the literal realization of the physical limitations and conditions of the medium and of the positive advantages to be gained from the exploitation of these very limitations.[34]

Although it might seem as if Kandinsky is fully aware of the flatness of the picture surface, "he came to conceive of the picture ... as an aggregate of discrete shapes; the color, size, and spacing of these he related so insensitively to the space surrounding them ... that this [space] remained inactive and meaningless; the sense of a continuous surface was lost, and the space became pocked with 'holes.'"[35] Aside from this purely technical shortcoming, Greenberg sees one clear sign of relapse by Kandinsky into academic art: for, "having begun by accepting the absolute flatness of the picture surface, Kandinsky would go on to allude to illusionistic depth by a use of color, line, and perspective that were plastically irrelevant ... Academic reminiscences crept into [Kandinsky's paintings] at almost every point other than that of what they 'represented.'"[36]

In another accusation of insensitivity to medium, Greenberg

---

[33] Greenberg, *The Collected Essays and Criticism: Arrogant Purpose*, 6.

[34] Ibid., 5.

[35] Ibid.

[36] Ibid.

complains that "the consistency of [Kandinsky's] paint surface and the geometrical exactness of his line seem more appropriate to stone or metal than to the porous fabric of canvas."[37] Finally, his supposed failure to master what the avant-garde was really all about led Kandinsky to become an insecure and eclectic stylist. As Greenberg puts it, "the stylistic and thematic ingredients of Kandinsky's later work are as diverse as the colors of Joseph's coat: peasant, ancient, and Oriental art, much Klee, some Picasso, surrealist protoplasma, maps, blueprints, musical notation, etc., etc."[38] Greenberg concludes with a few concessions and a single crowning damnation:

> [Kandinsky] was and will remain a large and revolutionary phenomenon—he must be taken into account always; yet he stays apart from the mainstream and in the last analysis remains a provincial. The example of his work is dangerous to younger painters.[39]

But Greenberg's description of the dangers of Kandinsky seems to hinge too much on a single debatable point. He cautions that Kandinsky's exact line would be more appropriate for stone or metal than canvas, yet he immediately concedes that the same is true of Mondrian, whom Greenberg regards as a truly great artist despite that stony-metallic exact line. He also tries to warn us that "academic reminiscences" creep into Kandinsky, which should mean that Kandinsky has a lingering tendency to take his medium for granted. But even if this turned out to be sweepingly true for the whole of Kandinsky's work, it would not follow that it *must* be true for any art that adopts the abstractions of cubism while downplaying its relation to the flatness of the medium. Revolutions are often fuelled when heirs adopt only one portion of their forerunners' legacies while refusing the others. As Greenberg himself repeatedly admits, there is not just one way to make great art, and what succeeds in one era will fail in others—precisely because the

---

[37] Greenberg, *The Collected Essays and Criticism: Arrogant Purpose*, 5.

[38] Ibid.

[39] Ibid., 6.

same techniques are fresh at one moment and banal in the next. He even makes the surprising admission that Duchamp was right to be "wild" early on as a way of escaping the "cubist vise," which suggests Greenberg's firm awareness that even the greatest styles can become suffocating prisons.

Just like the Renaissance-era growth of perspectival illusionist painting, the reverse movement towards painting that exploits the *limitations* of the flat canvas can reach a point of decadent banality. Were Duchamp, surrealism, and Kandinsky truly *relapses* from cubism in the way that Greenberg claims? Or were they not instead more like probes seeking a new planet, quite apart from the question of whether they succeeded in finding it? Nonetheless, it is dangerous to call Greenberg "old-fashioned," as many of his opponents do. His keen intelligence deserves more than that, as does his literary brilliance. For his critical work and his spiritual guidance of the shift in avant-garde art from Paris to New York, Greenberg is no doubt one of the half-dozen or so most important intellectual figures the United States has produced. Moreover, *everyone* becomes old-fashioned someday, and those who dance on Greenberg's tomb will eventually be danced upon in turn, viewed as outdated in their own right.

What will it look like when this happens? Let us assume for the sake of argument that surrealism produces no further avant-garde revolution, since its basic principles have been thoroughly explored. The same holds for abstraction, a known quantity for just as long, even if its lifespan was longer. Duchamp's wager of continually questioning what counts as art may have a few years of life left in it, and hence we are still prepared to be impressed by "a row of boxes ... a mere rod ... a pile of litter ... projects for Cyclopean landscape architecture ... the plan for a trench dug in a straight line for hundreds of miles ... a half-open door ... the cross-section of a mountain ... stating imaginary relations between real points in real places ... a blank wall, and so forth."[40] But this too will eventually become old and tired, if it is not already so,

---

[40] Greenberg, *The Collected Essays and Criticism: Modernism with a Vengeance*, 302.

and something different will need to awaken to surprise us.

What will this new thing be? We have already considered the "academicism" of Duchamp and surrealism, and the "provincialism" of Kandinsky, and have stipulated a future in which all are spent forces along with Greenberg's School of Flatness. What else is left? It could be many things, but we have only encountered one other possibility in the course of our discussions: the *first* kind of provincialism, different from Kandinsky's second kind. To refresh our memories, Kandinsky's sort of provincialism was said to be "that of the artist—generally from an outlying country—who in all earnest and admiration devotes himself to the style being currently developed in the metropolitan center, yet fails in one way or another really to understand what it is about."[41] The other kind of provincialism, which we have not yet discussed, is that of "the artist, academic or otherwise, who works in an outmoded style or in a vein disregarded by the metropolitan center."[42]

At first it might sound as if this sort of artist cannot be a candidate for cutting-edge status, since the word "outmoded" suggests otherwise. But Greenberg already gives us an example of one such "outmoded" artist working in a vein disregarded by the metropolitan centre, and indeed one of the greatest artists: Paul Cézanne, whom he considers in a beautiful 1951 essay entitled "Cézanne and the Unity of Modern Painting."[43] The opening claim of that essay is that the apparent eclecticism of avant-garde art in 1951 is merely an appearance. Great figures do not exhaustively accomplish what they aim to achieve, and always leave behind a tangle of loose threads for their successors to tie together. Greenberg views the late nineteenth century, and Cézanne in particular, as the origin of these threads. Even as great a movement as cubism was able to benefit speedily from the untied threads of Cézanne:

---

[41] Greenberg, *The Collected Essays and Criticism: Modernism with a Vengeance*, 3-4.

[42] Ibid.

[43] Clement Greenberg, *The Collected Essays and Criticism: Affirmations and Refusals, 1950-1956*, vol. 3, ed. John O'Brian (Chicago: University of Chicago Press, 1993), 82-91.

Picasso's and Braque's Cubism, and Léger's, completed what Cézanne had begun, by their successes divesting his means of whatever had remained problematical about them and finding them their most appropriate ends. These means they took from Cézanne practically ready-made, and were able to adapt them to their purposes after only a relatively few trial exercises.[44]

But the truly interesting topic of Greenberg's essay on Cézanne is the opposite topic: not Cézanne as the far-seeing grandfather of later trends, but as the struggling admirer of the classical painters before him. It is the story of the artist who does not simply extrapolate from the threads of his immediate forerunners, but who attempts to bring back something important that recent revolutions had prematurely left behind. So it was with Cézanne and the Impressionists. As Greenberg unforgettably puts it:

[Cézanne] was making the first—and last—pondered effort to save the intrinsic principle of the Western tradition of painting: its concern with an ample and literal rendition of the illusion of the third dimension. He had noted the Impressionists' inadvertent silting up of pictorial depth. And it is because he tried so hard to re-excavate that depth without abandoning Impressionist color, and because his attempt, while vain, was so profoundly conceived, that it became the turning point it did … Like Manet and with almost as little appetite for the role of revolutionary, he changed the course of art out of the very effort to return it by new paths to its old ways.[45]

The danger faced by all modernisers is the danger of robotic extrapolation. They assume that the previous revolution performed innovation X, and therefore the next revolution must perform double-X or triple-X: since the Enlightenment advanced by denouncing superstition and defending reason, the next phase of history requires a campaign of utter persecution against all "irrational" people, and so forth. Extrapolation

---

44 Greenberg, *The Collected Essays and Criticism: Affirmations and Refusals*, 90.
45 Ibid., 83-84.

273

has its historical moments, and those lucky enough to live in such moments can complete their work rapidly at a young age thanks to struggling prior mentors, as did Picasso and Braque in their analytic cubist period. Others must struggle slowly like Cézanne (or Kant) to find the new principle of an age, painstakingly retrieving the old while not abandoning what is new, and perhaps dangling dozens of loose threads that others in the following generation can tie together as they please. If we follow Greenberg in treating art since 1960 as the reign of Neo-Dada, then what is most valuable in the past that this period sacrificed and left behind? What outmoded provincial might emerge as the Cézanne of the coming era?

Not Objects so Much As Images

A Response to Graham Harman's "Greenberg, Duchamp, and the Next Avant-Garde"

Bettina Funcke

School of Visual Arts

Editors' Note: This response was delivered at the *Art, Information, and Philosophical Objects* event held at Columbia University on 8 March, 2013.

I WANT TO START BY MAKING SOME comments on what you have written in your essay on Clement Greenberg and Marcel Duchamp, Graham. I was especially interested because I have also written about these two figures in my book *Pop or Populus: Art between High and Low*.[1] I want to say first of all that your paper is dense and complex, but ultimately open-ended and speculative. And this is what makes it exciting.

As I see it, you are taking Greenberg's criticism as a model that might once again be interesting or relevant, not because of his strict emphasis on formalism, but because he is known to us as the art critic who decreed what was right and what was wrong, and who therefore tried to predict what was to come next in art, or what *should* or *should not* be the next step. His judgments were moralistic, e.g. calling Wassily Kandinsky a dangerous influence for young artists, or describing Duchamp as a dead end. So, essentially you are looking to this viewpoint as a kind of inspiration, and then posing the question yourself

---

[1] Bettina Funcke, *Pop or Populus: Art between High and Low* (New York: Sternberg Press, 2009); see in particular chapters 1 and 2.

of what might come next and how we might get to this next step in the evolution of art and its criticism.

You write, "Over the past decade, there has been a growing sense that Greenberg is becoming readable once again, while Duchamp's legacy was perhaps on the verge of becoming overexploited."[2] And this is maybe because Greenberg was writing from what he saw as a point of exhaustion; in his view Duchamp was entirely played out and we needed to find a new direction. He was seeing land art, conceptual art, and minimal art as basically bankrupt derivatives of Duchamp. That may not be something that we agree with now, but it may be that, forty years later, we can finally sort of come to the same conclusions as Greenberg: OK, you were not right about the art of the 1970s, but *now* we have caught up with you, because now everything feels exhausted to us, too. And we recognise, of course, that this feeling of exhaustion, that things have been overexploited, is perennial.

I still would not necessarily agree that the period since the 1960s is a neo-Dada period, i.e., Duchampian, because I think that view, which was Greenberg's, leaves out the influence of Andy Warhol, whom he could not really deal with, and who shifted the terrain again. But then again Warhol, like Duchamp, is another strain of art whose legacy may be over-exploited, as you put it.

So, I cannot give an answer to the question of what is coming next, but I want to contribute to the discussion by coming from a slightly different angle, which is to fill in another side of Duchamp's work which, I think, has really come to influence the art of the last few decades, more so than the readymade in fact. This is his play with information and documentation, with the very reception of his own work, through printed and editioned representations. It is an interference into art history. This is something that basically falls outside of Greenberg's investigation, and is not really addressed by the 6-point critique that you mention. Just to recap those points:

---

[2] Graham Harman, "Greenberg, Duchamp, and the Next Avant-Garde" in this volume.

Duchamp rejects quality or taste; is primarily interested in shock value; uses transgressive material; privileges the concept; overestimates his own radicality; and is an academic artist who takes his medium for granted.

The thing is, these points of critique seem to make sense only as long as we focus on the readymades and other objects as *objects* per se, ignoring their context, their discourse, their perverse histories, and everything that Duchamp worked so hard to put into place, a practice which is now much more common because of his work. As an example, let's take a look at the most famous (and as such the most exhausted) readymade: the *Fountain*.

Few people saw the original *Fountain* in 1917. Like almost all the readymades, the original had gone missing, its dimensions never even recorded. Never exhibited, and lost or destroyed almost immediately, the *Fountain* was actually created through Duchamp's media manipulations rather than through the creation-myth of his hand selecting it in the showroom, the status-conferring (and, for Greenberg, would-be shocking) gesture to which the readymades are often reduced. A week after the Society of Independent Artists refused to exhibit the work, Duchamp transported the urinal to Alfred Stieglitz's 291 Gallery, where Stieglitz photographed it under theatrical lighting in front of an expressionist painting. This is the only remaining visual trace of the original *Fountain*. This photograph has been reproduced in countless publications, and also served as the model for the edition of *Fountain* produced in 1964 by Arturo Schwarz, in collaboration with Duchamp. A critical commentary on the work, which, apart from the photographic reproduction, is all that allows for its inscription into what we might call the archive, appeared a month later without attribution in the second and final issue of *The Blind Man*, a journal published not coincidentally by Duchamp. So the object disappears, but its semi-fictional documentation and narrative produced a guarantee, a shortcut to history through photography and writing.

With the original lost, the questions of what is a copy, what is an editioned object, and wherein the authorisation of ex-

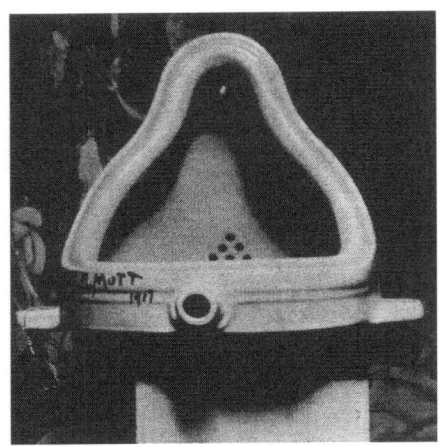

original

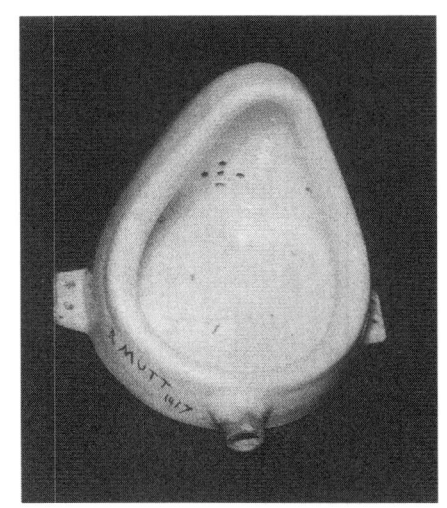

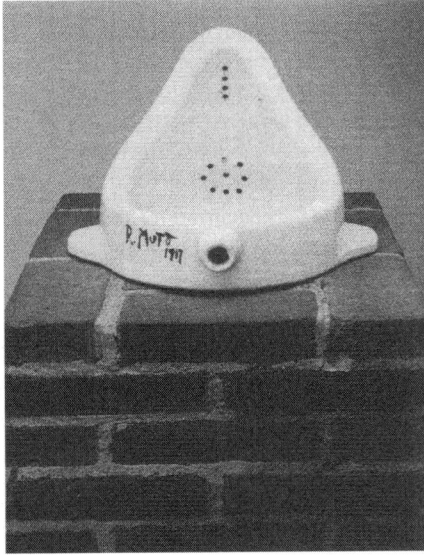

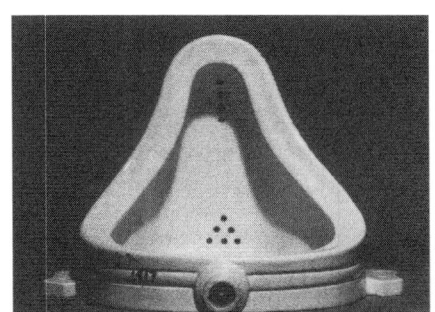

ecuting a work lies, are raised for the first time and remain complex and ambiguous. For example, the *Fountain*'s entry in the catalogue raisonné, *The Complete Works of Marcel Duchamp*, lists and depicts next to the original three additional urinals that embody later versions of the work.[3] Next to the original is one Sidney Janis selected in 1950 in Paris at the request of the artist; then there is one from 1963, selected by Ulf Linde for Duchamp's retrospective at the Moderna Museet, Stockholm; and, last, there is the 1964 edition of eight replicas produced under the artist's supervision from the photo by Stieglitz.

In *Fountain*'s elegant model, the artwork does not occupy a single position in space and time; rather, it is a palimpsest of gestures, presentations, and positions, as Seth Price suggests in his essay *Dispersion*. He writes:

> Duchamp distributed the notion of the *Fountain* in such a way that it became one of art's primal scenes; it transubstantiated from a provocative objet d'art into, as Broodthaers defined his *Musée des Aigles*: "a situation, a system defined by objects, by inscriptions, by various activities…"[4]

In short: it turned art into discourse. Duchamp made sure to photograph the original, to publicise it, to archive it, and then to totally twist the trail. Had anyone previously done such work with copies and editions within the realm of high art?

Once art defines itself as an activity primarily manifested in the larger domain of distribution, it encounters new and illuminating problems, as in the case of Duchamp's editions of his readymades created with Arturo Schwarz. Things declared to be readymades were, mere decades later, no longer industrially produced, or had become untraceable. The objects in question thus had to be reconstructed by hand and at great expense from sketches or photographs. The 1964 edition of *Fountain* was reproduced by a Milanese ceramicist with the aid of Stieglitz's photograph of the original. After Duchamp had authorised the designs for the copies, the "genuine copies of the readymades" were now—nearly forty years after they had been selected from among ordinary objects—seemingly

---

[3] Marcel Duchamp, *The Complete Works of Marcel Duchamp*, rev. and exp. pbk. ed., vol. 1, ed. Arturo Schwartz (New York: Delano Greenidge Editions, 2000), 648–50.

[4] Seth Price, *Dispersion* (Self-published, 2002), http://www.distributedhistory.com/Dispersion2008.pdf (accessed March 18, 2013).

conventional sculptures, handcrafted to imitate mass-produced articles. As Martha Buskirk has noted:

> For the readymades, Duchamp had developed new ways of establishing authorship that would operate in tandem with their testing of the boundaries of the work of art. If Duchamp's initial gesture of choosing the readymade referred to mass production, the later forms of reproduction through which the readymades cycled secured their status as art.[5]

From 1930 to 1940, Duchamp spent his creative energy mainly on the reconstruction of miniature replicas of earlier works. Most of the pieces from that period took the form of multiples: *La boîte-en-valise* (an edition of 300, completed in 1941) included miniature replicas of the readymades, reproductions of the works in glass or celluloid, collotype prints of the paintings, drawings, and commercial prints (some black-and-white, others hand-coloured), as well as photographs of the readymades, of the optical apparatus, and of Duchamp's studio, all manipulated in various ways. In order to reproduce some of them, he had to visit his collectors and take notes. The notes in Duchamp's 1934 *Green Box*, in an edition of 300, were thought to be the only extant notes about *The Large Glass*. Duchamp, however, had more. In 1966, thirty-two years after publishing *The Green Box*, he produced *The White Box* or *A l'infinitif* in an edition of 150, which contained additional notes. These were translated and typographically transferred into English by Richard Hamilton and Ecke Bonk, a so-called typotranslation published as a book in 1967, also under the authorisation of Duchamp.

I want to stop and point out that all these examples do not invalidate Greenberg's critiques. Obviously Greenberg would have seen all of this as a confirmation of his doubts about the direction in which Duchamp was taking art. But this is how Duchamp allowed the work to enter a larger conversation and to circulate through cultural realms way beyond the exhibi-

---

[5] Martha Buskirk, "Thoroughly Modern Marcel" in *The Duchamp Effect: Essays, Interviews, Round Table*, ed. Martha Buskirk and Mignon Nixon (Cambridge: MIT Press, 1996), 200.

tion hall or gallery. Greenberg underestimated the power of this; he may have been right about the eventual waning of the readymade as a model, but there were a lot more powerful tools in Duchamp's toolbox: the way he made manuals for his own work, the status of the copy and the editioned object, the tweaked reproduction of one's work, the way art can turn into discourse, his thoughts on the fourth dimension and other quasi-mathematical and quasi-scientific aspects, and so on. In comparison, if you look at a painting by Jackson Pollock, you can admire the work, you can take something away in terms of attitude, experience, or freedom, but there are not so many concrete strategies to take away and use in your own work.

It is not in fact so much about objects now, but about images and their particular kinds of materiality; and now that we are in the realm of the digital, the image can migrate and transform much more rapidly and with all sorts of new forms. This is today's over-exploited legacy of Duchamp, not the readymades as shocking new sculptural form. It is Duchamp's work of documentation, information, altered photographs, forgeries, identities, narrativising, and transferrals.

I want to switch gears now. Graham, the last sentence of your essay is "What outmoded provincial might emerge as the Cézanne of the coming era?"[6] You are referring to Cézanne going back to pick up perspectival space and trying to synthesise it with contemporary strategies, and you are pointing to this as a possibly interesting new approach, or a direction for artists today, who retrieve passed-over elements and basically run them through a contemporary filter. With regard to this, there is a case study I would like to share.

I want to go back to the 1970s and look at certain pieces by Robert Whitman. Whitman is not exactly overlooked, but certainly not as well-known as he should be. He is mainly known for his performances from the 1960s and '70s, and his *Cinema Pieces* from as early as 1963, in which installations of everyday objects, like a shower, sink, or window, became screens

---

[6] Harman, "Greenberg, Duchamp, and the Next Avant-Garde," in this volume.

onto which he projected films showing these objects in use. He also worked over many years with Bell Labs engineer Billy Klüver and the Experiments in Art and Technology group, which brought him into contact, crucially, with the Xerox machine. A Xerox machine is interesting as a transitional technology. Unlike a camera, it is not based on a chemical development process; it does not really refer to the world of photography. It is electronic, it is electrostatic, and it sweeps across whatever you place on its flatbed, and puts it together in one image. So we are just one step away from the scanner, which is what is interesting here.

The contemporary artist collaboration Guyton/Walker, consisting of Wade Guyton and Kelley Walker, uses a scanner as one of their main tools, and a whole component of their work comes out of something Whitman did in 1974 when he had a fellowship at Xerox. The photocopier was not a common artist's tool at the time; you had to have this kind of access. What Whitman started doing was Xeroxing sliced fruit, and fish, and other food.

To return to the present, Guyton and Walker both saw the 2003 Whitman exhibition at Dia Art Foundation, where Guyton was working. In the exhibition, there is a 1976 poster announcing an earlier Whitman show at Dia that includes a sliced lime and a sliced orange placed on the flatbed of the Xerox and turned into a flat graphic element. These Xeroxed fruit slices then became the cover for Dia's book, *Robert Whitman: Playback*.[7] And this turned directly into a series of works in which Guyton/Walker started putting sliced fruit, particularly limes, through their scanner. What is different now is that the scanner brings the fruit not simply to the page, but into digital space, where you can do all kinds of things to a file. You turn the lime orange, you blow it up, and you pervert it. It is open to manipulations and applications in various formats, and to printing on different kinds of objects and surfaces.

---

7 *Robert Whitman: Playback*, ed. Lynne Cooke, Bettina Funcke, Karen Kelly (New York: Dia Art Foundation, 2003).

You can see here the naked file as information first of all, a Photoshop document. The image was then printed by inkjet in various compositions onto different surfaces and objects: a paint can, canvas, sheetrock, the ubiquitous building material, itself part of an installation, and most recently, as depicted, laminated onto a table.

These artists are not the new Cézannes, by the way! But I *am* interested in taking up your idea, Graham, of past elements gaining a new relevance when they are brought to contemporary strategies that create a strange synthesis.

I want to close with the image of this table because it brings to mind another question. I wonder how, in thinking about the strangeness of how the scanner takes in the world of objects, and how these images are output through printing technologies in so many adaptable ways in order to cover the world of objects, we might possibly approach an understanding of your notion of "the third table" through the work of art.

This is a concept you wrote about in a notebook for dOCU-MENTA (13)'s *100 Notes – 100 Thoughts* publication series, which I edited.[8] I don't want to presume to discuss this notion in too much detail but I will summarise briefly: the first table is the one that scientists would call the "real" table, which is a collection of materials, described in terms of the laws of physics. The second table is the table that humanists would find more real, and this is a table as we know it in everyday life, a familiar object inscribed in social use and customs and so on. You however say that neither of these tables is the real table, that there is a third table, which lies between the two, and which may belong to the culture of the arts. It is a table that is to some degree unknowable, it is a philosophical/ artistic table, and I will leave it at that.

In closing, I am hoping that in future discussions we can go a bit further into how an object-oriented philosophy might somehow change how we think about art, what art is, where its place is, and where it may be going.

---

[8] Graham Harman, *The Third Table*, dOCUMENTA (13) 100 Notes – 100 Thoughts Series (Ostfildern: Hatje Cantz, 2013).

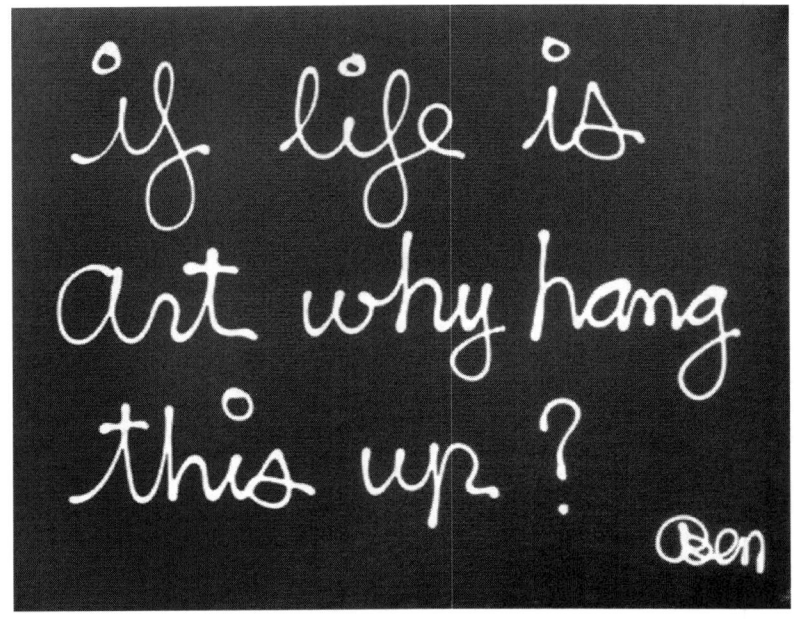

Ben Vautier, *If life is art why hang this up?*, 1990.

Strategic Invisibility
The Zero Point of Modernism and the Avant-Garde

Thomas Gokey

"Anti-art is life, nature; true reality is the one and all."
—George Maciunas, *Fluxus Codex*[1]

Introduction: Art and Life

LET US BEGIN WITH A HEIST. ON Sunday August 20th, 1911 Vincenzo Peruggia hid overnight in the Louvre. He was an Italian nationalist who mistakenly believed that the *Mona Lisa* had been stolen from his native Italy, and he aimed to steal it back. At least that was the story he would tell the press later on after he was captured and he became a national hero. In the meantime, what was the harm in making a little bit of money selling forgeries of the missing painting? On Monday morning, when the Louvre was closed to the public, he emerged from his hiding place wearing his official white smock, which is issued to the museum staff. In broad daylight he walked up to the *Mona Lisa* and removed it from the wall. It was as simple as that. In a stairwell of the Louvre he removed the wooden panel from the frame, tucked it under his smock, and left the building. Because it was common for the museum staff to remove artworks for various reasons it took a full day before anyone even noticed it was actually missing. At first he hid the painting behind a pile of firewood at his apartment. That is where it was when the

---

[1] Jon Hendricks, *Fluxus Codex* (New York: Harry N. Abrams, 1988), 23.

287

police came to interview him as they did all of the museum staff. Standing in the same room as the hot booty (*L.H.O.O.Q.*) they were none the wiser. Later he would hide it for two years in a customised secret compartment in the bottom of a trunk. Peruggia seemed to have gotten away with it, and he really might have if he had not tried to sell the infamous painting.

What is the *Mona Lisa*? On the one hand it is an image, a fictional three-dimensional depth representing an otherwise forgotten Italian woman of the merchant class from the fifteenth century. But of course it is much more than that. It is one of the most widely reproduced images in history. In countless art history surveys it is reproduced through various printing techniques, most commonly using Ben-Day dots, tiny points of pure CMKY colour which our brains combine into the shapes and forms of the familiar image. The *Mona Lisa* is reproduced on t-shirts, posters, postcards, rendered in pixels and just about every other medium conceivable, even paint balls.[2] Indeed it has become an icon in its own right, the image of all other images, the very symbol of painting itself. Clearly it is a painting or an artwork if anything is. If we think of it slightly differently, however, we might describe the *Mona Lisa* as a thin skin of pigment suspended in linseed oil on a 13 millimetre thick piece of poplar measuring 77 cm by 54 cm. The paint, like all of Da Vinci's paints, was something of a scientific experiment in its own right. It was made of ground glass, precious stones, plants and wax, all of which were cooked to different temperatures. Over the years the pigment has undergone chemical changes as it continues to interact with the light and air. The colours have darkened slightly, and the paint itself is cracking. Due to humidity the poplar has also developed a healthy crack. In the eighteenth century a skilled craftsman fitted two walnut butterfly braces into the back of the panel to keep the crack from growing further. The poplar itself has warped and continues to change shape with changes in temperature and moisture.

---

[2] To watch the Mythbusters Jamie Hyneman and Adam Savage create the Mona Lisa using 1,100 paintball guns see www.youtube.com/watch?v=fKK933KK6Gg (accessed September 30, 2013).

But how do these two senses of the *Mona Lisa*, the *Mona Lisa as an image* and the *Mona Lisa as a thing*, relate to one another? And in which does the ontological status of the work of art lie, in the immaterial image or in the material support, or in the composite of both? Whether images are perfectly flat spectres, or whether images are real things among other real things, has been one of the questions that have continually driven the history of art forward almost since its inception.[3] In twentieth century art we can see this dynamic shift between the emphasis of pure spectral flatness in high modernism and the re-emergence of the image-as-object with minimalism and post-minimalism. In many ways, the questions raised by speculative realism are more apropos for that era. We can imagine a counterfactual history in which a turn towards weird realism from within continental philosophy takes place in the late 1960s and a young Donald Judd latches on to a kind of object-oriented ontology to do battle with Michael Fried. For Fried, the modernist artwork needed to separate itself from its own material support, from the element within itself that was not art but merely life which Fried termed its "objecthood." In his famous criticism of minimalism, Fried writes that a modernist work of art is "in some essential respect not an object."[4] In a way it is a pity that speculative realism did not develop within the context of minimalism. We can imagine a healthy exchange between the arts and theory in which speculative realism helps the minimalists articulate the materiality of the image.[5]

---

[3] The very origin of painting is focused on this question and identifies images with the shades of the dead. See the legend of the Corinthian maid and the origin of painting in Pliny the Elder, *Natural History Books XXXIII-XXXV*, trans. H. Rackman (Cambridge: Harvard University Press, 1952), 373. For the influence of this legend on classical painting, see Robert Rosenblum, "The Origin of Painting: A Problem in the Iconography of Romantic Classicism," *The Art Bulletin* (1957), 39:4, 279-90.

[4] Michael Fried, *Art and Objecthood* (Chicago: University of Chicago Press, 1998), 152.

[5] Robert Jackson has written a brilliant interpretation of Fried through the lens of OOO in which he focuses on the role of the beholder for Fried and the distinction between theatricality and absorption. See Robert Jackson,

Instead, the situational dynamic in which speculative realism has emerged is a different one, and the problem that artists are using speculative realism to articulate now concerns a re-thinking of relational aesthetics. The art of the 1990s was almost totally dominated by relational work that focused either on the way the viewer completes or creates the artwork by coming into relation to it, or artwork which sought to produce new social relationships and used these relationships as its medium.[6] While there is much that is valuable and fascinating about relational aesthetics, indeed my own artwork is often relational, we are starting to see the pendulum swing back towards artistic practices that are curious about the remainder that escapes these relationships, usually thought in terms of the material or real in excess of all relation. The question many of today's artists seem to be asking is about the status of the *Mona Lisa* when it was placed behind the pile of firewood. When no one knew it was there, when Peruggia was absentmindedly cooking his food, enjoying a walk, or sleeping, was the *Mona Lisa* still an image or a painting or an artwork in any sense? Or was it a colourful piece of wood, only slightly different from the firewood it was temporarily hidden behind and maybe potential kindling that could have been added to a fire?

Both of these questions, the relationship between the image and thing and the artwork's relationship to human consciousness, share a common underlying question about the boundary between art and life. It would seem that aesthetics, like politics and ethics, would provide the most difficult terrain for the various speculative realisms because such

---

"The Anxiousness of Objects and Artworks: Michael Fried, Object Oriented Ontology and Aesthetic Absorption," *Speculations* (2011), 2, 135-68, and his sequel presented in this issue. The present essay is in part a response. I do not disagree with anything in Jackson's reading; instead this is an attempt to use OOO to offer a reading of the other path in the dispute between Fried and the minimalists.

6 Nicolas Bourriaud remains *the* definitive critic of relational aesthetics. See Nicolas Bourriaud, *Relational Aesthetics*, trans. Simon Pleasance and Fronza Woods (Dijon: Les presses du réel), 2002.

areas necessarily involve human consciousness and values. If "there is no difference that does not make a difference,"[7] then one of the differences that human beings make is the difference between art and life. I hope to show that the boundary between art and life is inviolable because it is produced and maintained by human consciousness itself. In this regard, I am defending a qualified relational aesthetics. But even if we accept that humans produce the distinction between art and life, to what degree can material things use this capacity that humans have to their own ends? If humans produce values everywhere we go, to what degree can brute facts utilise humans to marshal values of their own? I see a potential in what I am calling strategic invisibility for artworks to operate in a semi-autonomous manner but only when they operate on the other side of what I will call a zero point, an internal impasse built into the very logic of the modernist and avant-garde projects.

Modernism

The history of modernism can be thought of as a narrowing path which whittles itself away until it comes to an impasse. Modern painting arguably begins with the invention of the photograph. When Paul Delaroche saw a daguerreotype for the first time, he is rumoured to have announced: "From today, painting is dead."[8] Photography forced a kind of John Henry crisis for painting. How could painting justify its continued existence when representation could be achieved "better" through new technological methods? This forced painting to retreat into itself, to discover what it could do that no other media could, "to entrench it more firmly in

---

[7] This is Levi Bryant's ontic principle. Levi Bryant, "The Ontic Principle: Outline of an Object-Oriented Ontology" in *The Speculative Turn: Continental Realism and Materialism*, ed. Levi Bryant, Nick Srnicek, and Graham Harman (Melbourne: Re.press, 2011), 263.

[8] Quoted in Geoffrey Batchen, "Ghost Stories: The Beginnings and Ends of Photography," *Art Monthly Australia* (1994), 76, 4-8.

its area of competence,"[9] to find a safe house where neither photography nor any of the other media could break-in and steal its turf. The history of modernist painting is a history of several different routes through abstraction until they wind up in more or less the same place: complete flatness and pure colour. If the logic of modernism is to "purify" each medium, even if we have to use scare quotes around the word "pure" as Greenberg always did, then there is an approximate level of "purity" beyond which it is seemingly impossible to advance further. Modernism sharpens itself to a point.

The invention of the monochrome is a particularly illustrative crisis point. In 1921 Alexander Rodchenko produced three monochromes, one of each primary colour. Rodchenko claimed: "I reduced painting to its logical conclusion and exhibited three canvases: red, blue, and yellow. I affirmed: this is the end of painting."[10] In a way he was right, this was the internal impasse of modernism. Ad Reinhardt became *the* definitive painter of this endpoint, painting one black monochrome after another from 1953-1967. He called them his "ultimate paintings" and claimed he was "merely making the last painting which anyone can make."[11] In 1992, Clement Greenberg said that nothing happened in the past thirty years.[12]

Although a number of modern painters reached similar dead ends each in their own way, Kasimir Malevich's *Black Square* stands apart because it was conceived not just as an aporia of painting but as a portal to a new and stranger world.

[9] Clement Greenberg, "Modernist Painting," *The Collected Essays and Criticism: Modernism with a Vengeance, 1957-1969*, vol. 4, ed. John O'Brian (Chicago: University of Chicago Press, 1993), 85.

[10] Alexander Rodchenko, "Working with Majakowsky" in *From Painting to Design: Russian Constructivist Art of the Twenties* (Cologne: Galerie Cmurzynska, 1981), 191.

[11] Ad Reinhardt, *Art as Art: The Selected Writings of Ad Reinhardt*, ed. Barbara Rose (Berkeley: University of California Press, 1991), 13.

[12] "In the summer of 1992, Greenberg spoke for a small group in New York. He claimed that perhaps never in history had art 'moved so slowly.' Nothing, he insisted, had happened in the past thirty years." Arthur C. Danto, *After the End of Art: Contemporary Art and the Pale of History* (Princeton: Princeton University Press, 1997), 105.

Ad Reinhardt with several paintings.

Rather than the dead end of a pure flat surface it was more like Alice's looking glass. When he first exhibited the *Black Square* at the *0.10 Last Futurist Exhibition* in 1915, it caused a scandal. Indeed it was a *scandalon* in the technical sense of the word, a stumbling block that simultaneously bars the way forward while providing the foundation for a new quest, both the capstone for an old paradigm and a cornerstone for a new one. Critics read the *Black Square* as the death of painting and the death of God. For Malevich, it was teeming with new possibilities. It was as much a rebirth as it was a death, as much an Alpha as an Omega. In this regard, Malevich's black monochrome, while a near visual twin, was the anti-Reinhardt. Malevich's closest pupil, El Lissitzky, describes the *Black Square* the following way:

> When we have a series of numbers coming from infinity ...6, 5, 4, 3, 2, 1, 0... it comes right down to the 0, then, begins the ascending line 0, 1, 2, 3, 4, 5, 6... ... We are saying that if on the one side the stone of the

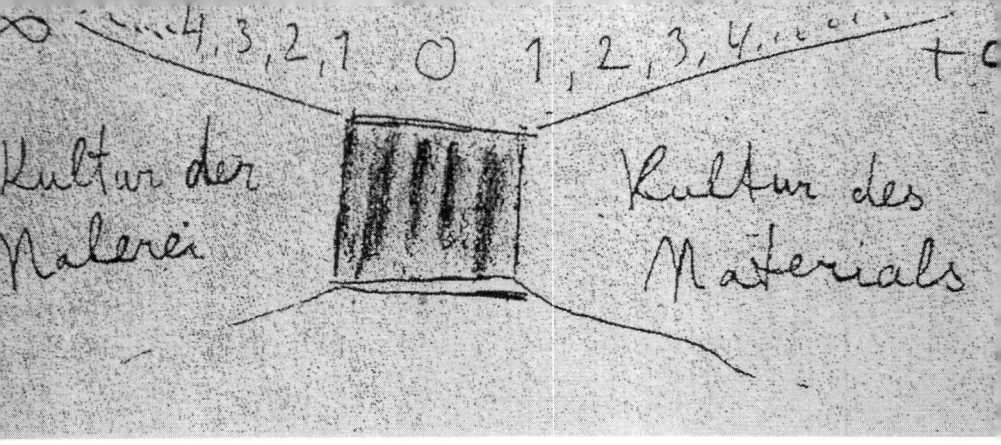

Drawing by El Lissitzky explaining Malevich's *Black Square* as the zero point of modern painting, 1922

square has blocked the narrowing canal of painting, then on the other side it becomes the foundation-stone for the new spatial construction of reality.[13]

It is helpful here to contrast an artist like Piet Mondrian to someone like Reinhardt. Mondrian, for example, shows a continued development towards abstraction until he reaches a kind of dead end in his mature *de stijl* paintings. Like Reinhardt he seems to stall out at this point for a number of years until we get to *Broadway Boogie Woogie. De stijl* is a kind of zero point for Mondrian and on the other side representation is re-introduced in bizarre ways. The flat grid of the painting's surface becomes the city, painting becomes jazz.

The exhibition *As Painting* curated by Stephen Melville, Philip Armstrong and Laura Lisbon at the Wexner Center in 2001 is such a fascinating exhibition precisely because it seeks to follow this logic of painting underground, through the zero point of modernism, and map the places that it tunnels. The thesis of *As Painting* is that painting thinks itself, it forms a kind of generative program where one object that

[13] El Lissitzky, "New Russian Art: A Lecture (1922)" in *El Lissitzky: Life, Letters, Texts*, ed. Sophie Lissitzky-Küppers, trans. Helene Aldwinckle and Mary Whittal (Greenwich: New York Graphic Society, 1968), 333-34.

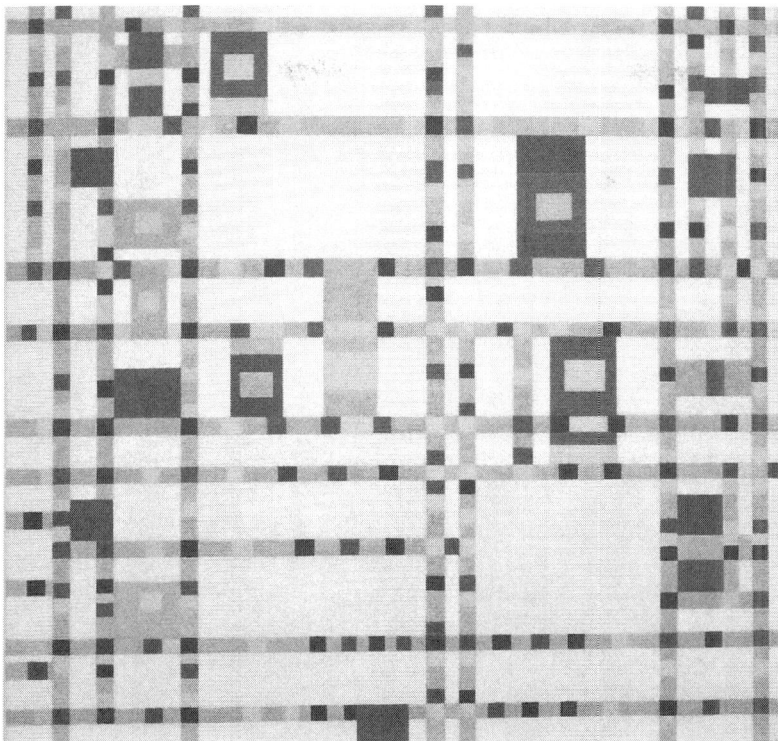

Piet Mondrian, *Broadway Boogie Woogie*, 1943, oil on canvass

counts as a painting in turn creates new conditions under which other objects can come to be seen as paintings and so forth. The exhibition itself is populated with 110 things, the vast majority of which would not ordinarily be recognised as paintings. It included artworks such as Robert Smithson's *Slantpiece*, a mirror slanted against a wall in a pile of rock salt, Daniel Dezueze's *Cube* built out of layered wooden lattices, conceptual drawings by Mel Bochner and installations by Imi Knoebel consisting of stacked plywood with lacquered surfaces that look like the storage room for building supplies. The conceit of the exhibition is that all of these are meant to be seen *as paintings* rather than, simply, as objects. We can only identify these objects as paintings historically, that is to say that these objects participate in the historical outworking of the logic of painting as a medium. What counts as a painting is historically contingent. High modernist painting created new historical conditions under which something like minimalism could become (one of) the step(s) beyond modernism. In *As Painting* we see modernism turn itself inside out, pulled through the buttonhole of the zero point, painting becomes sculpture, image becomes thing, surface becomes mass.

In his marvellous catalogue essay "Counting/As/Painting" Stephen Melville draws a straight line between an important footnote in Fried's "Art and Objecthood" and Heidegger's as-structure.[14] If as-structure is the idea that all consciousness is consciousness of something "*as*" something, what then is the as-structure of painting? Fried here is commenting on a passage from Greenberg that reads, "the observation of merely these two norms [flatness and the delimitation of flatness] is enough to create an object which can be experienced as a picture: thus a stretched or tacked-up canvas already exists as a picture—though not necessarily as a *successful* one."[15] Now Fried:

> Moreover, seeing something *as a painting* in the sense that one sees the tacked-up canvas *as a painting*, and being convinced that a particular work can stand comparison with the painting of the past whose quality is not in doubt, are altogether different experiences: it is, I want to say, as though unless something compels conviction as to its quality *it is no more than trivially or nominally a painting* ... This is not to say that painting has no essence; it is to claim that the essence—i.e. that which compels conviction—is largely determined by, and therefore changes continually in response to, the vital work of the recent past.[16]

---

14 Stephen Melville, "Counting/As/Painting" in *As Painting: Division and Displacement*, ed. Philip Armstrong, Laura Lisbon, and Stephen Melville (Cambridge: MIT Press, 2001), 1-26.

15 Clement Greenberg, "After Abstract Expressionism," *Art International* (1962), 6:8, 30, original emphasis.

16 Fried, *Art and Objecthood*, 169 n.6, my emphasis.

The history of painting has an agency of its own. What counts as a painting is not nominated as such by an artist or critic so much as it is by other pre-established paintings. Paintings are actants in their own right that use human consciousness parasitically to think according to their own logic. One painting can step up and "vouch for" another object's status as a painting, thereby altering the very as-structure of what can count as a painting allowing new objects to be caught and identified as paintings and so forth. Note that Fried nearly endorses Duchamp's position, that a tacked up canvas—a readymade canvas if you will—can only be seen as painting *in a nominal sense*. This is exactly what Duchamp discovered and called "pictorial nominalism" and which Thierry de Duve has fleshed out into a fully formed theory of art.[17] What happens when painting passes through the zero point of modernism is that paintings can pick out and nominate other objects as painting in a semi-autonomous way. I say semi-autonomous because I take it for granted that paintings can only exist as paintings for human consciousness. If you removed all human consciousness and everything like human consciousness, the *Mona Lisa* would still exist, but only as an object or thing, or as non-art as indeed everything would be non-art, but not as a painting or an artwork.

Fried's objection to minimalism was that it did not suspend its relationship to its own objecthood. For all artworks, not just the modernist ones Fried championed, the line between art and non-art runs through the artwork itself. This is perhaps the clearest way to understand the difference between what Fried calls absorption (which Fried supported) and theatricality (which he opposed). Absorptive art suspends its relationship to its own material support, the part of it-

---

[17] One of the notes for *The Large Glass* from 1914 reads: "A kind of *pictorial Nominalism*." Marcel Duchamp, *The Writings of Marcel Duchamp*, ed. Michel Sanouillet and Elmer Peterson (Cambridge: Da Capo Press, 1989), 78. See Thierry de Duve, *Pictorial Nominalism: On Marcel Duchamp's Passage from Painting to the Readymade*, trans. Dana Polan (Minneapolis: University of Minnesota Press, 1991), and Thierry de Duve, *Kant after Duchamp* (Cambridge: MIT Press, 1996). If Melville is the best reader of Fried, then de Duve is by far the best reader of Duchamp.

self that is non-art, whereas theatrical art like minimalism identifies with the aspect of itself that is non-art. Duchamp said the same thing from the other way around, noting that any artist who purchases a tube of paint at the art store is purchasing a readymade thing and that all paintings are just assisted readymades. It is to readymades that we now turn for they pose another zero point, this time at the very heart of the as-structure itself.

The Avant-garde

In 1913, in one of the many notes for *The Large Glass*, Duchamp wrote the following on the back of a card:

Speculations
Can one make works which are not works of "art?"[18]

I take this to be the fundamental formula which animates the logic of avant-garde. Just like the course of modernism, the course of the avant-garde will reach an internal impasse at roughly the same time in history. In this case it will dead end in the readymade, forcing Duchamp to adopt new tactics like quitting art for chess or trying to limit the number of readymades he "made," all the way up to adopting a strategic invisibility.

Avant-garde art as I am using the term is not just innovative art. We can see the history of art develop and innovate all throughout history, such as the innovations of Cimabue's depiction of the human form or the discovery and application of perspective. Rather, in order for a work of art to be avant-garde it must renegotiate the border between art and life. "Life" as it is used here is simply the conventional term artists have settled on to signify the set of all things that are not art. An avant-garde work of art takes place on the "life" side of the boundary between art and life, thereby redrawing that boundary. I take Courbet to be the first avant-garde artist and

---

[18] Duchamp, *The Writings of Marcel Duchamp*, 74. The bold text is in the original.

Gustave Courbet, *The Stone Breakers*, oil on canvas, 1849-50,

The Stone Breakers to be the first avant-garde painting. For a long time, violating the boundary between art and life simply meant violating social conventions about what counted as art, painting labourers rather than aristocrats, painting them in the course of their labour rather than posing for the audience, painting torn clothing rather than tidying up reality, etc.

One way of thinking about what Duchamp was trying to do with readymades is that he was trying to make a work of art that was not present-at-hand in Heidegger's sense, that is to say Duchamp was trying to make a work of art that would not present itself to human consciousness as a work of art to be contemplated or appreciated by aesthetic judgement. The first readymades that he ever exhibited were not exhibited as art or as readymades, instead they were exhibited secretly even while being in plain view. We do not know where they are any more. Maybe they are floating around anonymously somewhere or more likely they are in pieces, some in landfills. Art historians are not even sure which objects they were. The consensus seems to be that one of the first readymades

299

was probably his hat rack, placed in the front of the gallery Bourgeois near the door in 1917. People entering the gallery would place their hats on the hat rack without thinking about it, never considering it a work of art at all, completely oblivious to the idea that they had just encountered a work "by" Duchamp. They used it absentmindedly *as a hat rack.*

The avant-garde, in order to function as a redrawing of the frontier between art and life, requires this very frontier. This frontier might shift, indeed any work of avant-garde art will shift it, and the history of the avant-garde (which we should remember is a military term) is the history of a kind of colonial encroachment of art into the territory of life. The readymade announces a kind of globalism where this frontier disappears, art gains a totalitarian dominance and life has nowhere left to hide. Like self-replicating carbon-based nano-bots, art threatened to swallow up all of life.[19] One tactic that Duchamp adopted in an attempt to maintain this boundary was to simply create an artificial limit to the number of readymades he would "make" in a given year. "I realized very soon the danger of repeating indiscriminately this form of expression and decided to limit the production of 'readymades' to a small number yearly. I was aware at that time, that for the spectator even more than for the artist, art is a habit forming drug and I wanted to protect my 'readymades' against such contamination."[20] Duchamp tried to quarantine his readymade against the pandemic spread of art. Should we read the readymade as an object that marks the boundary between art and life, a kind of herma marking a territory beyond which art should not tread, or as an object that is neither art nor life but a zone of indistinction between the two? I would suggest not, for two reasons. First, the anxiousness of the work of art comes from being internally split by life and art. The boundary line runs through the work of art itself. This

---

[19] See Ransom Riggs, "How to Destroy Civilization with Nanotechnology," *mental_floss* http://mentalfloss.com/article/21077/be-amazing-movie (accessed August 31, 2013).

[20] Duchamp, *The Writings of Marcel Duchamp*, 142.

is Duchamp's example of the tube of paint as a readymade.[21] A painting by Van Gogh is an assisted readymade. Van Gogh purchased readymade tubes of paint and simply rearranged these colours. Even when artists mixed their own paint we just push the point at which they are assisting readymades back one step further. Second, when we come to regard a readymade as a work of art, human consciousness again splits the readymade in two and establishes the boundary line between art and life within the readymade itself, converting it into a work of art. The problem is that as soon as you see the readymade *as a readymade* it ceases to be a readymade in some true sense. If every object of life can come to be seen as readymade and any readymade seen as such becomes art, what becomes of the avant-garde?

Duchamp tried to quarantine *life* against the pandemic spread of art. But he could have no such luck against the culture industry which quickly sweeps in behind the advances of the avant-garde co-opting and assimilating it as art history. The culture industry has left us no place to hide. No place that is, unless we adopt an absolute strategic invisibility. Suzi Gablik begins her 1984 book *Has Modernism Failed?* the following way:

> The art dealer and critic John Bernard Myers once asked Marcel Duchamp how many people he thought *really* liked avant-garde art, and Duchamp replied, "Oh, maybe ten in New York and one or two in New Jersey." That was back in 1945.[22]

She then goes on to detail the massive expansion of the multi-billion dollar market for avant-garde art that was able to instantly commodify and completely neutralise any external avant-garde advances or resistance. The situation is no doubt even worse today where art fairs dominate the cultural field. In the holy war between modernism and kitsch, kitsch emerged victorious. In the battle between the culture industry

---

[21] See "The Readymade and the Tube of Paint" in de Duve, *Kant After Duchamp*, 147-98.

[22] Suzi Gablik, *Has Modernism Failed?* (New York: Thames and Hudson, 1984), 12.

and the avant-garde, the culture industry won in a rout. The state of cultural production today can only be expressed by a Leonard Cohen lamentation: "everybody knows the war is over / everybody knows the good guys lost."[23] But is there any way to continue to fight the good fight? Is there any way to remain faithful to the revolutionary ideals of the avant-garde? The only way to resist instantaneous assimilation to the culture industry is to become strategically invisible to it. This is how I read Duchamp's claim that he had given up art for chess, as a strategic manoeuvre to shake a tail (or as Picabia might put it, the task of the avant-garde artist is to avoid having one's artwork caught by the tail). The landscape had already changed by 1965 when Duchamp claimed that, despite the fact that there were vastly more people who *really* liked avant-garde art, there was no longer any avant-garde left.

> Duchamp asserted at the time, "There is no avant-garde art today. And if there were, it would be so totally underground art that no one would see." As a quintessential "exercise in strategic invisibility," Duchamp then used a torch in the [University of Minnesota] grad sculpture studio to sign his name in soot on a piece of metal, and inscribed his signature in pieces of wet clay that were subsequently fired.[24]

Fried had said that a tacked up canvas might be seen as a painting, but not necessarily as a successful one. It fails at painting by being merely a readymade canvas. One way to understand what is meant by strategic invisibility is to ask what it would mean to be a *successful* readymade. A successful readymade can never be seen as such; or put otherwise, a true avant-garde work of art could never appear as an avant-garde work of art. Like a meteor that burns itself up as it enters Earth's atmosphere never actually reaches Earth, a readymade

---

[23] Leonard Cohen and Sharon Robinson, "Everybody Knows," *I'm Your Man* (Columbia Records), 1988.

[24] Micaela Amateau Amato, "Duchamp as Stealth Artist," *Art in America* (2000), 88:7, 19.

burns itself up as it crosses the boundary between life and art. Sheldon Nodelman describes strategic invisibility as the ability to evade being recognised as a work of art:

> But in a larger sense, Duchamp's entire artistic activity since the "definitive incompletion" of the *Large Glass* in 1923 was an exercise in strategic invisibility, giving rise to objects and events which—because they were apparently too impermanent or unimportant or insubstantial, or because they eluded established genre conventions, or because they confused or diluted authorial identity—evaded recognition as "works of art."[25]

Piggybacking on Melville, we might ask: what counts as a work by Duchamp? Nodelman notes the fun fact that while the 1969 edition of *The Complete Works of Marcel Duchamp* contained 421 known works, the most recent edition contains 663 known works. A whole army of art historians are going back and adding all of these apparently insubstantial items. In this way we can say that anything that is recognised as one of Duchamp's readymades in some real sense fails to be one of Duchamp's readymades. Likewise we can say that any successful readymades are ones that avoid detection as art and remain merely objects of life. What makes them different from mere objects of life is that they participate in the outworking of the logic of art history, albeit a history that is inaccessible to human consciousness.

It becomes possible to imagine that the boundary between art and life no longer holds or might be obliterated altogether. This seems to be the position that Allan Kaprow held. At times he described his happenings in terms of strategic invisibility. "Once, the task of the artist was to make good art; now it is to avoid making art of any kind."[26] Or again, "Leaving art is the art ... I define it as that act or thought whose identity as art

---

[25] Sheldon Nodelman, "The Once and Future Duchamp," *Art in America* (2000), 88:1, 37.

[26] Allan Kaprow, *Essays on the Blurring of Art and Life*, ed. Jeff Kelley (Berkeley: University of California Press, 2003), 81.

must forever remain unknown. That is, to answer the initial question What is Art?, art could (but might not) be simply doing art, whatever that is, as long as it can't be identified."[27] But it soon becomes clear that his real goal is not to make "art" on the side of "life" that nobody ever notices, but instead to make us really and truly notice our lives while we live them.

At the end of Thornton Wilder's *Our Town*, when Emily has died and only now that her life is gone can she truly notice how magical it had always been, she cries "Oh, earth, you're too wonderful for anybody to realize you." She turns to the Stage Manager and asks "Do any human beings ever realize life while they live it?—every, every minute?" The Stage Manager replies, "No. The saints and poets, maybe they do some."[28] Allan Kaprow was such a saint, someone who tried to cultivate a habit of hypervigilance, of truly seeing what he was looking at, of really noticing life every, every minute. Kaprow's hypervigilance seeks to turn everything in the world, at every given moment, into a broken tool. It is as if he turned to Heidegger's carpenter and said "look, look at what you are doing. Feel—no really truly feel—the weight of the hammer as you swing. Listen to the sound of the wood rattle as the hammer strikes the nail. Take joy in its momentum. Feel the vibrations in your elbow as it lands. Notice the way the light changes as you swing. Take pleasure in the hammering while it happens for even this simple happening can disclose the whole world." If Fried says that we are literalists most of our lives, Kaprow would say we are not nearly literalist enough. Creating his own Latour litany, Kaprow declares,[29]

Objects of every sort are materials for the new art: paint, chairs, food, electric and neon lights, smoke, water, old socks, a dog, movies, a thou-

---

[27] Kaprow, *Essays*, xxix, original emphasis.

[28] Thornton Wilder, "Our Town," *Three Plays by Thornton Wilder* (New York: Bantam Books, 1957), 62.

[29] Latour litany is a term coined by Ian Bogost to describe a long list of assorted objects that Bruno Latour frequently uses in his books to shock us into noticing the awful abundance and variety of reality.

sand other things that will be discovered by the present generation of artists. Not only will these bold creators show us, as if for the first time, the world we have always had about us but ignored, but they will disclose entirely unheard-of happenings and events, found in garbage cans, police files, hotel lobbies; seen in store windows and on the streets; and sensed in dreams and horrible accidents. An odor of crushed strawberries, a letter from a friend, or a billboard selling Drano; three taps on the front door, a scratch, a sigh, or a voice lecturing endlessly, a blinding staccato flash, a bowler hat—all will become materials for this new concrete art.[30]

John Cage also does the same thing. At first it might seem that his furniture music (a beloved term he borrowed from Erik Satie) is music that is meant to be strategically invisible, but it soon becomes clear that his real goal is to make us notice all of the other furniture in the world. For Cage the proper response after encountering his compositions is to immediately abandon them to become constantly aware of the world around you, to become hypervigilantly aware of it. What we see here is that Kaprow and Cage's inheritance of Duchamp's legacy does not seek to make strategically invisible artworks on the "life" side of the art/life divide, but to make the life side of this division glaringly visible to us. It would seem that both Kaprow and Cage really truly believed that they could blur the boundary entirely and abandon it completely. Yet upon further investigation by the next generation of Fluxus artists, it becomes evident that the boundary is maintained by human consciousness itself. Artists like Ben Vautier spent years honestly pursuing the goal of obliterating the distinction between art and life but ended up concluding that the boundary is inviolable.

We are trying to do non-art but non-art cannot exist because it is art. And we are trying to do life-art but life-art cannot exist because it is either art or life. If it is life it's life and nobody knows about it. It's my mother-in-law opening the tap and she doesn't care. And if she finds

---

[30] Kaprow, *Essays*, xx.

out it's *Drip Music* by George Brecht then she starts thinking that it's art. So you can't get one into the other. It's one and another and that's important.[31]

The limit point that the avant-garde runs into is built into the as-structure itself. The point is that after the avant-garde was forced underground, it is no longer possible for human consciousness to see that dividing line between art and life, even as the line's very existence is produced by human consciousness. At this very moment, in the very space you are reading this text, you could be entertaining readymades the way one might, without knowing it, be entertaining angels. A pair of trousers hanging over a chair, the window in the library, the very floorboards, a passenger sitting next to you on the subway who is stiff from sitting still so long and begins to fidget, any of these could be, without anyone realising it, the greatest work of avant-garde art the world has ever known. Except that the world can never know it for if the world knew it, it would destroy it. When the police interviewed Vincenzo Peruggia in his apartment while the *Mona Lisa* was buried under a pile of firewood, one of those pieces of firewood might have been the true work of avant-garde art. George Maciunas's favourite piece was said to be George Brecht's *Exit* because it was something that everyone did every day without realising it and as such became a strategically invisible work of art.

The Avant-Garde and Justice

At first glance, axiology would seem the toughest terrain for the various speculative realisms to deal with. There are parallels between the strategically invisible aesthetics of the avant-garde and the strategically invisible ethics of someone like Emmanuel Levinas. For Levinas, justice cannot show

---

[31] Ben Vautier, quoted in *The Misfits: Thirty Years of Fluxus*, directed by Lars Movin (Copenhagen: The National Film Board of Denmark, 1993), video. The relevant clip from this interview can be viewed at www.youtube.com/watch?v=wifEeopqg3o&feature=share&list=UUKJRuwRVnoagrL6OL_5ioWw (accessed August 31, 2013).

itself as such without becoming self-righteousness for the same exact structural reason that Vautier outlined between art and life. True justice for Levinas is not the justice of the ego. The justice of the ego is merely self-righteousness. The problem is that to even recognise something as justice is to instantaneously convert it into a self-justification. One can never know if one is doing justice and one can never even write a history of justice without turning it into a history of injustice for the same reason that Jacques Derrida demonstrated that one can never write a history of madness without turning it into a history of reason.[32] Levinas writes, "The just person who knows himself to be just is no longer just. The first condition of the first as of the last of the just is that their justice remains clandestine to them."[33] As soon as I say "I am just" or even "this deed is just" it ceases to be just and instead becomes mere self-righteousness. This is not to say that justice does not happen or operate in the universe, only that we cannot perceive it as such.

The avant-garde has always been linked to a utopian justice. Like the avant-garde, justice operates in a strategically invisible way, for the two are really synonymous. Justice exists and operates, but it does so clandestinely and can only do so clandestinely. You can see the same dynamic play out in the history of Christian theology. What does it mean to be justified by the radical outside? Here the primary concern was a way of trying to avoid Pelagianism, one that I believe ultimately is impossible to avoid. We can only be more or less Pelagians, just like, as Derrida said, we can only ever be more or less generous narcissists.[34] Every theory of justice, every

---

[32] See Jacques Derrida, "Cogito and the History of Madness" in *Writing and Difference*, trans. Alan Bass (Chicago: University of Chicago Press, 1978), 31-63.

[33] Emmanuel Levinas, "Transcendence and Height" in *Basic Philosophical Writings*, ed. Adriaan Theodoor Peperzak, Simon Critchley, and Robert Bernasconi (Bloomington: Indiana University Press, 1996), 17.

[34] "There is not narcissism and non-narcissism. There are narcissisms that are more or less comprehensive, generous, open, extended. What is called non-narcissism is in general but the economy of a much more welcoming and hospitable narcissism." *Points...: Interviews, 1974-1994*, ed. Elizabeth Weber,

doctrine of justification, ultimately collapses into a version of Pelagianism for the same reason that every war is always a just war in the eyes of the aggressors. We can actually watch the moment in Luther's commentary on the book of Romans where he slips up and his radical vision of justification from the wholly other through a general economy of grace falls back into a restricted economy of works.

> God does not want us to redeem us through our own, but through external, righteousness and wisdom; not through one that comes from us and grows in us, but through one that comes to us from the outside; not through one that originates here on earth, but through one that comes from heaven. Therefore, we must be taught a righteousness that comes completely from the outside and is foreign. And therefore our own righteousness that is born in us must first be plucked up ... Even though a person with all his natural and spiritual gifts may be wise before men and righteous and good, God will not on that account look upon him as such, especially if he regards himself so ... Therefore we must in all these things keep ourselves so humble as if we still had nothing of our own. We must wait for the naked mercy of God, who will reckon us righteous and wise. *This God will do if we have been humble and have not anticipated God by justifying ourselves* and by thinking that we are something.[35]

This radical exterior justice gets converted into an if/then statement in exactly the same way that a strategically invisible work of avant-garde that takes place on the side of "life" gets converted into art. But it also provides us with a way of

---

trans. Peggy Kamuf (Stanford: Stanford University Press, 1995), 199. Compare this to Vautier: "Fluxus in America try to keep onto the impersonality research. Impersonality means the non-ego research of John Cage which did not succeed but was very interesting as a tentative because I don't believe you can do anything non-ego. Man [sic] is a hundred percent ego and even when he becomes a non-egoist it is pure ego non-ego. You cannot get non-ego but you can get a new statement on ego which is non-ego. Complicated huh?" Vautier, quoted in *The Misfits*.

[35] Martin Luther, *Lectures on Romans, Glosses and Schoilia: Luther's Works*, vol. 25, ed. Jaroslav Pelikan (St. Louis: Concordia Publishing House, 1986), 136, my emphasis.

Sign at the inaugural lecture of the University of Strategic Optimism

seeing how speculative realism could approach issues of axiology. If every difference makes a difference, then one of the differences that human consciousness introduces is value. Yet the location where these values take place can still be outside human consciousness. Art and ethics are both dependent on the existence of human consciousness (or something like human consciousness) in the sense that if you removed all human consciousness, there would no longer be any difference between things that are art and things that are not art, nor would there be any ethics. Billiard balls might continue to collide into things without humans, but never *as* an assault. Fire might continue to burn cotton but never *as* arson. Yet although human consciousness produces ethics in a Levinasian sense, the real work of ethics happens outside of human awareness.

Today it is taken as a matter of dogma that the avant-garde is no longer possible, that it was a historical period that came to an end. The exact date at which it ended is hard to pin down, but sometime between May '68 and November '89, the door to the future closed seemingly forever. History, we were told, had ended.[36] Global capitalism and liberal democracy are now

---

[36] Francis Fukuyama, *The End of History and the Last Man* (New York: Free Press, 1992).

the only possibility. There is no alternative. The avant-garde and its ideals had a good run, but to pine for them now is pointless. The best thing to do is to make your peace with the current order of things. Look, you can still paint and sculpt and hang art on the wall, they can never take that from you. But the *avant* of the avant-garde is now closed. The reading I am offering rejects this account. In contrast, it holds that the history of justice is a secret one, and that, clandestinely, it still marches on. Likewise, the avant-garde as it passes through the zero point of the readymade is liberated from the human to follow its own devices on the side of life. Without realising it, we may be participating in justice or in the avant-garde, which amount to the same thing. History is not over, events are still possible, they just continue invisibly.

The Anxiousness of Objects and Artworks 2

(Iso)Morphism, Anti-Literalism and Presentness[1]

Robert Jackson

University of Lancaster

Look at a stone and imagine it having sensations. – One says to oneself: How could one so much as get the idea of ascribing a *sensation* to a *thing*? One might as well ascribe it to a number! – And now look at a wriggling fly and at once these difficulties vanish and pain seems to get a foothold here, where before everything was, so to speak, too smooth for it.
—Ludwig Wittgenstein, *Philosophical Investigations*[2]

A S ITS TITLE INDICATES, THIS contribution is a continuation of my article published in this very journal in 2011, where I first attempted to align the principles of Graham Harman's object-oriented ontology (OOO) with Michael Fried's art criticism.[3] Since then, three important and surprising events have occurred which the present essay takes as its task to integrate and elaborate on.

Firstly, Harman himself has published, presented, and publicly blogged on similar connections between Clement

---

[1] I extend my thanks to Ridvan Askin and Andreas Hägler whose invaluable insights refined any muddled judgements and their patient editing work immeasurably enhanced my earlier drafts.

[2] Ludwig Wittgenstein, *Philosophical Investigations*, trans. G. E. M. Anscombe, 3rd ed. (Oxford: Blackwell, 2001), 83e.

[3] See Robert Jackson, "The Anxiousness of Objects and Artworks: Michael Fried, Object Oriented Ontology and Aesthetic Absorption," *Speculations* (2011), 2, 135-68.

Greenberg's modernist principles of the avant-garde and his own philosophy of objects.[4] In consideration of the fact that Fried was arguably Greenberg's most famous protégé alongside Rosalind Krauss, this adds an impetus for critical development. As is the norm with any deliberation on Fried's criticism, the essay will also gather central insights from the work of his philosophical compadre and close friend Stanley Cavell.

Secondly, the expansion of speculative realism not only continues to proliferate in-between distinct disciplines outside of philosophy—including the arts—but the movement itself has exposed a critical fault-line which can be separated into two distinct, contradictory philosophical orientations. The essay will borrow Quentin Meillassoux's distinction between demonstration and description,[5] and in so doing, illuminate

---

[4] For a very brief exposition of Harman's broad influence by Greenbergian literary criticism, see the recently published Graham Harman, *Weird Realism: Lovecraft and Philosophy* (Winchester: Zero Books, 2012), 19-21. As for public talks, I can only cite the most explicit lectures and presentations in this area from 2012 and the beginning of 2013. Graham Harman, "Greenberg, Heidegger, McLuhan, and the Arts," presentation given at Pacific Northwest College of Art, Museum of Contemporary Craft, January 22, 2013. The audio for this lecture can be found at http://untitled.pnca.edu/multimedia/show/6380/ (accessed February 19, 2013). Graham Harman, "Non-Relational Aesthetics: An Object-Oriented Look at Contemporary Art," presentation given at The School of Art and the Center for the Arts in Society, Carnegie Mellon University, October 23, 2012. Graham Harman, "The Next Avant-Garde," keynote delivered at the Aesthetics in the 21st Century conference, University of Basel, September 13-15, 2012. For references to Graham Harman's weblog posting, see Graham Harman, "where Greenberg and McLuhan meet," Object-Oriented Philosophy, http://doctorzamalek2.wordpress.com/2011/10/27/where-greenberg-and-mcluhan-meet/ (accessed February 1, 2013); Graham Harman, "Greenberg and McLuhan," Object-Oriented Philosophy, http://doctorzamalek2.wordpress.com/2011/07/05/greenberg-and-mcluhan/ (accessed February 1, 2013); Graham Harman, "Robert Jack[s]on on my Greenberg posts," Object-Oriented Philosophy, http://doctorzamalek2.wordpress.com/2011/06/21/robert-jackon-on-my-greenberg-posts/ (accessed February 1, 2013); and Graham Harman, "Greenberg as a writer," Object-Oriented Philosophy, http://doctorzamalek2.wordpress.com/2011/05/20/greenberg-as-a-writer/ (accessed February 1, 2013).

[5] See Ray Brassier, Graham Harman, Iain Hamilton Grant and Quentin Meillassoux, "Speculative Realism," *Collapse* (2007), 3, 391-392. For the rest of the article, I will distinguish my own appropriation of these terms as

how the critical demands of this philosophical distinction in speculative realism can be associated with the critical demands of Fried's distinction between "Literalism and Presentness,"[6] or as it is better known, "Theatricality and Anti-theatricality."[7] My use of Meillassoux's fault-line in this essay is exactly that: *a critical use*, and not a purely descriptive, or empirical one. I will not attempt to deliberately align these terms, as Meillassoux does, with a single viewpoint or a school of thought, but with a general orientation of conflict: such a conflict, I claim, can also be traced in the terrain of aesthetics, by means of juxtaposing conflicting theoretical viewpoints.

Thirdly, in September 2011, Fried published his latest collection of essays on contemporary art criticism called *Four Honest Outlaws*.[8] In these four essays, Fried discusses works by contemporary video artist Anri Sala, sculptor Charles Ray, painter Joseph Marioni, and Douglas Gordon, whose work crosses different types of media. I have included this work primarily because I consider it to be an important progression in Fried's later career; a snapshot of a modernist thinker who is not only opening up his modernist conviction to other media (in this case video projection), but is also indirectly revealing new claims on anthropomorphic absorption and presentness taking place within non-human reality. These new claims unfold under the catchphrase of *empathic projection*, which I argue is not just central to Fried's late criticism (at least in *Four Honest Outlaws*), but in combination with

---

Demonstration and **Description**, capitalised and in boldface.

[6] Michael Fried, "Art and Objecthood," *Artforum* (1967), 5, 12-23. Reprinted in *Minimal Art: A Critical Anthology*, ed. Gregory Battcock (Berkeley: University of California Press, 1995), 116-47; *Aesthetics: A Critical Anthology*, ed. George Dickie and Richard J. Sclafani (New York: St Martin's Press, 1977), 438-60 and *Looking Critically: 21 Years of Artforum*, ed. by Amy Baker Sandback (Ann Arbor: UMI Research Press, 1984), 61-68. Subsequent citations are taken from *Art in Theory 1900-1990: An Anthology of Changing Ideas*, ed. Paul Wood and Charles Harrison (London: Wiley-Blackwell, 2002), 822-34.

[7] Michael Fried, *Absorption and Theatricality: Painting and Beholder in the Age of Diderot* (Chicago: The University of Chicago Press, 1980).

[8] Michael Fried, *Four Honest Outlaws: Sala, Ray, Marioni, Gordon* (New Haven: Yale University Press, 2011).

Harman's philosophy of objects has the potential to unveil a general aesthetic relationship between objects. This relationship I call *isomorphism*.

Part 1

Harman and Greenberg: Radicalising Anthropomorphism

If one is convinced by Harman's maxim that philosophy must primarily align itself with a primordial aesthetics (rather than analytic logic, rational science or militant politics),[9] then one could assert the following challenge as a loose provocation: an OOO non-relational aesthetics must be associated with a Greenbergian high modernist criticism, rather than any philosophical deliberation in recent art theory.[10] Such a challenge will require taking the metaphorical theories of modernist criticism into a realist direction, rather than rejecting them outright or keeping them within the confines of correlationism.

In order to do so, my aim is to develop the deep relevancy between OOO and the modernist criticism of Greenberg and Fried in an effort to understand how the connection between them *radicalises* certain critical boundaries between anthropomorphic art and its objecthood. Art's autonomy is meaningless if a beholder is unable to at least acknowledge some haggard form of distinguishing one from the other, and to get straight to the heart of the intervention, the critical role of the beholder may not just be a matter of human discourse.

So why high modernism? At first pass, the high modernist sensibility evokes the opposite goals of Harman's philosophy, for it privileges human opticality (in the modernist sense) and a deep, self-knowing sense of privilege, where the impact of a critic's decision relegates non-art to "mere" objecthood.

---

[9] Graham Harman, "On Vicarious Causation," *Collapse* (2007), 2, 221.

[10] For prominent examples of such theory, see Jacques Rancière, *The Emancipated Spectator* (London: Verso, 2011) and Alain Badiou, *Handbook of Inaesthetics* (Stanford: Stanford University Press, 2004).

However, consider two prominent criticisms usually levelled at both positions: the charge of conservatism for trying to cut off objects in general and artworks in particular from their social and political relational context, and an ever-present dismissal based on the joint endorsement of categories such as limit, naiveté, taste, quality and essence to describe the art object's determinate character. To adopt an old saying, the enemy of an enemy is a friend (paradoxically, Greenberg was, in his harsher articles, nothing if not his own worst enemy at times).

The key term which modernist critics used to distinguish art from the mundane is *anthropomorphism*; namely the attribution of human characteristics to an impersonal world, thing, animal, machine, or a god. As J. M. Bernstein points out, Greenberg's formalism originated in, and was a reaction to, what he saw as the demythologisation of anthropomorphism inherent to a particular historical response within modernity according to which only reductive strategies of reason and logic should be associated with genuine progress and understanding.[11] Scepticism demonstrates the forward march of progress, whilst irrational superstition is purged and abandoned. As Bernstein writes:

> Beginning with Descartes's methodical doubting of appearances, modernity has construed its rationality as a critical overcoming of the endless displays and temptations of anthropomorphic understanding—the projecting of human meaning onto an inhuman or indifferent material world. If, the argument runs, things only have meaning through what we project onto them, then in themselves things are meaningless and thus ought to be understood in the *visionless medium of pure mathematics*. The same movement of demythologisation that fashioned the death of God is carried forward by a rationalism that limits meaning and value to the satisfaction of human desires and interests as processed through a practical reasoning that is instrumental, means-ends rational, through and through. *All else is mythology and illusion.*[12]

---

[11] J. M. Bernstein, *Against Voluptuous Bodies: Late Modernism and the Meaning of Painting* (Stanford: Stanford University Press, 2006), 124-26.

[12] Ibid., 123, my emphases.

Despite sharing similar historical and cultural tendencies, Greenberg's celebration of abstraction (ultimately guided by Kant) *defended* the human limits of anthropomorphism against visionless pure reasoning and rational justification.[13] Painting cannot be demythologised from a non-anthropological view from nowhere, otherwise it ceases to operate as an independent artwork of depth and quality which connects with reality through its own allusive form. Instead, what is primary in aesthetic experience are the Kantian relations of finite *intuition* and *description* of an independent entity: a failed demonstration which the beholder or artist can never deduce. In Greenberg's words, modernist practice must justify itself from the inside of a *limiting condition*, which "does not offer theoretical demonstrations."[14] If Enlightenment's criticism came from processing the outside through the cold light of reason and knowledge, modernist art attempts to *process the outside through the sensual light of intuition and allusion.* In Greenberg's words, it "criticizes from the inside, through the procedures themselves of that which is being criticized."[15]

This refusal of demonstration is what keeps modernist artworks shorn of political and cultural baggage, never dependent on external reason or context, but on a passive and "heightened cognitiveness without cognition."[16] For Greenberg, aesthetic justification was an end to itself, "not to be

---

[13] Bernstein, *Against Voluptuous Bodies*, 124.

[14] Clement Greenberg, "Modernist Painting," first published in *Arts Yearbook* (1961), 4, and reprinted with revisions in *Art & Literature* (1965), 4, 193-201 and in *Art in Theory 1900-1990: An Anthology of Changing Ideas*, ed. Charles Harrison and Paul Wood (Oxford: Blackwell Publishers, 1992), 754-60. All citations are taken from Clement Greenberg, "Modernist Painting," in *Modern Art and Modernism: A Critical Anthology*, ed. Francis Frascina and Charles Harrison (London: Harper and Row, 1982), 9, cf. 5-10.

[15] Ibid., 5.

[16] Clement Greenberg, "The Language of Esthetic Discourse," in *Homemade Esthetics: Observations on Art and Taste* (Oxford: Oxford University Press, 1999), 65. The second part of *Homemade Esthetics* transcribes Greenberg's Bennington Seminars delivered over nine nights during April 6-22, 1971. On the third night and in response to a question asked at the Q&A concerning the similarity between Greenberg's concept and the apparatus of seeing, Greenberg explains his idea of "cognitiveness without cognition" thus:

obtained from any other kind of activity," to the extent that the proper practice of artistic competence would reveal the unique nature of its medium, in its own right.[17] An aesthetic medium establishes a timeless essence in which "each art [must] determine, through the operations peculiar to itself, the effects peculiar and exclusive to itself."[18] Refusing reliance on anything outside the medium, abstraction removes the representational image, which could always be subject to demystifying critique, and decides on the optical space of a painting to transcend its image. Greenberg's commentary consists in following the practice of artists who test a medium's conventions, and whose continual testing of conventions determines which ones are either essential or dispensable in different movements. According to Greenberg, such testing reveals that flatness (and the delimitation of flatness) in abstract expressionism and modernist painting in general has the status of essential quality and truth.

As Bernstein states, painting for Greenberg was a *human* practice: "the world as seen, the seen world, is not the world as a thing in itself, but precisely the world as the internal correlate of the seeing eye."[19] To summarise this in Greenberg's words (and Bernstein correctly cites this passage):

I think one of the ways in which you can stab at saying what art does to you is that it puts you in a state of heightened cognitiveness. Not cognition, but cognitiveness. It's somehow as though you've risen above impediments to knowledge or awareness, but not on the basis of anything specific, that you are specifically aware of. Now, I come back to good old Kant who said that the pleasure of art consists in the free play of reason together with intuition or imagination. These faculties are stimulated at the same time: *there's nothing there for you to know*, there's just something there to intuit, and there's nothing there for the understanding to really absorb as information.

Clement Greenberg, "Night Three: April 8th, 1971" in *Homemade Esthetics*, 113, my emphasis.

[17] Greenberg, "Modernist Painting," 5.

[18] Ibid.

[19] Bernstein, *Against Voluptuous Bodies*, 124-25.

the making of pictures, in the flat, means the deliberate choice and creation of limits. This deliberateness is what Modernism harps on: that is, it spells out the fact that the limiting conditions of art [that is, the flatness of the picture-support] have to be made altogether human limits.[20]

For Greenberg, the joint fusion of human convention and a medium's limiting condition of form is not simply a matter of tweaking physical constituents to suit particular purposes. Quoting one of Greenberg's famous commenters, Thierry De Duve, "it comprises know-how, cultural habits, working procedures and disciplines."[21] The consensus in convention in a specific medium is fragile and momentary, and it is the *form of the work itself* (such as the flatness in painting) which makes the subject matter of decision and judgement not only visible, but also offers *access* to its content and quality.[22] The form is hidden, and it is the hiddenness of the form's constraint, which "puts pressure" on the aesthetic judgement of the artist and the beholder—such constraints remodel content and the decisions of the artist, thus transgressing aesthetic quality. Judgement in Greenberg's eyes cannot be reduced to a formulaic, knowledgeable realm of visionless reason, nor is it purely inferred from any autonomous realm of conscious reasoning—rather "judgement" in this sense is provoked by the medium itself. In Greenberg's words, "the artist receives judgements-decisions-inspiration, if you like—from this medium as he works in it."[23] The historical remodelling of the work's form cannot be found as "art" in a generic knowledgeable sense, but in the specificity of the medium: painting, video, sculpture, music, poetry, etc.

---

[20] Greenberg, "Modernist Painting," 9.

[21] Thierry de Duve, "The Monochrome and the Canvas" in *Kant after Duchamp* (Cambridge: MIT Press, 1999), 210.

[22] Ibid., 210.

[23] Clement Greenberg, "Judgement and the Esthetic Object" in *Homemade Esthetics*, 42-23.

Although this commentary is far from deliberative, there are key points we can bring forward into the discussion which are already evident in Fried's early criticism. Even though Greenberg's criticism was at base Kantian, and thus immediately dwells within the realm of correlationism (that *only the highest quality of art* encloses the material world within the limits of human activity), it ultimately seeks to counter a demonstrative and non-anthropomorphic epistemology by upholding the intuitive realm of the aesthetic bound by the limitations of the respective medium operating in the background. We cannot exactly specify what conditions Greenberg had in mind when he aligned human limits with a medium's own, but whatever they are, it is at least clear that the form of such a medium remains *intrinsically* correlated with artists and viewers. Thus, the artist's and viewer's "morphisations"—to put it rather awkwardly—are *always already* conditioned judgements of the withdrawn formal capacities of a medium. Aesthetic judgement cannot be known and processed into *extrinsic* mechanical form, but only passively intuited *intrinsically,* from the inside. As the later Greenberg writes elsewhere:

> Your aesthetic judgement, being an intuition and nothing else, is received, not taken. You no more choose to like or not like a given item of art than you choose to see the sun as bright or the night as dark.[24]

Demonstration and Description

Having shown what Greenberg's criticism attempted to defend, we can associate the stakes of his criticism with a more familiar philosophical sort of distinction. Once the philosophical position of correlationism is rejected in speculative realism, an incompatible discord in continental philosophy is let loose, and this discord operates between two broad orientations. Freely drawing on Meillassoux's distinction, we can

---

[24] Clement Greenberg, "Intuition and the Esthetic Experience" in *Homemade Esthetics,* 7.

assign the terms **Demonstration** and **Description** to these orientations.[25] Note here that in using these terms, I do so in an extremely general sense, without ascribing a particular role, function, or argument of any author as an overriding factor to them.

First there is **Demonstration**: a passive, inert material reality can be epistemologically demonstrated through the formal, inferential properties of thought and *an extrinsic principle of the fact*, so that thought becomes radically divorced from a non-anthropomorphic being. This position is shared both by Meillassoux and Ray Brassier in their joint commitment to explaining the truth of reality *rationally*. The very reality of thought itself is to be uncovered, and in doing so, seeks to uncover the "in-itself" through a visionless absolute understanding, as a significant (yet the culmination of a contingent) rational achievement.

But there is also **Description**: reality is composed of fundamental entities, objects, things, forces and powers which exist in their own right; the relations of which, in their specific limitations or groundings, are no different in kind from the epistemological limits of cognition. *This is an intrinsic principle of the thing.* The limitations of the correlation between thinking and being are radicalised and hypostatised such that they are turned into the characteristics of relationality in general. The descriptivists subdivide into substance ontologists (Harman, Levi Bryant), the radical empiricists of networked actants (Bruno Latour), and the panpsychist, vitalist dynamists of active matter (Iain Hamilton Grant, Steven Shaviro, Jane Bennett). **Description**, in this sense, does not solely include phenomenological descriptive claims, but appeals to a broader importance of ontological "being"; that is, the modality of entities, which "describe," "withdraw," "intensify" or "affect" *with as much exuberant metaphysical importance as cognition.*

---

[25] I have written about the detailed differences between these two orientations in the short essay "Demonstration and Description" in *And Another Thing*, ed. Katherine Behar and Emmy Mikelson (New York: Punctum Books, forthcoming).

What is important here is the utterly incompatible nature of both orientations, *precisely insofar as correlationism was a pre-synthesis of both*. No middle way is possible, because correlationism *was that middle way*. Like a Hegelian dialectic stuck in reverse gear, speculative realism fractures the correlate into these two halves *and only these two*. Fuse both **Demonstration** and **Description** together and you arrive back at correlationism; that the world cannot be known in itself, *and* only be internally related by human thought. The key split between the two lies in how reality is accounted for within the ontological *importance or unimportance of knowledge and mastery in human thought.*

In **Demonstration**, the discontinuity of thought from material reality must be explained in emergent materialist terms through rational knowledge, whilst in **Description** any discontinuity or continuity between thought and the reality of objects, occasions, assemblages or processes is understood to be *different in degree* and not ontologically special in kind. Elsewhere, Steven Shaviro has argued that this central axis marks two extreme speculative positions at base, *eliminativism* and *panpsychism*.²⁶ This latter position, which entails **Description** as I have just defined it, has recently been attacked by Meillassoux as a lamentable strain of "subjectalism."²⁷ This neologism was coined by Meillassoux to capture the history (since Berkeley) of thinking absolute thought as an *ontological* category, a lineage that encompasses not only Diderot's "Hylozoism,"²⁸ Schelling's "Freedom," Nietzsche's "Will to

---

²⁶ Steven Shaviro, "Eliminativism and/or Panpsychism," talk given at the OOOIII conference in New York and the SLSA conference in Kitchener, Ontario. Available online: http://www.shaviro.com/Blog/?p=1012 (accessed on June 30, 2013).

²⁷ Quentin Meillassoux, "Iteration, Reiteration, Repetition: A Speculative Analysis of the Meaningless Sign," lecture given at the Freie Universität Berlin, 20 April 2012. It is available online: http://oursecretblog.com/txt/QMpaperApr12.pdf, trans. Robin Mackay (accessed June 30, 2013).

²⁸ The inclusion of Diderot here by Meillassoux is quite telling for my argument, especially if one considers Fried's infamous research on Diderot and premodernist art (although on Fried's part, there would not be any link between Diderot's panpsychism and his art criticism). See Fried, *Absorption*

Power," and Deleuze's "Larval Vitalism," but also Hegelian idealism, despite the obvious conflicts between these positions (this is why for example Grant's position cannot be located outside this divide and Meillassoux is right to include him in the opposing faction: human knowledge and phenomena for Grant are the *products* of nature, not a special rational achievement).

It follows then that speculative realism *simply is* this incompatible splintering, this fracture, and its existence *emerges from this schism*. **Demonstration** argues that thought itself can fruitfully prove or deduce knowledge of itself and thus reality, whilst **Description** argues that thought never fully deduces any in-itself and has little ontological significance or achievement in doing so, since its ontological significance is not superior to any other kind of possible relation between entities. Once correlationism is rejected, there is no middle way to stake a claim apart from these two broad orientations of "what is": *either reality must be epistemologically demonstrated or reality must be described in terms of real ontological variance.* Once one side is chosen, the other recedes from view.[29]

Demonstration justifies itself in two ways: in the first way, it aligns itself with the *rational* rejection of anthropomorphism, endorsing a visionless absolute knowledge (as attributed to Brassier and especially Meillassoux); in a second (but related)

---

and Theatricality. For my claim that Fried's notion of "Absorption" is related to Harman's notions of "allure" and "withdrawal," see Jackson, "The Anxiousness of Objects and Artworks," 156-62.

[29] As a side note, it increasingly appears that because speculative realism manifests itself as this contradictory fracturing of the correlate into these two specific modalities, there are only three possible moves forward. The first move is already taking place, with **Demonstration** and **Description** both making their progressive strides in each orientation, whilst also being stretched and pulled apart more vigorously within certain trench war debates. The second move simply re-embraces correlationism and all of its anti-realist flaws. The third move, finally, requires the difficult, yet more elusive, necessary and creative step in reconciling both orientations *without inadvertently arriving back at correlationism* and repeating the gesture that the world can only ever be internally related. In other words, how does one reconcile the "thinking reality/existing beyond thought" discord without immediately embracing the easy option of anthropocentric anti-realism?

way, it aligns itself with the *sceptical or absolute* rejection of anthropomorphism—which is to say, that for **Demonstration** it makes little to no sense to speak of an unthinkable ontology outside of ourselves (similar to Meillassoux's notion of strong correlationism). The former way takes the progressive step of attaining knowledge through the rational capabilities of thought *knowing, progressively mastering and uncovering* its own materialist, contingent functioning, its own reality. The sceptical onslaught of the latter way demonstrates the reality of finitude *as such*, rather than merely bathing in its givenness.

The impact that **Demonstration** has on aesthetics is the crux here. **Demonstration** has little concern with allusive strategies of sensual apprehension for its own purposes. Intuition is not an end goal. It is worth noting that Meillassoux in particular has a philosophical investment in Duchamp, although this influence remains, as of writing, unpublished.[30] Regardless of any possible speculation concerning Duchamp's role in Meillassoux's system, his role in **Demonstration** will become clear under the topic of generic objects and appearance in part two of this essay. Brassier's early writings on noise and sonic practice are perhaps a more deliberate provocation to eliminate any sensual judgement from aesthetic taste, to the point of endorsing a "destitution of the aesthetic";[31] one which "exacerbates the rift between knowing and feeling by splitting experience, forcing conception against sensation."[32] **Demonstration**, in whatever form it takes, cannot abide the apprehension of Kantian disinterest, nor be satisfied with its rejection of empirical "gratification."[33]

---

[30] See Harman's interview with Meillassoux in Graham Harman, *Quentin Meillassoux: Philosophy in the Making* (Edinburgh: Edinburgh University Press, 2011), 173-74.

[31] Ray Brassier, "Genre is Obsolete," in *Noise & Capitalism*, ed. Mattin and Anthony Iles (San Sebastian: Arteleku Audiolab, 2009), 60-71.

[32] Ray Brassier, "Against an Aesthetics of Noise," *Transitzone*, nY, 2009, <www.ny-web.be/transitzone/against-aesthetics-noise.html> (accessed November 30, 2012).

[33] Immanuel Kant, *Critique of Judgement*, trans. Werner S. Pluhar (Indianapolis:

With Harman's position so utterly invested in his variant of **Description**, it should be clear why his own version of speculative realism so readily embraces Greenbergian criticism. The modernist discovering or illumination of sensual representation operates *through an anthropomorphic discovery of involuntary aesthetic description* (however, we must also realise that other philosophers of **Description** may clearly reject Greenberg's aesthetic criticism, particularly Grant and definitely Shaviro).[34] Meillassoux's charge that "subjectalism" conveys a "non-materialist form of absolutism"[35] is accurate here in terms of rejecting the reductive and correlated understandings of "materialism," yet is perhaps inaccurate in characterising the status of thought as absolutising (Harman, for instance does not assign any primordial level of cognitive phenomena, such as memory, to objects).

Whatever relation fits, we can suggest that the relationship between Harman and Greenberg is part of a wider framework within which works of art are *essential, discrete things*, that actually *matter* and that cannot be replaced with social determinacy, analytic reduction or scientific deduction. The artwork is a transformation of an object—it outlines a dark shape, a silhouette, as Bernstein might say—which has the potential to allusively bridge finite understanding and material world.[36]

In this regard, if Fried and Greenberg are left as they are, they can only stretch towards a "weak correlated" variant of **Description**. Their criticism can never speak about the

---

Hackett Publishing, 1987), 47. Here, I am referring to Steven Shaviro's extraordinary reading of Kant's aesthetics. Shaviro reads Kant's description of beauty in experience in light of a Whiteheadian metaphysical *affective event*. See Steven Shaviro, *Without Criteria: Kant, Whitehead, Deleuze, and Aesthetics* (Cambridge: MIT Press, 2009), 4-5.

[34] Steven Shaviro, "The Actual Volcano: Whitehead, Harman, and the Problem of Relations" in *The Speculative Turn: Continental Materialism and Realism*, ed. Levi Bryant, Nick Srnicek, and Graham Harman (Melbourne: Re.press, 2011), 288-89, cf. 279-90.

[35] Meillassoux, "Iteration, Reiteration, Repetition," 3.

[36] Bernstein, *Against Voluptuous Bodies*, 126.

material world in itself. The next step is to *radicalise* this modernist sensibility so that it becomes a speculative one, and to suggest how aesthetics not only bridges the finite limits of human intuitions, *but bridges the finite limits of all objects*. What if Greenberg's limiting condition was not a feature of art as a human discipline, but a basic feature of an ontology that features aesthetics as the general and fundamental mode of causal relation?

This is the work Harman has already begun. Besides Harman's theory of allure in *Guerrilla Metaphysics* and "Vicarious Causation," there are other developments and implications to consider. Thus, Harman values in Greenberg what he also values in thinkers of technology like Marshall McLuhan, namely that such critics not only identify a central interaction between the present-at-hand sensual figure, content, or foreground and the withdrawn, real background of medium and form, they also grasp how creative movements of ripe discovery and fresh surprise can be retrieved and historically stimulated within the throws of decadence and monotony.[37] In the second instance, such a discovery of creative progress is indicative of Harman's recent critical trajectory; that new movements, new methods and new principles emerge as a result of retrieving outmoded ideas in aesthetics and philosophy, left behind by previous modernisers in recent history.[38] I shall now turn to Fried and Cavell who add another layer to this logic.

---

[37] This relationship is expanded on briefly in the keynote lecture "Everything is Not Connected" delivered at the *Transmediale* festival in February 2012 and published in Graham Harman, *Bells and Whistles: More Speculative Realism* (Winchester: Zero Books, 2013), 100-127. For an extensive treatment, see Harman's contribution to this volume.

[38] The outstanding essay which extrapolates this sense of aesthetic progress is Greenberg's "Cézanne and the Unity of Modern Painting," written in 1951 and published in Clement Greenberg, *The Collected Essays and Criticism: Affirmations and Refusals, 1950-1956*, vol. 3, ed. John O'Brian (Chicago: University of Chicago Press, 1993), 82-91.

Speculations V

A Paradigm Shift of the Senses: Fried's Anthropomorphism

Whilst Fried supported Greenberg's views on the finite limits of human anthropomorphism in modernist convention, he rejected the view that painting had an unchanging and timeless essence. For him, such a position led down a "cul-de-sac artistically and theoretically" (for instance, how could anything new emerge in foregrounded convention if its formal, backgrounded essence remains fundamentally unchanged?).[39] Fried believed that the authentic way to think of essence *was historical*: artists discovered conventions, which in the present moment and in response to the vital work of the past turned out to be essential to the medium in question. Such an acknowledgement could only be both beholden to the recent past and subject to change. Fried's modernism did not seek to "overthrow or supersede [or] break with the pre-modernist past, but rather ... attempt[ed] to equal its highest achievements, under new and difficult conditions that from the first were recognised by a few writers and artists stacking the deck against the likelihood of success."[40]

Thus Fried's own strategy for defeating scepticism lies in aligning human limits with historical pressures and bursts of conviction. Indeed, in a footnote to his famous essay on the artist Frank Stella, "Shape as Form," Fried cites Thomas Kuhn's The Structure of Scientific Revolutions, inferring that Kuhn's infamous "paradigm shifts" may offer an insight into the mechanism of revolutions in art.[41] As Caroline A. Jones and Vasso Kindi argue (the former more polemically), Fried's articulation of Greenberg's modernist criticism "was indebted to the matrix of ideas circulating around Kuhn ... many of

---

[39] Fried, *Four Honest Outlaws*, 8.

[40] Michael Fried, "How Modernism Works: A Response to T.J. Clark" in *Pollock and After: The Critical Debate*, ed. Francis Frascina (New York: Harper and Row, 1985), 70.

[41] Michael Fried, "Shape as Form: Frank Stella's Irregular Polygons" in *Art and Objecthood* (Chicago: The University of Chicago Press, 2004), 99, n.11, cf. 77-99.

them mediated by the cogent philosophy of Stanley Cavell."[42] A detailed exposition which evenly accounts for these different approaches (along with their critics) is beyond the word limit of this essay, and is better suited to be pursued elsewhere. Instead, I will turn to a brief discussion of how Fried's position relates to Harman's own approach.

Kindi's essay deftly unpacks the controversial anti-Hegelian nature of Kuhn's scientific revolutions, insofar as they are "nothing typically rational," nor "objectively ascertainable."[43] Kindi also examines the conflicting methods of these approaches, as commentators often misconstrue that both Fried and Cavell favour the discovery of "genuine" essence in the establishment of new conventions compared to a medium's history (that the essence of painting is recovered and restored from its past), whilst Kuhn removes any presentation of essential progress in science, because the breaking of scientific tradition is a clean, destructive *break* from its past. However, Kindi argues that the two disciplines are not so different.[44] Like Kuhn, Cavell does not push an essentialist tradition, but a project of brutal re-conceptualisation, and a resistant but anxious learning of a language initiated by the joint internal criticisms of both art and science.[45]

---

[42] Caroline A. Jones, "The Modernist Paradigm: The Artworld and Thomas Kuhn," *Critical Inquiry* (2000), 26:3, 523. Jones articulates the polemical critique that Kuhn's evolutionary metaphor lends itself to an essentialist and teleological conceptualisation of progress in modernist art and especially Fried's criticism, insofar as Fried's modernist project becomes the only paradigm which deserves to be dominant. Unsurprisingly, Fried was not amused and wrote a rejoinder to Jones's essay; see Michael Fried, "Response to Caroline Jones," *Critical Inquiry* (2000), 27:4, 703-05.

[43] Vasso Kindi, "Novelty and Revolution in Art and Science: The Connection between Kuhn and Cavell," *Perspectives on Science* (2010), 18:3, 298.

[44] Kindi also reveals the mutual indebtedness of Kuhn and Cavell in their respective understandings of their different disciplines after regularly meeting at Berkeley from 1956 onwards; see Kindi, "Novelty and Revolution," 284-85. See also Thomas Kuhn, *The Structure of Scientific Revolutions* (Chicago: The University of Chicago Press, 1970), xiii; and James Conant "An Interview with Stanley Cavell" in *The Senses of Stanley Cavell*, ed. Richard Fleming and Michael Payne (Lewisburg: Bucknell University Press, 1989), 35-72.

[45] Kindi puts it thus:

In my view, Kindi all too carefully avoids the problems of essence that the philosophical tenor of modernist aesthetics and scientific paradigm shifts pose. Harman's object-oriented ontology indicates a potentially profound change of understanding of this literature. In this vein, the reasons why Fried, Cavell and Kuhn's conceptions of revolution are similar are not to be found in their favouring a re-conceptualisation of the concept of essence.[46] Instead, each thinker repeatedly misunderstands that essence is real *but can never be ultimately known or forever mastered, and as such the modernist aesthetic generated from this historical allusion can never be teleological.* Successive interpretations may seemingly be progressively

---

They consider particular revolutionary developments (for instance, Modernism in art or the Chemical Revolution in science) in order to understand and elucidate what radical novelty involves. Both art and science are marked by the high value they attach to the mastery of a tradition which, according to Kuhn and Cavell, far from committing these disciplines to a confining conservative practice, constitutes the condition for bringing about revolutionary changes. Scientists, confronted with anomalies (i.e., deviations from what tradition inclines them to expect), seek to restore order while artists, striving for originality and excellence, measure up to the standards of past achievements. In their effort to recover what has been lost, practitioners of both fields break new ground and, consequently, redefine their respective disciplines. This is not an attempt to uncover an already given, atemporal, essence but a dynamic process of re-organization and re-conceptualization. Cavell's talk of essence must be seen in this light. In his view, essence is redefined with each attempt to preserve it. The result is not a continuous, piecemeal advancement, but a re-vision involving breaks and the redrawing of boundaries. Here, Cavell's analysis again meets Kuhn's, who understood revolutions in science as re-conceptualizations.

Kindi, "Novelty and Revolution," 306.

[46] It is telling here that Kindi reverts back to the idea that the newness of a revolution in art or science is something that anthropomorphism initiates, rather than a genuine, fresh encounter with an allusive hidden layer of the real world. Or in other words, revolutions are internally related to human history only. Kindi thereby repeats Greenberg's axiom that the limiting conditions of art and science must *altogether be* human limits. To quote Kindi once more: "What it means, I think, is that we take huge responsibility in what we do and what we bring about. The new is not something we stumble upon which we need to seize so that a revolution occurs ... it is something *we* initiate, *we* bring about by looking, in a way, backwards, to our history and our past achievements." Kindi, "Novelty and Revolution," 305, my emphases.

more truthful in closing in on the object in question, but this is only an allusive shift, not a direct one. Regarding Kuhn, Harman has already indicated how this might be mapped:

> A paradigm is not an arbitrary principle constructed by a social community in a contingent time and place and imposed by the power of the mob, but rather the rule of a unified scientific object beyond all nail-filing arguments and contradictory evidence and public cataloguing of its traits ... "Normal science," like normal perception, tidies up our lists of known properties and fixes previous inconsistencies in our map of things, but does nothing to shift the underlying field of objects that are accepted as real. *Allure*, with its severing of objects and qualities, *is the paradigm shift of the senses.*[47]

Under this view, the dual paradigmatic roles of modern art and the sciences are one of temporally exposing or retrieving a new revelation from the essences of withdrawn real objects within the caricature of a work's content. The role of the artist is to trace the contours of this withdrawn essence through the content; to inscribe a practice within it and through it, whilst being never entirely sure of the consequence that emerges from the output. Whilst Fried's ultimate contribution to high modernist criticism is to follow artists who inscribe what Harman calls a "paradigm shift of the senses" (a model which still informs Fried's twentieth century criticism, as well as his more famous historical research), we can see in object-oriented ontology an initial outlay towards a rejuvenation of theorising essence within an arts context, which rejects the sole dependency on an internal anthropomorphic correlate. Although neither Fried, nor Cavell, nor Kuhn would ever endorse this reading, Harman's intervention loosely signals why aesthetics is bound to causal relation and helps recalibrate the repeated (failed) efforts of modernist art theory and the philosophy of science to jointly allude to an object's withdrawn essence.

---

[47] Graham Harman, *Guerrilla Metaphysics: Phenomenology and the Carpentry of Things* (Chicago: Open Court, 2005), 152, original emphases.

Things and Objects: Contemporary Literalism

Meanwhile, consider the contemporary art-world's indirect dealings with the speculative turn so far. The take-up of speculative realism in the art world has, arguably, been predominantly aligned with OOO and more broadly the growing opposition to anthropocentric thought. Whether artists have been directly influenced by the proponents of OOO, actor-network theory, and the new materialisms or not, it certainly seems that a change has occurred concerning the understanding and exposure of the nature of materiality after years of framing it through human orientation. The artist's materials are no longer passive or inert, but are reworked and re-contextualised to "let loose" their inherent, dynamic creativity.

This renewed democracy of things, the sociality of objects, can be traced in a number of shows which attempt to understand how the agency of units and "things" shapes viewer interactions, from the famous *THING: New Sculptures from Los Angeles* show at the Hammer Museum in 2005, to Steven Claydon's exhibition *Strange Things Permit Themselves the Luxury of Occurring* at the Camden Arts Centre in 2008, to the show *Material Intelligence* at Cambridge's Kettle's Yard in 2009. This new sensibility towards the aesthetic imperative and agency of things is also what brought Katherine Behar and Emmy Mikelson to curate the 2011 show *And Another Thing* at the CUNY.[48] The curators sought "to dislodge the human from the center of discussion, to enrich the concept

---

48 Hammer Museum, *THING: New Sculptures From Los Angeles*, Exhibition, Los Angeles, February 6, 2005 - June 5, 2005. Camden Arts Centre, *Strange Events Permit Themselves the Luxury of Occurring*, Exhibition, London, December 7, 2007 - February 10, 2008. Kettle's Yard, *Material Intelligence*, Exhibition, Cambridge, May 16, 2009 - July 12, 2009. The website for the exhibition show at Kettle's Yard featuring Claire Barclay's *Stillstill* (2009) is here: http://www. kettlesyard.co.uk/exhibitions/mi_catalogue/index.html (accessed October 20, 2013). CUNY Graduate Centre, *And Another Thing*, Exhibition, New York, September 14, 2011 - October 29, 2011.

of being, and to open the very world itself to all things that comprise it" using the minimalist work *Base 5 Aluminum Stack* (2005) by Carl Andre as a starting point: a work which simply "is what it is."[49]

Moreover, the art theoretical literature surrounding this shift is expanding. Rikke Hansen's 2008 essay "Things vs. Objects" in *Art Monthly* was specifically written to address art's return to things. According to Hansen, works such as Superflex's *Copy Right* (2007) and Hans Schabus's *Next Time I'm Here, I'll Be There* (2008) have a "bearing on the way we perceive and critique the social." Such works need the beholder to work, but are "never determined by the subject alone," and instead "engage directly with the form of sociality that is produced by things; artworks that, momentarily, make objects stand out against the backdrop of everyday life."[50] More recently, in his review of *dOCUMENTA 13* in ArtForum, Daniel Birnbaum argued that there was a productive conflict between the trauma-led artworks focusing on human conflict and reconciliation, and artworks which explicitly focused on the thingliness of actants and objects (or as *dOCUMENTA's* catalogue attests: "[t]his vision is shared with, and recognizes, the shapes and practices of knowing of all the animate and inanimate makers of the world, including people").[51]

Elsewhere, artists and writers Pil and Galia Kollectiv have described this mode of artistic practice as an "anti-aesthetic which asks us to consider the changing nature of our relationship to objects," whilst at the same time criticising it for disabling political action:

[49] Katherine Behar and Emmy Mikelson, "Curatorial Statement," *And Another Thing,* http://andanotherthingexhibition.wordpress.com/curatorial-statement/ (accessed June 20, 2013).

[50] Rikke Hansen, "Things vs. Objects: Rikke Hansen on the Public Life of Things," *Art Monthly* (2008), 318, http://www.artmonthly.co.uk/magazine/site/article/things-v-objects-by-rikke-hansen-jul-aug-2008 (accessed February 10, 2013).

[51] Daniel Birnbaum, "Documenta 13," *ArtForum* (October 2012), http://blog.urbanomic.com/sphaleotas/archives/id_34514/id_34514.htm (accessed February 10, 2013). Carolyn Christov-Bakargiev, "Artistic Director's Statement," in *Introduction to dOCUMENTA (13) - Press Release*, <http://d13.documenta.de/uploads/tx_presssection/3_Introduction.pdf> (accessed June 20, 2013).

> The vague sociality inscribed in the recognition of the thingly character of objects withdrawn from our consciousness seems insufficient in this context as the basis of the transformative power promised by art throughout modernity. At best it suggests a kind of Romantic failure—of consciousness, and of matter that threatens to collapse, but probably never will given the polished, well-heeled environments into which it is gathered.[52]

On a side note, Pil and Galia Kollectiv misunderstand the philosophical literature somewhat. They mistake the political implications of equality (what should be) with the ontological implications of equality (what exists) and neglect the nuanced differences between an actor-network distribution of the social and the discrete, object-oriented metaphysical *withdrawal* from the social. That said, their meandering critique is not the only problem here; whilst the curation of things and our relationship to them speeds on, both forms of aesthetic commentary miss the larger ontological picture.

I propose that a more fundamental link with OOO should perhaps avoid assumptions which take objects in art discourse too *literally*, as if any encountered, re-contextualised, or re-focused object or unit of matter is worth exhibiting in a gallery because it can perform its own thingly stage theatrics for the beholder *as such*. Whilst it may provide a positive, entirely honourable and worthy antidote to the banal merry-go-round of relationality and the creative malaise of participation-oriented art in the mainstream art-world, the paradigm's dominance is hardly contested.

The reason why New Sculpture's "thingliness" has sincerity, yet lacks aesthetic teeth, attests to the proposed Greenbergian challenges which OOO may pose for artistic practice as a

---

[52] Pil and Galia Kollectiv, "Can Objects Perform? Agency and Thingliness in Contemporary Sculpture and Installation," paper delivered at the Sculpture and Performance conference at the Henry Moore Institute, March 24, 2010, http://www.kollectiv.co.uk/Object%20Orientations.html (accessed February 10, 2013). You can also listen to an audio recording of the paper here: http://www.henry-moore.org/hmi/events/multimedia-recordings/sculpture-performance-conference-archiveaudio/pil-and-galia-kollectiv (accessed October 20, 2013).

historical challenge; for if artists continue to enter shows and create works which disregard human meaning in favour of speculation, gathering disparate interests in the non-human world, there must be an adherence to the philosophical and critical stakes of that speculation. Such an adherence will, in the end, be more closely aligned with and more specific to the stakes of speculative realism proper and result in artistic practices which prevent literal illustrations of the philosophical ideas or unnecessary concoctions operating from different philosophical positions and consequences. Art is far too important to illustrate conceptual achievements.

It is not enough to demand that an anti-anthropocentric artwork "is what it is" simply because it illustrates a theoretical point about things *in relation to a beholder.* It is because speculative realism offers two rather different and incompatible versions of the noumenal "is" in relation to the beholder that this rift exposes specific issues and competing tensions between *a viewer and the artwork,* or to be more specific, between *the thought of the viewer* and *the being of the artwork.* The construction of the work must either demonstrate "what is" for the beholder's appearance, or it offers an internal allusive finite description within the thing itself, both in human and non-human modalities. New Sculpture carries some unfortunate but latent minimalist baggage in its history, and as we will see, this means it cannot fully come to terms with its confident interest in a thing's independence.

To create a work which simply presents a "thing" in a space, no matter how weird, cannot take advantage of the allusive, anti-literal properties inherent to its speculative **Description.** An OOO aesthetics has to fully reconcile itself with this limited descriptive gesture because any object, *including the artwork itself,* always withdraws from the beholder. Not only this, but it also has to reconcile itself with the separate, but more pressing, aesthetic issue that the relationship between the beholder and work can never be centralised in accordance with the primacy of human beholders. In short, whilst the return to literal things is welcome in art practice, this setting cannot ignore the sustained historical and critical problems of the inclusion or exclusion of the beholder. How can an aesthetic which embraces the performative independence of materials and objects deal with its beholders?

Literalism and the Theatrical

Art criticism can take solace in this discord. Fried's famous text "Art and Objecthood," published in *ArtForum* in June 1967, highlighted the stakes involved in what was a crucial moment of activity in contemporary art (in Fried's case, the stakes of American modernist sculpture), one that may reveal or indeed retroactively manifest itself in delicate aesthetic differences within continental philosophy today. The inherent conflicting consequences of the different positions attributed to speculative realism may be explored in the context of the multitude of conflicting interpretations as they arose from "Art and Objecthood." For instance: mundane objects vs. artworks, generic vs. specific, non-gesture vs. gesture, immanent vs. transcendent, contingency vs. purpose, hollowness vs. depth. The most central critical dichotomy for the purposes of this essay, however, is *anti-anthropomorphism vs. anthropomorphism*.

Reading "Art and Objecthood" again today, one is still struck by Fried's polemical sting and blunt criticism of Donald Judd and Robert Morris's minimalist work. Reiterating Fried's basic charge, minimalism (or literalism, a term which Fried still prefers) operated as a kind of theatre, which brought out *the wrong sort of anthropomorphic relationship* compared to the more authentic high modern one. Distinct emphasis was placed on the relationship between the beholder and the work, meaning that any relationship within the work itself as a separate entity or separate mechanism had been made irrelevant. What mattered was the beholder's experience within a relational situation and each experience became commensurable with every other, insofar as *each duration of experience "was" the work* so to speak. The situation of the viewer literally replaces or stands in for the work itself, which in Fried's view brought out an inferior relationship. Fried's key point is that the beholder's subjective response cannot stand in for the object itself—*the pure experience of the work is not the work.* Whilst the relevance of one's conviction is subject to change, the self-determining autonomous nature of the work itself cannot be.

In contrast, relations in modernist works such as Morris Louis's *Alpha-Pi* (1960) or Frank Stella's early paintings do take place within the works' objecthood. Their formal purpose, for Fried, is precisely to defeat and suspend meaninglessness and scepticism. The job of the artist is to construct an object— entirely specific, unified, portable and self-sufficient—that offers more than the ordinary, which means finding in the historically contingent medium something *more* than simple contingency, discovering the sensual paradigm shift within the work itself. The minimalist/literalist projection took objecthood too far and made it literal, empty, and false, which put it "at war [with the] modernist sensibility as such."[53] This was a war which Fried lost of course—quite spectacularly as he admits—to the point where his polemical arguments against minimalism inadvertently influenced mainstream art's subsequent rejection of the art object.[54] This is what Lucy Lippard influentially summarised as conceptual art and system art's dematerialisation of the art object.[55]

For the purposes of this essay, Fried's importance lies in reminding us of the ontological difference between modernist aesthetic values and the new, contemporary view on objecthood. Is it not the case that the dividing line between **Demonstration** (in the sceptical sense) and **Description**

---

[53] Fried, "Art and Objecthood," 830.

[54] Fried, *Four Honest Outlaws*, 10-11. Fried is quite explicit here:

The important point ... is that my arguments did not prevail in the world of contemporary art; on the contrary, the overwhelming impetus of new art during the 1970s and indeed the 1980s ... was nothing but theatrical in my pejorative sense of the term, to the extent that it has sometimes seemed to me that I might inadvertently have contributed to that development.

[55] See Lucy Lippard, *Six Years: The Dematerialization of the Art Object from 1966-1972* (New York: Praeger Publishers, 1973), republished with a new introduction by the University of California Press in 1996.

(in the high modernist sense) maps onto the dividing line between objecthood and art respectively?

By aligning objecthood with **Demonstration**, I could be called up for misunderstanding the usual reading here. For instance, according to Pil and Galia Kollectiv, Jan Verwoert's 2007 talk "Make the Prop Talk" spoke of a return to Fried's theatricality through the performance of New Sculpture and how the use of generic sculptures was a vehicle for staging performative social practices.[56] What is more, surely Fried's hatred of minimalism and the focus on individual units makes this arch-modernist critic susceptible to a harsher critique than ever before.

Verwoert's view is not unreasonable, for there is a deep link between Fried's theatricality and New Sculpture. But that does not inevitably mean Fried's endorsement of modernist criticism should be rejected in this light. If one remembers, Fried's life-long hatred of theatrical artworks was not because they were simply objects, although there is an element of truth to this (in Fried's eyes, as in Greenberg's, "a good work of art" is meaningless—the quality and significance of contemporary works of art lies in their historicised medium specificity). Instead, Fried charges minimalism with a two-step movement: it distances itself from commitment to internal relations whilst concomitantly the beholder's situation becomes the exclusive focus of viewing the work, even demonstrating that the *beholder's situation actually becomes the work* and vice-versa.

So the question we seek is this: what was it about the minimalist sensibility of a Judd "Block," a Smith "Die" or a Morris "L Shape" that induced such a sceptical view in Fried's criticism? And, more to the point, why am I arguing that these sensibilities indicatively support variants of **Demonstration** as opposed to variants of **Description**? Even more to the point, how does this relate to the art world's increasing embrace of material objects today?

---

[56] Jan Verwoert, "Make the Prop Talk—On Putting Performance Back into Sculpture" in *The Showroom Annual 2006/7*, ed. The Showroom (London: The Showroom, 2008), 30-31.

Fried was sensitive to two particular qualities of the minimalist enterprise: its literal, generic quality together with its hollowness. Both qualities mean more or less the same thing—the general requirement of the literal object is for it to be "just what it is," utterly holistic and commanded by its totality. The emptiness of, say, Tony Smith's Die (1962) or Judd's Untitled (1966), with their hollowed-out interior, revealed their explicit, epistemological intention, namely that of being pure surface standing in for nothing. Smith was not concerned with the discrete thing in itself but the literal emptiness of the thing, the fact that there was no-thing and nothing behind it. Fried puts it this way: literalism "is inexhaustible… not because of any fullness—that is the inexhaustibility of art—but because there is nothing there to exhaust, it is endless the way a road might be: if it were circular, for example."[57] The literalist work offers a diminished, impoverished source of aesthetic appreciation in that it literally is nothing and the thing demonstrates this. The modernist aesthetic not only privileges a work which is something, but also stresses that its aesthetic fullness operates in the relationship between the beholder's and artist's judgement of quality as a playing out within the limiting condition of the work.

More recently in a 2007 lecture, Stephen Melville elucidated on the nuances of Fried's argument and revealed certain ontological assumptions inherent to it.[58] Fried's definition of "theatre" does not simply signify the presence of the gesture-less work and its architectural relational lighting within the exhibition, but is symptomatic of Judd's and Morris's profound epistemological declaration. Minimalism is a sceptical performance declaring that "nothing" is operating behind the facade of the inert work and that it can only ever

---

[57] Fried, "Art and Objecthood," 831.

[58] Stephen Melville, *"Art and Objecthood": A Lecture* (Barcelona: Museu d'Art Contemporani de Barcelona, 2007). The booklet is available online here: http://www.macba.cat/uploads/20080915/QP_15_Melville.pdf (accessed August 20, 2013). I owe a great debt and sincere gratitude to Thomas Gokey, who introduced me to Melville's text.

be "what it is."[59] This is why the work itself becomes unnecessary for the beholder's aesthetic judgment. The visionless realisation that "nothing is there" in reality only requires a literalist demonstration of an exhibited object to support it, the deliberate satisfaction of the beholder's *experience* that there can be no barrier between appearance of the thing and the thing itself, whereas Fried believed that illusion was essential to the modernist conviction.[60]

A brief but rich quote from Melville on the links between Fried's definition of theatre and Cavell's essay "The Avoidance of Love: A Reading of *King Lear*" should be sufficient here:

> Theatricality means ... **something like what is left of theatre once the drama "itself" has ceased to count or vanished altogether.** ... It begins with the old story of someone in the audience who rushes onto the stage to stop the terrible thing going on there. The butt of this joke is evidently someone deeply naive, who does not know what theater is, and the point of our telling it is presumably the satisfaction we take in knowing better than him. "But what mistake," Cavell writes, has the yokel in the theater made, and what is *our way*? He thinks someone

---

[59] Here I am following Melville's lead in conjunction with Cavell's writings on "generic objects":

> The object set before us and claiming to be there as a "specific object" Fried sees as all too clearly a variation on what Cavell describes as a "generic object" and understands as a crucial relay within the standard epistemological or skeptical performance.

Melville, "Art and Objecthood," 12.

[60] This is why Jeff Wall in his 2003 essay "Frames of Reference" stresses the importance of Fried's concern with illusion in pictorial arts, both in painting and (much later) photography. Here is Wall on Fried's understanding of literalism/objecthood:

> I read "Art and Objecthood" to say that if an artwork simply cast its lot with physicality and immediacy, it lost its essential possibility as serious art and was reduced to a repetitive staging of the encounter between an object or group of objects in the world and a person looking at that object. *It soon became obvious that it was arbitrary what the object was ... Fried showed that illusion is essential.*

Jeff Wall, "Frames of Reference" in *Selected Essays and Interviews* (New York: The Museum of Modern Art, 2007), 178, my emphasis.

is strangling someone. —But that is true. Othello is strangling Desdemona. —Come on, come on; you know, he thinks that very man is
putting out the light of that very woman now. —Yes, and that is exactly
what is happening. —You're not amusing. **The point is that he thinks
something is really happening, whereas nothing is really happening.
It's play acting.** The woman will rise again to die another night. ... **The
trouble is that I really do not understand what I am being asked, and
of course I am suggesting that you do not know either.**[61]

Theatricality is not simply defined by the inclusion of the
beholder as the literal criticism of a slickly polished, well-lit
situation (a stupid point which I also fell for in my earlier
essay)—rather theatricality is predominantly defined by its
sceptical attitude emphasising that nothing is really going
on when the play-acting is eliminated: when the work is *no
longer naive, no longer gullible*, no longer full of transcendent
depth, concealing a reality behind it. Instead, it is flattened
into a literal immanent facade of itself. Therein, minimalism only produces the ability to demonstrate, or to reduce
everything to the appearance of the beholder.

So too is Cavell helpful in articulating that, for Fried, the
objects of minimalism were not specific (that is, to be described
in detail), but the result of being "generic objects": they focus
entirely on the beholder's relationship to them. A literalist
object simply "is," but only insofar as it demonstrates that
it also has a part which cannot be experienced. The lack of
parts in a generic object requires the beholder to inspect them
in a situation, rather than behold this appearance from the
start. It is inherently meaningless, deliberately constructed
to exude no depth, and is thoroughly expunged of any anthropomorphic traits. In this sense, any argument on the
aesthetic effect generated by the literalist work cannot be
grounded in its distinguishable traits or qualities (even the

---

[61] Melville, "*Art and Objecthood,*" 9, italics original emphasis, italics and bold
my emphases; missing quotation marks in the original. Melville's citations
are from Stanley Cavell, "The Avoidance of Love: A Reading of *King Lear*"
in *Must We Mean What We Say? A Book of Essays*, updated ed. (Cambridge:
Cambridge University Press, 2002), 328.

trait of quality is expunged) as all aesthetic effects generated by any beholder's perspective become commensurable with that of any other. Cavell's "generic objects" are not presented for their features, but specifically presented without features, *which forces the beholder to look for them, without finding them.* The moment the beholder moves, "the 'parts' disappear, or else we see what had been hidden from view"—which in turn bequeaths new hidden parts to be revealed by the beholder and a new view from within the situation.[62]

As an added side effect, each generic object becomes substitutable in equal measure:

> The "generic object" is defined in its employment by its lack of features, and so is not arguable in the way we can argue over our recognition of fully-featured objects ... specific objects, in Cavell's sense, are distinguishable through their close contact with other specific objects, generic objects merely substitute for one another without establishing any other contrasts.[63]

In a brief note, Melville makes the correct statement (in my opinion) that Duchamp's *Fountain* (1917) is unique in discounting its qualities and features in favour of a disconcerting generic frame within which all content can be considered substitutable. In this light, he suggests, Fried's complaint about objecthood was not about objects at all, but the "no-thing that we do not see, thus not a synonym for 'object' but something more like its opposite."[64]

Bernstein's treatment of Fried's critique (and of Judd specifically) is even more explicit on the matter. The anthropomorphic power of signification within traditional painting was (for Judd) exhausted and the future of its signification "required elimination."[65] Bernstein argues that Judd's "art and

---

[62] Stanley Cavell, *The Claim of Reason: Wittgenstein, Skepticism, Morality, and Tragedy* (Oxford: Oxford University Press, 1979), 302.

[63] Melville, "*Art and Objecthood*," 12.

[64] Ibid., 13.

[65] Bernstein, *Against Voluptuous Bodies*, 128.

criticism ultimately belong to the tradition of Enlightenment rationalism" and that the

> material item ... no longer depends for its holding in the visual field through anthropomorphic assumptions, but literally appears as an object, a mere thing, in the same way that natural objects appear for the natural scientist as constituted through quantities that escape the vagaries of human perceivings and doings. *Judd wishes to achieve for artworks an analogue of the perspectiveless appearing that is the telos of absolute knowing: a view from nowhere.*[66]

Note here the crucial resemblances between Judd's intentions and **Demonstration**. As Bernstein rightfully grasps from the consequences of Fried's argument, Judd wanted to eliminate the descriptive aesthetic, morphised assumptions we make about artworks and instead craft a literal encounter with the object as it appears, without allusion, without depth, without essence. The literalist object would be fully known, within the beholder's "perspectiveless appearing": another way of saying that the object's appearance (all it is) can be known with or without the beholder's perspective, privileging the ultimate reality of human perspective all by itself.

The correlationist rub reappears. It is the contingency of the beholder which requires this "nothing" to be known and demonstrated, as if they alone were capable of realising the literal truth of the nothingness upon which the aesthetic experience rests. Thus **Demonstration**, as I have described it in the aesthetic sense, becomes an *impoverished anthropomorphism. There is no absolute knowing; only a view from nowhere, which still is a human view from nowhere.* This view transforms something with substantial anthropomorphic depth into a no-thing, deliberately constructed *not* to be anthropomorphised, precisely as it eliminates any visual projection of human characteristics.

The question that follows is whether minimalism achieves its **Demonstration**. But as Bernstein writes, "art cannot utterly remove the viewer from the viewed, but it can aspire to

---

[66] Bernstein, *Against Voluptuous Bodies*, 128, my emphasis.

neutralise viewing by decentering the viewer and disorienting and dehumanizing the visual field."[67] This neutralisation is the chief method of literalism's broad attempt to create an aesthetic anti-anthropomorphism. It seeks to *demonstrate* the neutralisation of the beholder's appearance so as to render explicit, or present to them, how the work is constituted by nothing, for nothing, because the situation of both work and beholder (which is only the beholder's appearance) is pure surface. It is this sense of demonstrable "absence" that Fried has been actively fighting against throughout his career in favour of anthropomorphic presentness.[68]

The principle problem of New Sculpture is this anti-anthropomorphic attitude of exhibiting works as situational, literal, essenceless surfaces, rather than exhibiting works which allude to the hidden essence of things through the beholder's *naiveté*. This is why Fried is vital for contemporary aesthetics, because his critique in "Art and Objecthood" works in exactly this way. *It becomes problematic for New Sculpture to both endorse the independence of things, whilst at the same time constructing works which have historically neutralised the beholder's situation.* We are, in effect, talking about two different types of aesthetic relation: one pure surface, the other pure morphism.

---

[67] Bernstein, *Against Voluptuous Bodies*, 128, my emphasis.

[68] To reiterate, OOO is quite a novel realism, insofar as its realism is not conditioned by a common sense, perspectiveless reality of things "simply as they are." Rather, OOO is an ontology of real essential objects, which have their own modes of perception and relationships towards other objects, or what Ian Bogost calls "metaphorism." See Ian Bogost, *Alien Phenomenology, or What It's Like to Be a Thing* (Minneapolis: University of Minnesota Press, 2012), 61-83.

The being of real objects is defined not by being simply real in a view from nowhere, but being real in having a view from somewhere, i.e. from something real. With ontology being the study of what there is, OOO simply extends this insight into all irreducible units—which is to say all units are capable of a perspective of some description, and reality is the total sum of these entities coupled with their perspectives. This is what makes OOO a particular kind of post-correlationist philosophy, insofar as it extends the correlate—minus the privileging of demonstrative reason—to all entities and all relations of being (or at the very least, it decentralises the correlate but keeps its finitude).

Fried argues that Minimalism can never entirely shrug off internal anthropomorphism, and so it has to disguise it, even dissimulate its inherent anthropomorphism into an empty shell of art; or as he states: "what is wrong with literalist work is not that it is anthropomorphic but that the meaning and, equally, the hiddenness of its anthropomorphism are incurably theatrical."[69] The result of this endeavour manifests itself in a work which has the opposite effect of anything resembling an OOO object. The structuring of the work, together with the situation it generates, utterly exhausts itself in its effect on the beholder, or as Bernstein puts it so wonderfully again,

> minimalist works create what might be termed "the art effect" without anything substantial corresponding to that effectivity ... If the sense of such works is the situation they compose, then they are not separate or independent from the viewer, and they are relational: poles or elements of a relational situation. Being only elements of a situation, deriving their identity from the situation they create, minimalist works lack any "in-side," any internal complexity or depth that would token their separateness or autonomy ... They simulate the manner of an aesthetic encounter without there being anything of significance to encounter.[70]

Whilst pages and pages of academic sweat have been spilled since the fallout of Fried's 1967 essay, the aesthetic stakes which he diagnosed still hover precariously in the arts and will continue to do so. This is not to say that Fried's diagnosis was fool-proof, only that he highlighted the fault-lines of the most important schism in the recent history of art. This is the ongoing problem with art practice attempting to justify itself as anti-correlationist, via foregrounding the independence of autonomous things: *by abandoning anthropomorphism, it removes any "in-side" of that complex autonomy from the very start.* Devoid of any characteristics which may be morphised by the beholder, the autonomous thing becomes arbitrary in the wake of eliminating givenness *as such.*

---

[69] Fried, "Art and Objecthood," 827.

[70] Bernstein, *Against Voluptuous Bodies*, 133.

Likewise, the immediate challenges that OOO brings in the name of aesthetics (not just to current philosophy or the arts but also to already existing models of anti-anthropocentric theory), consist in the injunction to return to an *anti-literal mode of conviction*, with the necessary addition that humans are no less capable of an anti-literal perspective than desks, motherboards and ice-laden comets. In other words, what real characteristics (or qualities) of objects allow other objects to be morphised by them? The task then is to show this continuity, and to show how such an alternative, anti-literal aesthetics of autonomous objects can be carved out of Fried's historical and critical trajectory since "Art and Objecthood."

Metaphysical Objects of Presentness

Against the viewer's duration of experience and the literalism of objecthood's strange, exhaustive stage presence, Fried defines the authentic experience of anti-literal art as "presentness"—yet another term and worldview he shares with Cavell—and, much later, as "absorption." Both terms express a Kantian delight in the finite miscommunication and disinterest of aesthetic experience *within* the fullness of anthropomorphic appreciation. Presentness is described as "metaphorical [but] (not literal) instantaneousness,"[71] where "at every moment the work itself is wholly manifest."[72] In the first instance the use of the term is an explicit rebuttal of the literalist manifestation of presence, designed to expose the "bad" anthropomorphism of minimalism. The literalist object of presence simply is, insofar as it deliberately has no essence, whereas the absorptive object of presentness attempts the much harder task of bringing the hidden reality of the world before the involuntary givenness of the anthropomorphic beholder. In this vein, Cavell says of painting and photography:

---

[71] Fried, *Four Honest Outlaws*, 10.

[72] Fried, "Art and Objecthood," 832.

To maintain conviction in our connection with reality, to maintain our presentness, painting accepts the recession of the world. Photography maintains the presentness of the world by accepting our absence from it. The reality in a photograph is present to me while I am not present to it; and a world I know, and see, but to which I am nevertheless not present ... is a world past.[73]

Thus, for example, the presentness in painting for Cavell "would be painting's latest effort to maintain its conviction in its own power to establish connection with reality—by permitting us presentness to ourselves, apart from which there is no hope for a world."[74]

The differences between the works of presence and presentness can be traced in the differences between **Demonstration** and **Description** in relation to how the beholder is meant to critically relate to a work. The work of presentness exists as a whole, a unity of instants which need not require the beholder's presence to complete it. Unlike the "bad" anthropomorphic literalist artwork of presence, the autonomy of the work does not require the beholder to exist for what it is. For every moment that the work exists, it does so instantaneously, maintaining as much conviction in the beholder as it did in the previous moment. Anthropomorphic description is all we have to relate to such an aesthetics of presentness in a world whose objects continue to exist without us and recede interminably. Any aesthetic quality must be generated from the mechanism of the work itself, only the beholder must be *present* for this quality and may have the ability to be enthralled by it. In doing so, the beholder projects their inherent, finite perceptive limitations onto the work of art. In contrast, a work that exudes presence is only committed to a surface of presence taking place in the beholder, with nothing behind it.

By what criteria must the work appeal to different treatments of the beholder? For Fried, the anti-theatrical artwork

---

[73] Stanley Cavell, *The World Viewed: Reflections on the Ontology of Film* (Cambridge: Harvard University Press, 1979), 23.

[74] Cavell, *The World Viewed*, 23.

is defined by its refusal to acknowledge the beholder's presence, whilst paradoxically remaining worthy of being present. The aesthetics of presentness is afforded asymmetrically, *when the beholder is present for the artwork, yet the deep essence of the artwork is never present for the beholder as such.* Now, it can be said that this is exactly what Judd sought to do, with the use of simple natural shapes that attempt to "naturalise" the beholder's vision, yet this is the crux of the reading given here: the focus on neutralising *the beholder's epistemological vision in the ontological world,* against the focus on *the beholder accepting the recession of the ontological world.*

Fried's life-long project as a critic has been to trace those historical moments when variants of theatricality and anti-theatricality surface in and out of a medium's convention. In the same manner that Fried and Cavell's high modernist, historical conviction was unabashedly correlationist, so too is presentness: the world of presentness is only internal, and without us it is nothing but absent. But my central aim here is to radicalise presentness and follow a similar anti-presence metaphysics as outlined by OOO and **Description** more broadly: a metaphysics of non-human aesthetic description. What is needed is an abandonment of anthropo*centrism* and an endorsement of anthropo*morphism*, latent in Fried's endorsement of human limitations, which brings with it an understanding of various isomorphisms within the realm of objects. What we do not need in art is an impoverished anthropomorphism masquerading as an anthropocentric generic object: *art objects need to get specific.* As Jane Bennett puts it in *Vibrant Matter*:

> A touch of anthropomorphism, then, can catalyze a sensibility that finds a world filled not with ontologically distinct categories of beings (subjects and objects) but with variously composed materialities that form confederations. In revealing similarities across categorical divides and lighting up structural parallels between material forms in "nature" and those in "culture," anthropomorphism can reveal isomorphisms.[75]

75 Jane Bennett, *Vibrant Matter: A Political Ecology of Things* (Durham: Duke University Press, 2010), 99.

But unlike with Bennett's rejection of substantial form in favour of relational, vital matter, there does exist a similarity between Harman's allure and Fried's paradigmatic shift of the anthropomorphic senses. We may only have a finite morphised access to the world, but that does not preclude real morphised relationships happening beyond and within that access.

An authentic artwork, present to the beholder, is never "nothing" for Fried, but instead is unveiled in a perpetual creation of itself as something intense, essential and inexhaustible, and not as a thing of literal presence in duration. Similarly, if the literalist work has an obsession with the duration of the subject's experience of the relational situation (and not the work), the anthropomorphic experience of presentness within the high modernist work "has no duration."[76] The work of presentness cannot be completely contingent on the beholder in order to work, but Fried's more controversial suggestion refuses minimalism's conviction that the artwork is contingent on time to function.[77]

Consider then, the striking similarity in the following quote from Harman's 2011 essay "The Road to Objects":

> According to the object-oriented model *only the present exists*: only objects with their qualities, *locked into* whatever their duels of the moment might be. In that sense, time seems to be illusory ... *time does not exist simply because only the present ever exists*.[78]

---

[76] Fried, "Art and Objecthood," 832.

[77] The literature on minimalism's inherent relationship to time is vast. Suffice it to say that a minimalist work as such is contingent on time, for its manifestation is dependent on repetition and infinite configuration. For instance Morris's *Untitled (Three L-beams)* (1965) requires the pieces to be placed in varying positions, so that beholders are unable to view the work in identical fashion. Once again it is the neutralisation of a fixed point of view which marks the passing of time in continuation with the presence of the work. For a more relevant, extended historical analysis of this effect, together with a deeply critical exposition of Fried see Pamela Lee, *Chronophobia: On Time in the Art of the 1960s* (Cambridge: MIT Press, 2006).

[78] Graham Harman, "The Road to Objects," *continent.* (2011), 3:1, 179, my emphasis.

Harman's anti-durational claim, no matter how controversial, fits his object-oriented ontology precisely because *this ontology only contains objects in the present,* not objects grounded by the primacy of time, space and relationality.[79] Essential objects come first, and the conflicts between them *account for the illusion of time.* Time and space are *produced by objects,* or to be more specific, they occur as withdrawn relationships in-between the presences of each object's wake. *Harman's intervention has been exactly this point: that all relations are contingent on objects, and never the other way round.*

Fried's justification for an aesthetic presentness is an odd one, and is never elucidated into a full blown metaphysical claim with much depth (he is an art critic, poet and historian, not a philosopher). Nevertheless, these brazen descriptions are meant to offer somewhat tenuous attempts at bridging Harman's Leibnizian intervention and Fried's conception of presentness. It is my conviction that Harman's object-oriented philosophy provides the metaphysics adequate to Fried's criticism and, conversely, that Harman's philosophy warrants a radicalised Friedian approach to art. With this in mind, I now turn to a final discussion of Fried's theoretical elaborations, to push forward how isomorphism may operate in contemporary art.

---

[79] There is a notable analogy in science, in the para-academic work of theoretical physicist Julian Barbour. Barbour has, independently from academia, worked on a counter-factual history of theoretical physics, where the adoption of Einstein's theory of general relativity is replaced by the earlier theory of relativity as developed by Ernst Mach. Barbour advocates the controversial and tendentious view of a timeless physics, where time does not exist, thus circumventing irresolvable issues attached to Einstein's theory (for example attempts to prove causative agents such as dark energy). For Barbour, reality is not partly contingent on the external existence of a space-time dimension. Instead, its changes can be explained entirely from the actual content of matter, the configuration of which is subject to change within the operations of timeless matter itself. For further reading, see Julian Barbour, *The End of Time: The Next Revolution in our Understanding of the Universe* (Oxford: Oxford University Press, 1999).

Iso-Morphism: Empathic Projection within Non-Humans

As I argued in my earlier essay, presentness within an artwork operates when the work deliberately withdraws from an explicit method of relational execution and never attempts to seek out the beholder's presence, whilst at the same time being paradoxically constructed by the beholder's anthropomorphic finitude. For Fried this manifests itself in beholders being entirely absorbed in their actions, feelings and thoughts, completely unaware of their situation vis-à-vis the artwork. Presentness thus institutes a "supreme fiction" in the beholder absorbed in and persuaded by the work's depth such that they are convinced they were not "really there, or ... had not been taken into account."[80] The work has to convey the illusion of a pictorial depth, a supreme fiction, which surpasses and trumps its material basis. This is not to say that an inanimate, stretched canvas covered in dry chemicals is not real. Rather, for Fried, the aesthetic encounter is defined by critically showing how the beholder's *representation* of the work trumps its material basis, its thingliness. As soon as either the material basis of the work itself or the beholder's presence is deliberately made explicit (that is, the work is no longer needed and becomes contingent purely on the beholder to exist), theatricality ensues and absorption is cut short.[81] As soon as any hint of the figure's obliviousness is found to be staged or acted, the ontological primacy of absorption makes room for a literal impression on the beholder, ruining the aesthetic effect, exhausting the experience and retaining only appearance.

---

[80] Fried, *Absorption and Theatricality*, 96.

[81] Fried describes the following Diderotian shifts in the construction of the *tableau*, which indicate how subtle changes can transform an absorptive painting into a theatrical one: "action is replaced by posing, expression is replaced by grimace, grace and naiveté by mannerism, and the entire painting is inflected by falsity." Fried, *Four Honest Outlaws*, 169.

Empathic Projection: A History

Before I move on to Fried's writings on the work of contemporary artists Douglas Gordon and Anri Sala, I feel that a punishingly brief summary of Fried's published work on art history is necessary in order to give the reader a taste for how Fried understands how anti-theatrical presentness has been and continues to be historically opposed to theatricality. This summary will not follow the chronological order of Fried's publications on the issue, but rather, for the reader's ease, the chronological order of the artworks and periods discussed. In doing so, I hope to elucidate Cavell and Fried's notion of *empathic projection*, which will become essential for my speculative intervention into Fried's work, for the operation of empathy lends itself to a nuanced discussion of aesthetics within the framework of OOO (that said, I do not endorse that it is the only method).

In *The Moment of Caravaggio*, Fried locates the initial invention of the absorptive "mechanism" in the early Caravaggio's *Penitent Magdalen* from 1596-97. The work depicts a young woman who is entirely devoid of outward expression and completely absorbed in her thoughts, actions, and feelings. As opposed to the "spectacular" representations of Magdalene which depicted her in a state of "histrionic remorse,"[82] Caravaggio managed to retrieve this context and to force this imagery into the present moment of the immediate everyday: by inviting the beholder to "see the woman in his painting as wholly absorbed in painful thoughts and feelings—thoughts and feelings that, the painting suggests, lie too deep for expression in any more demonstrative form."[83] This discovery is significant for Fried, insofar as it unleashes within the beholder an "intense inwardness," and the "discovery of the basic truth that human beings tend strongly to

---

[82] Fried, *Four Honest Outlaws*, 207. Here Fried is thinking of Magdalen's theatrical portrayal in Titian's *Penitent Magdalen* of 1533.

[83] Michael Fried, *The Moment of Caravaggio* (Princeton: Princeton University Press, 2010), 76.

project—that by and large they cannot *not* project—*a conviction of inwardness.*"[84] Subsequently Caravaggio exploits this discovery, this "moment," throughout his short (and eventful) artistic career, by repeatedly evoking the beholder's inwardness as projected onto the work.

Fried's most well-known historical trilogy *Absorption and Theatricality* (1980), *Courbet's Realism* (1990) and *Manet's Modernism* (1996) recounts, starting with the mid-eighteenth century, similar but more explicit pictorial issues which were already at stake in Denis Diderot's pre-modern celebration of absorption and raised prominently in Chardin's *Young Student Drawing* (1733-8) and *The House of Cards* (1737). The internal dynamic of these works, and the Diderotian project as a whole, reached its climax in Edouard Manet's revolutionary *Dejeuner sur l'herbe* (1862-63). The success of the woman's gaze and her "facingness" subjects the beholder in a strikingly non-absorptive manner, to such an extent that some acknowledgement of the beholder became central to the ambitious French tradition of modern art, and especially Manet.[85] Naturally, this opposition became an issue once again in "Art and Objecthood," where the historical pressures of literalism/theatricality posed similar issues for modern art in the late 1960s and early 1970s, as discussed earlier.

But at the turn of the twenty-first century, Fried forcibly moved back into the territories of contemporary art criticism: first with the 2008 publication *Why Photography Matters as Art as Never Before*, where to the art world's surprise (and Fried's own) he argued that the artistic and ontological projects of anthropomorphism, as associated with high modernism, were being taken up once more in contemporary photography, albeit for vastly different reasons. Jeff Wall's *Adrian Walker, Artist, Drawing from a Specimen in a Laboratory in the Dept. of Anatomy at the University of British Columbia* (1992) is one of the more famous examples; a piece which seemingly cap-

---

[84] Fried, *The Moment of Caravaggio*, 76-77, my emphasis.

[85] Michael Fried, *Manet's Modernism: Or, The Face of Painting in the 1860s* (Chicago: The University of Chicago Press, 1996), 405.

tures the absorption of the draftsman completely unrelated to the world around him. Despite this refreshing turn, Fried admits that some theatricality is manifest in the presentness of Wall's pieces (i.e. the subjects are posing for Wall and the beholder) and brands this view "to-be-seenness," a sort of "good" or "better" theatricality.[86]

More intriguingly still, Fried's most recent and largely ignored publication *Four Honest Outlaws* points towards the beginnings of a non-human anti-literal presentness within the work of artists working today. It presents what is in Fried's eyes a resurgence of the modernist conviction, even in primarily temporal media that would have been previously considered utterly theatrical (such as video projection). In what I consider to be a long overdue admission, Fried briefly suggests that the vitality of the modernist movement is not tied to historical, conventional media.[87] In "Art and Objecthood," Fried's largely formalist view, much like Greenberg's, was that theatre operated *between* the arts, which is to suggest that anything between the historical media of the arts (such as sculpture or painting) could only be confined to objecthood.[88] But in *Four Honest Outlaws*, and on evidence of the four artists under interrogation, Fried is no longer persuaded by the suggestion that the historical nature of the medium functions so exclusively in either Sala's video work or the interdisciplinary work of Gordon (Marioni's paintings and Ray's sculptures are not discussed in this context). Fried is certain that these artists are investigating the absorptive mechanism in new vital methods that escape the traditional media of modernism. This is a notable and important development in Fried's later criticism which should not be ignored.

---

[86] Michael Fried, *Why Photography Matters as Art as Never Before* (New Haven: Yale University Press, 2008), 58-59.

[87] Fried, *Four Honest Outlaws*, 204.

[88] This is the respective famous passage:

> The concepts of quality and value—and to the extent that these are central to art, the concept of art itself—are meaningful, or wholly meaningful, only within the individual arts. What lies between the arts is theatre.

Fried, "Art and Objecthood," 831.

But what is far more important is a certain speculative reading which emanates from Fried's account of Gordon's video installation *Play Dead: Real Time* (2003). Gordon's work depicts the repeated action of Minnie, an elephant, who is commanded to "play dead," that is, she sits down, plays dead, stands up and walks in a circle. Fried's own viewing took place at the New York Gagosian, Chelsea, in March 2003, where the arrangement of the projections consisted of two semi-transparent large screens positioned in an angle of ninety degrees to each other, with a television monitor on the floor.

In the first instance, Fried reflects on the appearance that Gordon's elephant "may be described as absorbed in what she is doing."[89] In Fried's eyes, Minnie's response to the call of her trainer, absent from the video piece, exudes a self-determination of the subject, entirely focused on the rules that are given:

> the fact that *Play Dead* depicts an animal (and such an animal) puts a new and different complexion on the whole topic of the subject's awareness of being beheld, and *a fortiori* of being photographed or filmed. That is, we cannot doubt—the projections leave no room for doubt—that Minnie was aware of her trainer and the others sharing the gallery space with her. But in what precisely, with respect to the issues that interest us, did that awareness consist? For example, is it remotely conceivable that she understood that she was being filmed for subsequent exhibition? Obviously not. Nor do her actions ... convey the least sense of self-consciousness, mannerism, or theatricality.[90]

Part of the delight about Fried's reading of *Play Dead* is the difficulty of the questions he himself poses whilst trying to honestly account for the empathic nature of Gordon's piece. He is, as he admits, "on ontologically shaky ground here" in attempting to speak of what Minnie is absorbed by in the piece.[91] Yet that "shaky ground," I claim, is only Fried

---

[89] Fried, *Four Honest Outlaws*, 171.

[90] Ibid., 173.

[91] Ibid.

wrestling with the fact that the anthropomorphic tropes of anti-literal absorption can be witnessed and extended *beyond* the modernist limits of human sensibility. All of the aesthetic effects of quality that Fried endorses and promotes are clearly and utterly evident in Gordon's *Play Dead*, within something undoubtedly non-human, direct and real, and yet never a lesser subject of empathic acknowledgement.

Who thought that a critic like Fried, the arch-reactionary critic who supposedly despises the anti-modern fallout of post-formalism, could find a video projection of an elephant playing dead so utterly captivating? Yet he is right. Gordon's work is so inexorably strange, haunting, intensely anthropomorphising, that it fosters empathy as much as any work playing up to human subjectivity. The beholder is ultimately absorbed in "an intense but also in the present instance largely gratuitous or unearned emotional response to Minnie."[92] Notice for example the intense expressiveness of Minnie's eyes, the willingness she depicts in order to obey the rules of the absent trainer, the "freakishness but also the nobility of her massive head," her fixed, expressionless, waiting stare, and her effort-laden determination to simply stand up.[93] The success of *Play Dead* lies within the beholder's finite projection of Minnie's own absorption, which, quoting Fried again, "elicit[s] such feelings, and … promote[s] a consciousness in the viewer of his or her tendency to project empathically."[94] This is to suggest that beholders project onto and into the work their real empathy towards the non-human subject. They do not just "see" Minnie, or possess a discernible "identification" of Minnie, but empathically project a sensual morphism "with" Minnie, even though Minnie is not "literally" there, and especially not as a literal thing in a situation. Human beholder map their traits onto Minnie's own present situation, without this mapping occurring explicitly. Fried also notices this mechanism at work in Gordon's *10 ms $^{-1}$* (1994)

---

[92] Fried, *Four Honest Outlaws*, 175.

[93] Ibid., 176.

[94] Ibid.

and especially Anri Sala's *Time After Time* (2003), a video depicting an emaciated horse, completely abandoned by the
side of a road in Tirana;[95] a piece which "all but defies the
viewer not to empathize."[96]

The crucial question that Fried must tackle is what separates
Gordon and Sala's video pieces from other similarly-minded
theatrical video works, which usually require the subject's
personal experience to be entirely part of the literal situation
(one has in mind Bruce Nauman or the ghastly theatrical video
work of Bill Viola here). Here Fried is still adamant that the
work makes no appeal to different subject positions, or to an
"experience standing in for the work," as theatricality would
aver.[97] Instead the effect of empathic projection is *built into
the work* from the start as a specific effect, which is to say that
"the emphasis falls on the structurally imposed recognition
of the 'mechanism,' not the nuances of a particular subject's
personal experience of it."[98]

One might be tempted to assert that only humans could
be indicative of this phenomenon due to the finite universal
framework of sensation which they share qua living things.
But on further inspection, I am not convinced. For instance,
consider the equally absorptive, equally anti-theatrical computational artwork *Avec Determination* (2000-2001) by the
algorithmic artist Antoine Schmitt. In this procedural piece,
the artist constructs an automated struggle, a procedural torture of sorts: the struggle of an algorithmic creature caged in
a coded box, beholden to a gravitational pull—an ever present
limit, never released. There is of course a shift of medium from
time-based video to a computer algorithm, a puzzle solver, a

---

[95] *10 ms⁻1*, an early piece by Gordon, is a video loop depicting a fragment of a
medical film, where a World War I soldier is utterly shaken by psychological
damage and who, like Minnie in *Play Dead*, also struggles to stand up and
walk with determination. Whilst Fried admits that Gordon's mechanism in
10 ms⁻1 borders on the level of being sadistic, it is nonetheless capable of
aesthetic conviction and absorption regardless of the beholder's reaction to it.

[96] Fried, *Four Honest Outlaws*, 211.

[97] Ibid., 177.

[98] Ibid., 210.

step-by-step procedure, a recipe. Each creature that Schmitt codes has different goals—to stand, to walk, to jump, to step, to resist, to push—and they are impeded in real time, by other algorithmically constructed forces continually acting on it *in the present*. The goals are determined, but the autonomous reality of the creatures' actions are never perfect nor the same. Built with intention and intensity, the other algorithmic rules which surround it force errors of judgement (much like the rules given to Minnie). This is then a much more explicit form of the autonomous mechanism Fried favours.

As Schmitt states, we are but helpless spectators, entirely beholden to the algorithm's movement—the slightest shift of the mouse perturbs its journey for the worse we might add, smashing it into the sides without damage. It is invincible and yet tortured. "For each of these creatures," Schmitt states, "I try to approach a certain essence of being … The function of the image is to enable us to apprehend their mode of being. The interaction itself is only a minimal link between their reality and ours."[99] Like Gordon's *Play Dead* (and for entirely different reasons), *Avec Determination* commands our projection, and is just as intense. Like Minnie, the role of the beholder is sealed off from its struggle, yet we behold it anyway—and we do so by witnessing the work's strange perpetual creation of itself. The reality of the mechanically inanimate cannot be disregarded in modernist conviction, or as Schmitt candidly muses, "they are silent creatures, struggling against their environment, which we are a part of."[100]

This is all the more startling insofar as Cavell's descriptive theory of empathic projection in his famous *The Claim of Reason* was originally written to stave off external world scepticism and mind scepticism: the point that we cannot reducibly prove self-consciousness in other human creatures, or doubt it, in any case. Cavell described empathic projection as a "dummy concept for something that must be the

[99] Antoine Schmitt, "avec determination (with determination)," *Antoine Schmitt Website* http://www.gratin.org/as/avecdetermination/ (accessed February 1, 2013).

[100] Ibid.

basis of my claims to read the other."[101] In other words, it is perfectly plausible that the sceptic can doubt the existence of other minds, or other subjects, but empathic projection nonetheless suggests that we acknowledge the existence of *something specific* outside of ourselves, even though it is projected and unknowable. In Cavell's words, another human could just possibly be "an automaton, a zombie, an android, an angel, an alien of some unheard of kidney," yet whatever it is, we find ourselves empathically projecting, or finding a common trait in that external thing, even if our knowledge about it eventually turns out to be incorrect.[102]

It cannot be a coincidence that the withdrawn nature of the phenomenological object plays an identical role in Harman's philosophy, not simply in the way that acknowledgement "goes beyond" knowledge, but also in the added suggestion that humans do not play the starring role in empathically projecting their inwardness towards other things.[103] The only thing that stops us from perpetually empathising with specific human and non-human objects is the banality of the everyday as expressed in the objecthood of mundane art. What is needed then is an *aesthetics of the isomorphic*. This is an aesthetics of asymmetrical causation, where the inwardness of objects or units corresponds to their local neighbourhood, blind only to themselves. Following Harman's intervention, what is crucial in isomorphism is the ability for the aesthetic effect to occur in a non-anthropocentric manner, without the acknowledgment of a human beholder; i.e. the primordial logics of projection, absorption and presentness occur between neighbour cat and catnip, sodium and chloride, lemon juice and salmon flesh, wheat and flame, as well as the work of art and beholder. Any such beholding thing cannot "step outside" empathic projection, much like the correlationist, who cannot escape their own correlation. This is a direct consequence of **Description**.

---

[101] Cavell, *The Claim of Reason*, 440.

[102] Ibid., 423-24.

[103] Ibid., 428.

Speculations V

The necessary question that must be asked in light of *Play Dead* and *Time After Time* is how other objects themselves also empathically project. Is this "mechanism" to which Fried ascribes such an importance capable of a projection all by itself and if so, can artists take advantage of it? The important point to emphasise here is that whilst human beholders are locked into their own traits of projection, such other isomorphic projections need not correspond to narrowly human attributes. The function of "projection" in isomorphism takes on a simple form of self-determination. To take the liberty of paraphrasing Fried, by virtue of its determinate essence, an object *cannot avoid* projecting its own aesthetic inwardness onto other objects, yet it also cannot avoid accepting the "presentness" of recession, which traps its contents.

There is something here in Fried's later work, a wider metaphysical significance of his theory of absorption and presentness that needs to be fast-forwarded into fuelling the current technologies of the ambiguous. Perhaps a twenty-first century aesthetics will not be about a return to objects in the literal sense, but about a realist explosion of isomorphisms: any mindless, inanimate, cephalic or a-cephalic beholder in its withdrawn inwardness has the potential to be, in a realist manner, absorbed through its own projected presentness of withdrawal.

Post Script

The Wittgenstein epigraph is taken up by Fried in *Four Honest Outlaws* to illustrate the consequences of another work by Douglas Gordon. *B-Movie* (1995) is a small fragmented video, similar to Gordon's *10 ms $^{-}1$*, where an upturned fly struggles to flip to its natural state. The beholder empathically realises the fly's pain through their own inwardness. Following Harman, could we not realise that the fly may project its own inwardness onto us, during our darkest struggles?

The Alien Aesthetic of Speculative Realism, or, How Interpretation Lost the Battle to Materiality and How Comfortable this Is to Humans

Roberto Simanowski

City University of Hong Kong

ANYONE INTERESTED IN THE central issues of media studies will also have an interest in speculative realism or object-oriented ontology, particularly when it comes to the question of the extent to which the respective subject of research has a life of its own. Media studies and speculative realism both discuss whether agency is with the people using an object or technology or with the objects and technologies themselves. While speculative realism may ask "Do people kill people or does the gun kill people?" media studies debates whether technologies represent social practices or are imposing their own constraints and rules on humans. Presuming the latter—i.e., that agency lies with the gun and the acting media—represents a perspective based on the independent existence of technologies and objects. Voting for the former corresponds to an anthropological point of view or to an anthropocentric one, as speculative realism terms it.

The pejorative connotation of this characterisation is intended; speculative realism objects to any privilege humans may claim over entities. It does so even if the privilege is actually a disadvantage, if, for example, one assumes—in the philosophical tradition since Immanuel Kant's Copernican

Revolution—that objects only exist in relation to human perception, that they are nothing more than the products of human cognition. The assumption that the known does not exist without the knower, such "correlationism," as Quentin Meillassoux calls it, is a "negative privilege" since it rejects all possible knowledge of an absolute: "it is the claim that we are closed up in our representations—whether conscious, linguistic, or historical—with no sure access to an eternal reality independent of our specific point of view."[1] The answer of speculative realism to such anthropocentrism is anthrodecentrism, claiming not only that objects exist independently of human perception but also that they relate to one another on their own. If speculative realism—evoked here predominantly in its object-oriented guise—overcomes correlationism in the name of objects, it also overcomes the epistemological nihilism that modern and postmodern philosophy have passed on to us.

Part of the proclaimed anthrodecentrism is an aesthetics that replaces human agency by the self-expression of objects. Ian Bogost, in particular, advocates such "Alien Aesthetics," as he terms it, which does not centre around the human perception of objects but around objects' perceptions of humans, aiming at "the secret lives of things."[2] This paper explores such claims with respect to two examples Bogost presents and discusses, asking to what extent the alien aesthetics of speculative realism has been anticipated and supported by certain aesthetic theories and artistic practices since the end of the twentieth century, and exploring how useful this philosophical movement is for describing the mode of being of certain artworks. While the driving question of my consideration is the ethics of aesthetics, the central subject of this paper is the relationship between art and interpretation. My thesis is that these aesthetic and artistic developments aim

---

[1] Quentin Meillassoux, "Presentation by Quentin Meillassoux," *Collapse* (2007), 3, 427.

[2] Ian Bogost, "The New Aesthetic Needs to Get Weirder," *The Atlantic*, http://www.theatlantic.com/technology/archive/2012/04/the-new-aesthetic-needs-to-get- weirder/255838 (accessed June 6, 2013).

at overcoming both correlationism and the psychological burden of destabilised meaning in their own ways, either by evading interpretation or by turning to statistics.

1. The Aestheticisation of Society, or, The Postmodern Condition Is Aesthetic Insofar as it Is Epistemologically Nihilistic

A general statement, though not the only possible one, about the function of art conceptualises art as the negation of what the world is and of who we are, as place of the other, as the experience of alienation and deconstruction. Art does so not only by presenting other ideas and concepts of being, but also and first of all by denying a stable signifier. "All artworks—and art altogether—are enigmas," Adorno notes, "it is their incomprehensibility that needs to be comprehended."[3] The essential role of art is to undermine any automatism and certainty in the process of signification. Hence, in his 1999 book *The Sovereignty of Art: Aesthetic Negativity in Adorno and Derrida*, German philosopher Christoph Menke aptly titles one of his chapters "The Aesthetic Experience of Crisis."[4]

There are various attempts to escape such experience. Susan Sontag's seminal essay "Against Interpretation" identifies one of them in a certain hermeneutic approach: "In a culture whose already classical dilemma is the hypertrophy of the intellect at the expense of energy and sensual capability, interpretation is the revenge of the intellect upon art. Even more. It is the revenge of the intellect upon the world. To interpret is to impoverish, to deplete the world—in order to set up a shadow world of 'meanings'."[5] People who have not used the term interpretation for a long time probably like this quote. However, they should also remember that the essay

---

[3] Theodor W. Adorno, *Aesthetic Theory*, ed. Gretel Adorno and Rolf Tiedemann, trans. Robert Hullot-Kentor (New York: Continuum, 2004), 160, 157.

[4] Christoph Menke, *The Sovereignty of Art: Aesthetic Negativity in Adorno and Derrida* (Cambridge: MIT Press, 1999), 215-40.

[5] Susan Sontag, "Against Interpretation" in *Against Interpretation and Other Essays* (New York: Noonday Press, 1966), 7.

was published three years before Guy Debord's book *Society of the Spectacle* and that in 1996, in the afterword "Thirty Years Later" to the anniversary issue of the essay collection *Against Interpretation*, Sontag adopts a different tone. Given the ongoing "transvaluation of values," the shift from symbolic concerns to intensities of direct sensual stimulation, and the arrival of "the age of nihilism," Sontag distances herself from her original attack on interpretation.[6] At the end of the century, giving up the search for meaning has turned out to be a much more efficient and popular strategy for escaping the experience of crisis than the fixation of meaning.

At the same time, interpretation is no longer aiming at stabilising meaning. In his 1994 book *Beyond Interpretation: The Meaning of Hermeneutics for Philosophy* (engl. 1997), Italian philosopher Gianni Vattimo speaks of a "nihilistic vocation of hermeneutics"—this is the title of the first chapter—which is to dissolve "the principle of reality into the Babel of interpretations" and to "reveal the world as a conflict of interpretations" without the prospect of reconciliation.[7] In this perspective, interpretation has the opposite effect of what Sontag assumed in 1964. In addition, the "age of nihilism" that Sontag deplores in 1996 is now attested positive ethical consequences: "the guiding thread of nihilism" is "the reduction of violence, the weakening of strong and aggressive identities, the acceptance of the other, to the point of charity."[8] Vattimo is not the only one who, back in the 1980s and 1990s, asserted the moral, antifundamentalist effects of putting any claim of truth or "correct" interpretation into

---

[6] Susan Sontag, "Thirty Years Later" in *Against Interpretation and Other Essays* (New York: Picador, 2001), 311.

[7] Gianni Vattimo, *Beyond Interpretation: The Meaning of Hermeneutics for Philosophy*, trans. David Webb (Stanford: Stanford University Press, 1997), 39-40.

[8] Vattimo, *Beyond Interpretation*, 73. Vattimo further elaborates: "Thinking that no longer understands itself as the recognition and acceptance of an objective authoritarian foundation will develop a new sense of responsibility as ready and able, literally, to respond to others whom, insofar as it is not founded on the eternal structure of Being, it knows to be its 'provenance'." Vattimo, *Beyond Interpretation*, 40.

the perspective of the context from which it arises. Against the interpretation of postmodern perspectives as ethically cynical, Vattimo and others considered such renunciation from the illusion of an absolute truth as a call for accepting difference and thus as an adequate foundation of multicultural society in a global world.[9]

Highlighting the link between Vattimo's epistemological nihilism and Menke's aesthetic experience, I should also point to the German philosopher Wolfgang Welsch, who in the early 1990s extensively discussed aesthetics as the new key currency—or "Leitwährung"—and the "homo aestheticus" as the new prevalent figure in contemporary society.[10] According to Welsch, we are experiencing two forms of aestheticisation. The shallow one—"Oberflächenästhetisierung"—is marked by the beautification of the living environment and the creation of neologisms such as shopertainment, eatertainment, edutainment, and infotainment.[11] Deep aestheticisation—"Tiefenästhetisierung"—constitutes the loss of a reliable perspective on reality as we know it from the experience of art.[12] This kind of *epistemological* aestheticisation—"epistemologische Ästhetisierung"[13]—is the most serious and effective form of aestheticisation; Welsch traces

---

[9] Vattimo is well aware of the fact that the proposed nihilistic—or, as he also puts it, "antimetaphysical"—vocation of hermeneutics is itself nothing more than interpretation based on a specific western perspective that may be rejected as another grand narrative after the end of all grand narratives. His offer to solve the postmodern version of Epimenides' Cretan Paradox by understanding the post-metaphysical hermeneutic as the most adequate interpretation of modernity does not explain why other, non-western cultures should adopt the proposed positive perspective on nihilism. The issue to what extent the libertarian postmodern *Farewell to Truth* (New York: Columbia University Press, 2011), as the title of a recent book by Vattimo reads, is conducted in favour of or in opposition to the oppressed cultural paradigms of others remains, as far as I can see, unsolved.

[10] Wolfgang Welsch, "Ästhetisierungsprozesse—Phänomene, Unterscheidungen, Perspektiven" in *Grenzgänge der Ästhetik* (Stuttgart: Reclam, 1996), 14, 18.

[11] Ibid., 10.

[12] Ibid., 10, 21.

[13] Ibid., 21.

it back to Kant (the "transcendental aesthetic" in the *Critique of Pure Reason*), Friedrich Nietzsche, Paul Feyerabend, and Richard Rorty and calls it the legacy of modernity.[14] In this light, the postmodern condition is aesthetic because it is epistemologically nihilistic: alienation and deconstruction leave the fenced system of art to become the primary mode of perception and cognition.

This take on nihilism—that there is no objective meaning and universal value—is clearly different from Ray Brassier's, one of the representatives of speculative realism, who declares himself a nihilist exactly because he believes in truth. Brassier reads meaninglessness as the purposelessness of existence. To him, "we understand nature better than we did, but this understanding no longer requires the postulate of an underlying meaning"; human rationality has abandoned theologically inflected metaphysics, cognitive progress in intellectual history has left us without any "metaphysical narrative about the ineluctable forward march of Spirit."[15] Brassier's nihilism is less serious and epistemologically more comfortable than Vattimo's, for it is at least sure of its own foundation.

However, while the "homo aestheticus" certainly has become accustomed to the beautification of everyday life, and while the iPad and Facebook generation enjoys beautification in technology and communication, the question is whether one can also cope with the demise of truth. Are people strong enough to accept "weak thought" as the new philosophical paradigm required by any anti-foundational hermeneutics?[16] Are people ready to be supermen, to apply the common but improper translation of Nietzsche's term *Übermensch*? Because this is what the painful but necessary emancipation from the

---

[14] Welsch, "Ästhetisierungsprozesse," 43, 53.

[15] Ray Brassier, "I Am a Nihilist Because I Still Believe in Truth," *Kronos* (2011), http://www.kronos.org.pl/index.php?23151,896 (accessed June 6, 2013).

[16] The concept of "weak thought" is Vattimo's central contribution to the postmodern debate. It considers thought incapable of knowing the state of being, which is why it cannot determine universal ("strong") values valid for all human beings.

illusion of an absolute truth and historic progress requires.[17] The recourse to new or old metaphysical foundations such as God, however, means, as Vattimo states in an essay about the return of religion, to fail the challenge of Nietzsche's Overhuman.[18]

A more demanding way of holding on to strong thinking and the idea of truth are science and statistics. As the quantitative turn in the humanities demonstrates, there is a new "longing for evidence" (*Sehnsucht nach Evidenz*), as the title of a special issue of the *Zeitschrift für Kulturwissenschaften* read in 2009. Desire for evidence is the desire to control of which Sontag had accused art critics. Postmodern aesthetics—such as Jean-François Lyotard's aesthetics of the sublime in the 1980s—reacted to this desire by refusing meaning altogether. Since the 1990s, however, there has been—as an extrapolation of that refusal rather than a response to it—a return of the real in art which in recent years was taken up by digital media artists who are developing an aesthetics of statistics. Section 2 discusses this development as a precursor to the alien aesthetics promoted by Bogost and other advocates of speculative realism.

2. Events and Objects in Art, or, Turning Attention from Meaning to Materiality

In his writings on aesthetics following his description of the erosion of grand narratives in *The Postmodern Condition*, Lyotard focuses on the event and intensity of the moment at the expense of message and signification. In "The Sublime

---

[17] Gianni Vattimo, *The Transparent Society* (Baltimore: Johns Hopkins University Press, 1992), 9-10.

[18] Gianni Vattimo, "The Trace of the Trace" in *Religion*, ed. Gianni Vattimo and Jacques Derrida (Stanford: Stanford University Press, 1998), 82. Given the fact that Nietzsche himself always disdained the masses' escape into hedonism, the hedonism and distraction, characteristic of our society of the spectacle can hardly be seen as an answer to the end of truth that faces the challenge of Nietzsche's Overhuman. There is a fundamental difference between weak thought and no thought, the latter being closer to strong than to weak thinking.

and the Avant-Garde," he famously states that "a work of art is avant-garde in direct proportion to the extent that it is stripped of meaning" and asks: "Is it not then like an event?"[19] In an interview about the unrepresentable, Lyotard notes: we do not consume the occurrence but its meaning.[20] As a consequence, Lyotard proposes an aesthetics of the sublime that cannot be grasped by reason but interrupts control-seeking discourse. The sublime artwork is the artistic materialisation of philosophical nihilism and of what Welsch calls *epistemological aestheticisation*. It is the challenge to live without meaning, the demand to embrace this challenge like Nietzsche's Overhuman does. In a sequence that recalls Sontag's insistence on an erotics in place of a hermeneutics of art, Lyotard notes: the energy encountered in an artefact will make a noble man dance, while a bad (occidental) person will start to talk.[21]

Lyotard's aesthetics of the sublime establishes the perception of incomprehensibility *before* interpretation. Menke, who focuses on the aesthetic experience as crisis *through* interpretation, takes issue with Lyotard's theory of "asemantic effects" and his concept of the artwork as "an epiphany of an unarticulatable meaning" and distances himself from a

---

[19] Jean-François Lyotard, "The Sublime and the Avant-Garde" in *The Lyotard Reader*, ed. Andrew E. Benjamin (Malden: Blackwell, 1989), 210.

[20] Jean-François Lyotard, "Das Undarstellbare—wider das Vergessen: Ein Gespräch zwischen Jean-François Lyotard und Christiane Pries" in *Das Erhabene—zwischen Grenzerfahrung und Größenwahn*, ed. Christiane Pries (Weinheim: VCH, Acta humaniora, 1989), 344.

[21] Jean-François Lyotard, *Essays zu einer affirmativen Ästhetik* (Berlin: Merve, 1982), 49. Sontag, "Against Interpretation," 14. In his 1976 essay "The Tooth, the Palm," Lyotard presents his idea of the "energetic theater," in which the gesture of the body is liberated from the duty of signifying; thus the clinched fist no longer represents the pain caused by a toothache but stands on its own. Lyotard saw the sensual perception of energy transmitted by an artefact in its entire presence, as pure intensity, without turning it into a sign subject to hermeneutic or semiotic analysis. The "business of an energetic theater," he notes, "is not to make allusion to the aching tooth when a clinched fist is the point, nor the reverse." The tooth and the palm no longer have a relationship of signifier and signified; they "no longer mean anything, they are forces, intensities, present affects." Jean-François Lyotard, "The Tooth, the Palm" in *Performance: Critical Concepts in Literary and Cultural Studies*, vol. 2, ed. Philip Auslander (London: Routledge, 2003), 31, 30.

perspective on art that promotes the embrace of "pure, meaningless materiality." As Menke states, the "discernment of the vacillation of aesthetic signifiers stands in contrast with an unmediated rehabilitation of the material determinations of aesthetic objects, as proclaimed, for instance, in Lyotard's model of an affirmative aesthetics."[22] In German aesthetic theory, the embrace of pure, meaningless materiality has explicitly been advocated by Hans Ulrich Gumbrecht in his concept of the culture of presence replacing the allegedly dominant culture of meaning or hermeneutics. Gumbrecht favours the aesthetic experience as a sensual connection to the world, as the experience of moments of intensity such as the polyphone complexity of a Mozart aria, the touchdown in football, the death blow in bullfighting, or "'special effects' produced today by the most advanced communication technologies" as possibly "instrumental in reawakening a desire for presence."[23] Gumbrecht's list reveals how closely affiliated aesthetic theory has become with the culture or entertainment industry and how affirmative it is towards the status quo.[24]

The strategy of avoiding the nihilistic vocation of hermeneutics by turning attention from meaning to materiality can also be found in contemporary artistic practice. Here a way of dealing with epistemological nihilism is turning to the objects to let them speak for themselves. In 1996, US-American critic Hal Foster announced *The Return of the Real*, discussing "The Artist as Ethnographer," as one of the book's chapters is entitled.[25] In 1997, the exhibition *Deep Storage, Arsenale der Erinnerung: Sammeln, Speichern, Archivieren in*

---

[22] Menke, *The Sovereignty of Art*, 153, 270, 45-46.

[23] Hans Ulrich Gumbrecht, *Production of Presence: What Meaning Cannot Convey* (Stanford: Stanford University Press, 2004), xv.

[24] For a detailed critical discussion of Lyotard's aesthetics of the sublime, Hans Ulrich Gumbrecht's culture of presence as well as similar aesthetic theories such as Erika Fischer-Lichte's and Dieter Mersch's aesthetics of the performative, see my *Digital Art and Meaning: Reading Kinetic Poetry, Text Machines, Mapping Art, and Interactive Installations* (Minneapolis: University of Minnesota Press, 2011), 1-26, 208-230.

[25] Hal Foster, *The Return of the Real: The Avant-Garde at the End of the Century* (Cambridge: MIT Press, 1996).

der Kunst in the *Haus der Kunst* in Munich explored art as a collection of objects from the real. In 2002, French curator and art theoretician Nicolas Bourriaud noted in his book *Postproduction* that artists today remix what they find rather than compose from scratch: "Notions of originality (being at the origin of) and even of creation (making something from nothing) are slowly blurred in this new cultural landscape marked by the twin figures of the DJ and the programmer, both of whom have the task of selecting cultural objects and inserting them into new contexts."[26] However, referring to Guy Debord's *Methods of Detournement* published in 1956—which announces *détournement* as a kind of political use of Duchamp's readymade-concept giving objects and situations a different, enlightening meaning by a specific appropriation—Bourriaud also emphasises that the aesthetics of postproduction still puts the found objects into a specific perspective, making the artist herself present in the object.[27] This situation changes once the objects become data collected by the computer.

The exhibition *Collect the WWWorld: The Artist as Archivist in the Internet Age* in Basel in 2012 (*Haus für elektronische Künste*) contained Evan Roth's "Personal Internet Cache Archive" of 2010, which presents images his computer automatically stored in the cache while Roth was browsing the internet.[28] The collection is not a result of the artist's deliberate decision but rather represents a new form of Walter Benjamin's optical unconscious, showing the images Roth may have seen only briefly during his browsing session. Another work in this exhibition is Travis Hallenbeck's "Flickr Favs" of 2010, a book

---

[26] Nicolas Bourriaud, *Postproduction. Culture as Screenplay: How Art Reprograms the World* (New York: Lukas & Sternberg, 2002), 13. Bourriaud's examples are, among others, Thomas Hirschhorn's and Rirkrit Tiravanija's environments of objects, though both, as Claire Bishop makes clear in an essay in 2004, are quite different in their postproductive art. Claire Bishop, "Antagonism and Relational Aesthetics," *October* (2004), 110, 51-79.

[27] Bourriaud, *Postproduction*, 35.

[28] Evan Roth, "Personal Internet Cache Archive," http://www.haus-ek.org/de/content/evan-roth (accessed June 6, 2013).

which on each of its 315 pages presents 36 images taken from Flickr.com.[29] In contrast to Christian Boltanski—an earlier representative of archive art, who in his work *Album de la famille D.* (1972) composes a specific narrative by a montage of 150 images taken from the photo album of a friend—Hallenbeck does not present a careful choice of images. He has no narrative to convey but lets the randomly chosen images speak for themselves. While in the postproductive, ethnographic work of artists such as Boltanski, Thomas Hirschhorn, or Rirkrit Tiravanija, the return of the real is rather the return of the artist *to* the real, in online based works such as Roth's and Hallenbeck's, the artist truly withdraws from any creation and production and presents the objects—the photographs they have not taken—free from human intervention.

In his talk "Seeing Things" at the Third Object-Oriented Ontology Symposium in September 2011, Ian Bogost presented the "snapshot aesthetic" of the American photographer Garry Winogrand as an example of objects speaking for themselves:

> His works are not commentaries, they are precisely the opposite. Garry Winogrand makes photographs not to capture what he sees, but to see what he will have captured. That's what it means to take photographs to see what the world looks like in photographs.[30]

By evoking Winogrand's photographs as documents teaching us "to see the world of things as things in a world, rather than our world, with things in it," Bogost considers Winogrand's work an example of unmediated access to the object itself. This way—and suitable to the specific context of his talk—Bogost presents an example of overcoming "correlationism."[31]

---

[29] Travis Hallenbeck, "Flickr Favs," www.flickr.com/photos/cosmic_disciple/favorites (accessed June 6, 2013).

[30] Ian Bogost, "Seeing Things," talk at the Third Object-Oriented Ontology Symposium, 15 September 2011, www.bogost.com/writing/seeing_things_1.shtml (accessed June 6, 2013).

[31] Kant's correlationism is, as Bogost notes in his book *Alien Phenomenology*, the common enemy of speculative realism. Bogost's own reasoning of this enmity—he basically dismisses Kant for not having travelled enough—is quite insightful regarding the theoretical rigor of one of the most popular

Rather than discussing whether Bogost's claiming of Winogrand for object-oriented ontology is appropriate, I want to ask to what extent Bogost's claim could be extended to the medium as such. As Siegfried Kracauer notes in his 1927 essay on photography, the medium captures the given as a spatial continuum regardless of the meaning it has for us.[32] In this perspective, photography per se represents the world rather than our understanding of the world. Jean Baudrillard drives this perspective even further, stating that with photography the object can prevail with its "discontinuity and immediacy" against the will of the perceptive subject; the "magical eccentricity of the detail" blocks out the "view of the world," the "'approach' to things."[33] Since the nature of photography is indexical, this medium promises the prevailing of the real—or objects, for that matter—over its observer. Baudrillard detects an antagonism between, on the one hand, "the philosophy of the subject and the contemplating gaze—of stepping back from the world in order to grasp it" and, on the other, "the anti-philosophy of the object, of the disconnectedness of objects, of the random succession of part-objects and details."[34]

If Baudrillard were still alive, he may have attacked object-oriented ontology and considered photography its natural medium. He would be as wrong as Bogost is to claim Winogrand for his cause. Both neglect the well-established argument that rather than reality, a photographer documents

---

representatives of this new philosophy: "The speculative realists share a common position less than they do a common enemy: the tradition of human access that seeps from the rot of Kant. Even if tales of Kant's infamous introversion are overstated, they are true enough to have birthed this irony: the blinkered state of philosophy-as-access arrives on the coattail of a man who never strayed far from the Prussian town of Königsberg. For more than two centuries, philosophy has remained mousy and reticent, a recluse." Ian Bogost, *Alien Phenomenology, or What It's Like to Be a Thing* (Minneapolis: University of Minnesota Press, 2012), 4-5.

[32] Siegfried Kracauer, "Photography," trans. Thomas Y. Levin, *Critical Inquiry* (1993), 19:3, 421-43.

[33] Jean Baudrillard, *Photographies 1985-1998*, ed. Peter Weibel (Ostfildern: Hatje Cantz, 2000), 132, 130.

[34] Baudrillard, *Photographies*, 132.

her specific relationship to that reality. There is no escape in photography from correlationism, unless photographs are taken automatically: by surveillance cameras, Google Street View or other devices operating on their own behalf, including commercialised intelligent cameras.[35] To the extent that those devices autonomously take pictures and analyse and share them with other devices, they indeed seem to take on a life of their own independent of human action. Are they becoming players in their own right? Do they imagine *us*, as advocates of the new aesthetic claim? Do they illustrate the perspectives of objects, which Bogost notes, under the term "carpentry," as one of the practices of his *Alien Phenomenology*? Section 3 explores these questions by discussing the movement of the new aesthetic and some examples that do or do not serve to reveal the secret lives of things.

3. The New Aesthetic, or, The Secret Lives of Things and the Ethics of Cool

The new aesthetic was officially introduced at the 2012 South by Southwest conference with the panel "The New Aesthetic: Seeing Like Digital Devices": "Slowly but increasingly definitively, our technologies and our devices are learning to see, to

---

[35] Cameras with face detection are designed to warn their users when someone blinks or automatically take a picture when somebody smiles. Such intelligent media, which are programmed according to specific perspectives (that one should not blink but smile on a photograph), do not take *the* human out of the equation but the concrete human in concrete situations. As a *Time* article reports, this technology is so undetermined by the specific situation that it even becomes racist, e.g., when it interprets Asian people as having blinked because the face recognition software is programmed according to white peoples' eye forms. This is especially ironic given that the camera accused of such racism was a Nikon. See Adam Rose, "Are Face-Detection Cameras Racist?" *Time*, 22 January 2010, www.time.com/time/business/article/0,8599,1954643,00.html (accessed June 6, 2013). Jon Rafman's work of 2009 "The 9 Eyes of Google Street View," which was part of the *Collect the WWWorld* exhibition, presents strange images which Google certainly would have discarded if its street view photographing were overseen by people: a baby strolling alone along the street, a body on the ground. See http://www.haus-ek.org/de/content/jon-rafman (accessed June 6, 2013).

hear, to place themselves in the world."[36] The new aesthetic is "striving towards a fundamentally new way of imagining the relations between things in the world," as artist and researcher Greg Borenstein states in a blog entry which also links the new aesthetic movement to the philosophical movements of object-oriented ontology and speculative realism.[37] Borenstein holds: as much as object-oriented ontology "advocates a philosophical process of 'speculation' about, as Bogost says, 'what it's like to be a thing,'" the new aesthetic aims "to dig out what it's like to be a thing born of our contemporary technological era ... It's an attempt to imagine the inner lives of the native objects of the 21st century and to visualize how they imagine us."[38]

The assumption that objects imagine *us* stands in such contrast to traditional perspectives that it ensures this new aesthetic the attention it needs. However, this movement—if it is a movement at all—has been harshly criticised in Bruce Sterling's "Essay on the New Aesthetic" regarding the incoherence of visual objects assembled under the new aesthetic banner. To Sterling, the "New Aesthetic wunderkammer" is nothing more than a "glitch-hunt," a "heap of eye-catching curiosities [that] don't constitute a compelling worldview."[39]

---

[36] SXSW Schedule: "The New Aesthetic: Seeing Like Digital Devices." http://schedule.sxsw.com/2012/events/event_IAP11102 (accessed June 6, 2013). For a report on this panel, see James Bridle, "Report from Austin, Texas, on the New Aesthetic Panel at SXSW," 14 March 2012, http://booktwo.org/notebook/sxaesthetic (accessed June 6, 2013).

[37] Greg Borenstein, "What It's Like to Be a 21st Century Thing," The Creators Project, http://thecreatorsproject.com/blog/in-response-to-bruce-sterlings-essay-on-the-new-aesthetic#4 (accessed 6 June, 2013).

[38] Ibid.

[39] Bruce Sterling, "An Essay on the New Aesthetic," 2 April 2012, Wired Blog, www.wired.com/beyond_the_beyond/2012/04/an-essay-on-the-new-aesthetic (accesssed April 10, 2013). Sterling lists the various works assembled in this wunderkammer: "Satellite views. Parametric architecture. Surveillance cameras. Digital image processing. Data-mashed video frames. Glitches and corruption artifacts. Voxelated 3D pixels in real-world geometries. Dazzle camou. Augments. Render ghosts. And, last and least, nostalgic retro 8bit graphics from the 1980s."

In addition, Sterling addresses the new aesthetic's implicit nostalgia with old dreams about artificial intelligence and glorious Turing machines debunking the anthropomorphisation of "thinking machines" as part of the "mental chains of the old aesthetic."[40] Computers, Sterling underlines, lack perception, intelligence, taste and ethics; they are built and programmed by humans who should not project their own qualities into their products.

Sterling's criticism has prompted many comments, some of them even harsher towards the new aesthetic than Sterling's essay.[41] Among the responses in favour of the new aesthetic, not every contribution really supports the cause. If, for example, Borenstein lists Adam Harvey's *CV Dazzle*—this project aims to protect humans against face detection algorithms through wearing a set of hair, makeup, and fashion designs that disorient the algorithms of computer vision (CV)—as the quintessential new aesthetic project, he actually draws attention to humans' relationship to objects rather than to objecthood itself.[42] This is exactly what Bogost takes up in his article "The New Aesthetic Needs to Get Weirder": "The New Aesthetic stops short of becoming an object-oriented aesthetics partly by limiting itself to computational media, and partly by absconding with the lessons of object-aesthetics into the realm of human concern."[43] To Bogost, the concern of a new aesthetic should not be the impact objects have on *us* but "paying attention to the secret lives of things": "we

---

[40] Sterling, "An Essay on the New Aesthetic," n.pag.

[41] See comments assembled in The Creators Project Staff, "In Response To Bruce Sterling's 'Essay On The New Aesthetic'," 6 April 2012, The Creators Project, http://thecreatorsproject.com/blog/in-response-to-bruce-sterlings-essay-on-the-new-aesthetic (accessed June 6, 2013).

[42] Borenstein, "What It's Like," n.pag. For *CV Dazzle* see Adam Harvey, "CV Dazzle: Camouflage from Face Detection," April 2010, http://ahprojects.com/projects/cv-dazzle (accessed June 6, 2013).

[43] Bogost, "The New Aesthetic," n.pag. Bogost critically refers to Borenstein's notion that new aestheticians "want to know what CCTV [Closed Circuit Television, i.e., surveillance cameras] means for social networks, what book scanning means for iOS apps, and what face detection means for fashion." Borenstein, "What It's Like," n.pag.

have to resist drawing the conclusion that they exist for our benefit—even if we ourselves created them."[44] How can we think objects without thinking of them in relation to us?

An ironic example of the secret lives of things may be *The Secret Lives of Numbers* (2002) by Golan Levin, which presents a graph of every number from zero to one million, showing the popularity of each number according to statistics gathered from a Google search. The work undertakes an anthropomorphisation of numbers and suggests that we see the ranking of numbers not according to their natural ordering system but rather their "fame." *The Secret Lives of Numbers* is an ironic example of what Bogost is looking for, since it does not really reveal the secret life of *things* but the secret or rather unconscious perspectives humans have on things or numbers respectively. The secret lives of numbers are determined by human culture, i.e., the paradigm of ranking, which Levin addresses by ranking numbers not according to their numerical quality but according to the quantifiable frequency of their appearance. *Klout Score*, which was invented in 2008 and represents a person's online influence as a number between 1 and 100, reveals post festum how political Levin's work is.[45]

To Bogost, however, a really new aesthetics does not concern itself "with the way we humans see our world differently when we begin to see it through and with computer media that themselves 'see' the world in various ways." A really new aesthetics rather "ask[s] how computers and bonobos and toaster pastries and Boeing 787 Dreamliners develop their *own* aesthetics."[46] Such alien aesthetics, as Bogost coins his version of the new aesthetic, is not centred on the human perception of objects

[44] Bogost, "The New Aesthetic," n.pag.

[45] Another work detecting the secret life of non-human objects in relation to human perception is Christian Nold's *Bio Mapping*, which started in 2004. People go for a walk wearing a biomapping device that measures their galvanic skin response as an indicator of emotional arousal in conjunction with their geographical location. The resulting maps visualise where people feel stressed and excited and hence present reality depending on how it is perceived. See Christian Nold, "Bio Mapping / Emotion Mapping." http://biomapping.net (accessed June 6, 2013).

[46] Bogost, "The New Aesthetic," n.pag., original emphasis.

but rather the other way around. Bogost illustrates his idea referring to *Tableau Machine* (2007) by Adam Smith, Mario Romero, Zachary Pousman, and Michael Mateas, an artwork that interprets, through the use of overhead video, activities in its environment and expresses, based on a set of design grammars, its interpretation of these activities by displaying a sequence of abstract images. This "non-anthropomorphic system" illustrates distinctions with distinct outputs which are absolutely meaningless to any human observer. *Tableau Machine* is, as the authors state, an "alien artist," an instance of "alien presence"—*alien* because it does not understand human behaviour while humans do not understand the system's representation of their behaviour.[47]

Bogost's reading of *Tableau Machine* is not the only possible one. He himself implicitly suggests a different, opposite reading, stating that "Romero and his collaborators hoped to disrupt the assumption that ubiquitous computing is good for task support."[48] Disrupting the paradigm of useful data processing does not so much point to the secret life of an object—or the experience of a home in the case at hand—but to a specific relationship humans entertain with computing and data. In this light, the foundation of alien aesthetics is not an "alien artist" or "alien presence" but the artistic act of alienation responding to the phenomenon—and imposition—of ubiquitous computing.

Ubiquitous or pervasive computing is a model of information processing beyond the desktop by bringing it out into the

---

[47] Adam Smith, Mario Romero, Zachary Pousman, and Michael Mateas, "Tableau Machine: A Creative Alien Presence," presentation at the Association for the Advancement of Artificial Intelligence, 2008, www.cc.gatech. edu/-mromero/smith_romero_pousman_mateas_2008.pdf (accessed June 6, 2013). Such abstract commentary on activity in a room where a machine is installed has been programmed before. An example the authors of *Tableau Machine* mention is AARON, a program developed since the 1970s that creates abstract drawings by the British painter and information designer Harold Cohen. Another example is *Untitled 5* (2004) by Camille Utterback, which uses body-tracking software to change an abstract wall projection in response to the user's activities in the exhibition space.

[48] Bogost, "The New Aesthetic," n.pag.

environmental background of everyday objects and activities. It provides tacit information in the environmental background, which is why Mark Weiser and John Seely Brown entitle their 1996 essay about ubiquitous computing "Designing Calm Technology."[49] Examples of such calm technology are strings mounted into the ceiling of an office space whirling with diverse degrees proportionally to the amount of traffic on the internet, or a fountain translating the currency rates of Yen, Euro and Dollar in real-time into the water-jet of the fountain.[50] Although ubiquitous computing exposes humans to information less obtrusively, it does so more pervasively. Information becomes omnipresent, invisible to perceptual consciousness but affective at the level of microsensation, for it will move from the background to centre stage the moment one turns attention to the object. This is an ethical issue: a fountain conveying information on currency rates has lost its innocence to the laws of information society.

As long as the output of ubiquitous computing allows interpretation and task support, as Bogost puts it, it may be an alien way of presenting data but does not represent alien aesthetics or phenomenology, to use Bogost's terms. The moment it becomes abstract and unintelligible, as in the case of the *Tableau Machine*, calm technology turns cool according to Alan Liu who, in his 2004 study *Laws of Cool: Knowledge Work and the Culture of Information*, defines cool as "a 'way of looking' at the world of information that exceeds the utilitarian sense of either presenting or receiving information."[51] Liu bestows this specific "way of looking" with ethical implica-

---

[49] Mark Weiser and John Seely Brown, "Designing Calm Technology," *Power-Grid Journal* (1996), 1:1, www.ubiq.com/hypertext/weiser/calmtech/calmtech.htm (accessed June 6, 2013).

[50] The first example is given by Weiser and Brown; it refers to Natalie Jeremijenko's 1995 work *Live Wire*, which is placed in the office environment of the Xerox Palo Alto Research Center Computer Science Lab. For the second example, see Koert van Mensvoort, "Datafountain: Money Translates to Water" www.koert.com/work/datafountain (accessed June 6, 2013).

[51] Alan Liu, *The Laws of Cool: Knowledge Work and the Culture of Information* (Chicago: University of Chicago Press, 2004), 184.

tions: as "an ethos of information that is against information, the uselessness of useful information, the use of information to abuse information." Cool is the awareness of the information interface rather than of the information itself; it is the prevalence of the form by which content is presented over the content itself; the "eroticism of *technique*"; it is the replacement of the utilitarian approach to reality by a hedonistic one.[52] *Tableau Machine* is an example of such "abusive" use of information; just as other works of mapping art such as Camille Utterback's *Untitled 5* (2004) and Mark Napier's *Black & White* (2002) are.[53] Rather than presenting an object alien to the human perceiver, such works represent the alienation of information from human beings through human programming. They are not about the secret life of objects but about the secret revolt of humans against the imposition of the information age. Like photography, they represent not reality but a certain relationship to reality. The only way to document reality bypassing the human relationship to it is the automatic documentation of human action.

---

[52] Liu, *The Laws of Cool*, 185-86, 183, 236, original emphasis.

[53] The online work *Black & White* reads the os and 1s on the CNN server and visually translates them into black-and-white patterns moving horizontally and vertically over the screen. Thus, Napier sensualises the data retrieved into an abstract visual object, a "non-cognitive 'visualization'" that gives up the significance of the source data, to borrow from Richard Wright's article on data visualisation. See Richard Wright, "Data Visualization" in *Software Studies: A Lexicon*, ed. Matthew Fuller (Cambridge: MIT Press, 2008), 84. For a detailed discussion of *Black & White* as well as other examples of non-cognitive (and cognitive) mapping art, see Simanowski, *Digital Art and Meaning*, 158-86. For my discussion of other artworks—such as the installations *Text Rain* (1999) by Camille Utterback and Romy Achituv and *Bit.Fall* (2006) by Julius Popp—in the context of ubiquitous computing and the ethos of cool, see Roberto Simanowski, "Text as Event: Calm Technology and Invisible Information as Subject of Digital Arts" in *Throughout: Art and Culture Emerging with Ubiquitous Computing*, ed. Ulrik Ekman (Cambridge: MIT Press 2012), 191-204.

4. Trust in Numbers, or, The Truth of Numerical Narratives

Section 3 ended with the notion that correlationism in photography can only be overcome by photographs taken automatically. A specific way of generating such photographs is data tracking, as promoted in the *Quantified Self* community that is gathering in about 40 groups worldwide, tracking data in order to gain *self knowledge through numbers*—as the slogan at quantifiedself.com reads. A famous example of such revealing of the secret lives of data is Nicholas Felton's *Annual Reports*, which presents statistical information about his mundane life since 2005: how often he used the subway, taxi, bus, airplane, a ferry or a chairlift; how often he visited a museum or attended a birthday party; how many hours he was in the gym; how many books and book pages he read; and how many beers he drank from which countries. Which books he read we do not learn, nor what effect they had on him. A more prevalent and influential, but also more complex example of overcoming correlationism in relation to one's own actions is Facebook's *Timeline*, the "diary" or, rather, log book of the twenty-first century that reports and stores everything one does online automatically and in real-time regardless of one's own perspective. Other examples of how culture is being redesigned on the grounds of statistics are the countings of views, likes, shares, and comments online.[54]

Such data tracking is "photography" to the extent that there is a physical correspondence between the signifier and the signified. The recorded data of shared links, visited videos, and music listened to on the internet are as indexical as photography for they directly result from the action they represent. From a media ontological perspective, *Timeline* can

[54] For an early report on the quantified self movement, see Jamin Brophy-Warren, "The New Examined Life: Why More People Are Spilling the Statistics of Their Lives on the Web," *Wall Street Journal*, 6 December 2008, http://online.wsj.com/article/SB122852285532784401.html (accessed June 6, 2013). For an extended discussion of Felton's *Annual Reports* and Facebook's *Timeline* as numerical and "photographic" data tracking, see Roberto Simanowski, "The Compelling Charm of Numbers: Writing For and Thru the Network of Data" in *Remediating the Social*, ed. Simon Biggs (Edinburgh: ELMCIP, 2012), 20-27.

be considered textual photography (*Textfotografie*), to adapt the term "linguistic photography" (*Sprachfotografie*) coined by German art critic and media theorist Boris Groys to describe the fact that the computer does not store the *meaning* of a text but every single word. The main unit of the text is no longer the sentence but the word, Groys concludes, and he adds that, like in photography, the central element is no longer the "visual expression" (*der malerische Ausdruck*) but the object.[55] One can even go further and suggest that the single letter is the actual object of linguistic photography; because not a single one is lost when *Timeline* stores who shared what with whom and when with what comment. This is even true for one's texts, status updates, and comments on Facebook, which are equally documented, word by word, letter by letter. There is no retrospective entry into the diary giving the gist of what one has done or uttered, because now the diary is itself what it reports: the event *is* the report. What now comes true is what Bogost incorrectly claimed for Winogrand's photographs as examples of unmediated access to the object itself.

To be sure, the results of photographic data tracking can be a source of interpretation again, with the implications of distortion or appropriation by the specific perspective of the perceiver. However, the effect of correlationism comes after the recording; the human perception is preceded by algorithmic perception. As long as Felton lists how many books he read in a year—even if he had documented which books they were—he lets data speak for itself. The corruption of this data starts when he tries to answer the question what the books mean to him, when he starts reflecting and interpreting his relationship to the entities and actions of his life.

At the beginning of this essay, I announced my thesis that there are developments in aesthetic theory and artistic practices that try to overcome correlationism by either evading interpretation or by turning to statistics. While *Tableau Machine* and the other examples of "cool resistance" to information

---

[55] Boris Groys, "Der Autor im Netz" in *Kursbuch Internet: Anschlüsse an Wirtschaft und Politik, Wissenschaft und Kultur*, ed. Stefan Bollmann and Christiane Heibach (Mannheim: Bollmann, 1996), 385.

represent the earlier, the data tracking projects by Felton and others as well as Facebook's "photographic" *Timeline* exemplify the latter. These algorithmic analyses of human actions and relationships the data tracking represents, this replacement of the diffuse self- and world-perception through precise and incorruptible numbers is a response to our nihilistic situation and epistemological aestheticisation that is quite different from the turn to materiality and pure presence. It is the response to the end of grand—and small—narratives by *numerical narratives*, as Felton names them.[56] It contributes to the *Pursuit of Objectivity in Science and Public Life* as Theodor M. Porter subtitles his 1995 study *Trust in Numbers*.[57] The trust in numbers as well as the trust in algorithmic "dataveillance" is the return of truth avoiding the nihilistic vocation of hermeneutics by computing. It not only has the "appearance of being fair and impersonal."[58] It also takes the human out of the equation—as much as this is possible.[59] Avoiding the human factor in documenting human behaviour, this kind of data tracking and textual photography thus embodies what speculative realism and object-oriented ontology try to accomplish: a kind of anthrodecentric anthropocentrism that reverses the "negative privilege" manifest in correlationism by a "de-privileging promotion," reassuring the knower that the known really exists. It allows humans to reclaim control by letting the objects of knowledge speak for themselves or—in the case of pure presence—by altogether avoiding

---

[56] Nicholas Felton, "Numerical Narratives," lecture at UCLA Department of Design Media Arts, 15 November 2011, http://video.dma.ucla.edu/video/nicholas-felton-numerical-narratives/387 (accessed June 6, 2013).

[57] Theodor M. Porter, *Trust in Numbers: The Pursuit of Objectivity in Science and Public Life* (Princeton: Princeton University Press, 1995).

[58] Porter, *Trust in Numbers*, 8.

[59] To be sure, there is human authorship also in data analysis and information graphics. Felton is an excellent example here; he avoids any sexual and monetary reporting because he finds it "distasteful." Nicholas Felton, "FAQ," Feltron, http://feltron.com/faq.html (accessed June 6, 2013). In addition to the aggregation of data, the specific way of their visualisation and textual annotation demands human decisions and follows cultural rules.

the "experience of crisis" Menke localises in the undertaking of interpretation.[60] It is a response to the postmodern condition of the contingency and relativity of knowledge and cognition that misses both the "nihilistic vocation of hermeneutics" Vattimo advocates in *Beyond Interpretation* and the "emancipatory 'confusion' of dialects" he welcomes in *The Transparent Society*.[61]

---

[60] Menke, *The Sovereignty of Art*, 215.

[61] Vattimo, *Beyond Interpretation*, 39; Vattimo, *The Transparent Society*, 10.

Art and Guerrilla Metaphysics

Graham Harman and Aesthetics as First Philosophy[1]

Francis Halsall

National College of Art and Design, Dublin

The room was suddenly rich and the great bay-window was
Spawning snow and pink roses against it
Soundlessly collateral and incompatible:
World is suddener than we fancy it.

World is crazier and more of it than we think,
Incorrigibly plural. I peel and portion
A tangerine and spit the pips and feel
The drunkenness of things being various.

And the fire flames with a bubbling sound for world
Is more spiteful and gay than one supposes -
On the tongue on the eyes on the ears in the palms of one's hands -
There is more than glass between the snow and the huge roses.

—Louis MacNeice, "Snow"[2]

Introduction

MACNEICE'S POEM SHOWS HOW beautiful poetry, like beautiful philosophy, tells us things about the world and our place in it that we might have otherwise overlooked. As Simon Critchley says in response to Wallace Stevens's poetry:

[1] I am very grateful for the careful, patient and thoughtful comments made by the reviewers (Philipp Schweighauser, Andreas Hägler, Ridvan Askin) on earlier versions of this paper.

[2] Louis MacNeice, "Snow," in *Collected Poems* (London: Faber and Faber, 2002), 30.

At its best, poetry offers an experience of the world as meditation, the mind slowing in front of things, the mind pushing back against the pressure of reality through the minimal transfigurations of the imagination ... Poetry increases our feeling for reality by allowing us to see it, to focus on that which we normally pass over in our everyday activity: the world.[3]

Critchley's observation forms the main theme of this essay which is about poetry more generally conceived—which I identify as the focus of aesthetic reflection and judgment—and Graham Harman's version of speculative realism; what he calls object-oriented philosophy.[4] My argument is that as well as employing the aesthetic concept of "allure" Harman's philosophical position in general is underwritten by a tacit aesthetics. That is, aesthetic reflection and judgment are employed in metaphysical speculation into what a mind-independent reality might be like. This is a distinct strategy within speculative realism which I will identify with an aesthetic turn in contrast to the mathematical/objectivist strategies exemplified by Meillassoux and Brassier. From this follows the claim that art practice can also be a form of philosophical speculation; that is, art can be a form of what Harman calls guerrilla metaphysics.[5]

To develop this argument I unpack Harman's claim that aesthetics is first philosophy. In arguing this Harman explicitly draws on a tradition (starting with Aristotle) where first philosophy is used to denote ontology, taken to mean the "description of the basic structural features shared by all

---

[3] Simon Critchley, *Things Merely Are: Philosophy in the Poetry of Wallace Stevens* (London: Routledge, 2005), 88-89.

[4] "My first use of the term 'object-oriented philosophy' was in the late 1990's, before there was any such thing as Speculative Realism, and long before I had heard of Brassier, Grant or Meillassoux. The wider umbrella term 'Object-Oriented Ontology' (OOO) was coined by Levi Bryant in 2009." Graham Harman, "The Current State of Speculative Realism," *Speculations* (2013), 4, 26.

[5] Graham Harman, *Guerrilla Metaphysics: Phenomenology and the Carpentry of Things* (Chicago: Open Court, 2005).

objects,"[6] and thus the attempt to describe reality in general. My conclusion goes beyond Harman's use of allure as a theory of causal relations in claiming that aesthetic and philosophical reflections are congruent. There are three dimensions to this conclusion.

First, I argue that the phenomenological strategy of epoché, in which the world as it is lived is bracketed in order to focus on its givenness to consciousness, is an act of aesthetic reflection as well as a philosophical one. I argue that Harman begins from this phenomenological starting point but, similar to his inversion of Heideggerian hermeneutics, focuses on what phenomenology has bracketed, namely the world beyond its conscious manifestation. Hence there is, in the epoché (and the focus on what it excludes), an aesthetic foundation to his whole project.

Second, because in the epoché aesthetic reflection coincides with philosophical reflection art (as a socially and historically privileged site of aesthetic reflection) can be philosophically significant. In short, works of art can provide a means to both aesthetic and philosophical reflection. Or, experiencing art through aesthetic reflection can be a way into certain forms of philosophical reflection on the world and its objects. The key point is that certain forms of artistic and philosophical practice are comparable in so far as both are open to aesthetic judgement.

Hence, third, a flip-side to the claim that art can be philosophical is that certain forms of philosophy are like art. This is to say that certain styles of philosophical speculation are also creative forms. The content of those forms is: (i) not provable empirically because they allude to a world that withdraws from consciousness; these forms point towards something beyond experience and hence outside empirical verification. And (ii), this content is also not verifiable a priori because this would lead back to some form of transcendental idealism.

Instead, such speculations are proposed in the spirit of our aesthetic judgments; that is, as looking for approval

---

[6] Graham Harman, "Vicarious Causation," *Collapse* (2007), 2, 204.

or consent by appearing plausible and through appeal to a common sense (the Kantian sensus communis), rather than resting on empirical or conceptual proofs.

The Mathematical/Aesthetic Axis of Speculation

The implications of my argument are that the well-documented differences between positions associated with speculative realism might be reconceived along a slightly different axis: the mathematical/aesthetic one, reflecting both the commitments of the main players and an ancient philosophical rift originating in Plato.

The dual challenge faced by both sides of the mathematical/ aesthetic axis of speculative realism is that we view the world, not from a god's eye view, but from within subjectivity. So: (i) there is a paradox that thought must begin from consciousness (this is, by necessity, unavoidable for thought) whilst seeking to go beyond its horizon into that which exists independently of thinking; (ii) we must attempt to explain how consciousness can emerge from the pre- or unconscious world.

In attempting to treat a world independent of minds in a philosophically serious manner speculative realists position themselves in opposition to the dominant tendencies within contemporary philosophy in general and the continental tradition in particular. These tendencies are the transcendental aspects of the Kantian tradition, of idealism, and of phenomenology, all of which argue that the two starting points for philosophy in general and for ontology in particular are firstly consciousness, and secondly the relationship of that consciousness to the world. These are the traditions of what Harman calls the "Philosophy of Human Access"[7] and what Quentin Meillassoux names correlationism and which rest on the apparently tautological statement that we cannot think of anything without thinking about it; or, in Harman's words: "If we try to think of a world outside human thought, then we

---

[7] Graham Harman, *Prince of Networks: Bruno Latour and Metaphysics* (Melbourne: Re.press, 2009), 102-03.

are *thinking* it, and hence it is no longer outside thought. Any attempt to escape this circle is doomed to contradiction."[8]

There are different (often conflicting) strategies for attempting this move beyond correlationist thinking. However, there is some agreement that these strategies can be generally characterised by two distinct positions. On the one hand there is the position of Quentin Meillassoux and Ray Brassier. This is grounded in objectivism or mathematism and attempts to rehabilitate the access of thought to the absolute. As Brassier says:

> [Meillassoux] hopes to demonstrate mathematical science's direct purchase on things-in-themselves ... The claim is that mathematical thought enjoys direct access to noumena precisely insofar as the latter possess certain mathematically intuitable characteristics, to which all rational knowledge must conform.[9]

In short, Meillassoux argues that mathematics offers a way of thinking de-subjectivated (and non-correlated) nature on the basis of its formal, logical operations. Brassier's position is similar; that is, he defends a scientism which claims that the slow but steady work of the sciences will get us ever closer to the absolute even if it can never, ultimately, reach its goal. This is the mathematical side of the axis.

On the other hand, there is the position of Harman and others for which Meillassoux has coined the term "subjectalism" intended to capture a kind of anti-materialism that is nevertheless speculative. Of Harman Meillassoux says that he

> hypostasizes our subjective relation to things by projecting it into the things themselves. [This is a] very original and paradoxical subjectalism, since he hypostasizes the relation we have with things that, according to

---

[8] Graham Harman, *The Quadruple Object* (Winchester: Zero Books, 2011), 63, original emphasis.

[9] Ray Brassier, *Nihil Unbound: Enlightenment and Extinction* (Basingstoke: Palgrave Macmillan, 2007), 69.

him, withdraw continually from the contact we can make with them. But the implicit form of this withdrawal is given by *our relation* to things.[10]

This can be re-cast as the aesthetic side of the axis for the reasons given below.

Harman's Weird Realism

Amongst artists, critics and curators Graham Harman has become the most well-known member of the speculative realists. His writing has appeared in magazines like *Artforum*, artists' catalogues, and in the context of major exhibitions such as Documenta 13.[11]

Harman makes several references to aesthetics in relation to his own philosophical work. These include the claims that "aesthetics may be a branch of metaphysics," and "aesthetics becomes first philosophy."[12] He has also addressed the relationship between philosophy and art practices: "Yet what if the counter-project [of philosophy as a rigorous science] of the next four centuries were to turn philosophy into an art? We would have 'Philosophy as Vigorous Art' rather than Husserl's 'Philosophy as Rigorous Science'."[13] By introducing "allure" as a metaphysical term Harman argues that "aesthetics is first philosophy, because the key problem of metaphysics

[10] Quentin Meillasoux, "Iteration, Reiteration, Repetition: A Speculative Analysis of the Meaningless Sign," trans. Robin Mackay, http://oursecretblog.com/txt/QMpaperApr12.pdf (accessed July 31, 2012), 7, original emphasis.

[11] Graham Harman, "The Best Books of 2011," *Artforum* (Dec. 2011); Graham Harman, *The Third Table/Der dritte Tisch*, dOCUMENTA (13): 100 Notizen—100 Gedanken Series (Ostfildern: Hatje Cantz, 2012); Graham Harman, "Rogue Planets" in *Woran glauben die Motten, wenn sie zu den Lichtern streben* by Ralo Mayer (Nuremberg: Verlag für moderne Kunst, 2011), E30-E40; Graham Harman, "It is Warm Out There/Il fait chaud là-bas" in *Intimately Unrelated/Intimement sans rapport* by Isabel Nolan (Sligo and Saint Étienne: The Model/Musée d'art moderne de Saint-Étienne Métropole, 2012), 58-95.

[12] Harman, "Vicarious Causation," 221.

[13] Harman, *The Third Table*, 15.

has turned out to be as follows: how do individual substances interact in their proximity to one another."[14] Here allure is used to explain "not just a theory of art, but a theory of causal relations in general."[15]

As with other speculative realists the central focus of Harman's realism is a mind-independent reality that exists beyond the correlation of consciousness and world. According to Harman, this world is populated by objects which have relations with one another. Consequently, the philosopher should not restrict themselves to talking about the relationship of consciousness to world and how we access reality. Instead, Harman argues, philosophers should direct their attention toward "all nonhuman reality."[16]

This is obviously a seductive position for many artists because it gives a theoretical support to an attractive proposition: that works of art have an autonomous identity. This proposition supports two further beliefs that an artist might have: that art objects and their meanings will elude their audience; and that an artist is not fully responsible for the things they produce.

In certain philosophical circles this has also proved tantalizing because it promises a way out of those philosophical trajectories (in both the continental and analytic traditions) that lead away from the world and toward forms of transcendental idealism that bracket consideration of any aspect of reality which is not available for human consideration.

Harman claims that he "rejects any privilege of human access to the world, and puts the affairs of human consciousness on exactly the same footing as the duel between canaries, microbes, earthquakes, atoms, and tar."[17] However, as he is at pains to point out, this is not merely a naive realism[18] that

---

[14] Graham Harman, "Aesthetics as First Philosophy: Levinas and the Non-Human," *Naked Punch* (2012), 9, 30.

[15] Ibid.

[16] Harman, *Guerrilla Metaphysics*, 18.

[17] Harman, "Vicarious Causation," 189.

[18] "Adjectives can also play a distracting/masking role, as I've said on this

generally accepts the existence of reality as it is given (and is made available to empirical observation, scientific naturalism or physical materialism) without further philosophical reflection. Speculative realism speculates on the metaphysical grounds of a mind independent reality. Harman actually claims that his realism is a *weird realism*: "Philosophy must be realist because its mandate is to unlock the structure of the world itself; it must be weird because reality is weird."[19] He is pursuing "a model of reality as something far *weirder* than realists had ever guessed."[20] Here "weird" is a term appropriated from H.P. Lovecraft who explains it thus:

> The true weird tale has something more than secret murder, bloody bones, or a sheeted form clanking chains according to rule. A certain atmosphere of breathless and unexplainable dread of outer, unknown forces must be present; and there must be a hint, expressed with a seriousness and portentousness becoming its subject, of that most terrible conception of the human brain—a malign and particular suspension or defeat of those fixed laws of Nature which are our only safeguard against the assaults of chaos and the daemons of unplumbed space.[21]

In Harman's appropriation of Lovecraft's weirdness[22] we can already see evidence of an aesthetic judgment at play.

---

blog before. Accusing someone of *naive* realism isn't just invective. It's also a way of masking the true charge: realism. The true charge is that the person is a realist. But since the accuser has no good argument against realism, they create a distraction by denouncing *naive* realism, leaving us to assume vaguely that the person isn't so extreme as to hate all realism, but only the 'naïve' kind, whatever that might be in opposition to the less naive kinds." Graham Harman, "On the Abuse of Adjectives, Scare Quotes, etc.," Object-Oriented Philosophy, http://doctorzamalek2.wordpress.com/ (accessed May 14, 2012).

[19] Graham Harman, "On the Horror of Phenomenology: Lovecraft and Husserl," *Collapse* (2008), 4, 334.

[20] Graham Harman, "The Well-Wrought Broken Hammer: Object-Oriented Literary Criticism," *New Literary History* (2012), 43:2, 184, original emphasis.

[21] H.P. Lovecraft, *Supernatural Horror in Literature and other Literary Essays* (Rockville: Wildside Press, 2011), 19.

[22] See also Graham Harman, *Weird Realism: Lovecraft and Philosophy* (Winchester: Zero Books, 2012).

For Harman, his *style* of philosophy can be judged as having more in common with the weird and wild speculations of the pulp-fiction texts of horror and science fiction than with the accepted philosophical traditions. This is a significant point to which I will return later as it acknowledges an equivalence between certain modes of thinking and aesthetic activities such as fiction writing. For now, I stress that Harman makes Lovecraftian weirdness a pervasive and central aspect of all of reality, from science fiction to mathematics to speculative physics:

> Even a cursory glance at the physics literature reveals a discipline be-witched by strange attractors, degenerate topologies, black holes filled with alternate worlds, holograms generating an illusory third dimension, and matter composed of vibrant ten-dimensional strings. Mathematics, unconstrained by empirical data, has long been still bolder in its gambles. Nor can it be said that science fiction is a marginal feature of literature itself. Long before the mighty crabs and squids of Lovecraft and the tribunals of Kafka, we had Shakespeare's witches and ghosts, Mt. Purgatory in the Pacific, the Cyclops in the Mediterranean, and the Sphinx tormenting the north of Greece.[23]

Inverting Heidegger

Harman's starting point for his weird realism is an audacious reading and *inversion* of Heidegger. This strategy of inversion, in which he reads Heidegger against the grain of his thinking and reception, appears again in the use of the phenomenological epoché which is also used in a manner contrary to its mainstream application.

In chapter 1 of *Tool Being* Harman revisits the Heideggerian pair of the ready-to-hand (*zuhanden*) and the present-at-hand (*vorhanden*).[24] Harman uses the well-known example of the

---

[23] Harman, "On the Horror of Phenomenology," 334.

[24] Graham Harman, *Tool Being: Heidegger and the Metaphysics of Objects* (Chicago: Open Court, 2002), 13-100.

hammer from *Being and Time*.[25] On the one hand, there is the ready-to-hand hammer which is used according to our concern for it as a piece of equipment to hammer in nails; that is, as a tool enmeshed within a "global system" of human uses and human meanings. On the other hand, there is the present-at-hand entity of the broken hammer as an inert and meaningless thing that has become suddenly present to us in its phenomenal particularity.[26] But, Harman argues, there is surplus to both the readiness-to-hand of the tool and the presentness-at-hand of the broken hammer. This surplus or excess is what Harman calls the "tool-being" of the hammer itself as object that is independent of the system of relations within which it is positioned. This object withdraws. It withdraws from the network of human uses in which it is ready-to-hand, *and* it also withdraws from the condition of presence by which it appears as present-at-hand.

> In other words, the opposition is not really between tools on one side and broken tools on the other, but between the withdrawn tool-being of things on one side and both broken and non-broken tools on the other. After all, the functioning pragmatic tool is present for human praxis just as the broken tool is present for human consciousness. And neither of these will suffice, because what we are looking for is the thing insofar as it exists, not insofar as it is present to either theory or praxis.[27]

What Harman proposes, therefore, is a reading of Heidegger which draws directly on his critique of the philosophy of presence yet which attends to its other side, or that which it ignores. Hence, objects become entitled to withdraw into a shadowy, occult, weird realm in which they are autonomous in three ways: (i) autonomous in respect to systems of human uses and meaning; (ii) autonomous from presence as

---

[25] Martin Heidegger, *Being and Time*, trans. J. Macquarrie and E. Robinson (New York: Harper and Row, 1962), 98 ff.

[26] And, "we should emphasize that [Heidegger's] 'presence at hand' has multiple meanings, and that all of these meanings ultimately refer to relationality." Harman, *The Quadruple Object*, 52.

[27] Harman, *The Quadruple Object*, 54.

phenomena; (iii) and also, *crucially*, autonomous from one another.

But, importantly, this does not wall off a noumenal world, in-itself, beyond consciousness about which nothing can be thought, or said or done. Instead, a *speculative* realism is proposed in which there is an attempt to speculate about objects as they are, independent of human observations. Features of this object-oriented philosophy include:

(i) A definition of the object as radically irreducible. This definition encompasses simple, complex, composite, actual and imaginary entities. Objects in this sense are not reducible to the instances of their appearance, their qualities, relations, or moments. In this, Harman's philosophy entails a substance ontology.

(ii) The claim that "intentionality is not a special human property at all, but an ontological feature of objects in general."[28] This means that objects have intentional relations to one another in which neither object is completed, defined or exhausted by that relationship alone. The example from *Tool-Being* is of a washing machine sitting on a frozen lake. These two objects are in a relationship with one another. While the machine pushes down on the ice, the ice resists the weight of the machine. Yet "the important factor is that the heavy object, while resting on the ice as a reliable support, [does] not exhaust the reality of that ice," and the washing machine "reacts to some features of the lake rather than others—cutting its rich actuality down to size, reducing that relatively minimal scope of lake-reality that is of significance to it."[29] Harman calls this an intentional relationship.

(iii) The claim that objects relate to one another not directly, but vicariously; that is, some aspect (the substantial inner core) of the object withdraws from the relation. Objects interact vicariously because they do so only through some aspect of the object entering into the relationship. At the heart of every object is a conflict between its *real* identity

---

[28] Harman, "Vicarious Causation," 205.

[29] Harman, *Tool Being*, 223.

(its withdrawn and inaccessible nature) and its *sensual* appearance (the aspect of, or mode by which the object appears to other objects). Harman refers to this conflict in terms of allure. Allure explains the moments when the relationship between the different identities of a thing becomes apparent: "Allure is a special and intermittent experience in which the intimate bond between a thing's unity and its plurality of notes somehow partially disintegrates"[30] as "allure alludes to entities as they are, quite apart from any relations with or effects upon the other entities in the world. This deeply *non-relational* conception of the reality of things is the heart of object-oriented philosophy."[31]

Allure, then, is how Harman introduces aesthetics into his metaphysical program. Aesthetic reflection attends to the alluring elements of an object which can only, qua sensual object, be sensually experienced. Aesthetic reflection thus reveals how its objects are, in part, abstracted from a system of things and meanings:

> The eidetic features [or essence] of any object can never be made present even through the intellect, but can only be approached indirectly by way of allusion, whether in the arts or in the sciences. Copper wires, bicycles, wolves and triangles all have real qualities, but these genuine traits will never be exhausted by the feeble sketches of them delivered to our hearts and minds. A proton or volcano must have a variety of distinct properties, but these remain just as withdrawn from us as the proton and volcano themselves.[32]

Thus, aesthetic reflection takes advantage of aesthetic experience and offers the promise of glimpses of reality *beyond* experience. So, aesthetic reflection provides a means, different to that of the formal abstractions of mathematics and logic, of thinking beyond the correlation. And artistic practices might constitute a guerrilla metaphysics in that they offer a

---

[30] Harman, *Guerrilla Metaphysics*, 143.

[31] Harman, "The Well-Wrought Broken Hammer," 187.

[32] Harman, *The Quadruple Object*, 28.

way into thinking non-conceptually, beyond the correlation of consciousness and world.

Thinking beyond the Correlation

The now standard speculative realist position begins from a critique of phenomenology in that it exemplifies the problems inherent to correlationism and castigates it for philosophically prioritising questions of human access to reality over and above that reality itself. However, if Harman is right that "all human relations to objects strip them of their inner depth, revealing only some of their qualities to view,"[33] then we face the problem of how to think beyond the context of the system of human relations with the world into which we find ourselves flung.

Harman claims that "we never occupy a formless sensory medium, but only a landscape of determinate things, even if these things seduce us with a full arsenal of what seem like kaleidoscopic surface effects."[34] But not only do things in the world seduce us; they are meaningful to us as well. In other words, we are already enmeshed in a system of objects *and* structures of meaning. The problem with this lies in how one might disentangle such claims to meaning from the path toward transcendental idealism to which they seem to necessarily lead. This problem, Ray Brassier argues, is the fundamental problem of philosophy:

> That the articulation of thought and being is necessarily conceptual follows from the Critical injunction which rules out any recourse to the doctrine of a pre-established harmony between reality and ideality. Thought is not guaranteed access to being; being is not inherently thinkable. There is no cognitive ingress to the real save through the concept. Yet the real itself is not to be confused with the concepts

---

[33] Graham Harman, *Towards Speculative Realism: Essays and Lectures* (Winchester: Zero Books, 2010), 124.

[34] Harman, *Guerrilla Metaphysics*, 180.

through which we know it. The fundamental problem of philosophy is to understand how to reconcile these two claims.[35]

What Brassier points to here is the difficulty, if not impossibility, of ever absenting ourselves from familiar systems of human meanings and relations. This becomes unthinkable because such absenteeism would seem to require leaving consciousness behind. If, as Harman says, "the default state of reality is that I am protected by firewalls from the objects lying outside me"[36] then the implication would seem to be that we can only ever peer over those firewalls by which we are surrounded to those cold and distant horizons beyond but cannot walk amongst these landscapes and explore their contours.

Hence, whilst gesturing toward reality, Harman's object-oriented philosophy problematically proposes that the world withdraws into a shadowy and weird realm beyond human thinking. This seems to deny philosophical access to a domain of reality where objects reside. Harman's argument thus has the potential to undermine philosophical attempts to provide knowledge of a mind-independent reality. Reality might be there, but it cannot be fully known through the operations of human thought.

For his part Harman does not propose that there is a true logic that gives privileged access to reality. This distinguishes him from Quentin Meillassoux, who claims that this is possible via foundational mathematics and set theory. Harman instead admits:

> nothing can be modelled adequately by any form of knowledge, or by any sort of translation at all. In its primary sense an object is not used or known, but simply what it is. No reconstruction of that object can

---

[35] Ray Brassier, "Concepts and Objects" in *The Speculative Turn: Continental Materialism and Realism*, ed. Levi Bryant, Nick Srnicek and Graham Harman (Melbourne: Re.press, 2010), 47.

[36] Graham Harman, "Response to Nathan Coombs," *Speculations* (2010), 1, 147.

step in for it in the cosmos ... [this has] profound consequences for the theory of knowledge, since it implies that no scientific model will ever succeed in replacing a thing by listing its various features. Access to the things themselves can only be indirect.[37]

My response to this problem is to argue that aesthetic practices offer strategies for such modelling. My claim here is twofold. First, that the way Harman arrives at his conclusions is through the familiar phenomenological move of the epoché or the bracketing out of the world in order to focus on the immediate objects of consciousness (albeit, as we shall see, in an inverted form). And second, that the epoché is a form of aesthetic reflection. Hence, I hold that after the epoché in which the world is put out of action Harman does something strange and audacious. He attends to that which phenomenological reflection has traditionally ignored: that which has been bracketed out. Further, I propose that epoché is grounded in an aesthetic act of perceptual differentiation and performative disinterest. In other words, the philosophical move of bracketing involves a form of aesthetic reflection. In turn this means not only that certain forms of artistic and philosophical practice are similar insofar as both promote instances of aesthetic reflection *but also* that aesthetic reflection can provide a means of thinking beyond the correlation of mind and world.

Epoché

The emblem of Husserlian phenomenology is the epoché, the method of philosophical bracketing. For Edmund Husserl, the epoché required the bracketing (to "parenthesise") of judgments, pre-conceptions, beliefs and attitudes toward the world:

> We put out of action the general positing which belongs to the essence of the natural attitude; we parenthesize everything which that posit-

---

37 Harman, *The Quadruple Object*, 73.

ing encompasses with respect to being; thus the whole natural world which is continually "there for us," "on hand" and which will always remain there according to consciousness as an "actuality" even if we chose to parenthesize it.[38]

This would lead back to the fundamental nature or essence of things as they appear to consciousness in perception, leading to on the one hand a descriptive phenomenology, and on the other an "eidetic" reduction concerned with pure essences.[39] The purpose of the reduction is to concentrate philosophical reflection upon a particular set of concerns in relation specifically to consciousness (that is the "phenomenological residuum" or "the whole of absolute being").[40] This includes a suspension (or putting "out of action") of both our assumed beliefs about the world and the natural attitude. The natural attitude is characterised by a belief in a mind-independent reality to which we can have access. It thus both underwrites and is underwritten by scientific methods and knowledge which work on the assumption that the world is knowable.
Husserl says:

Clearly required before everything else is the epoché in respect to all objective sciences. This means not merely an abstraction from them, such as an imaginary transformation, in thought, of present human existence, such that no science appeared in the picture. What is meant is rather an epoché of all participation in the cognitions of the objective sciences, an epoché of any critical position-taking which is interested in their truth or falsity, even any position on their guiding idea of an objective knowledge of the world. In short, we carry out an epoché in regard to all objective theoretical interests, all aims and activities

---

[38] Edmund Husserl, *Ideas Pertaining to a Pure Phenomenology and to a Phenomenological Philosophy, First Book*, trans. F. Kersten, (The Hague: Nijhoff, 1983), 60-61.

[39] As Dan Zahavi observes: "It has become customary to say, in the course of his writings Husserl introduces several different *ways* to the transcendental reduction: The *Cartesian* way, the *psychological* way, and the *ontological* way." Dan Zahavi, *Husserl's Phenomenology* (Stanford: Stanford University Press, 2003), 47.

[40] Husserl, *Ideas*, 113.

belonging to us as objective scientists or even simply as [ordinary] people desirous of [this kind of] knowledge.⁴¹

For Husserl's supporters and critics alike the epoché is the route into transcendental idealism. Yet even though it begins from a position of radical doubt, the epoché is not a strategy for radical scepticism. It is, instead, part of a systematic strategy to first identify and then exclude that which is not relevant to the question of the mind-world relationship. The epoché temporarily cleaves consciousness from the world in order to focus on consciousness. It positions the world as separate from us. In that, it does something which we do not normally do, namely attend to the "given-ness" or appearance of the world in our experience. Yet as Zahavi observes, this does not deny the existence of the world, but rather puts speculation on its constitution temporarily on hold:

> It is of crucial importance not to misunderstand the purpose of the epoché. We do not effect it in order to deny, doubt, neglect, abandon, or exclude reality from our research, but simply in order to suspend or neutralize a certain dogmatic attitude toward reality, that is, in order to be able to focus more narrowly and directly on the phenomenological given—the objects just as they appear. In short, the epoché entails a change of attitude toward reality, and not an exclusion of reality.⁴²

What Zahavi identifies in his account of epoché is that Husserlian phenomenology (at least in its early phase) was metaphysically neutral:

> it is not difficult to characterize Husserl's position in *Logische Untersuchungen*. It is metaphysically *neutral*. To be more specific, Husserl's early phenomenology is neither committed to a metaphysical realism nor to a metaphysical idealism ... It is exactly this metaphysical neutrality which is behind Husserl's repeated claim that the difference

---

⁴¹ Edmund Husserl, *The Crisis of European Sciences and Transcendental Phenomenology*, trans. D. Carr (Evanston: Northwestern University Press, 1970), 135.

⁴² Zahavi, *Husserl's Phenomenology*, 45.

between a veridical perception and a mis-perception is irrelevant to phenomenology.[43]

And hence the controversial Husserlian claim in the *Logical Investigations* that there is no difference between an hallucination or a perception of a book should be read as meaning that there is no difference to it as an object of consciousness to be examined. This does not mean that both perception and hallucination are equally real; but rather that such a question of their difference does not fall to phenomenology to answer. In other words the primary interest for phenomenological research is not the natural world which remains within the domain of the natural sciences and the object of empirical research. Instead, the interest of phenomenology is particular to consciousness and the relationship (or correlation) of mind and world. The particular questions addressed by Husserlian phenomenology are *not* ontological ones. Hence, throughout his career Husserl claimed an ontological neutrality for phenomenology. For example, in the introduction to the first volume of his *Logical Investigations* Husserl distinguishes phenomenology from metaphysics and says that "the question as to the existence and nature of the external world is a metaphysical question."[44] Much later in his career, in the *Crisis of European Sciences*, he makes the related claim that "the point [of phenomenology] is not to secure objectivity but to understand it."[45]

Hence, the critiques of phenomenology as being inherently correlationist conflate epistemological questions (regarding the knowability of the world) with ontological ones (regarding the existence of the world) which were not part of the original phenomenological project. The point here is to recognise that strategies of speculative realism on both sides of the mathematical/aesthetic axis are not incompatible with

---

43 Zahavi, *Husserl's Phenomenology*, 40, original emphasis.

44 Edmund Husserl, *Logical Investigations*, vol. 1, ed. Dermot Moran, trans. J. N. Findlay (London: Routledge, 2001), 178.

45 Husserl, *The Crisis of European Sciences*, 189.

phenomenology, in much the same way that other activities such as science, sociology, painting and cooking are not. They are engaged in different activities with different objects of reflection. Phenomenology is concerned with the *meaning* of the world for us; speculative realism with the underlying structures of that world which lie beyond human meaning.

Inverting Epoché

Harman's object-oriented philosophy, by attempting philosophical voyages into a metaphysical space beyond consciousness, is an inversion of what was originally intended as the project of phenomenology. It thus reverses the epoché and pays attention to what is left over from its operations in much the same way as Harman also does with Heidegger's hammer and its "tool-being."

In this vein, a comparison can be made between Zahavi's claim that philosophy, in the guise of phenomenology, should suspend naivety (which is what the epoché does) and Graham Harman's claim that philosophy should attempt to recapture naivety:

> Instead of beginning with radical doubt, we start from naiveté. What philosophy shares with the lives of scientists, bankers, and animals is that all are concerned with objects … Once we begin from naiveté rather than doubt, objects immediately take centre stage … But whereas the naive standpoint of [this book] makes no initial claim as to which of these objects is real or unreal, the labor of the intellect is usually taken to be *critical* rather than naive. Instead of accepting this inflated menagerie of entities, critical thinking debunks objects and denies their autonomy.[46]

Harman, then, whilst beginning from the same methodological starting point as phenomenology, namely the epoché in which world is bracketed out from mind, moves beyond what was ever possible via the phenomenological method into a

---

[46] Harman, *The Quadruple Object*, 5-7.

realm of speculations. His concern is to shift attention away from the relation of mind to world to the realms that lie beyond this relation and which we can only speculate on and creatively imagine. The real can only enter the picture tangentially through allusive and alluring metaphors and poetic acts.[47] To accept this means to say that some philosophical speculation is synonymous with fiction and may be similarly mediated through aesthetic judgment.

Aesthetic Epoché

Maurice Merleau-Ponty outlines what is at stake in the phenomenological reduction in the opening pages of *The Phenomenology of Perception*:

> The best formulation of the reduction is probably that given by Eugen Fink, Husserl's assistant, when he spoke of "wonder" in the face of the world. Reflection does not withdraw from the world towards the unity of consciousness as the world's basis; it steps back to watch the forms of transcendence fly up like sparks from a fire; it slackens the intentional threads which attach us to the world and thus brings them to our notice; it alone is consciousness of the world because it reveals that world as strange and paradoxical.[48]

Whilst Merleau-Ponty famously argues that the phenomenological reduction is never fully achievable and that "the most important lesson which the reduction teaches us is the impos-

---

[47] As Paul J. Ennis observes: "Harman's object oriented ontology proposes that it is language, *in particular metaphor*, which offers the path of least resistance to the 'things themselves'." Paul J. Ennis, *Continental Realism* (Winchester: Zero Books 2011), 33, my emphasis. In a similar vein Brassier argues: "In actuality, the more closely we try to stick to describing the pure appearing and nothing but, the more we end up resorting to a descriptive register which becomes increasingly figurative and metaphorical; so much so, indeed, that it has encouraged many phenomenologists to conclude that only figurative and/or poetic language can be truly adequate to the non-propositional dimension of 'meaningfulness' harboured by 'appearing'." Brassier, *Nihil Unbound*, 28.

[48] Maurice Merleau-Ponty, *The Phenomenology of Perception*, trans. Colin Smith (London: Routledge, 2002), xv.

sibility of a complete reduction,"[49] he also claims that this is no reason to not incorporate it into the phenomenological toolbox and that "the incompleteness of the reduction ... is not an obstacle to the reduction, it is the reduction itself."[50]

In short, Merleau-Ponty argues that although a complete indifference toward the natural attitude is not possible, the attempt to achieve it is philosophically necessary. In this he seems to prefigure Harman's position that philosophy begins from seemingly non-philosophical activities like "wonder" or naivety. Such claims are also compatible with Husserl's own observations that the philosopher should be creative in searching out new ways of experiencing and thinking, and that philosophical activities involve forms of creativity similar to other aesthetic activities:

> Extraordinary profit can be drawn from the offerings of history, in even more abundant measure from those of art, and especially from poetry, which are, to be sure, imaginary but which, in the originality of their forms [Neugestaltungen], the abundance of their single features and the unbrokenness of the motivation, tower high above the products of our own phantasy and, in addition, when they are apprehended understandingly, become converted into perfectly clear phantasies with particular ease owing to the suggestive power exerted by artistic means of presentation.[51]

Hence creative imaginings are a means not only of philosophising but also of communicating that philosophising to an audience.

Art as Epoché

I am thus lead to my first conclusion: that aesthetic experience is a route to a bracketing of the natural attitude and is

---

[49] Merleau-Ponty, *The Phenomenology of Perception*, xiv.

[50] Maurice Merleau-Ponty, *The Visible and the Invisible*, trans. Alphonso Lingis (Evanston: Northwestern University Press, 1968), 178.

[51] Husserl, *Ideas*, 160.

therefore a way into the two different activities of phenomenological reflection *and* its mirror image (or excluded other),
speculative metaphysics. Hence my claim: objects and spaces
of art, as socially and historically privileged sites of aesthetic
experience, reflection and judgment, have the potential to be
philosophically meaningful on their own accord.

This account of art as a means to the epoché is consistent
with the Kantian account of the disinterestedness of aesthetic
judgement. In the Kantian account, aesthetic judgments are
not subsumable under a determinate (*bestimmend*) concept
yet they are made as if they were so through an appeal to a
common sense; this is the celebrated antinomy of taste.[52] Here
a certain disinterestedness is assumed by which certain personal attitudes *and determining concepts* are put out of action.
The connection between the epoché and the Kantian account
of aesthetic reflection is something that Husserl also noticed.
In the short "Letter to Hofmannsthal" he writes:

> For many years I have attempted to get a clear sense of the basic problems
> of philosophy, and then of the methods for solving them, all of which led
> me to the "phenomenological" method as a permanent acquisition. It
> demands an attitude towards all forms of objectivity that fundamentally
> departs from its "natural" counterpart, and which is closely related to
> the attitude and stance in which your art, as something purely aesthetic,
> places us with respect to the presented objects and the whole of the
> surrounding world. The intuition of a purely aesthetic work of art is
> enacted under a strict suspension of all existential attitudes of the

---

[52] "(1) Thesis: A judgement of taste is not based on concepts; for otherwise
one could dispute about it (decide by means of proofs). (2) Antithesis: A
judgement of taste is based on concepts; for otherwise, regardless of the
variation among [such judgements], one could not even so much as quarrel
about them (lay claim to other people's necessary assent to one's judgement)."
Kant's famous solution to the antinomy is that "a judgement of taste must
refer to some concept or other, for otherwise it could not possibly lay claim
to necessary validity for everyone. And yet it must not be provable from a
concept, because while some concepts can be determined, others cannot,
but are intrinsically both indeterminate and indeterminable." Immanuel
Kant, *Critique of Judgment,* trans. Werner Pluhar (Indianapolis: Hackett
Publishing, 1987), 211-12.

intellect and of all attitudes relating to emotions and the will which
presuppose such an existential attitude. Or more precisely: the work
of art places us in (almost forces us into) a state of aesthetic intuition
that excludes these attitudes.[53]

Here Husserl is proposing that the phenomenological method
of suspending natural attitudes is analogous to aesthetic experience in which there is a disinterested focus on the form
of the object of aesthetic reflection. Both involve a judgement
following from that reflection: the epoché as concerns the
object of cognitive judgment; the aesthetic experience as
concerns the object of aesthetic judgement. This suggests and
prefigures the complex interconnection of aesthetics and
philosophy that Merleau-Ponty was to develop, particularly
in his later work.

Art, as a focus of aesthetic attention, can provide instances of
strangeness and wonder when the world becomes something
that can no longer be taken for granted. This happens for
both the artist and the viewer. Art, in Niklas Luhmann's terms,
retards perception; it slows it down and makes it observable:

art aims to retard perception and render it reflexive—lingering upon
the object in visual art (in striking contrast to everyday perception)
and slowing down reading in literature, particularly in lyric poetry ...
Works of art by contrast [to everyday perception] employ perceptions
exclusively for the purpose of letting the observer participate in the
invention of invented forms.[54]

The artist can view the world, strategically, as if it were unfa-
miliar (and not through the natural attitude) in order to work
out the way in which it can be re-presented according to the
specificities of their medium. And these specificities might

53 Edmund Husserl, "Letter to Hofmannsthal," trans. Sven-Olov Wallenstein,
Site (2009), 26/27, 2; originally in *Husserliana Dokumente, Briefwechsel, Band
7: Wissenschaftlerkorrespondenz* (Dordrecht: Kluwer, 1994), 133–36.

54 Niklas Luhmann, *Art as a Social System*, trans. Eva Knodt (Stanford: Stanford
University Press, 2000), 14.

be material (such as qualities of paint), technical (methods of working) and conventional (protocols and styles).

This is what Merleau-Ponty interpreted in certain early modernist painters, namely that they viewed the world as weird because they were viewing it according to the specificities of the medium of painting. The painter intuitively experiences the world as a phenomenologist:

> painting thrusts us once again into the presence of the world of lived experience. In the work of Cézanne, Juan Gris, Braque and Picasso, in different ways, we encounter objects—lemons, mandolins, bunches of grapes, pouches of tobacco—that do not pass quickly before our eyes in the guise of objects we "know well" but, on the contrary, hold our gaze, ask questions of it, convey to it in a bizarre fashion the very secret of their substance, the very mode of their material existence and which, so to speak, stand "bleeding" before us. This was how painting led us back to a vision of things themselves.[55]

Thus, for Merleau-Ponty, viewers of art are drawn into and made complicit in the weirdness of the world. This happens even if they are not involved in the technical issues of producing the work of art because they look upon what the artist has produced. In other words art, "in a bizarre fashion" allows us to apprehend *otherwise withdrawn* substance. The lemons, mandolins, bunches of grapes and pouches of tobacco of the studio are re-presented as strange and autonomous; as withdrawing from us.

Even when something potentially familiar is presented, this is done so in a way in which its usual meanings are suspended. It is because we know that it is art that we do not run on stage and stop Othello from murdering Desdemona. It is because we know that it is art that we do not take a piss in Duchamp's *Fountain* (1917).

The spaces of display for art are spaces of social differentiation, where everyday life appears suspended. For example,

---

55 Maurice Merleau-Ponty, "Lecture 6: Art and the World of Perception," *The World of Perception*, trans. Oliver Davis (London: Routledge, 2004), 69-70.

what Brian O'Doherty calls the "White Cube"[56] of the modern art gallery (the paradigm of which is MoMA, in New York) is designed to provide a privileged and distinct space of display and observation. It has white walls that are an abstraction from everyday life; and it is regulated by certain accepted behaviours (do not talk loudly, do not run etc.). The gallery, in other words, is a space apart from other social spaces and thus serves a bracketing function in spatial terms.

Works of art are weird objects and we encounter them in weird spaces. And we encounter them in weird ways. They are probably not something that we encounter in the everyday run of events in our lives; and even if they are, when we view them *as art* then we view them in a certain weird way. To be clear, works of art are no weirder in themselves than other objects of the world. It is rather that when viewed as art (from a particularly human perspective) then they: (i) are treated as distinct for the cultural and historical reasons that art has become recognised as such and (ii) have this weirdness of address as part of their meaning. It is because of this weirdness that they remain open to interpretation and continue to present us with something of a puzzle; that is, how to deal with them.

Harman's position leads to accepting that all objects are intrinsically weird because they withdraw from thought and from each other. They only ever show their sensual surface to whatever other object happens to stand in relation with them. Yet, as I claim here, we do not encounter this deep weirdness without engaging in philosophical reflection. Art provides this, I argue, by promoting a way of thinking about *all* objects; it brings their weirdness into view through implying a hidden depth to them which is never fully disclosed.

If there is a philosophical significance to art objects and the spaces they occupy, then this significance is not that they illustrate certain didactic theories such as how to live a better life, or what the role of politics is (even though they might). It

---

[56] Brian O'Doherty, *Inside the White Cube: The Ideology of Gallery Space* (Berkeley: University of California Press, 2000).

does not even lie in their capacity for representation as they can be weird in themselves. It is rather that the spaces and objects of art demand of (or perhaps extort from) us a particular frame of mind which—when couched in terms of aesthetic reflection—is inherently reflexive, perhaps philosophical.

Philosophy as Vigorous Art

My second conclusion presents another inversion; it is the flipside to the first conclusion which proposes a similarity in artistic and philosophical practices in that both are mediated by aesthetic reflection and judgment. It is that certain philosophical speculations—like works of art—may be judged aesthetically. What this means is that the tasks of speculative metaphysics and modes of aesthetic reflection, far from being incompatible, might actually be mutually reinforcing.

Merleau-Ponty began unpacking the intertwining of ontology and aesthetics in his later work. In "The Intertwining—The Chiasm" he claims:

> Already our existence as seers (that is, we said, as beings who turn the world back upon itself and who pass over to the other side, and who catch sight of one another, who see one another with eyes) and especially our existence as sonorous beings for others and for ourselves contain everything required for there to be speech from the one to the other, speech about the world.[57]

However, Merleau-Ponty continues that such speech about the world is the language *of* the world, rather than language which represents it in human terms. The role of both philosophy and poetry then, is to capture the origin of meaning. It seeks to capture the "wild-being" of the world as it precedes human reason. So, if it is to reflect a real world which is weird (as Harman claims it is) then its only hope in doing so is by gesturing toward it by aesthetic means. In these terms, the whole world is an aesthetic object, but one that is revealed further through aesthetic reflection:

---

[57] Merleau-Ponty, *The Visible and the Invisible*, 155.

The whole landscape is overrun with words as with an invasion, it is henceforth but a variant of speech before our eyes, and to speak of its "style" is in our view to form a metaphor. In a sense the whole of philosophy, as Husserl says, consists in restoring a power to signify, a birth of meaning, or a wild meaning, an expression of experience by experience, which in particular clarifies the special domain of language. And in a sense, as Valéry said, language is everything, since it is the voice of no one, since it is the very voice of the things, the waves and the forests. And what we have to understand is that there is no dialectical reversal from one of these views to the other; we do not have to reassemble them into synthesis: they are two aspects of the reversibility which is the ultimate truth.[58]

There are two ways of reading Merleau-Ponty's claim here. The first is as a strong correlationist one in which the world is thoroughly enmeshed in human meanings and not knowable in-itself. A second reading, however, proposes that things have a language of their own which we might ventriloquise in acts of poetry. Poetry in all its forms, be they visual, verbal, gustatory or whatever, is our clumsy, human attempt to speak the "drunkenness of things being various."[59]

The second conclusion, then, is that Harman's metaphysical speculations into the world populated by countless objects which lie beyond the horizon of human knowledge are fundamentally poetic. They are a poetry born from an aesthetic act of wonder in the face of the world. Such poetry does not admit of verification in the terms of other modes of philosophical thinking and standard epistemic procedures. This does not mean that it is without meaning, but rather that the way in which it is to be judged is through aesthetic judgement of taste rather than empirical or conceptual verification.[60]

[58] Merleau-Ponty, *The Visible and the Invisible*, 155.

[59] MacNeice, "Snow," 30.

[60] A related argument concerning the validity of art historical judgments is made in Francis Halsall, "Making and Matching: Aesthetic Judgement and the Production of Art Historical Knowledge," *The Journal of Art Historiography* (2012), 7, http://arthistoriography.wordpress.com/7-dec2012/ (accessed September 26, 2013).

In the first moment of the *Critique of Judgement* Kant argues for the subjective purposiveness of judgements of taste. Subjective purposiveness gives us a model for how synthesis can be achieved between speculations into a weird world beyond human reason and their objects. Importantly, there can be no empirical or objective concept, such as truth, that regulates the validity of the speculations. Instead a subjective purposiveness is at work:

> What is formal in the presentation of a thing, the harmony of its manifold to [form] a unity (where it is indeterminate what this unity is [meant] to be) does not by itself reveal any objective purposiveness whatsoever. For here we abstract from what this unity is as a purpose (what the thing is [meant] to be) so that nothing remains but the subjective purposiveness of the presentations in the mind of the beholder. Subjective purposiveness [is] merely a certain purposiveness of the subject's presentational state and, within that state, [an] appealingness [involved] in apprehending a given form by the imagination. Such purposiveness does not indicate any perfection of any object whatever, [since] no object is being thought through any concept of a purpose.[61]

In short, like a judgement of something beautiful for Kant, some philosophical speculations into a world beyond consciousness cannot be proved; that is, they are neither empirically nor conceptually demonstrable. They are nonetheless still made in the faith of their communicability through appeal to an audience that is hoped will agree with them. Certain forms of speculative philosophical thought are creative imaginings and aesthetic acts in their own right. Here we find a perhaps unlikely ally in Meillassoux whom I had placed on the other side of the mathematical/aesthetic axis. Meillassoux says:

> Philosophy is the invention of strange forms of argumentation, necessarily bordering on sophistry, which remains its dark structural double. To philosophize is always to develop an idea whose elaboration and defense require a novel kind of argumentation, the model for which

---

[61] Kant, *Critique of Judgment*, 74.

lies neither in positive science—not even in logic—nor in some supposedly innate faculty for proper reasoning. Thus it is essential that a philosophy produce internal mechanisms for regulating its own inferences—signposts and criticisms through which the newly constituted domain is equipped with a set of constraints that provide internal criteria for distinguishing between licit and illicit claims.[62]

In this sense forms of philosophising like Harman's guerrilla metaphysics are like works of art. They are to be evaluated not according to their validity in correspondence with a transcendental set of truth conditions. But rather they are to be judged aesthetically. In other words, these speculations can never be proved, only contemplated. And their effectiveness is to be judged aesthetically, as a matter of taste.

---

[62] Quentin Meillassoux, *After Finitude: An Essay on the Necessity of Contingency*, trans. Ray Brassier (London: Continuum, 2006), 124.

Images I Cannot See

Magdalena Wisniowska

Royal Academy Schools

Primary Aesthetics

CONFRONTED WITH A CALL FOR the rehabilitation of the distinction between primary and secondary qualities, I cannot help but turn towards the discussion of aesthetics, specifically of a Kantian kind.[1] The call belongs to Quentin Meillassoux, as expressed at the very beginning of his seminal essay *After Finitude*; what is at stake in such a call is modern philosophy's relation to the absolute.[2] For we learn that ever since philosophy has rejected the "pre-critical" or "naïve" distinction between the sensible qualities of an object and its more fixed, mathematical properties, there is nothing which does not fall under the spell of subjectivation.[3] Not only is there no outside of the correlation between thought and being, the correlate itself—whether this is, according to its modern incarnation, language or consciousness—cannot be grasped. For fear of substantiation and a fall back into

---

[1] I am drawing on Immanuel Kant, *Critique of Judgment*, trans. Werner S. Pluhar (Indianapolis: Hackett, 1987).

[2] Quentin Meillassoux, *After Finitude: An Essay on the Necessity of Contingency*, trans. Ray Brassier (London: Continuum, 2008).

[3] Ibid., 3.

naivety, philosophy remains in its glass cage, destined to look outside while trapped within.

Not only does Meillassoux's argument seem utterly convincing, there is precious little one could say in response. Correlationism does seem to be the dominant mode of thinking. This implies that the rehabilitation of the distinction between primary and secondary qualities is both urgent and necessary. Where then does aesthetics come in? Why would anyone wish to turn, at this very moment—to Kant? While it is true that the centrality of correlation prevents modern critical philosophy from considering the two concepts of being and thought independently from one another, there is nevertheless one place in which at least the concept of thought is confronted in a more direct manner. As Kant's third critique explains, pleasure associated with the beautiful is different from the satisfaction derived from the agreeable or the good because it consists of the experience of our faculties of thought at work. The aesthetic judgement of taste is pleasurable because we feel our faculties, the very faculties conditioning the human subject, at play.[4]

One could respond to this privileging of aesthetic experience with scepticism. Indeed, it is far from clear how the sensing of the faculties could lift the spell of subjectivation when it is the human subject who is doing the sensing. Yet this moment of aesthetic pleasure described by Kant gains significance once we consider what incites Meillassoux to break with the correlationist circle. As modern critical philosophy cannot think outside of the central correlation, it cannot think the problem of origin, whether this concerns the formation of the universe or the emergence of the conditions of knowledge that it seeks to determine; this despite the fact that in Kantianism the transcendental subject is always instantiated in the empirical body.[5] Kant, by ascribing aesthetic pleasure

---

[4] See Kant's treatment of the free-play of imagination in Kant, *Critique of Judgment*, 61-64.

[5] For Meillassoux, the body is one of the conditions for the "taking place" of the transcendental thus rendering the correlationist argument (that the problem of the ancestral confuses the empirical and transcendental) invalid.

to the feeling of the faculties in free play, takes the first tentative step towards thinking how transcendental conditions themselves might be generated. Accordingly, the sensation of the quickening of the faculties becomes a key moment for generations of post-Kantian thinkers working on this problematic.[6] In so doing, Kant might also be considered as taking the first step towards thinking outside of the critical remit, the taste for beauty being something like a taste for the unconditioned or absolute.

At this point, a clarification is in order. The above account is heavily skewed towards one post-Kantian thinker in particular, the French philosopher Gilles Deleuze. Although Deleuze is perhaps better known for his critique of representation and the broader rejection of Kantian philosophy as a whole, many recent studies have nevertheless placed his aesthetics within the Kantian context that I have outlined above.[7] According to these readings, Deleuze's engagement with Kant revolves around the problem of genesis.[8] Taking up the post-Kantian slogan of "real" and not "possible" experience, his concern is not the definition of the transcendental conditions that

---

See Meillassoux, *After Finitude*, 22-26.

[6] I am using the term "post-Kantian" very loosely in a Deleuzian sense. Key figures would be Salomon Maïmon, Johann Gottlieb Fichte and Friedrich Wilhelm Joseph Schelling. See the section on the relationship between Kant and Deleuze in Joe Hughes, *Deleuze and the Genesis of Representation* (London: Continuum, 2008), 16-18.

[7] Deleuze's best-known critique of representation is found in the chapter "The Image of Thought" in his *Difference and Repetition*, trans. Paul Patton (London: Continuum, 2009), 164-213.

[8] Daniel W. Smith is one of the first to offer this Kantian reading. See for instance his short essay "Deleuze's Theory of Sensation: Overcoming Kantian Duality" in *Deleuze: A Critical Reader*, ed. Paul Patton (Oxford: Blackwell, 1996), 29-56. A similar reading is taken up by Joe Hughes in *Deleuze and the Genesis of Representation* and *Deleuze's Difference and Repetition: A Reader's Guide* (London: Continuum, 2009) as well as by Christian Kerslake, *Immanence and the Vertigo of Philosophy: From Kant to Deleuze* (Edinburgh: Edinburgh University Press, 2009). Levi Bryant addresses the question of genesis within a speculative realist context in "Deleuze's Transcendental Empiricism: Notes towards a Transcendental Materialism" in *Thinking between Deleuze and Kant: A Strange Encounter*, ed. Edward Willat and Matt Lee (London: Continuum, 2009), 28-48.

allow for the possibility of knowledge, but to track knowledge's genetic constitution. In other words, Deleuze asks how representation comes about, under what circumstances it is generated. One could argue that he rethinks the first critique from the point of view he discovers in the third precisely by taking up the key moment of aesthetic pleasure: the fact that free play occurs prior to determination in judgement and that this free play involves the mutual quickening of the faculties.[9]

The possibility that intrigues me here is that of what I would like to call a "primary aesthetics." If indeed in aesthetic experience we confront transcendental conditions directly and these conditions are the conditions of real genesis rather than the conditions of mere possibility, this would mean that we confront a world prior to emergence, that is, we confront not the object as it is "for us," but as it is "in itself," as true substance.

Working with Meillassoux's distinction between primary and secondary qualities, an aesthetics that is primary in nature would thus bring us face to face with the absolute. The question is, to what extent is this the case? Does Deleuze in his recasting of Kant's critical project take that tentatively offered step and bring us closer to Meillassoux's absolute? Or does Kant's all-encompassing subjectivity somehow intervene? To what extent does the correlationist contract stating the primacy of the correlation between thought and being stay intact?

In answering these questions, Deleuze's discussion of Samuel Beckett's television play ...*but the clouds...* in "The Exhausted" strikes me as particularly relevant, dealing as it does with both the problem of emergence and the extent to which the conditions of emergence can be confronted. The play was first broadcast by BBC2 in 1977 and published in *Ends and Odds* later in the same year. Deleuze's essay subsequently served as a postscript to the play's first French translation and was republished as "The Exhausted" in the English translation of

---

[9] Joe Hughes makes a very similar argument in *Deleuze and the Genesis of Representation*, 17-18, and throughout *Deleuze's Difference and Repetition*.

Critique et Clinique.[10] Both the play and Deleuze's discussion of it centre on an image of a woman's face, a close-up "reduced as far as possible to eyes and mouth."[11] We learn the manner of her appearance from the play's single male protagonist: that she can appear and immediately disappear, that she can also appear, linger and disappear and finally that she can appear, mouth the words "but the clouds" and then disappear—all of which takes place when the protagonist is seated in his darkened room. Deleuze describes this moment in which Beckett "makes the image" in a unique way, a way that cannot be found in his other uses of the term.[12] The image here is "not a representation of an object but a movement in the world of the mind."[13]

Beckett makes an image, an image that is "not a representation" but a "movement," furthermore "a movement in the world of the mind." He makes such an image through a very particular and elaborate process, which Deleuze calls the process of "exhaustion."[14] Within the context of the essay, this is the logical and physiological exhaustion of possibility, set in contrast to the realisation of possibility characteristic of everyday life. Whereas the realisation of the possible in the everyday is limited to the choices that we might make and the aims we might follow, exhaustion rejects any such decisions,

---

[10] I will be using Gilles Deleuze, "The Exhausted" in *Essays Critical and Clinical*, trans. Daniel W. Smith and Michael A. Greco (London: Verso, 1998), 152-74.

[11] Samuel Beckett, "...but the clouds..." in *Collected Shorter Plays* (London: Faber, 1984), 257.

[12] Deleuze, "The Exhausted," 169. The concept of the image appears frequently in Deleuze's work. Notably, he critiques the "image of thought" in *Difference and Repetition* alluding to the subjective presuppositions of Cartesianism. There is also the image of *Bergsonism*, trans. Hugh Tomlinson and Barbara Habberjam (New York: Zone Books, 1991) and the movement and time images of the *Cinema* Books: *Cinema 1*, trans. Hugh Tomlinson and Barbara Habberjam (London: Continuum, 2005) and *Cinema 2*, trans. Hugh Tomlinson and Robert Galeta (London: Continuum 2005).

[13] Deleuze, "The Exhausted," 169.

[14] Ibid., 152-54.

leading us to discover a world that is "prior to birth."[15] The image thus is the culminating point of the exhaustive process, the moment in which the state of exhaustion is reached, "the final word, 'nohow'."[16] And while we can understand this culminating point in a Spinozian way, as following the pattern set out by the Spinozian God,[17] its Kantian sense is equally clear. The world "prior to birth" is the world prior to representation: the world before the givenness of sensation and before the subject-object distinction that constitutes all cognitive experience. The exhaustion of the image is the moment in which the conditions of possible (Kant) or, rather, real (Deleuze) experience have become manifest.

The Exhausted

Our task then is a simple one. To establish whether Deleuze is a speculative realist or not, we must interrogate Deleuze's text—"The Exhausted"—with reference to Meillassoux's arguments concerning primary and secondary qualities. However seductive our reading of the process of exhaustion as a kind of reaching out towards the absolute may be, we must first establish the extent to which Deleuze's superior empiricism breaks with the Kantian transcendental contract. Does Deleuze consider subject and object independently or always relative to one another? Does he think the separation of being and thought or only their correlation? Deleuze may indeed be best known for his critique of representation, but Meillassoux has shown that such a critique, however convincing, is of itself insufficient to overcome the correlationist bind.[18] Does Deleuze, then, like so many others, fall into the trap of

---

[15] Deleuze, "The Exhausted," 152, 156.

[16] Ibid., 170.

[17] This is the most common interpretation of Deleuze's essay. See for instance Audrey Wasser, "A Relentless Spinozism: Deleuze's Encounter with Beckett," *SubStance* (2012), 41:1, 124-36.

[18] See for example Meillassoux's critique of Heidegger in Meillassoux, *After Finitude*, 8.

correlationism or is he able to avoid what Meillassoux terms the "correlationist circle" or "two-step"?[19]

Before answering, we must consider the argument of "The Exhausted" more closely. I have already mentioned the distinction with which Deleuze begins his essay (and its Spinozian framework). Possibility is either something we can realise or something we can exhaust. While we realise possibility constantly every time we choose to pursue one aim over another, the exhaustion of possibility occurs only within art. Only in art can we grasp all possible aims and goals in their totality and at once, in all contradiction, without the accompanying need for realising one possibility or another. As we have already seen, this kind of exhaustion has two aspects. On the one hand, there is a logical exhaustiveness associated with the construction of "inclusive disjunctions"; on the other hand, there is physiological fatigue.[20] Of central importance is the final of Deleuze's introductory distinctions. Whereas the realisation of the possible is tiring for the subject, the fatigue arising from exhaustion is the consequence of the objective exhaustiveness of "the combinatorial."[21]

In "The Exhausted" Deleuze argues that Beckett achieves such a double exhaustion of possibility through his specific use of language. Once again a distinction is in order, following the pattern set by the first. On the one hand, we have everyday life where language readies possibility for realisation by establishing plans, goals and aims. On the other hand, we have art which in contrast seeks to give the possible a "reality that is proper to it."[22] In this manner, we have come across a crucial point of relevance for our speculative realist inflected account of a Deleuzian aesthetics. If, as Meillassoux argues, language is one of the two modes through which correlationism dominates modern philosophical thought, we can see how exhaustion might be able to offer one way of reaching

---

[19] Meillassoux, *After Finitude*, 8.

[20] Deleuze, "The Exhausted," 154-55.

[21] Ibid., 153.

[22] Ibid., 156.

outside of the proverbial glass cage. Through his use of language, Beckett makes the nature of the correlate that binds us visible. At the very least, we know what we are to reach out of.

Deleuze attributes to Beckett a schematic approach, a gradual exhaustion of language that takes place in three distinct stages, each coinciding with one period of Beckett's creative output. According to this scheme, there is a first language of names found in the early novels and plays; a second language of voices that dominates Beckett's work from the *Unnameable* onwards; and finally, a third language of spaces and images which, although born in the novel *How It Is* and present in a number of theatre works (Deleuze lists *Happy Days*, *Act without Words* and *Catastrophe*), is associated most closely with the late television plays: *Quad*, *Ghost Trio*, ...*but the clouds*... and *Nacht und Träume*.[23] Each of these three languages exhausts the possible in its own particular way.

The first of these languages is perhaps easiest to grasp, as it concerns the more logical aspect of the process of exhaustion. Deleuze considers the daily task of language to be the establishment of aims, goals and preferences that ready the possible for realisation. Thus, we can see that the construction of inclusive disjunctions associated with exhaustiveness necessarily impacts the naming function of words as numeration replaces language's more familiar grammatical structures. The consequence of the combinatorial is that it exhausts its own object, those discrete entities that it so carefully enumerates. To refer to the example given by Deleuze, Murphy can only "partake" his daily five biscuits "in their fullness" when he stops treating them as different sorts of biscuit to be eaten and begins to think of all their possible combinations, 120 in total.[24]

The second language carries out this process of exhaustiveness one step further by including in the construction of the inclusive disjunction all those voices that emit the names of language one. With this second kind of inventory, we can see

---

[23] Deleuze, "The Exhausted," 159.

[24] Ibid., 153.

more of the physiological consequences of logical exhaustiveness. While fatigue, or at least weariness, accompanies Murphy in his confrontation with the five different sorts of biscuit, the decision facing the characters of Beckett's later novels and plays concerns not a distinct set of objects but these characters' very own sense of selfhood. So exhausted is Mahood in *The Unnameable* that he becomes no more than Worm—"the unnameable" or "the exhausted one"—at the limit of any sense of self.[25] Yet the aporia of the play is such that we learn of the character of the selfless Worm indirectly, through the initial character of Mahood. Language two thus confronts us with the bind of the narrator's voice, the notion of the individual subject who speaks.

In the third and final language, the process of exhaustion with its logical and physiological aspects is given substance in that it becomes self-sufficient. Deleuze describes this final language as consisting of spaces and, crucially for my argument, "images."[26] Exhaustion here is no longer a logical process carried out by one character or another; neither is it the drawn out process of the character's physiological exhaustion. The respective exhaustions of languages one and two allow for the appearance of images (and to a lesser extent spaces) which seem to bypass the relation of distinct object to individual subject. Deleuze describes these images in terms of "the indefinite" or "the singular," as no more than "a woman, a hand, a mouth, *some* eyes."[27] These images, independent of all specifics, are not objects—woman, hand or mouth—but processes; or rather, the images in Beckett's work are always in process. The effort required to make an image in its indefinite state—the construction of languages one and two, the "loosening" of the "grip of words" and the "drying up" of the "oozing of voices"—is so great that it is impossible to sustain.[28] The image, as Deleuze insists, has by

---

[25] Deleuze, "The Exhausted," 157-58.

[26] Ibid., 158-59.

[27] Ibid., 158, original emphasis.

[28] Ibid., 159.

its very nature only a "short duration"; it lasts for the shortest of times.[29] Indeed, the prime characteristic of the image is the violence with which it explodes. However, it also needs to be stressed that there is no one who exhausts or explodes this mysterious image. It does so out of its own self-accord.

We can find the best example of this self-dissipating image in *...but the clouds...*, Beckett's 1977 television work. Here, the protagonist attempts to recall the way in which a woman had previously appeared to him. We see both his re-enactment of his daily routine (coming indoors from the right; returning to his chamber to change from his day clothes into his night clothes and vice versa; exiting to the left) and the image of a woman's face (which appears and disappears; appears and lingers; appears, lingers, mouths the words of W. B. Yeats's 1928 poem "The Tower" and disappears). But crucially, the woman who appears to the protagonist is not a consequence of his active thought. The play begins with the protagonist correcting himself. He first states, "When I thought of her, it was always night. I came in—." But very soon he adds, "No that is not right. When she appeared it was always night. I came in—."[30] The woman is not the object of the subject's thought. She appears, whether the subject thinks of her or not. Despite the meticulous detail with which the protagonist recounts his daily activities, there is a sense that the woman appears whatever action he might take. Deleuze identifies this moment of the woman's appearance as the moment in which Beckett finally makes the image.

Movement and Darkness

At this stage in Deleuze's argument, we reach the key point of any comparison between his aesthetics and Meillassoux's speculative realist denunciation of correlationism. For it is here that Deleuze describes the image that appears to the protagonist of *...but the clouds...* as "not a representation of

---

[29] Deleuze, "The Exhausted," 161.
[30] Beckett, "...but the clouds...," 259.

an object but a movement in the world of the mind."[31] The image is not what we see before us. It is not the face of the woman that somehow materialises to the man seated at his desk. Instead, it is a movement of the mind, where the term "mind" takes on a meaning different to that familiar from our discussion of correlationism. Thought here is neither the one pre-given faculty nor the ensemble of the Kantian pre-given faculties working in harmony. For Deleuze, thought belongs to the three passive syntheses, a series of discordant and violent impulses and drives which constitute a system of the dissolved self.

But before making any such claims, I would first like to limit my examination to the argument Deleuze presents in "The Exhausted." First of all, to understand the nature of Beckett's image, we must consider more of "the darkness" that invariably accompanies it. When first discussing the nature of language three, Deleuze describes the moment of the image's self-dissipation as "a singular darkness."[32] Darkness is also a central feature of Deleuze's analysis of *...but the clouds....* Once the woman's appearance announces "the end of the possible," we are faced with "eternal darkness, the dead end of the black night."[33] Of this eternal darkness, Deleuze writes:

> There is no longer an image, anymore than there is a space: beyond the possible there is only darkness, as in Murphy's third and final state, where the protagonist no longer moves in spirit but has become an indiscernible atom, abulic, "in the dark ... of ... absolute freedom." This is the final word, "nohow."[34]

Deleuze here once again refers to Beckett's earlier novel, specifically to the chapter dedicated to the justification of the expression "Murphy's mind."[35] In the "riotous potpourri

---

[31] Deleuze, "The Exhausted," 169.

[32] Ibid., 161.

[33] Ibid., 170.

[34] Ibid.

[35] Samuel Beckett, *Murphy* (New York: Grove Press, 2011), 107-13.

of many metaphysical systems"[36] that this chapter contains, Murphy's mind is presented as "hermetically closed," a "hollow sphere"[37] which nevertheless holds the entire universe within. Murphy discovers that in order to move within this universe and to enjoy its treasures he must first let his body be at rest. Just as exhaustion has both logical and physiological aspects, Murphy's law of inversion involves both the mental and the physical.

In the elaboration of the law of inversion that follows, Beckett describes Murphy's mental acrobatics in more detail, dividing the closed and hollow sphere of his mind into three distinct zones: the light, the half-light and the dark. When Murphy first lays at rest, he travels through a zone that resembles the world outside, its mental forms corresponding quite closely to the outside's physical ones for which they act as a kind of parallel. Within the zone of light, Murphy has the childlike pleasure of manipulating those experiences which in the outside world lie beyond his control: he can, for instance, reprise a kick he has received. Providing that he rests a little bit more, he can enter the second zone of half-light, one step further removed from the physical in that it consists of forms which have no parallel. This second world he can no longer manipulate and the only pleasure available to him is this world's contemplation at a distance. At the ultimate point of rest, Murphy reaches the third, most distant and final zone of darkness which stands in stark contrast to the other two. It contains no forms, whether parallel or otherwise. Indeed, Beckett notes that it contains "no elements or states."[38] Thus, it cannot be manipulated, nor is it something which Murphy can contemplate. Of this last zone Beckett writes:

> The third, the dark, was a flux of forms, a perpetual coming together and falling asunder of forms. The light contained the docile element

---

[36] John Fletcher, "Samuel Beckett and the Philosophers," *Comparative Literature* (1965), 17:1, 54.

[37] Beckett, *Murphy*, 107.

[38] Ibid.

of a new manifold, the world of the body broken up into pieces of a toy, the half-light, states of peace. But the dark neither elements nor states, nothing but forms becoming and crumbling into the fragments of a new becoming, without love or hate or any intelligible principle of change. Here there was nothing but commotion and the pure forms of commotion. Here he was not free, but a mote in the dark of absolute freedom. He did not move, he was a point in the ceaseless unconditioned generation and passing away of line.[39]

We can see straightaway that the darkness of *…but the clouds…* and the darkness of the third zone of Murphy's mind are one and the same. But what can we learn from their mutual resemblance? What is striking is that both the third zone of Murphy's mind and the equally dark, equally mobile mental world of the protagonist of *…but the clouds…* have no "I" in the traditional sense in that they have no one conscious unifying force. By this stage in Murphy's travels, the freedom associated with zones one and two—the ability to manipulate and con-template—is forsaken. Similarly, the exhaustion of language has reached a stage in which our ability to realise goals, plans and aims through the naming and voicing of possibility has been renounced. As Deleuze writes, "something is seen or heard" provided that "it is freed from the chains by which it was bound": the image is the consequence of us "tearing away all these adhesions."[40] As the protagonist of *…but the clouds…* reminds us, the image is not a product of his active thought. But this is not to say that there is no sense of self or unifying force within the thought both Beckett and Deleuze describe. "Motes," "atoms" and "points" seem to populate this dark and mobile world. What kind of thought, then, is this thought without the traditional subject-object distinction? Who does the thinking and what does this thought consist of? What kind of existence does this thought have?

I would like to argue that Deleuze's text raises the question of the relation of thought to being. Or more precisely, it

---

[39] Beckett, *Murphy*, 107.

[40] Deleuze, "The Exhausted," 158.

raises the question of how thought comes into being, emerging from a non-time and a non-space. The problem is, as in many of Deleuze's works, that of thought's genetic origin: this is what in "The Exhausted" Deleuze expresses as the Spinoza-tinted "before birth." In this vein, Deleuze addresses the same problem of temporality as Meillassoux, although he stages it rather differently. As we have seen the issue for Meillassoux is modern philosophy's relation to the absolute, a notion which, together with the distinction between primary and secondary qualities, he believes has been cast aside in philosophy's turn towards the transcendental. To point out some of the shortcomings of the transcendental turn, Meillassoux formulates the notion of the ancestral, the temporal state prior to all "givenness."[41] Very simply, this is the time of reference for any scientific statement that attempts to date the origins of the universe, the origins of earth, or life on earth. He argues that the correlationism dominating most forms of philosophy since Kant is incapable of thinking the absolute, because it is incapable of taking these kind of scientific statements literally. Kantians are incapable of thinking a being that is not manifest *to us*. For correlationism, the paradox of "a givenness of being anterior to givenness" is insurmountable.[42]

Deleuze brings the entire problem of temporality much closer to home. The "before birth" of "The Exhausted" does not relate to statements concerning our most distant past, but to those experiences taking place here and now. As any good Kantian knows, before any kind of experience becomes possible, certain conditions must be in place. These are the forms of sensibility, space and time, the pure concepts of understanding and the principles of reason. Where Kantianism falls short however, is in explaining how and from where

---

[41] Meillassoux, *After Finitude*, 14. Meillassoux explicitly uses the term "givenness," which can ultimately be traced back to Kant. In the *Critique of Pure Reason* the sensible is "given" as a manifold of time and space. See Kant's discussion of the transcendental aesthetic in the *Critique of Pure Reason*, trans. John Miller Dow Meiklejohn (London: Henry G. Bohn, 1855), 71-104.

[42] Meillassoux, *After Finitude*, 14.

these conditions have arisen. Notoriously, in the first critique, Kant merely adopts his twelve categories of understanding from the twelve forms of judgment that logic has inherited from Aristotle. Thus, Deleuze discovers another shortcoming at the heart of transcendental thought. Not only is Kantianism incapable of thinking statements concerning events which science believes took place 13.5 billion years ago, it is incapable of thinking its own genetic origin. Just as Kantians cannot think the emergence of being generally, they cannot think how the principles of their own thought came into being. Such are the questions that dominate Deleuze's work from *Difference and Repetition* onwards: how to account for the genetic origin of our thought? What are the conditions of "real" and not just "possible" experience?

Whatever account we choose to read,[43] in Deleuze, the genesis of thought begins with the intensive encounter. Every time something is sensed, thought is forced to think, precisely because it is confronted with something external and independent of it. It is important to understand that the sensible here is not the "empirical sensibility" found in Kant, but the Deleuzian "transcendental sensibility" consisting of discontinuous instants of material impressions, an intensive zone whose only rule is discontinuity.[44] Thought begins when the body attempts to interpret this violence of the intensive encounter unfolding the spectacle of the active and passive syntheses and thus establishing the representational realm of actuality and the sub-representational realm of virtuality with the latter grounding the former.[45] If we accept that De-

[43] In *Deleuze and the Genesis of Representation*, Hughes shows how works as diverse as *Difference and Repetition*, *The Logic of Sense*, trans. Mark Lester with Charles Stivale, ed. Constantin V. Boundas (New York: Columbia University Press, 1990) and *Anti-Oedipus: Capitalism and Schizophrenia*, trans. Robert Hurley, Mark Seem and Helen R. Lane (Minneapolis: University of Minnesota Press, 1983) all share the same structure. He makes a similar argument to include *Cinema 1* and *Cinema 2* as well as *What is Philosophy?*, trans. Hugh Tomlinson and Graham Burchill (New York: Columbia University Press, 1994) in *Deleuze's Difference and Repetition*, 179.

[44] Deleuze, *Difference and Repetition*, 176.

[45] See chapter two of *Difference and Repetition*, 90-163 for further details on

leuze's genetic account begins with the initial encounter of the sensible and ultimately grounds the active recognition of the object on the passive "ideal synthesis" of difference,[46] we can accept that the "movement" and "darkness" of the world of the image refers to this very realm of passive syntheses.

A straightforward comparison ought to make the similarities between the two accounts clear. To first reiterate the argument of "The Exhausted": for Deleuze, the image always has the status of the indefinite. It is not an object but a process. More so, it is a process which is not carried out by someone or something. We know that the central characteristic of the image is the violence with which it self-dissipates or explodes. Such images can be found in Beckett's late television plays, specifically in *...but the clouds...*, and, to illustrate the nature of the image present there, Deleuze alludes to Murphy's third state and the zone of darkness and flux. Let us consider then the Nietzschean way in which he describes the third passive synthesis in *Difference and Repetition*:

> The system of the future ... must be called a divine game since there is no pre-existing rule, since the game bears already upon its own rules and since the child-player can only win, all of chance being affirmed each time and for all times.[47]

The similarities between the two descriptions—of Murphy's third zone of darkness and *Difference and Repetition*'s system of the future—are pronounced. First of all, in both cases there is no question of a distinct object bound by a set of rules. Just as the system of the future does not conform to any pre-existing rule, the movement of the third dark zone follows no set principles. Not only does this final zone bear no relation to anything within the actual world; Beckett tells

---

this grounding process. Deleuze also refers to the passive synthesis in chapter three, 181-183, acknowledging Kant's "discordant harmony" as a model for his system of the dissolved self.

[46] Deleuze, *Difference and Repetition*, 203-04.

[47] Ibid., 142.

us that those forms that constitute its virtuality continually "become and crumble into new becomings without love or hate or any intelligible principle of change."[48] Secondly, both the mental world of Murphy's travels and the world of the divine game are not presided over by an individual subject possessing ready-made faculties. The player of the divine game is a child that, in its "innocence and forgetfulness," is synonymous with the new.[49] The system of the future is a consequence of the dissipation of the first and second passive syntheses in the third. The self of this third synthesis is thus appropriate to it, cut off from previously established bonds. Similarly, Murphy must lose those shreds of agency that he held in the brightness of the zone of light and the twilight of the zone of half-light. There is freedom in the last zone of his mind, but this is neither the freedom to manipulate particular events nor the freedom to contemplate forms not encountered before. Instead, it is the freedom of continual change, which he can only enjoy by becoming a "mote" in "the ceaseless generation of line," that is, a *dissolved* self.[50] Like the child-player of the divine game or the non-subject of the third passive synthesis, Murphy needs to become both innocent and forgetful.

If, then, there is a unifying force to the dark and mental world shared by both Murphy and the protagonist of *…but the clouds…*, it centres on this child figure taken up in movement and flux. Deleuze is famous for multiplying his definitions, and even by limiting ourselves to the consideration of *Difference and Repetition* we discover a number of synonyms for this figure in a variety of contexts: philosophical, scientific, psychoanalytic. However, for our purposes, the mathematical context of chapters four and five is particularly suggestive.[51]

---

[48] Beckett, *Murphy*, 112.

[49] Friedrich Nietzsche, *Thus Spoke Zarathustra*, trans. R.J. Hollingdale (New York: Penguin Books, 1969), 54-55. See also Hughes, *Deleuze's Difference and Repetition*, 133.

[50] Beckett, *Murphy*, 112.

[51] Deleuze, *Difference and Repetition*, 214-329.

Here, the Nietzschean child-player re-appears as the contingent or "aleatory point."[52] In modern day calculus, this point plays a comparable role to the child-player in Nietzsche's divine game. Just as the throw of the dice affirms all of chance, the aleatory point allows for the progressive reciprocal determination of differentials to occur. Without this point, the differentials may indeed be determinable but their status is of the yet to be determined. This aspect of Deleuzian thought is particularly relevant to any discussion of primary and secondary qualities and the concurrent claim that the subject-centeredness dominating modern philosophy renders it incapable of taking mathematical statements literally. According to Meillassoux, there is no conceivable property of the object in modern philosophy which can be considered independent of its relation to the subject. In Deleuze, we are witness to a rather remarkable twist. He shows that the genetic heart of subjectivity can be presented in objective mathematical terms.

Deleuze and Speculative Realism

By way of conclusion, let me engage more systematically with some of Meillassoux's arguments to see if there is indeed the possibility of a primary aesthetics. First in line is the claim with which Meillassoux ends his opening chapter: that modern philosophy is incapable of taking scientific statements regarding the emergence of being literally. All philosophy working in the critical tradition prefers to argue one of two things: either that the temporal problem is misunderstood as a problem of space, or that the problem confuses its empirical and transcendental levels.[53] According to the correlationist, the difficulty of the ancestral event is merely that of the unwitnessed or unperceived. The correlationist has no wish to discuss how organic bodies have come to appear but only how the science of emergence is possible. Needless

---

[52] Deleuze, *Difference and Repetition*, 181, 248-50, 354.

[53] Meillassoux, *After Finitude*, 18-27.

to say, Meillassoux dismisses both of these arguments. The problem of the ancestral is not that of the unperceived but of that which is prior to givenness, the non-given event or even the absence of givenness. And while it might seem that the levels at which the problem is discussed are different, Meillassoux insists that the conditions for the emergence of organic bodies and the science of emergence are one and the same. The human subject, too, needs to be instantiated. Hence his rehabilitation of the distinction between primary and secondary qualities becomes necessary. We are forced to think "outside ourselves."[54]

Of course, Deleuze does not think of events that occurred several billion years ago but of a genetic origin immanent to nature. Yet I have shown that the temporality in question is not dissimilar. In both cases, we are confronted with an event prior to givenness, a movement from non-being to being. It could be argued that this is precisely what Deleuze first traces in *Difference and Repetition*. The three passive syntheses with their productive disruption are his way of thinking how a world of representation, in other words, a world of givenness, might arise. Prior to such givenness is the Nietzschean system of the future with its lack of rules and child-player. It is the world of differentials and aleatory points. The affirmation of chance or the reciprocal determination of differentials explains how the determined develops from the undetermined, the known from the unknown. This emergence is also present in Beckett as the making of the image in ...*but the clouds*... so clearly shows. The appearance of the woman evokes a world in which there are no pre-existing rules and no pre-constituted subjectivity. Subjecthood here is a matter of chance and has all the spontaneity and innocence of Nietzsche's child-player.

In "The Exhausted," Deleuze affirms the non-being, or meontological status, of this dark and mobile world. Let us examine the initial distinction between the realisation and the exhaustion of the possible one more time. Whereas the

---

54 Meillassoux, *After Finitude*, 27.

realisation of the possible takes place in the here and now, exhaustion returns to a moment "prior to birth." Within this schema, the "possible" is that which "exists." Deleuze confirms, "There is no existence other than the possible." This would mean that the world of exhaustion—the world prior to birth—is of a non-existent order. Deleuze implies as much when he alludes to exhaustion as "nothing."[55] God, defined here as "the sum total of possibility," is also that which "merges with Nothing."[56] The challenge, then, is to think Beckett's constructions of languages one, two and three as effecting this "nothing." After all, we can see the television plays clearly enough; the image of the woman is very much apparent to the protagonist of ...*but the clouds*.... Yet we are told that once the image appears "there is ... the end of all possibility."[57] At that moment, existence is no more.[58]

Second in line is the question of correlationism itself. Is Deleuze a correlationist or not? Do the "primary aesthetics" of "The Exhausted" escape the bind of the correlationist circle? Or do they, like so much of modern philosophy, fall back into the correlationist double step?

To discuss fully Deleuze's take on the relation between thought and being is beyond the scope of this paper. Suffice it to say that it would require a more careful examination of Deleuze's three passive syntheses than I have provided. Specifically, such an examination would have to show how the epistemological trajectory that leads from violence of the intensive encounter to representation can be interpreted ontologically as the story of Being wrested away from beings and then restored back to them.[59] Central to this project

---

[55] Deleuze, "The Exhausted," 153.

[56] Ibid.

[57] Ibid., 161.

[58] By existence, I here mean the "given" existence of entities in the order of space and time. It is important to note that despite thinking beyond such "givenness," Deleuze does not wish to describe an ontological "leap" from non-being to being. See Deleuze, *Difference and Repetition*, 263.

[59] Deleuze, *Difference and Repetition*, 50-52, 66, 69, 80-81, 113-14, 141-42, 153.

would be the definition of two Nietzschean concepts, the "will to power" equated with this "world of intensities" and the "eternal return," associated more closely with "thought." If the will to power is understood as that initial intensive difference of the encounter, then the eternal return is the "affirmation, reproduction, repetition or return of difference."[60] The eternal return is the thought of our own affection, the affection of the self by the self, or as Blanchot put it, a kind of sign that signifies only itself.[61]

Turning towards the aesthetics of "The Exhausted," several points can be made without further discussing Deleuze's debt to Nietzsche. Firstly, the framework of "The Exhausted" is broadly speaking ontological in character. In a kind of reversal of Spinoza's logic,[62] the possible is defined as "existence," whereas God "merges with Nothing."[63] Yet the image towards which exhaustion aims is defined primarily in terms of thought. The image is "mental" in nature, encountered by the protagonist of *...but the clouds...* when he is seated in his "mental" chamber.[64] The tension between the two orders of being and thought is striking and reaches a certain kind of resolution in the comparison of the protagonist's mental state with the third dark zone of Murphy's mind.

When Beckett writes, "Here he was not free, but a mote in the dark of absolute freedom," this is suggestive of a very particular state of being. In the third zone of his mind, Murphy has no agency. He is not free to manipulate events as he was in the light of zone one. Neither has he the freedom to stand back and contemplate a new form of the world as was the case in the half-light of zone two. Within this third zone,

---

See also the summary in Hughes, *Deleuze's Difference and Repetition,* 61-65.

[60] Hughes, *Deleuze's Difference and Repetition,* 63.

[61] Maurice Blanchot, *Friendship,* trans. Elizabeth Rottenberg (Stanford: Stanford University Press, 1997), 173.

[62] See the more detailed discussion of this reversal in Asja Szafraniec, *Beckett, Derrida and the Event of Literature* (Stanford: Stanford University Press, 2007), 121.

[63] Deleuze, "The Exhausted," 153.

[64] Ibid., 169.

his freedom is irrevocably dissolved in the absolute freedom of movement. Ontologically speaking, there is no distinction between his state of freedom and the zone's absolute freedom. He retains determinability—he is, after all, a "mote" on a "line"—but his movement, his travels and his pleasure are all part of the general flux rendering him fundamentally undetermined. As a "mote" he is carried by "the ceaseless unconditioned generation and passing away of line."[65]

From the above, we can conclude that Deleuze does not think being and thought separately, but rather indicates that there is a moment at which the two are in fact indistinguishable. Within the third zone of darkness, Murphy's state of being is pure thought, and pure thought is being.[66]

Can we then see Deleuze as a speculative realist avant la lettre? His isomorphism of being and thought seems to preclude this. Deleuze's debt to Kant is undeniable, specifically the way in which his superior empiricism builds on the relation between the *Critique of Pure Reason* and the *Critique of Judgement*. It is also important to remember that Deleuze never wishes to deny the world of givenness and representation but attempts to explain how such a world might come into being. However, Deleuze completes his epistemological account by returning to an ontology much more pre-critical in flavour. He grounds his system of knowledge in the isomorphism between thought and being, Spinoza's idea of substance being one of the models for the third passive synthesis, the ideal synthesis of difference. How we interpret this gesture remains up for debate. We can limit it to the human mind in its conscious and unconscious states, but we can also open the transcendental field to being itself.[67]

---

[65] Beckett, *Murphy*, 112.

[66] Once more, an in-depth discussion of this relation between thought and being would require further study of Deleuze's reference to Blanchot in his formulation of the "aleatory point." See Deleuze, *Difference and Repetition*, 249-50 and compare this to Blanchot's discussion of "the central point" in Maurice Blanchot, *The Space of Literature*, trans. Ann Smock (Lincoln: University of Nebraska Press, 1989), 44-46.

[67] See Bryant, "Deleuze's Transcendental Materialism," 41-47.

The question then remains if the rehabilitation of the distinction between primary and secondary qualities is both urgent and necessary. I would argue that it is, if only to draw attention to these aspects of Deleuze's work which I have discussed above: the world "prior to birth," the non-existent, self-dissipating nature of the "image" and the relation of thought and being in the murky world of the "system of the future."[68] Perhaps only by reading Meillassoux's critique of transcendentalism can we find the absolute hidden within a Kantian tradition. And perhaps only then can we see the face of the woman appearing to the protagonist of *…but the clouds…* as some kind of an encounter with it.

---

[68] Deleuze, "The Exhausted," 152, 156, 169, 170; Deleuze, *Difference and Repetition*, 142.

Disegno
A Speculative Constructivist Interpretation

Sjoerd van Tuinen

Erasmus University Rotterdam

Speculation and Sufficient Reason

SINCE THE AIM OF THIS ISSUE IS TO stage an encounter between speculative philosophy and aesthetics, I should like to begin by distinguishing the concept of speculation that I feel most affinity with from other current conceptions. In a recent essay I argue why the principle of sufficient reason (PSR) is the speculative principle par excellence and not, as Quentin Meillassoux claims, only its irrational double.[1] Despite his critique of correlationism, Meillassoux's reading of the PSR converges not only with its Heideggerian interpretation as the original sin of Western philosophy, it is also indebted to the Kantian critique of the ontological proof, which culminated in Heidegger's critique of metaphysics as onto-theology precisely insofar as it targets the PSR for saying that "this or that entity must absolutely be *because* it is the way it is."[2] Hence, it is only logical for Meillassoux to draw on what

---

[1] Sjoerd van Tuinen, "Difference and Speculation: Heidegger, Meillassoux and Deleuze on Sufficient Reason" in *Deleuze and Metaphysics*, ed. Alain Beaulieu, Edward Kazarian, and Julia Sushytska (Lanham: Lexington Books, 2014), forthcoming.

[2] Quentin Meillassoux, *After Finitude: An Essay on the Necessity of Contingency*, trans. Ray Brassier (London: Continuum, 2008), 22-23, original emphasis.

is strongest in the correlationist tradition, even if only to turn it against itself. What remains of correlationism, in the end, is nonetheless precisely the critical, i.e., anti-metaphysical treatment of the PSR. Indeed, Meillassoux's rejection of the PSR in terms of the "principle of unreason" or "principle of factuality" forms the very core of his double criticist project: an investigation of the general conditions of possibility of scientific knowledge and of rational ideology critique.

By contrast, a more affirmative concept of speculation based precisely on the PSR can be found in Gilles Deleuze and the empiricist tradition of Henri Bergson, Alfred North Whitehead, John Dewey and more recently Isabelle Stengers—a tradition that, despite his occasional references to it, does not seem to fit Meillassoux's epistemological division of contemporary philosophy into correlationism, metaphysics or speculative idealism, and speculative materialism. After all, already Hume disconnected reason from what it grounds not only because he was a proto-critical thinker who rejected the presuppositions of a systematic order in nature (Meillassoux refers to this rejection as "Hume's problem"), but also, as Deleuze demonstrates so convincingly in *Empiricism and Subjectivity*, because he inquired into how such a system comes about. According to Kant, we have universally valid knowledge of the world because the transcendental subject's imagination schematises sense experience so that the categories of the understanding become applicable to it. By contrast, Hume's "schematism"[3] could never be a subjective system rendering possible empirical knowledge, as the subject is not an a priori ground, but itself an experimental and provisory actualisation of a virtual schema rooted in the impersonal and pre-individual intensity of experience. The schematism—or as Deleuze later calls it, the "diagram" or "abstract machine"—is a speculative system or "image of thought" that is elaborated

---

[3] Gilles Deleuze, *Empiricism and Subjectivity: An Essay on Hume's Theory of Human Nature*, trans. Constantin V. Boundas (New York: Columbia University Press, 1991), 65.

in and through experience.[4] As a consequence, sufficient reason is neither the ground that lies out there waiting to be discovered, nor is it merely a subjective form which we impose upon the world. Rather than belonging to an order of knowledge, it belongs to an order of production and subjectivation. As was already the case in Spinoza and Leibniz, the genesis of the system also implies the material genesis of the world "in and through the system."[5]

Does this proto-correlationist position, according to which anything totally a-subjective cannot be thought, necessarily disqualify Hume and his followers as speculative thinkers? Or is not the problem rather with Meillassoux and his "intellectual intuition" of the necessity of contingency, which in its purely formal "capacity-to-be-other relative to the given" risks remaining empty and irrelevant in the face of the here and now?[6] It is true that Meillassoux fuses absolute logical necessity with an equally absolute contingency of being and thus radically disconnects the domain of the thinkable from concrete experience. Yet while the principle of non-contradiction may well be sufficient in the hyper-chaotic domain of logical possibility, it becomes insufficient as soon as we are talking about real possibilities, which, as Kant and Heidegger knew well, are bound to temporal experiences. This is why Bergson replaces the possible/real opposition with that of the virtual/actual. Whereas conditions of possibility have a limitative relation to the real (correlationism), or are at best meaningless in the face of it ("anything is possible"), the virtual conditions of the actual are no less real than the actual since they are first of all its unconditioned or unformed potential of becoming other. Thus, while Meillassoux denies himself all means of accounting for real genesis by discarding the PSR *tout court*, Bergson merely disconnects the PSR from

---

[4] Gilles Deleuze, *Difference and Repetition*, trans. Paul Patton (London: Continuum, 2001), 131.

[5] Gilles Deleuze, *Desert Islands and Other Texts 1953-1974*, ed. David Lapoujade, trans. Mike Taormina (New York: Semiotext(e), 2004), 146.

[6] Meillassoux, *After Finitude*, 58-59.

the realisation of the possible. He does not seek a foundation for what already is, but rather schematises the consolidation of present becomings.

The same can be said of Deleuze, who proposes a new practical use of the PSR rather than a deconstruction or rejection of it. With Deleuze, the PSR is no longer a principle of identity, nor is it subordinate to, or in conflict with, the latter's inverse, the principle of non-contradiction. Rather, the PSR is the principle of difference. On the one hand, the PSR does refer to something necessary, a differential element, an intensive ground or necessarily existing milieu: life. But on the other hand, precisely because it refers to difference instead of identity, it is not a transcendent principle but an immanent one. It concerns what really makes a difference in life: thought. If Deleuze is indeed a classical metaphysician, as he often says, this is because he rejects the Kantian bifurcation between speculative and practical reason as a nominalist illusion. For Kant, ideas have uses that can be practical, religious or aesthetic, but no longer speculative or metaphysical. Thinking becomes metaphysical when it makes epistemological claims about what lies outside experience. In this sense, Meillassoux is right to call his attempt to go beyond correlationism speculative. But for Deleuze, ideas are always both speculative and practical. Even the Platonic idea concerns less the theoretical distinction between true and false knowledge than the pragmatic or dramatic distinction between claims to truth: "The problem of thought is tied to … the evaluation of what is important and what is not, to the distribution of the singular and the regular, distinctive and ordinary points … To have an idea means no more than this."[7] Put differently, the "speculative and practical object" of philosophy is not the representation of Truth, Justice, or Beauty, but their problematic, i.e., the overwhelming presence of their multiple immanent becomings.[8] Knowing, acting and judging

---

[7] Deleuze, *Difference and Repetition*, 189-90.

[8] Gilles Deleuze, *The Logic of Sense*, trans. Mark Lester and Charles Stivale (London: Continuum, 1990), 266.

are practical solutions that give form to an unformed frenzy (Being or Life as the groundless ground or *sans-fond*).[9] They are *real constructions* detected and evaluated by the "speculative investment"[10] or *amor fati* of thought and effectuated by the difference that forms their ground (the "dark precursor").[11] Such is the speculative immanence of thought and life, or reason and ground: like a flash of lightning distinguishing itself from the dark night without the latter distinguishing itself from it, "it is as if the ground rose to the surface without ceasing to be the ground."[12]

It is in a similar way that Isabelle Stengers defines her own version of "speculative constructivism": "The problem is not to ground, to define conditions for valid knowledge, but to care for the consequences of the event."[13] If to speculate is to think about something without knowing it, this means that it always involves some kind of risk. Whereas both Heidegger and Meillassoux interpret the PSR as the metaphysical principle that says that all that exists must be logically accounted for, Stengers treats it not as a principle of accountability but as a principle of prudence or active responsibility for the practical effects of our reasonings, no matter whether these concern truth, justice, or beauty. Thus, the PSR again becomes the principle of an ethics in the pre-Kantian sense, that is, an ethics of our actual becomings. To speculate with the PSR is to believe in a dispositional basis for future existence, thought and action and to be transformed by this belief. In other words, it is to speculate on the virtual becoming of what is actual, i.e., the real ideas inherent in the interstices of any actual situation. Whether in philosophy, science or art, speculative thinking is an art of pure expression or efficacy, an art of precipitating events: an art that detects and affirms the possibility of other

---

9 Deleuze, *The Logic of Sense*, 152-54.

10 Ibid., 238.

11 Deleuze, *Difference and Repetition*, 119.

12 Ibid., 28.

13 Isabelle Stengers, "William James: An Ethics of Thought?," *Radical Philosophy* (2009), 157, 9-17.

reasons insisting in a concrete situation as so many virtual forces that have not yet had the chance to emerge but whose presence can be trusted upon to make a difference.

Disegno: What Does it Mean to Have an Idea?

But let us stop pursuing this intra-philosophical discussion any further here. Instead, I want to develop my argument in a more practical way, namely by setting up a speculative relay within the utterly unfashionable beginnings of modern art history and theory of art in sixteenth century Italian mannerism—an undertaking typical of what Graham Harman in his contribution to this issue refers to as provincial retrieval. For it was then and there that the liberal arts began to systematise and rationalise their own practice raising the speculative question of what it means to have an idea, in other words, what the conditions are for the production of the new.[14] My aim is to propose an alternative to the usual neo-Kantian, humanist interpretations of this self-conscious, mannerist questioning that is more adequate to actual artistic practice. This is not only a way to put to the test the speculative project sketched above, including the claim that art is capable of thinking speculatively and not just practically by itself; it also enables us to better understand the connection between specifically artistic problems and their wider material, intellectual and spiritual contexts that drove the mannerists into speculation. After all, it was because of this connection that Erwin Panofsky in his classic *Idea* (1924) observed a clear parallel between mannerism and modern expressionism, a parallel which has to do with their shared interest in artistic ideas:

> Expressionism is related to mannerism in more than one sense, it comes with the particular speculation that guides us back to the paths followed by the metaphysics of art of 16th century theory, paths that seek

---

[14] Ernst Cassirer/Erwin Panofsky, *Eidos und Eidolon/Idea*, ed. John Michael Krois (Hamburg: Philo Fine Arts, 2008), 123.

to derive the phenomenon of artistic creativity from an extrasensory and absolute, or as we say today, cosmic principle.[15]

Mannerism is often said to begin with Michelangelo. Whereas Alberti warned artists against placing too much trust in their genius, advising them to confine themselves to the great model that is divinely created nature, Michelangelo relied on his *ingegno*, the power of his artistic mind to improve nature instead of merely imitating it. Nature for him was no more than an occasional cause calling forth the ideas virtually contained in the intellect. According to his most famous sonnet, he held that "the best artist has no concept [*concetto*] which some single marble does not potentially enclose within its mass, but only the hand which obeys the intellect [*intelletto*] can accomplish it."[16] Of course, the ancient and medieval tradition also knew this distinction between two successive stages in artistic creation, conception and execution. But even in the Renaissance, rules had been developed only for the second stage of the artistic process. With mannerism, by contrast, the new intellectual dignity of the liberal arts demanded reflection on the conception or design (*disegno*)—meaning drawing but also trained judgment and mental synthesis—and on the coordination of the two stages. Following the Neoplatonic tradition, the eye judges and the hand executes, but each under its own conditions. As Federico Zuccaro put it in a well-known passage: "For the thought [of the artist] has to be not only clear, but also free, and his spirit has to be released from and not limited by a mechanical dependence on such rules [of execution provided by the 'mathematical sciences']."[17]

[15] Panofsky, *Idea*, 149. This and all subsequent translations from German, unless otherwise indicated, are my own.

[16] Michelangelo Buonarroti as cited in Robert J. Clements, *Michelangelo's Theory of Art* (New York: New York University Press, 1961), 16.

[17] Federico Zuccaro as cited in Elizabeth Gilmore Holt, select. and ed., *A Documentary History of Art, Volume II: Michelangelo and the Mannerists, The Baroque and the Eighteenth Century* (New Jersey: Princeton University Press, 1982), 91.

According to classical humanist interpretations first inspired by Jakob Burckhardt and then ratified by Panofsky, what unites the eye of the artistic genius and the hand of the skilled craftsman is the conjunction of idea and mimesis. For Vasari, each of the three arts of design—painting, sculpture, architecture—still relied unequivocally on the mimesis of the visible perfection of nature. Subsequent theorists such as Danti, Lomazzo and Zuccaro, by contrast, sought the freedom of art in the imitation of the *concetto* or idea, which becomes the sufficient reason of the work of art. For example, Vincenzo Danti in his *Trattato delle perfette proporzioni* (1567) writes that "an artist should not simply copy (*ritrarre*) visible nature but should imitate it (*imitare*) in its purposes; that is to say, he should imitate the perfected intentional form of nature."[18] Whereas men such as Alberti and Leonardo were anxious to curb the latent artificiality of the idea by insisting on natural depiction, the conflict between realistic imitation and artificial improvement, objective matter and subjective manner now made its full appearance. With the doctrine of *disegno interno* or inward design (Zuccaro)—the drawing after an internal design guiding the hand that replaces the *disegno esterno* of external models that dominated Renaissance formalism—the idea could emerge as an autonomous standard of perfection, eventually becoming a pre-existent concept independent of nature and execution. Art thus no longer relies on knowledge of reality, but competes with it through its self-conscious *sapere dell'artifice*. It begins to develop its own, strictly artistic knowledge that is to be taught in special academies, e.g., the Florentine Academy of the *arti del disegno* which transformed art from studio craft into philosophical study, accompanied by critical literature on aesthetic problems. For the first time, concepts of art, criticism and art history are articulated as such and form a kind of closed circuit—a discourse—in which artists inspire critics and historians who write for well-trained practitioners.

---

[18] Cited in Panofsky, *Idea*, 121.

In a paradoxical way, then, the mannerist apology for artistic freedom tends to go together with an unequalled emphasis on the academic training and rational systematisation of creativity. Whereas in the Kantian aesthetic, the faculty to know nature would be strictly distinguished from the faculty to judge art, rendering the aesthetic Idea transcendent to all rational speculation, mannerism sought to unite idea and conceptual rule in terms of an "imitation taken to the limit."[19] On the one hand, this unity of idea and imitation explains Kant's rejection of mannerism in terms of the opposition of genius to docile "mannering" or "mimicry" (*Manierieren*), since in the latter the Idea disappears in the unimaginative following of the rules set up by the former.[20] At the limit of imitation, on the other hand, we already discover the aporetic tension between the subjective abhorrence of rules and the fascination with objective know-how, between irrational but creative genius and rational but pedantic craftsmanship. This tension may always have been at the core of art, but is now made productive self-reflexively for the first time in the very perfection by which classical models are twisted, deformed and contorted. Panofsky therefore argues that in mannerism the idea ceases to be merely a model, as it was in Renaissance classicism, and becomes properly plastic: from Vasari onwards, we witness not only the birth of art theory and art history, but first of all the beginning of reflections on the conditions of possibility of artistic creativity in general that was to culminate in the Kantian theory of artistic genius.[21] Henceforth, the history of art is able to define itself as the auto-movement of a strictly artistic idea of perfection and its perfected imitation, the *imitazione fantastica*.[22]

---

[19] Panofsky, *Idea*, 132.

[20] Immanuel Kant, *Kritik der Urteilskraft* (Frankfurt a. M.: Suhrkamp, 1997), §49, 256.

[21] Panofsky, *Idea*, 119-23.

[22] Georges Didi-Huberman, *Confronting Images: Questioning the Ends of a Certain History of Art*, trans. John Goodman (University Park: Penn State University Press, 2005), 46. "Vasari here becomes the first thinker about art to have

Now there are at least two well-known historical problems with this account of the mannerist idea that have important philosophical consequences. The first is that Michelangelo's reference to the intellect should not be understood in anachronistic subjectivist terms as the artist's individual and private genius. Artists cannot be abstracted from the "spark of divinity" (*scintilla di dio*) or divine sign (*segno di dio*, Zuccaro's quasi-anagram of *disegno*) that inspires them. The new status of the plastic arts relies on an argument from design: "Disegno is nothing other than divine speculation, which produces an excellent art; you cannot execute anything in sculpture or painting without the guide of this speculation and design."[23] Just as originality was not a value in itself and replication was an everyday practice in the artist's workshop (if they had one), the notion of *ingegno*, like that of perfection and *maniera*, was first of all used as a compliment that referred either to the divinity of the artist's hand and/or to the artist's social status.[24] In pragmatist-philosophical terms, this means that any privately enjoyed artistic experience or design remains incomplete without public embodiment: "What made Michelangelo or Beethoven great, what turned

---

questioned the reality of the 'thing in itself'." Didi-Huberman, *Confronting Images*, 110. Didi-Huberman summarises Panofsky's neo-Kantian adaptation of Vasarian academism in three "magic words": "the Renaissance is recast in terms of rationalist humanism and its conception of the history of art; imitation is recast by hierarchical subordination of figuration to signification; and the inevitable idea recast in an idealist use of Kant's transcendental schematism." Didi-Huberman, *Confronting Images*, xix. Moreover, he regards this art-historical academism as definitive for the "humanist conception of art in general": "a conception wherein *Mimesis* walked hand-in-hand with *Idea*, wherein the tyranny of the visible—the tyranny of resemblance and of congruent appearance—had managed to express itself perfectly in the abstract terms of an ideational truth or an ideal truth, of a *disegno interno* of Truth or of an ideal of Beauty ... all of which ultimately comes back to the same thing, namely *Sameness* as shared metaphysical authority." Didi-Huberman, *Confronting Images*, 88, original emphases.

[23] Anton Francesco Doni as cited in Stephen J. Campbell and Michael W. Cole, *Italian Renaissance Art* (London: Thames & Hudson, 2012), 496.

[24] See Patricia A. Emison, *Creating the "Divine" Artist: From Dante to Michelangelo* (Leiden: Brill, 2004).

them into geniuses, was not their genius as such, it was their attention to the qualities of genius, not in themselves, but in the work."[25]

The second problem is that the alleged rationalism of leading mannerist theorists—although a direct and necessary extension of practice—is hardly able to give an adequate description of what goes on in mannerist *art*, or indeed in any artistic practice. The question is even whether their focus on the imitation or representation of the idea is not fundamentally misguided.

It is true that mannerist discourse aims for conceptual knowledge about art. It constitutes art as an object of knowledge and thus provides a self-legitimation of art as a coherent and recognisable order of historical progression. Thus whereas in Cennino Cennini's old *Libro dell'Arte*, *disegno* was first of all a material practice that may or may not occupy the painters' mind, in Vasari it becomes the power of the mind to form purely mental pictures which, according to scholastic faculty psychology, is the fundamental faculty of judgment that relates the fine arts to all rational activities. For this reason, historians tend to focus on the epistemological purport of *disegno* and, as a consequence, take it as a figurative form of rational thought, even a metaphysical "system" of representation within the horizon of imitation as the final aim of art no less than of other, more explicitly knowledge-oriented practices.[26]

Yet, as Kant already saw, this epistemological conjunction of idea and imitation hardly enables us to cross the gap between theory and artistic practice. Art becomes philosophical, yet philosophy forgets art. Hence Georges Didi-Huberman's

---

[25] Étienne Souriau, *Les différents modes d'existence* (Paris: PUF, 2009), 161, my translation.

[26] Robert Williams, for example, has recently argued that in mannerism art seeks the status of a "*metatechne*," "a superintendency of knowledge, a form of knowledge, a mode of knowing that necessarily involves a mastery of other modes and is distinguished by being potentially, ideally, a mastery of all modes." Robert Williams, *Art, Theory, and Culture in Sixteenth Century Italy: From Techne to Metatechne* (Cambridge: Cambridge University Press, 2010), 4.

warning: "Imitation in the Renaissance is a *credo*, but it is not for all that a unifying principle."[27] But neither is the quasi-theological notion of the genius, in whom nature gives the rule to art without the artist himself being aware of it.[28] For the point is not that the speculative idea of art lies outside of knowledge, even less that a genius creates *ex nihilo* (i.e., spontaneously and thus without sufficient reason, as the Romantics claimed), but rather that knowledge of rules is only one aspect of the speculative search for sufficient reason, albeit often a necessary and important one. In reality, there is always a continuous circuit and indiscernibility between thinking, knowing and acting. Neither in artistic design nor elsewhere do we find the purely theoretical opposition between speculation and practice, conceptualisation and execution, genius and work. Creativity is not achieved at a single stroke but involves a whole series of translations and transpositions from sketch to *pentimento* to painting or from *bozzetto* to sculpture or building. This means that, as Dewey puts it, "wherever continuity is possible, the burden of proof rests upon those who assert opposition and dualism."[29] With Deleuze, we could add that, inversely, whenever such theoretical oppositions nonetheless persist, or even arise out of practical problems as so many necessary illusions, the task of philosophy is to demonstrate real continuity, even if this

[27] Didi-Huberman, *Confronting Images*, 74. There is indeed a rational system in Vasari, Didi-Huberman argues, but it is a cracked system, or rather, a "mended crack" that forever separates knowledge about art from the truth of art. What mends the crack is the floating signifier of *disegno*: "A totem-word reinvented and reinvested to decline the final, synchronic meaning of artistic activity in general understood as imitation." *Disegno* "is a descriptive word and it is a metaphysical word. It is a technical word and it is an ideal word. It is applicable to the hand of man, but also to his imaginative *fantasia*, and also to his *intelletto*, and also to his *anima*—as well as, finally, to God the creator of all things. It comes from the vocabulary of the studio, where it designates the form obtained on a support by the charcoal or crayon of the artist; it also designates the sketch, the work in gestation, the project, the compositional schema, and the layout of lines of force." Didi-Huberman, *Confronting Images*, 72, 80.

[28] Kant, *Kritik der Urteilskraft*, §46, 307.

[29] John Dewey, *Art as Experience* (New York: Penguin, 2005), 28.

implies that for once we do not heed the Deleuzian warning that philosophers do not listen carefully enough to what painters themselves say.[30]

This aim of demonstrating real continuity pertains especially to mannerism, in which the breakdown of the classical configuration of theory and practice heralds the breakthrough of a speculative regime of art. As Giancarlo Maiorino has pointed out, the Italian *perfettissimo*, so often used by sixteenth century theorists of art, puts the highest standard of classicism—perfection—into a superlative quantification that is logically redundant, thus pointing the idea-ideal toward construction rather than Kantian exemplification. From humanist "perfection" to the early mannerist "wholly perfect" (*perfetissimo*, Castiglione, Vasari) to the later mannerist "perfectly" (*perfettamente*, Danti), this hyperbolic excess "brought perfection within a 'modal' reach at the other side of the concept itself. Mannerism returned to the realm of practice what humanism had raised to ideal heights."[31] In other words, mannerism is based on a procedural excess that frees the difference of mimesis from the objective restrictions and standards of identity. As Gian Pietro Bellori would write a few decades later, it is based on a "*fantastica idea appoggiata alla pratica e non all'imitazione.*"[32] In the shift from the noun to the adjectival to the adverbial—a shift from idealisation to stylisation—it discovers an inventiveness and variability beyond measure: "The adverbial mode toned down teleological concerns, so that perfection brought out forms of a 'mannered' understanding of its own potential."[33] Subjective style thus becomes a speculative force that thrives upon its own precursory dynamics, a repetitive manner that gains strength

---

[30] Gilles Deleuze, *Francis Bacon: The Logic of Sensation*, trans. Daniel W. Smith (London: Continuum, 2004), 99.

[31] Giancarlo Maiorino, *The Portrait of Eccentricity: Arcimboldo and the Mannerist Grotesque* (University Park: Penn State University Press, 1991), 20, 3, 16.

[32] Giovanni Pietro Bellori, «Annibale Carracci» in *Le vite de' pittori, scultori et architetti moderni* (Rome: Mascardi, 1728), 1.

[33] Maiorino, *The Portrait of Eccentricity*, 30.

or expressivity from its own redundancy and empties out all objective matter and content: an "adjectival reduction" by which "excess took on itself, reversing matter into *maniera*."[34]

Thus, even if art now comes to need a theoretical legitimation, perhaps even *sub specie divinitatis* as is the case in the gnoseology of Lomazzo (which is based on Neoplatonism and Hermeticism) and Zuccaro (which is more Aristotelian), we should not mislead ourselves by saying that pre-Kantian aesthetics was somehow "rationalist" whereas almost no twentieth century philosopher would even consider having an idea in art as an intellectual affair. Instead of an epistemological interpretation, we should rather reconnect metaphysical speculation with its actual application in a material practice according to a singularising manner. As Zuccaro himself stresses throughout his *Idea of the Sculptors, Painters and Architects* (1607), the concept of inward design makes no sense when disconnected from practical work and sense experience. In art, there is no *intellectus speculativus* without *intellectus practicus*.[35] We can still call the actualisation of an idea a rationalisation or a process of speculative reasoning,[36] but that is to say that art generally thinks and is grounded directly in images, sounds and sometimes words. No reflection is needed to experience this plane of composition. It is true that with mannerism, art also begins to think indirectly, i.e., through concepts, but this has as little to do with a rationalist "aesthetics" in the modern sense as with postmodern conceptual art. Its rationality did not arise out of epistemology or philosophy, but out of art. As a consequence, whereas artists have the speculative ability to visualise things that are not there and therefore must have a clear idea of what they are doing, it does not follow that this idea must be detailed or distinct. The artistic idea is not a matter of rational contemplation

---

[34] Maiorino, *The Portrait of Eccentricity*, 27.

[35] Zuccaro as cited in Williams, *Art, Theory, and Culture in Sixteenth Century Italy*, 138.

[36] Gilles Deleuze, "Pericles and Verdi: The Philosophy of François Châtelet," trans. Charles T. Wolfe, *The Opera Quarterly* (2006), 21:4, 713-24.

but of sensible intuition, even if it must now be legitimated in terms of conceptual knowledge. It is closer to a confused passion or affective transition than to a distinct seeing. As a consequence, it is not distributed in whole-parts (clear light as synthesis analysable in distinct, but homogenous parts) relationships, but among heterogeneous and indivisible intensities, that is, in differential multiplicities. It is not found in the evidence of natural light, but in the differentiated light of an artificial chiaroscuro. As Leibniz observed, ideas of artists are usually clear but confused and thus inseparable from the obscure ground of their practice: "painters and other artists correctly know what is done properly and what is done poorly, though they are often unable to explain their judgments and reply to questioning by saying that the things that displease them lack an unknown something."[37] Or to put it in Deleuze's terms, artists are "visionaries" or "seers" of ideas, provided that thought and action, eye and hand, *aisthesis* and *genesis* are only the extremes of a continuum of experience and expression: "Ideas have to be treated like potentials already *engaged* in one mode of expression or another and inseparable from the mode of expression, such that I cannot say that I have an idea in general."[38]

Whether in art or in philosophy, then, thinking is a seeking-groping experimentation with the material ground. Ideas are always pragmatic, just as their eventual speculative conceptualisation always has a practical orientation. Despite some art historians' predilections for written sources over actual images, we should not maintain theoretical subjectivity independent of the objective execution of the work of art.

---

[37] Gottfried Wilhelm Leibniz, *Philosophical Essays*, trans. Roger Ariew and Daniel Garber (Indianapolis: Hackett, 1989), 24. Of course, this chiaroscuro rationality proper to sense perception and by extension to art was to be developed into a full-scale aesthetics by Alexander Gottlieb Baumgarten. See Jeffrey Barnouw, "The Cognitive Value of Confusion and Obscurity in the German Enlightenment: Leibniz, Baumgarten, Herder," *Studies in Eighteenth Century Culture* (1995), 24, 29-50.

[38] Gilles Deleuze, *Two Regimes of Madness: Texts and Interviews 1975-1995*, ed. David Lapoujade, trans. Ames Hodges and Mike Taormina (New York: Semiotext(e), 2006), 312.

What matters is not the self-legitimating intellectualism of the mannerists, but the practical forces that are relayed by it.[39] Once we apply this lesson of genealogy to the history of art, we can effectively reverse Zuccaro's speculative etymology of design from the theological metamorphosis of the physical world into a material metamorphosis of the idea—a reversal of Platonism. The real problem of mannerism, the intuition that forced it into conceptual speculation, is not that it is devoid of genius or the artistic idea, as Kant once suggested and as is still common sense today, but rather that the idea does not exist outside, and has to be found within, its manual expressions and its changing material conditions. And do we not already recognise in this reversal the Copernican revolution to which Deleuze refers as the complex unity of difference and repetition, of practice and speculation, one being the vehicle for the other, in which the "what" of representational content is entirely subsumed by the presentational and expressive "how"?

---

[39] Ultimately, the interpretation and evaluation of such forces is what necessitates a speculative approach to art history. As noted by Didi-Huberman, however, Panofsky's later re-edition of *Idea* features a preliminary warning (CAUTIUS!) that should protect his discipline from immoderations in the cognitive exercise of reason such as Aby Warburg's chiaroscuro rationalism. It is precisely this fear that led art history to the anti-speculative stance that it has consolidated until today: "Panofsky's *CAUTIUS* is not only a call for prudence; it is the cry of someone who went too far into the shifting sands of philosophical idealism, and who found only the worst branch—that of positivism, of iconography in a shrunken sense—to prevent his sinking and losing forever the singular truth of art images." Didi-Huberman, *Confronting Images*, 125, xxv. If Panofsky's iconography exorcised the very life of the image, however, Didi-Huberman's turn to semiology and the "phenomenology of the gaze" does not suffice to reverse Panofsky's reduction of "the permanence of crystal" to "the chronology of a story." Didi-Huberman, *Confronting Images*, 16-17, 13. Although it seeks to describe the "efficacy" of the visual as a "virtual" appearance or event such as it appears at the junction of a proliferation of possible meanings, it only includes the event of art in history as subjectively lived experience. Didi-Huberman, *Confronting Images*, 18-19. While a speculative approach seeks to actively reconnect with the very a-historical creative force in the historical genesis of such an experience, Didi-Huberman's ambition remains historicist and critical, i.e., namely to write a "true critique" or a "critical history of the history of art" as opposed to a "speculative" one. Didi-Huberman, *Confronting Images*, xx, 4, 25.

Idea and Maniera: From Leibniz to Bergson

If both genius and its ideas do not exist outside their material expressions, then it is no longer possible to interpret the mannerist theory of mimesis in hylomorphic terms as saying that the content lies waiting within the marble for its form to be hewn out. Of course, the authority of mannerist texts on art has led to precisely such an interpretation, which is idealist insofar as it would be the task of the intellect to recognise the form of this content and of the obeying hand merely to free it from the surrounding mass. It was precisely in these Aristotelian terms that Benedetto Varchi, a pupil of Michelangelo's, described the task of the sculptor as an inducing of "form" into "matter," as a drawing forth of "real" from "potential" existence. But when he complimented his master, "Signor Buonarroti, you have the brain of a Jove," Michelangelo responded "but Vulcan's hammer is required to make something come out of it."[40] The passage from the intellectual *concetto* to the hand that realises it entails much more than just a hylomorphic passage from matter to predetermined form, because the idea of the whole composition must constantly be rehearsed in a painstaking process of experimental construction. In the words of Charles de Tolnay that describe Michelangelo's *Day* and *Night* (1526-31):

> In a very real way the primitive form of the block had a decisive influence on Michelangelo's imagination. As he became absorbed in it, the inner image awoke in him; one can actually see how in his sculptures and reliefs he always allowed himself to be guided by the primitive form of the block, and in his frescoes by the dimension and shape of the surfaces at his disposal.[41]

More philosophically speaking, if the material work of art is not simply conceived in the image of its concept or idea, this

---

[40] Michelangelo Buonoarroti as cited in Robert J. Clements, *Michelangelo's Theory of Art* (New York: New York University Press, 1961), 35.

[41] Charles de Tolnay, *The Art and Thought of Michelangelo*, trans. Nan Buranelli (New York: Pantheon Books, 1964), 97.

means that mannerist imitation can no longer be interpreted in the classical terms of the real and the possible, the latter somehow resembling and limiting the former. In reality, as Bergson argues, possibility means only an "absence of hindrance," which the human intellect retrospectively turns into "pre-existence under the form of the idea":[42] "For the possible is only the real with the addition of an act of mind which throws its image back into the past, once it has been enacted."[43] In Aristotelian terms: *energeia* is prior to *dynamis*, the actual is prior to the potential. In order to understand what a truly creative act is, we therefore need an alternative to classical aesthetics in which thought precedes expression, and thus also to its scientific representative, art history or the rationalised study of creative processes.

It is striking that Bergson consistently illustrates his critique of possibility with examples from art before extrapolating his argument to the universe understood as global and continuous creation of unforeseeable novelty:

> When a musician composes a symphony was his work possible before being real? Yes, if by this we mean that there was no insurmountable barrier to its realisation. But from this completely negative sense of the word we pass, inadvertently, to a positive sense: we imagine that everything which occurs could have been foreseen by any sufficiently informed mind, and that, in the form of an idea, it was thus preexistent to its realisation: an absurd conception in the case of a work of art, for from the moment that the musician has the precise and complete idea of the symphony he means to compose, his symphony is done.[44]

It is absurd to think that a musician has a precise and complete idea of the symphony before it is realised, because in reality, creativity knows no retrograde movement, only intelligence

---

[42] Henri Bergson, *The Creative Mind: An Introduction to Metaphysics*, trans. Mabelle L. Andison (New York: Dover Publications, 2007), 83, 10.

[43] Bergson, *The Creative Mind*, 81.

[44] Ibid., 10.

does.[45] Indeed, the more general an idea is, i.e., the more possibility it contains, the emptier it is.[46] As a consequence, whereas "the technique of his art" and "the demands of the material" pertain to the knowledge of the artisan or the crafts-man, about the creativity of the artist—echoing Kant—"we know very little."[47] Poetic acts simply cannot be submitted to the reversible historical rationality of conditions of pos-sibility. No Zeitgeist, psychosocial or economic milieu, or technical development enables us to predict a priori what an act of generation will bring.

However, let us remember that Bergson distinguishes human intelligence, as the faculty of a posteriori remembrance, from the mind or spiritual life, which is the faculty of intuition (or as I am tempted to call it, a priori remembrance) and which is historically closer related to the Neoplatonist *intelletto*. To see something is not necessarily to know it. While the eye takes its legitimacy from the general idea, the mind takes its legitimacy directly from the singular and unforeseeable becoming of the visible itself. Intuitive ideas are generated in the mind's faculty of *fantasia*, a sub-rational but all the more speculative faculty of the mind, and therefore lack the generality of Platonic ideas. If things exist in time as much as in space, as intuition tells us, then we also see in time as much as in space. The intuition is the visionary ability to contract a multiplicity of abstract tendencies that enables the mind to recapitulate the constitutive elements of a concrete situation in "a simple thought *equivalent* to all the indefinite richness of form and color."[48] Now, is it not precisely in this sense that Lomazzo defined painting as the *perfezionatrice dell'intelletto*? As French cinematographer Robert Bresson says, to have a visionary idea is not to see what you are already thinking, but to think about what you see and to be the first

---

[45] Bergson, *The Creative Mind*, 10-11, 73, 75, 84.

[46] Ibid., 81.

[47] Ibid., 76.

[48] Ibid., 196, original emphasis.

to see what you see, the way you see it.[49] Accordingly, another interpretation of mannerist *disegno* opens up. In his essay on "The Life and Work of Ravaisson," a painter-philosopher, Bergson distinguishes the "intellectual intuition" of an idea in the mind from sensible intuition:

> This would be to extend the vision of the eye by a vision of the mind: without leaving the domain of intuition, that is, the intuition of things real, individual and concrete, to seek an intellectual intuition beneath the sensible intuition. To do that would be to pierce by a powerful effort of mental vision the material wrapping of things and to read the formula, invisible to the eye, which their materiality unrolls and manifests.[50]

Himself deeply influenced by Neoplatonism, Bergson claims that the "idea" as mental vision is simultaneously material and spiritual. It is no longer an ideal condition of possibility, but rather a material condition of reality, i.e., a matter-function, a virtual condition of the new. To have an idea is to move into, or adhere to, the *poiesis* of reality itself. It is to work back "from the intellectual and social plane to a point in the soul from which there springs an imperative demand for creation ... an impulse, an impetus received from the very depth of things."[51]

So what exactly is this ideal point in the soul that is intuitively present in the density of the real itself, i.e., in the depths of sensation-matter—or in the words of Michelangelo, "*della carne ancor vestita*"?[52] Long before Bergson, Leibniz gave us an important hint when in the preface to his *New Essays on*

---

[49] Robert Bresson, *Notes on Cinematography*, trans. Jonathan Griffin (New York: Urizen Books, 1975), 25, 57.

[50] Bergson, *The Creative Mind*, 190. This Bergsonist concept of "intellectual intuition," the model for which is art (or as Deleuze argues, the being of the sensible manifests itself in art), should be understood in contrast with that of Meillassoux, for whom the model is strictly logical.

[51] Henri Bergson, *The Two Sources of Morality and Religion* (Notre Dame: University of Notre Dame Press, 2006), 217.

[52] Michelangelo Buonarotti, *Le rime di Michelangelo Buonarroti, pittore, scultore e architetto*, ed. Cesare Guasti (Firenze: Le Monnier, 1863), 216.

Speculations V

the Human Understanding he invoked the analogy of veins in marble both to describe how pleats of matter surround living beings held in mass and how innate ideas are present in the soul. Leibniz substituted this analogy for that of the perfectly homogeneous and even surface of the blank tablet (*tabula rasa*) of Locke, who held that all truths originate in the senses. But his analogy also provides an interesting commentary on artistic production:

> For if the soul were like an empty page, then truths would be in us in the way that the shape of Hercules is in an uncarved piece of marble that is entirely neutral as to whether it takes Hercules' shape or some other. Contrast that piece of marble with one that is veined in a way that marks out the shape of Hercules rather than other shapes. This latter block would be more inclined to take that shape than the former would, and Hercules would be in a way innate in it, even though it would take a lot of work to expose the veins and to polish them into clarity, removing everything that prevents their being seen. This is how ideas and truths are innate in us—as inclinations, dispositions, tendencies, or natural virtualities [*virtualités*], and not as actions; although these virtualities are always accompanied by certain actions, often insensible ones, which correspond to them.[53]

Again, we must be wary of idealist interpretations. Ideas are not transcendental but virtual faculties, since they are never separable from empirical processes of actualisation.[54] Some

[53] Leibniz, *Philosophical Essays*, 294, translation modified. See also Gilles Deleuze, *The Fold: Leibniz and the Baroque*, trans. Tom Conley (Minneapolis: University of Minnesota Press, 1993), 4, 23, 146n19.

[54] In Dewey's commentary: "An innate idea is a dynamic relation of intelligence and some of its ideas. Intelligence has a structure, which necessarily functions in certain ways. Structure is not something ready-made. Rather it is the perfectly determined connections and relations which form the logical prius and the psychological basis of experience. Innate idea is a necessary activity of intelligence as it enters into the framework of all experience, not a faculty or potentiality. There is no hard and fixed division between a priori and a posteriori truths. They are 'real possibilities'." John Dewey, *The Early Works, 1882-1898, Volume 1, 1882-1888: Early Essays and Leibniz's New Essays* (Carbondale: Southern Illinois University Press, 2008), 307-10.

bodily action always "corresponds" to each minute perception in the dark depths of the soul, such that soul and body or subject and object are only different aspects or functions—functions of form and functions of matter—immanent to a single and same psychophysical continuum. At the same time, however, this continuum is an intermediary zone of immanence, an intensive chiaroscuro diversified by ideas that exceed their distribution in quality and extension. This means that, on the one hand, ideas constitute what François Jullien has called "the propensity of things," i.e., their implicit disposition to be (un) folded in a certain way, as if they were already by themselves accomplishing what the artist wants and for which the latter requires only a minimal force.[55] On the other hand, it does not follow that these ideas "resemble" their actualisation in the end product. If they did, they would be possibles. They would not be inclinations and dispositions, but fully developed models. In truth, we do not intuit our ideas as readymade and neither is there anything "natural" or "concrete" about them.[56] They are only "genitally innate" such that to invent is to find, *erfinden*, even if perfecting nature means to find in it what has never been found.[57] In other words, generative ideas are the "seeds of eternity" (Leibniz cites Scaliger) that do not exist outside of an infinite and continuous movement of development and differentiation.[58] Combining structure and genesis, expression and construction, the development of ideas is thus essentially a problem-solving process, not a process of modelling: "The virtual possesses the reality of a task to be done or a problem to be solved: it is the problem which orientates, conditions and engenders solutions, but these do not resemble the conditions of the problem."[59] It is

---

[55] François Jullien, *The Propensity of Things: Toward a History of Efficacy in China*, trans. Janet Lloyd (New York: Zone Books, 1999).

[56] *L'Abécédaire de Gilles Deleuze*, directed by Pierre-André Boutang (Paris: Editions Montparnasse, 2004), DVD, I.

[57] Deleuze, *Difference and Repetition*, 148.

[58] Leibniz, *Philosophical Essays*, 292.

[59] Deleuze, *Difference and Repetition*, 212.

in the same sense that Étienne Souriau defines the mode of existence of "work to be made" or "work to be done" (*oeuvre à faire*) as "virtual": every concretely existing thing responds to an abstract power of existence that urges its making as a restorative actualisation (*action* or *démarche instaurative*).[60] Instead of being distant, the virtual work and the actual work coincide or at least overlap in the manner or style in which the work is carried out.

However, Leibniz does not yet enable us to distinguish the specificity of the artistic conjunction of idea, matter and manner from their interrelation in general. In order to do so, we should develop the concept of the psychophysical continuum a bit further in terms of Bergson's *Matter and Memory*. On the one hand, Bergson teaches us that no (natural) perception is ever merely virtual, which means that every ideal vision is always directed towards some kind of material action and must itself be understood as "eventual action."[61] No mental intuition of an idea is therefore purely speculative. Rather, between vision and proprioception there is a vital intimacy, to which Bergson refers as the sensory-motor schema: a complex series of perceptions and actions which we know by heart and in which goal and movement, subject and object are fused together in an "immediate intelligence."[62] On the other

---

[60] Souriau, *Les différents modes d'existence*, 200. As Bruno Latour explains, instead of naming a redundant movement from matter to predetermined form, the concept of instauration (*restoration* and *instauration* have the same Latin etymology) describes a "growing existence," a "doing making (*faire faire*)" or "making exist" in such a way that the choice between what comes from the artist and what comes from the work is avoided: "saying of a work of art that it results from an instauration, is to get oneself ready to see the potter as the one who welcomes, gathers, prepares, explores and invents the form of the work, just as one discovers or 'invents' a treasure." Bruno Latour, "Reflections on Etienne Souriau's *Les différents modes d'existence*," trans. Stephen Muecke in *The Speculative Turn: Continental Materialism and Realism*, ed. Levi Bryant, Nick Srnicek and Graham Harman (Melbourne: Re-Press, 2010), 304-33. (In French the legal term for someone who discovers a treasure is "inventor").

[61] Bergson, *Matter and Memory*, 22, 17.

[62] Just as freedom is not confined to reflective will, but is also made flesh through motor habit, Félix Ravaisson argues that "as the end becomes fused with the movement, and the movement with the tendency, possibility, the idea,

hand, no perception is ever merely actual or material since it is always full of memories, i.e., the ideal contractions of time that are coexisting with, but independent from, the actual: "the past is only idea, the present is idea-motor."[63] Everything happens as if every actual perception was reflected in a crystal ball in which it communicates with memories, dreams, or retrospective possibilities that abstract themselves from the present. While these other, wider circuits between past and present can usually be discerned from actual perception, it is nonetheless necessary that we find both virtual and actual aspects of experience even in the smallest contraction of time, the one that is "the nearest to immediate perception."[64] It is even the very indiscernibility or "coalescence" of objective perception and subjective recollection in actual percep-tion—such that time splits itself in two at each moment as present and past, the one immediately chasing after the other in their "smallest circuit" (Bergson) or "immanence" (Deleuze)—that forms the condition of all other circuits of experience.[65] Even the most immediate perception has a vi-

---

is realised in it. The *idea* becomes *being*, the very being of the movement and of the tendency that it determines. Habit becomes more and more a *substantial idea*. The obscure intelligence that through habit comes to replace reflection, this immediate intelligence where subject and object are confounded, is a *real* intuition, in which the real and the ideal, being and thought are fused together." Félix Ravaisson, *Of Habit*, trans. Clare Carlisle and Mark Sinclair (London: Continuum, 2008), 55, original emphases.

[63] Bergson, *Matter and Memory*, 74, 24. Since ideo-motivity is still a too intel-lectualist notion, however, Deleuze points out that motivity is never based on an abstract representation *of* the idea, but on the repetition of the differential idea *in* real movement. "The movement of the swimmer does not resemble that of the wave, in particular, the movements of the swimming instructor which we reproduce on the sand bear no relation to the movements of the wave, which we learn to deal with only by grasping the former in practice as signs … In other words, there is no ideo-motivity, only sensory-motivity." Deleuze, *Difference and Repetition*, 23.

[64] Ibid., 127.

[65] Ibid., 130; Gilles Deleuze, *Cinema 2: The Time Image*, trans. Hugh Tomlinson and Robert Galeta (Minneapolis: University of Minnesota Press, 1989), 81. The fundamental splitting that constitutes the crystal is the "most fundamental operation of time"—and not merely the Heraclitean flow, as Meillassoux

sionary or hallucinatory quality to it. Although this presently appears only in paramnesia (the illusion of *déjà-vu*) in which the sensory-motor link or the organic linkage between man and world is momentarily interrupted, we are all clairvoyants in principle. We may be able to see for 100,000 miles when blinded sensory-motorically. Thus Bergson agrees with Leibniz and the mannerists that there is a "genetic and systematic priority of the idea with respect to the sense impressions."[66] We always see into the moving depth of chiaroscuro which constitutes the crystal, a psychophysical field of experience of which clear and distinct representation is only the kaleidoscopic effect. Subject and object, past and present, the possible and the real belong to the same living whole, the same psychophysical continuum. The ideal whole of the past is invisible, but virtually co-present with the actual, in which it appears as a hallucinatory fragment, a fissure or a cut in the sensory-motor schema.

But is it not precisely in aesthetic vision as opposed to natural perception that the whole of the past rises to its crystalline surface and is preserved *in itself*, i.e., as pure virtuality insisting outside all motor consciousness and in time alone? In natural perception, the crystalline quality of time appears indirectly, in more or less conscious states of recollection, imagination or dreaming: virtual experiences that are always already actualised *for themselves* in one psychological state or another, objectively mediated by the privileged perspective of organic and sensory-motor behaviour which accords them a capricious or intermittent allure within a "general system of commensurability."[67] By contrast, an aesthetic vision installs us in time in an immediate fashion. It is an expansion of the mind and of the mind alone, creating a purely temporal perspective that is no longer subordinate to an external,

---

interprets Bergson and Deleuze. Meillassoux, *After Finitude*, 64.

[66] Panofsky, *Idea*, 13.

[67] Deleuze, *Cinema 2*, 362 and Gilles Deleuze, *Cinema 1: The Movement-Image*, trans. Hugh Tomlinson and Barbara Habberjam (Minneapolis: University of Minnesota Press, 1986), 32.

spatial movement which measures and solidifies it but that is actual to a purely virtual or inner movement, a strange somnambulist thinking-feeling from the inside out. Such a vision is the speculative vision par excellence, since it is an intuition of subjective genesis and not of objective fact. But it is also the practical vision par excellence to the extent that all pre-given subjectivity disappears in pure activity.[68] A vision is not the suspension of all action, but the drawing in of all action into an intuitive occurrence that exhausts all means to discern the present from the past. This is why Deleuze and Guattari refer to it as a "contemplation" or "the mystery of passive creation."[69] Passive does not mean that there is no more action, but rather that it is no longer the subjectivity of the artist that mediates the idea. An artistic vision is the ascetic vision par excellence, since it is based on a break with the continuum of action-perception that normally hides the idea, "so as to let in a breath of fresh air from the chaos that brings us the vision."[70] To see is to take up an impersonal perspective and to be taken up by it; it is to go through "a curious stationary journey" that belongs only to the soul and not to

---

[68] The simultaneously speculative and practical nature is discussed by Deleuze as a trademark of structuralism, in which the idea appears as "resistant and creative force" that makes the virtual and the actual communicate, as the "mutation point [that] defines a praxis, or rather the very site where praxis must take hold." Deleuze, *Desert Islands*, 191.

[69] Gilles Deleuze and Félix Guattari, *What is Philosophy?*, trans. Hugh Tomlinson and Graham Burchill (London: Verso, 1994), 204, 212.

[70] See for example Ahab's vision of Moby Dick in Gilles Deleuze, *Essays Critical and Clinical*, trans. Daniel W. Smith and Michael A. Greco (London: Verso, 1998), 3, 116-17. Or, as Deleuze and Guattari put it elsewhere: "To be present at the dawn of the world. Such is the link between imperceptibility, indiscernibility, and impersonality—the three virtues. To reduce oneself to an abstract line, a trait, in order to find one's zone of indiscernibility with other traits, and in this way enter the haecceity and impersonality of the creator. One is then like grass: one has made the world, everybody/everything, into a becoming, because one has made a necessarily communicating world, because one has suppressed in oneself everything that prevents us from slipping between things and growing in their midst." Gilles Deleuze and Félix Guattari, *A Thousand Plateaus: Capitalism and Schizophrenia*, trans. Brian Massumi (Minneapolis: University of Minnesota Press, 1987), 280.

the acting body, since it connects body and environment in a single prosthetic and proprioceptive feeling-system.[71] In terms of Whitehead, such a vision marks a disruption in the organic functioning of the body in "perception in the mode of symbolic reference." The body is no longer the common ground between "perception in the mode of presentational immediacy," the absolutely clear and distinct consciousness of the extended world divided, spatialised and objectified as passive potentiality independent from actuality, and "perception in the mode of causal efficacy," the obscure and confused awareness of the extensive continuum as real potentiality antecedent to but co-functioning with actuality. Instead, vision consists of a clear but vague experience of which we are no longer sure to which mode of perception it belongs. We no longer know what is a symbol and what is a meaning, since it is an experience in which the past is lifted into the present and the present absorbed in the past.[72] Rather, it is a vision of time as transversal ground between multiple becomings, as an interstitial and nonorganic life in constant asymmetric self-distinguishing: "The visionary, the seer, is the one who sees in the crystal, and what he sees is the gushing of time as dividing in two, as splitting."[73]

---

[71] Deleuze, *Two Regimes of Madness*, 279-80.

[72] Alfred North Whitehead, *Process and Reality* (New York: The Free Press, 1978), 61-65, 84-85, 104-09, 121-26, 168-81, 220. Whitehead thus largely agrees with Bergson's analysis of normal perception as a spatialisation of time. The difference between Whitehead and Bergson is that for Whitehead, space is not just an illusion of the intellect but a real factor in the constitution of the well-founded phenomenon. See also Whitehead, *Process and Reality*, 114, 209-10, 312.

[73] Deleuze, *Cinema 2*, 81. If there is a break with correlationism in Bergson and Deleuze, then it can only be in the intellectual intuition of art, which reveals the interiority of the subject to time instead of vice versa: "The virtual image (pure recollection) is not a psychological state or a consciousness: it exists outside consciousness, in time, and we should have no more difficulty in admitting the virtual insistence of pure recollections in time than we do for the actual existence of non-perceived objects in space." Deleuze, *Cinema 2*, 80. It is true that we are not only in the absolute, as the absolute may also be in us. But it is in us only in the form of a cut. It is a discontinuity, not from its own, virtual point of view but from the point of view of our actual

Whereas Bergson consistently evaluates speculative vision as a pathological threat to vital interests,[74] Deleuze makes it constitutive of his concept of art as "objective illusion: it does not supress the distinction between the two sides [actual and virtual], but makes it inattributable." In aesthetic vision, actual perception (objective matter) crystallises as a whole with its virtual past (subjective manner) in an "original virtuality" such that actual and virtual, perception and imagination become "totally reversible" and appear in all their indiscernible composedness. Vision, in other words, is a matter of presence: "It is the virtual image which corresponds to a particular actual image, instead of being actualised, of having to be actualised in a *different* actual image."[75] And as a consequence, "the problem of art, the correlative problem of creation is the problem of *perception* and not memory."[76] Only when we immediately perceive our own action-movement directly in

representation of it. In itself, however, it can acquire a new, artificial form of subjectivity. With aesthetic vision, we thus move not only from art to life (expressionism), but also from life to art (constructivism). Indeed, to intuit conditions of real experience is already to materialise them in a new process of subjectivation—a process of "self-enjoyment" (Whitehead) or "the thinking-feeling of our active implication in the ever-rolling-on in the world to really-next-effects." Brian Massumi, *Semblance and Event: Activist Philosophy and the Occurrent Arts* (Cambridge: MIT Press, 2011), 37.

[74] Throughout his work, Bergson consistently opposes speculation to vital interest. To give but one example from *The Creative Mind*: "In this speculation on the relation between the possible and the real, let us guard against seeing a simple game. It can be a preparation for the art of living." Bergson, *Creative Mind*, 86; see also Bergson, *Matter and Memory*, 281. It should be noted, however, that his criticism of speculation is restricted to the Kantian understanding of speculative metaphysics: "The impotence of speculative reason, as Kant has demonstrated it, is perhaps at bottom only the impotence of an intellect enslaved to certain necessities of bodily life." Bergson, *Matter and Memory*, 241. This could easily be misunderstood as if the body were a hindering of the mind. However, as Bergson announces in the introduction to *Matter and Memory*, a non-Kantian understanding of speculation is still open: "metaphysics would not have been sacrificed to physics, if philosophy had been content to leave matter half way" between Descartes and Berkely. Bergson, *Matter and Memory*, x.

[75] Deleuze, *Cinema 2*, 69, 94, 80.

[76] Deleuze, *Two Regimes of Madness*, 296.

the mirror-image of the past and all retrospective illusions of other possibilities before their mimetic reminiscence and realisation are eliminated, are we dealing with "a work of esthetic art," as Dewey says, a work in which everything actual is saturated with one virtual idea alone: "Man whittles, carves, sings, dances, gestures, molds, draws and paints. The doing or making is artistic when the perceived result is of such a nature that *its* qualities *as perceived* have controlled the question of production."[77] Only in art does the immediate expression of the idea as virtual past coincide perfectly with the hallucination-construction of its own realisation in a new image of thought. "The work of art is artistic in the degree in which the two functions of transformation [conception and execution] are effected by a single operation."[78] Indeed, reflecting Bellori's late mannerist equation of "*la maniera, o vogliamo dire fantastica idea*,"[79] Deleuze too argues that art is based on the perfect unity of idea and style, the latter being "the formal structure of the work of art, insofar as it does not refer to anything else, which can serve as unity—afterwards."[80]

More than any other intuition, then, the intuition of an artistic idea implies a direct devotion to, and caring responsibility for, the inner vitality of the work in the process of being made. A purely artistic creation immediately and exclusively determines manner or style, to the extent that the latter completely absorbs all objective matter, including preexisting artistic styles and traditions. While classicism clearly distinguishes manner from matter, form from content, and accident from essence, thus guaranteeing the spatial identity and intelligibility of images throughout their execution, mannerism is interested in ontogenetic images as such—i.e., their absolute processuality, "where matter and manner meld."[81]

---

[77] Dewey, *Art as Experience*, 50, 155, original emphases.

[78] Ibid., 78.

[79] Bellori, "Annibale Carracci," 1.

[80] Gilles Deleuze, *Proust and Signs*, trans. Richard Howard (London: Allen Lane, 1973), 149.

[81] Brian Massumi, "Involutionary Afterword," *Canadian Review of Compara-*

Artistic intuition is like an extremely concentrated mould-ing of the work of art (manner) as it is struggling out of the adamantine block by discarding all the unmoulded shapes of foreign realisations (molecular matter) that impede and suspend its autonomous completion. Makers immerse their perceptive consciousness directly and completely in the real itself, not as it is but only as it becomes. Art then becomes the clear but confused expression and construction of material movements on a plane of composition connecting things and events in a singular process of individuation that en-compasses both artists and their material: "We are carried out beyond ourselves to find ourselves … The whole is then felt as an expansion of ourselves."[82] Here there is no *what*, only *that*. In its pure state, an artistic intuition permits no recognition. It is rather like a flash of lightning, "a dynamic unity that comes in self-exhibiting excess over its differen-tial conditions."[83] It is a purely speculative event: a sudden eruption of the past into a singular act in the present, unde-termined but always in determination, unformed but always in formation, informed by a single generative idea that sheds all illusions of other possibilities. From *idea* to *maniera*, from difference to repetition, from expression to construction, art is a non-theological or non-religious spiritualisation or animation that absorbs its material in an interior perspective cut out of time itself, unbeholden to any external or spatial finalities. It is "no longer motor or material, but temporal and spiritual: that which 'is added' to matter, not what distends it."[84] Although unintelligible to our sensory-motor schema and natural perception, art is therefore not a breakdown of life, but rather its breakthrough into a new, unnatural form: it is the very "bursting forth of life," even "the artist or out-pouring life" itself.[85]

---

tive Literature (1998), 23:3, 2013, http://www.anu.edu.au/hrc/first_and_last/works/crclintro.htm (accessed July 7, 2013).

[82] Dewey, *Art as Experience*, 50, 195.

[83] Massumi, *Semblance and Event*, 20.

[84] Deleuze, *Cinema 2*, 101.

[85] Ibid., 121, 192.

Speculations V
Manual Diagrams in the Age of Speculation

Let us summarise. According to the *Critique of Pure Reason*, the ideas of reason function as regulative principles in the transcendental schematism. Ideas systematise the way in which the manifold of sensible intuition is synthesised by the imagination into the unity of a particular image in order to subsequently make itself objectively recognised under the profile of a concept. Accordingly, *disegno* would move from image to concept and back so that the sensible and the intelligible, art and science converge in the production of art objects.[86]

From a Bergsonist point of view, by contrast, the idea is not outside of intuition, but belongs to it in the same way that the manner of its appearance belongs to the imagination. Firstly, there is neither imagination without intuition nor vice versa: "the work in the mirror and the work in the seed have always accompanied art without ever exhausting it."[87] The imagination (the virtual mirror image of the work) is evoked in order to express the intuition of the idea (the seed of the work in the process of being made), but the intuition itself is without image. Rather it is the *phantasteon* or *imaginandum*, "the unformed or the deformed in nature" in which the body schema disintegrates and the door is opened for new perceptions.[88] Only when taken together with the imagination (*maniera*) does intuition (*idea*) constitute "the *way* of seeing and feeling things as they compose an integral whole."[89] Secondly, the imagination, like the intuition, is not a faculty but a practice, itself constituted by processes of crystallisation, such that in fact "all that matters about the crystal itself is what we see in it, so the imaginary drops out of the equation."[90] In other words, the self-conscious man-

---

86 Didi-Huberman, *Confronting Images*, 130-33.

87 Deleuze, *Cinema 2*, 75.

88 Deleuze, *Difference and Repetition*, 320-21.

89 Dewey, *Art as Experience*, 278, original emphasis.

90 Gilles Deleuze, *Negotiations, 1972-1990*, trans. Martin Joughin (New York: Columbia University Press), 66. In the imagination, it is the manner of

ner of the imagination is inseparable from the material of its development, which is constituted by the unconscious "motor diagram."[91] Cognitive understanding is therefore not a separate faculty, but itself the product of a sensory-motor schema that slows down and filters the imagination by delimiting different possibilities, thus distinguishing between real and imaginary images. While it plays a crucial role in natural perception, in artistic vision the habitual perception of natural phenomena is reshuffled without detriment into the formation of new, unnatural images. These are not just capricious fantasies of a disturbed psyche, but real accelerations of spirit. While visible extension is the ordinary schema of ideas, the imagination as slowed down by the organic body, in artistic vision simulacra fly about in the hallucination of new intensities that provide the visionary schema in which the ideas of the intuition "shine like differential flashes which leap and metamorphose" and the ground rises up to the surface in a speculative moment or "spiritual ascension" that puts everything at stake.[92] From the heavy motor diagram

imagining that puts virtual ideas and actual cognitions in dynamic and creative interrelation. "The imaginary isn't the unreal; it's the indiscernibility of real and unreal ... [T]o imagine is to construct crystal-images, to make the image behave like a crystal ... It's not the imaginary but the crystal that has a heuristic role ... The imaginary is a rather indeterminate notion. It makes sense in strict conditions: its precondition is the crystal, and the unconditioned we eventually reach is time." Deleuze, *Negotiations*, 66. Or as we read in *Empiricism and Subjectivity*: "Nothing is done by the imagination; everything is done in the imagination. It is not even a faculty for forming ideas, because the production of an idea by the imagination is only the reproduction of an impression in the imagination. Certainly, the imagination has its own activity; but even this activity, being whimsical and delirious, is without constancy and without uniformity. It is the movement of ideas, and the totality of their actions and reactions. Being the place of ideas, the fancy is the collection of separate, individual items. Being the bond of ideas, it moves through the universe, engendering fire dragons, winged horses, and monstrous giants. The depth of the mind is indeed delirium, or—same thing from another point of view—change and indifference. By itself, the imagination is not nature; it is a mere fancy." Gilles Deleuze, *Empiricism and Subjectivity*, 23.

[91] Bergson, *Matter and Memory*, 136.

[92] Deleuze, *Difference and Repetition*, 146; Deleuze, *Cinema 2*, 267.

of the body to its spiritual transmutation in art, the mutual immanence of matter, manner and idea in the complex unity of intuition and imagination thus forms the solution to "the epiphany of the transcendental schematism of artistic production," while the cognitive intellect or general concept, which is adapted to matter alone, only comes afterwards.[93]

But how and why do we pass from normal or natural images to visionary images? Just as, psychologically speaking, visionary hallucinations are the result of a breakdown of the sensory-motor schema of natural perception, the mannerist will to speculate is intimately connected with a catastrophe in its socio-political grounds. Art will only become abstract and gain in aesthetic expressivity if its practical embedding in some wider milieu is somehow disrupted. We never speculate at will, as if speculation were some non-binding intellectual pastime occupation. Rather, speculation always answers a passionate cry, a painful restlessness that makes it both impossible and necessary to act. In fact, the clearest sign of some crisis of belief in the schema of the world is this treacherous tension between subjectivating reason and pre-subjective passion. Although traditionally art historians tend to associate the mannerists with their own social ideal of disinvolved *sprezzatura*, the grace of effortless accomplishment of some frivolous and contrived idea, I side with Arnold Hauser, who writes this about the mannerists: "They despaired of speculative thought, and at the same time clung to it; they had no high hopes of reason, but remained passionate reasoners."[94] In fact, the mannerist ideal of *sprezzatura* can only appear in response to a catastrophe of established schemata, amidst the "rage of disposition[s]" that leads to "the contingency of form in relation to the intelligible character

---

[93] Adi Efal, "Panofsky's Idea and Auerbach's Figura, Two Philological Iconodulist Experiments," *History and Theory, Bezalel* (2009), 14, 2013, http://bezalel.secured.co.il/zope/home/en/1252746792/1253042837_en (accessed June 18, 2013).

[94] Arnold Hauser, *Der Ursprung der modernen Kunst und Literatur: Die Entwicklung des Manierismus seit der Krise der Renaissance* (München: C.H. Beck, 1973), 15.

of the work."[95] Only what has no essence or reason becomes a matter of speculation. Situated between the Renaissance and the Enlightenment, what is lacking in mannerism is a belief in the existing grounds, a preparedness to be involved. Of course, this crisis is not yet the modern crisis of belief in "human reason" but rather "a crisis and collapse of all theological Reason" or a "cry of reason," as Deleuze calls it. Together with the baroque, mannerism is the temporary and provisional attempt to reconstitute a sufficient reason in the "long history of nihilism."[96] But whether in religion, in science, in philosophy, or in art, this is to say that all that is left of sufficient reason is a speculative trust in a future ground, a vision of "a new earth and people that do not yet exist."[97] Instead of referring to the mannerist age as "the age of criticism,"[98] I therefore prefer to call it "the age of speculation." The key here is that, as Massumi writes, "speculation is entirely active." Mannerism will only appear as disinvolved from a classicist perspective, i.e., a perspective in which art and politics are bound by the "eternal return of content," whereas in reality, it is manner that drags content along towards the excess invention of a new form of life.[99]

It is in this sense that I propose a speculative reinterpretation of the mannerist doctrine of the idea. Mannerism is not conceptual art. It is more an art of spirituality than of ideas. If the idea stands in opposition to material practice, spirituality sympathises with it. Instead of residing outside of the medium, it inheres within it. Any dematerialisation is only apparent, a trap. But this conjunctive immanence of

---

[95] Robert Klein, *Gestalt und Gedanke: Zur Kunst und Theorie der Renaissance*, trans. and ed. Horst Günther (Berlin: Verlag Klaus Wagenbach, 1996), 90.

[96] Deleuze, *The Fold*, 67-68, 41. See also Sjoerd van Tuinen, "Cinematic Neo-Mannerism or Neo-Baroque? Deleuze and Daney," *Image and Narrative* (2012), 13:2, 53-75.

[97] Deleuze and Guattari, *What Is Philosophy?*, 108.

[98] Baxter Hathaway, *The Age of Criticism: The Late Renaissance in Italy* (Westport: Greenwood Press, 1973).

[99] Massumi, *Semblance and Event*, 12, 150-54.

matter, manner and idea appears as such only in moments of crisis. Ideas always rise to the surface as breaks in a material process, in other words, as problems, not as solutions. "They are not interruptions of the process, but breaks that form part of it, like an eternity that can only be revealed in a becoming, or a landscape that only appears in movement."[100] This means that ideas are not outside practical matters, but rather form the outside *of* practical matters, their interstices and intervals. Ideas are the very passages of life within them. For Leibniz, these passages make up the ideal continuum of the universe in its impersonal and pre-individual state, a transfinite structure of disharmonious possibility in the mind of God;[101] for Bergson they constitute the Open Whole of the past that is virtually passing through each actuality. Either way, to have an intuition or vision of these passages is already to make a selection, to touch base with the groundless ground of the future itself. Timing is everything. Although in mannerism all possible intellectual traditions are mobilised to this speculative end, ideas do not yet concern the kind of cognitive knowledge which only comes afterwards, but rather a faith in something which is not yet there. Although it takes a continual practical effort to develop and sustain an intuition, this development is purely a matter of cultivation as opposed to method. And it is speculative, since it is a risky matter of stubborn perseverance and self-certainty about what one wants to do without knowing how to get there.

In Deleuze, this speculative conception of the idea as continuous with manner and matter returns in his concepts of the abstract machine as the world's immanent cause and of the diagram as a "state of the abstract Machine" as it returns

---

[100] Deleuze, *Essays Critical and Clinical*, 5.

[101] This is why the idea is the virtual object of complete determination (differentiation), the problematic structure insofar as it is complete but not insofar as it is actual since it never constitutes an integral whole, lacking the whole set of relations (differenciation) belonging to the actual existence of its solutions: "The elements, varieties of relations and singular points coexist in the work or the object, in the virtual part of the work or object." Deleuze, *Difference and Repetition*, 209.

in science, philosophy and art.[102] The diagram, Deleuze's transformation of the Kantian schematism, is a map of the future. It is not what the artist is the author of, but the set of asignifying and nonrepresentational signs which he puts to work and on which he relies. It does not specify the properties of the component parts of a concrete material assemblage, but only the ideal relations by which these free marks and traits of expressions could constitute a functional assemblage. When interpreted in terms of the diagram, *disegno* is no longer a matter of going back and forth between part and whole, as in classical sketch methods. Rather, it is the processing of abstract forces as information, in which the parts and the whole interact in a constructive gambling upon the real. The whole is not pre-set but emerges in an itinerant fashion, in which craft and design, matter and manner immediately answer to one another. And it is an open whole, structured by confusion, of which the parts are selected bottom-up, through their relations instead of the relations through their terms. Thus whereas in classical representation the potential idea slumbering in a given material is first "seen" by the eye of the intellect and then realised in manual work, mannerism—and here we should remember that Vasari speaks consistently of *maniera*, which derives from *mano* (hand), and not of *stile*—sets up a "frenetic zone in which the hand is no longer guided by the eye and is forced upon sight like another will."[103] Strictly speaking then, a diagram is not even an agent of design, but rather of breakthrough. It operates outside of established regimes of imagination. We see the signs of such an outside in the famous mannerist ideal of the *figura serpentinata*, a figure produced by a line of infinite variation, but also in the endless modulation of light in Venetian oil painting, the infinite manipulation of the veins in marble in sculpture, or in the constant play with dissonance in the polyphonic madrigal.

As a consequence, the disconnection between the stages of conception and execution is not at all a mannerist idea,

---

[102] Deleuze and Guattari, *A Thousand Plateaus*, 67.

[103] Deleuze, *Francis Bacon*, 137, 94.

but precisely a classical one. Mannerism simply no longer ignores or represses the artificiality or constructive aspect of the diagrams that may already have been at work in the nameless interstices of classicism. Rather, it is a pragmatic-speculative mode of thinking about what pre-artistic and non-artistic technologies and materials can bring in and activate. Diagrams are the groundless grounds that need to be worked over and worked out in the future, and in their eternal return even constitute "the future *per se*," the pure and empty form of time itself.[104] They are the elusive point where the innate and the genital, past and future merge in a speculative thought that produces that which it speculates on.

Implied in this diagrammatic understanding of mannerism as "manual intrusion" is, firstly, that the vision of the idea is itself transformed into an artistic *vision à la loupe* or a "close" and "haptic vision."[105] As Michelangelo writes, drawing his inspiration from Ficino's commentary on the *Symposium*, the aim of art is to "make of [one's] entire body one single eye."[106] In haptic experiences, there is no a priori division of labour. The eye itself now acts as if it were a hand, being no longer only a receptive organ but also an active one, whereas what is at hand is always close, without any sense of depth or horizon, internalised by the body in its entirety. Being neither models nor rules, we never meet the ideas as such. They are "artistic essences";[107] we only live through them or enact them in art. "As we manipulate, we touch and feel, as we look, we see; as

---

[104] Lars Spuybroek, *The Sympathy of Things: John Ruskin and the Ecology of Design* (Rotterdam: V2 Publishers, 2011), 162, original emphasis.

[105] Deleuze, *Francis Bacon*, 138, 152. Whereas clarity and distinctness form the ground of recognition, they explode into the "new clarity" (Deleuze, *Francis Bacon*, 161) or "inspired free vision" (Gilles Deleuze, *Spinoza: Practical Philosophy*, trans. Robert Hurley (San Francisco: City Lights Books, 1988), 14) of the "third eye" (Deleuze, *Cinema 2*, 265) that belongs to the groundless ground—an eye that is no longer mine, but that is itself a "vision-effect" or "appearance" belonging to the lived abstraction of the event. Massumi, *Semblance and Event*, 17, 51, 55, 72.

[106] Michelangelo as cited in Clements, *Michelangelo's Theory of Art*, 35.

[107] See the chapter "Essences and the Signs of Art" in Deleuze, *Proust and Signs*, 39-50.

we listen, we hear ... Hand and eye, when the experience is aesthetic, are but instruments through which the entire living creature, moved and active throughout, operates."[108]

Secondly, it follows that the complete execution of a work of art is not indispensable. Hence the extraordinary interest of Michelangelo's many drawings (*disegni*) used as studies for his paintings and sculptures. The conceptual character of *non finito* works of art such as the *Pitti Tondo* (1503-1504) or the *Prigioni* (1525-1530), moreover, reflects the artist's poetic virtuosity insofar as these works are inseparable from the manual act that executes them, rather than being reducible to some prefabricated idea in general. Indeed, it is precisely in this sense that Vasari appreciates the perfect control of Michelangelo's hand in *San Matteo* (1506): "In its sketched state it reveals the perfection to which it aspires and teaches all sculptors the manner (*maniera*) in which one carves figures from stone without harm."[109] Perfection, then, becomes an aspiration, not an endpoint that is already given. Or as we can argue with Souriau, Michelangelo's unfinished sculptures are not "failed projects" but "restorative trajectories." Perfection is not a question of existence, as this still presupposes a well-formed end product, but of *more* or *less* existence.[110] Form is constituted by both structure and action. Against the Aristotelian notion that form is active while matter is passive, we must uphold that forms are tending toward realisation in material processes themselves and that they are always between minimum and maximum states. They are formed by the "internal mold" of a given flow of matter, not as a prescription but as procedure, a motor schema, a digital code or genetic script.[111] After all, "the essence of a thing never

---

[108] Dewey, *Art as Experience*, 51-52.

[109] Giorgio Vasari as cited in Paul Barolsky, "The Artist's Hand," in *The Craft of Art: Originality and Industry in the Italian Renaissance and Baroque Workshop*, ed. Andrew Ladis and Carolyn Wood (Athens: University of Georgia Press, 1995), 9.

[110] Souriau, *Les différents modes d'existence*, 204, 207-08, 196.

[111] Spuybroek, *The Sympathy of Things*, 56.

appears at the outset, but in the middle, in the course of its development, when its strength is assured."[112]

Maybe this concept of a metastable perfection could also shed new light on the mystery of mannerist "resemblances." Both unformed chaos and conditions of the new, diagrams are the immanent becomings of the work of art in which the relation between model and copy is reversed. They constitute both the limit of imitation *and its threshold*, that is, the agitated zone where "the imitation of a primal model" constantly passes into "a mimesis that is itself primary and without a model."[113] It is in this sense that mannerist works of art are one with a virtuosity valued only for itself and judged by no external resemblance. In virtuosity lies the perfect unity of eye and hand, but also the immanence of matter, manner and idea. The mannerist *idea* does not preside over life but becomes coextensive with it. Rather than being general, it is a "concrete universal."[114] Perhaps this is the ultimate consequence of a truly pragmatist and materialist conception of spirituality: the mannerist paradox of a Neoplatonist overturning of Platonism based not on resemblances, but on manners of resembling. It demands an ethics of affirmation that replaces imitable models in space with the modulation of simulacra and the fictionalising productivity of time. Instead of an economy of originals we discover a dynamic pragmatics of immanent deviation that subsumes all content and renders the work of art a monument of time itself. Such a work is the work of the speculative artist par excellence, whom Deleuze calls the "forger."[115] For it is with the forger that the breakdown of the critical form of the true implies the breakthrough of the speculative powers of the false. To speculate or to have an idea is to metamorphose, to be done with judgment and

---

[112] Deleuze, *Cinema 1*, 3.

[113] Deleuze and Guattari, *A Thousand Plateaus*, 237.

[114] Deleuze, *Desert Islands*, 43.

[115] Deleuze, *Cinema 2*, 132.

to manipulate "forces, nothing but forces."[116] Unlike form, force has no essence: it has no "what," but only a "how" and a "that." Thus it also constitutes the expressive and constructive essence of mannerist *disegno*: "Manipulated chance, as opposed to conceived or seen possibilities."[117]

---

[116] Ibid., 139 and Deleuze, *Essays Critical and Clinical*, 134.

[117] Deleuze, *Francis Bacon*, 94.

33105303R00261

Printed in Great Britain
by Amazon